PANGS OF PARTITION

PANGS OF PARTITION

VOLUME I

The Parting of Ways

Edited by

S. SETTAR

INDIRA BAPTISTA GUPTA

INDIAN COUNCIL OF HISTORICAL RESEARCH

MANOHAR

2002

First published 2002

ISBN 81-7304-305-1 (Set)
ISBN 81-7304-306-X (Vol. I)

Published by
Ajay Kumar Jain for
Manohar Publishers & Distributors
4753/23 Ansari Road, Daryaganj
New Delhi 110002

Typeset by
A J Software Publishing Co. Pvt. Ltd.
New Delhi 110005

Printed at
Lordson Publishers Pvt. Ltd.
Delhi 110007

Contents

Introduction

The Partition of India is a much debated issue in the history of South Asia. One will never know exactly how many people died in the riots which accompanied it, but around seventeen million people had to relocate themselves across the newly drawn boundaries. The magnitude of such an uprootment is unprecedented in recorded history. In 1997, fifty years after the event, the Indian Council of Historical Research felt that it was time to review some of the established theories concerning Partition, focus attention on a wide array of individual and collective experiences of migration, trauma and the intense nostalgia of the displaced for the undivided past. The result was the present collection of essays representing various disciplines and showing the multiple strands of the historical evidence available on Partition.

The factors which led to Partition apart, the roles of individual leaders (and parties) who by their acts of omission and commission made it a *fait accompli*, have been discussed extensively. It is common knowledge that this complex issue has been made somewhat more complicated by the conflicting approaches of historians. At least three familiar pictures are before us: the imperialist (British); the Pakistani (Muslim); and the Indian (Hindu). However, some common issues have been raised by all these three advocates, such as: What led to Partition? Could it have been avoided? What is the share of the colonial power (divide and rule), India (Hindu domination and Congress authoritarianism) and Pakistan (Jinnah's intransigence and Muslim separatism)? Besides these, the role of individual leaders, 'accidental' factors and 'chances' that came by and other such issues, have also engaged all of them.

The imperialists regarded Partition as a natural consequence of the communal divide, the history of which could be taken back either to the Arab invasion of Sind or to the annexation of the Punjab by Mahmud Ghazni; what Indians and Pakistanis got in 1947 was only a generous hand out from them—a mere transfer of power. To the Indians and Pakistanis, on the other hand, independence was a hard won fruit, an outcome of a long and bitter struggle involving prolonged suffering and painful sacrifice. Perhaps, here ends the agreement between the two—they part ways to reiterate their individual compulsions and convictions to justify, condone and also to question the necessity of Partition as well as its consequences.

To a section of Muslims, partitioning the country was the only way out, if they were to escape the grip of the Hindu majority. They needed nothing less than 'double deliverance'—from the majority Hindus and from colonial authorities. To the majority of Indians (were they only Hindus?), the fears of the Muslims were unfounded. They held that the millennium old history of coexistence bears a testimony to this, and if there were occasional frictions between Hindus and Muslims, they were no different from frictions found in the history of any two communities or any two sects. The question of Muslim integration was never in doubt, for Indian culture was never claimed to have been created by Hindus alone. Also the Muslim share either in the national movement or in the National Congress was never questioned. In any case, the fear of the Muslims was proved unfounded in the end as a substantial section of this community found a secure home in India and are thriving as freely as any other community in independent India.

The present two volumes are organized on the principle of a certain complementarity. If the first volume, *Parting of Ways: History, Politics, Economics* can be termed to be a historian's history, the second, *Human Dimension: Culture, Society, Literature*, is a people's history. If the first maps the grand narrative of Partition with new perspectives on contemporary events and the leaders who played a prominent part in them, the second listens to the marginal voices and focuses on the popular culture of the period. If the first volume takes a scholarly view of the complex interplay of historical events during the closing years of the British Raj, the second takes off from where the first ends and reconstructs, with equal profundity, a microscopic view of the fall-out of Partition. Both volumes, however, supplement and sustain each other and offer an exciting range of discussion.

The seventeen papers, which constitute Volume I, deal with some familiar and some not so familiar problems. With a fresh perspective and new sources, they add, alter, strengthen and modify the prevalent arguments. The imperialist stand is questioned and reviewed by Bishwa Mohan Pandey. This issue also surfaces in some other papers. Lal Bahadur Varma, for example, reminds us of the two divergent approaches to Partition and of its impact on the writings of history books in India as well as in Pakistan. Partha Sarathi Gupta highlights the importance of documents as a corrective to stereotyped accounts.

The major concerns of about half a dozen papers relate to the role of personalities. V.N. Datta examines the acrimonious controversy surrounding the role of Lord Mountbatten in the Radcliffe Award, in the backdrop of the working of the Boundary Commission, the claims of political parties, and the Radcliffe Award itself. B.R. Nanda brings to light Gandhi's deep concern for the restoration of peace during the winter months of 1946-7, when the recrudescence of violence spread across the country. Gandhi remarked in June 1947: 'I find myself all alone.... Everybody is today impatient for independence. Therefore there is no alternative.' Chittabrata Palit goes into the positive aspects of Gandhi's satyagraha, his efforts to reconcile the warring communities and his final stand on Partition. When independence came, he reminds us, Gandhi was a broken man. 'Leave me alone to shed my tears', was all that he asked for.

Sucheta Mahajan goes into various aspects of the national movement and points out how it succeeded in building up a national consciousness sufficient to wrest independence and how the Congress party failed to keep the country united. Khwaja A. Khalique feels that the 'demand for Pakistan made in 1940 was a logical culmination of a long standing communal divide'.

Crucial contemporary issues, such as the role of the Constituent Assembly of India and the coalition politics in UP during 1937, which precipitated Partition, are discussed at length by S.K. Chaube and Salil Mishra. Kanchanmoy Mojumdar goes into the majority-minority syndrome and the widening of the Hindu-Muslim divide which was exploited by the local elements to their advantage in CP and Berar. The complex scenario in the North-West Frontier Province and the events that led to the worsening of the communal situation are brought out boldly by Parshotam Mehra. The happenings in the Oriya princely states, the role of some prominent tribal leaders and tribal politics in Central India as well as the North East, the role of the Akalis in Punjab, are the other issues which have engaged the attention of Jayanta Sengupta, K.S. Singh and Bir Good Gill, respectively.

The two papers of Dwijendra Tripathi and Shri Prakash take us to the politics of economics. The role and reactions of the capitalist class, both Hindu and Muslim, in the backdrop of contemporary political developments are analysed by Tripathi. The irrationality underlying the division of the country and the economic hardships it caused, both to India and Pakistan, are outlined by Shri Prakash.

The twenty-three contributions that constitute Volume II dwell on the consequences of Partition, captured by creative writers from non-conventional sources, but professional historians are not completely excluded from it. These papers fall broadly into four groups: personal reminiscences; recollections by contemporaries; impressions mirrored in creative literature; and events and incidents which inspired the visual media (in particular, films and paintings), narratives and popular culture. The rich mosaic of material spread out before us, should add a new dimension to our understanding of the saga and supplement our knowledge of it derived from archival sources. Personal narratives expose and enrich the hidden currents of history. Though an act of remembrance is always piecemeal, such bits and pieces could be effectively used to knit an interesting quilt of varied memories and emotions. Creative writers, poets and artists, who experienced Partition either personally or through others, have articulated with greater sensitivity, and have captured the multi-dimensionality of human suffering more realistically than some of the conventional historians. They do not get obsessed with the specifics of causes and results, they do not attempt at quantifying evidence, they do not believe it necessary to decorate their statements with quotes and notes, but the kind of stark reality that emerges from their works is hard to come by in conventional historical accounts.

Volume II begins with an essay by Krishna Kumar on the portrayal of Partition in school books of India and Pakistan. He observes that writers of both countries broadly share the state sponsored ideological biases in representing the events, which are then imprinted on young minds. R.K. Agnihotri doubts whether this 'Partition' could be regarded as final or complete, because unlike a mass of land an integrated psyche, characteristic of the northern parts of the subcontinent from the times of the Bhaktikal, cannot be fully or permanently fractured. As one of the victims of Partition who suffered the demographic dislocation Satish Gujral recalls, without any trace of malice or rancour, some significant moments from his experiences and traces the impact of riots, murder, brutality, indignity, abduction, rape and dislocation suffered by the innocent during and after Partition.

Three papers introduce us to different genres of creativity that deal with Partition. Though Partition does not form the main theme of Ritwick Ghatak's films, Partha Chatterjee finds its recurrent presence as a riveting memory image of that cataclysmic event. Badri Narain Tiwari discovers its multiple strands in the *nach* drama, folk songs and proverbs of the Bhojpuri region. Keshav Malik shows how Satish Gujral, the painter, handled the difficult and painful subject of Partition with conviction.

Bhisham Sahni, one of the most notable creative writers on Partition, has revealed his childhood experiences to Alok Bhalla. His recollections of the social milieu of the pre-Partition days, emphasize the harmony in which the religious affairs of different communities could be conducted in an atmosphere of tolerance. Reviewing the life, literature and politics of the two countries, Mrinal Pande observes that neither of them has recovered fully from the deep hurt suffered during Partition. Urvashi Butalia and Monmayee Basu, both from refugee families, draw from women and their experiences to weave moving tapestries of violence and indignity suffered by them. They explore history through the memories of the unknown and the anonymous to emphasize the rich benefits of placing the oral alongside the conventional evidence.

In the backdrop of a spate of literary activities in Punjab, K.S. Duggal situates himself amidst other creative writers to show how Partition was handled with commanding resilience and sensitivity by them. A recurring sentiment noticed by him is the wistful longing of the uprooted Punjabi to revisit his home and play fields. In what has been published in newspapers, magazines and journals during the fiftieth year of independence, Mushirul Hasan detects a common refrain, both in popular as well as in scholarly writings, that Partition was a colossal tragedy brought about by hot-headed and cynical politicians, who failed to grasp the implications of the division made along religious lines. Yet, he asserts, it is still possible for the people rather than the governments to make sense of the poignant writings of creative writers and poets. Nandi Bhatia also points out how literary works store the collective consciousness of the people and provide alternative sources of history. These 'marginal' experiences, though an intrinsic part of the Partition saga, would remain outside our reach, if the historian were to stick only to the official records.

Though Partition does not figure as the main theme in the plays and stories of Sharadindu Bandopadhyaya, Anindita Mukhopadhyay sees it as a grim backdrop in at least five of his stories. Sukrita Paul Kumar highlights the effective manner in which short stories captured the poignant moments of the Partition drama. Sadaat Hasan Manto's unique technique of telling stories has received wide acclaim. He mirrors what he sees. He does not attempt to seek solutions. Critically examining the English translations of some of his work by Khalid Hasan, Alok Bhalla sees several of these unique qualities sacrificed and he also raises some questions relating to the ethics of a translator.

An interesting aspect of Bengali literature is its total indifference to Partition, as virtually no short stories or novels of significance dealt with it. However, in contrast to this, its poetry was overwhelmingly preoccupied with this event. Total absence of it in one genre of literature and its dominant presence in another have confounded the historians of Bengali literature. Tapati Chakravarty makes an attempt to unravel this paradox. Holding Attia Hosain's novel *Sunlight on a Broken Column*, an 'aesthetically satisfying' work which 'presents the tragedy of partition with great objectivity', Naresh Jain highlights the changing Muslim attitude captured in this novel through the consciousness of a young Muslim girl of a *taluqdari* family, during the tumultuous decades of the 1930s and 1940s. Ameena K. Ansari takes up the tragic tale of Munshi Chitram or Dauji, a Hindu conversant with the Muslim idiom and a dedicated scholar of Persian. He refuses to give up his ancestral home in Pakistan and thus becomes a stranger, a 'metaphorical outsider', who faces the harsh realities of Partition in his own hometown.

Jayanti Chattopadhyay picks up two plays written and staged in the first decade after Partition and draws attention to the problems faced by the playwrights. Presenting pictures of Partition from different perspectives is Alok Bhalla's stories collected in three volumes. M. Asaduddin puts these volumes under scrutiny to show how these stories provide us with competing versions of truth and multiple points of view that lead to a richer and a more nuanced understanding of Partition. Kamlesh Mohan deals with a story that is based on a real incident of a mother looking for her lost son and in the process experiences the gory and dehumanizing conditions of a refugee camp. Taking up Khushwant Singh's *Train to Pakistan*, Shikoh Mohsin Mirza exposes the event that led to the transformation of a sleepy village 'into a cauldron of conflicting loyalties' on one August night of 1947, when a train load of massacred men, women and children arrives in the village.

Preparation of these two volumes was a great experience for both of us. What little we have achieved in these two volumes was made possible only by the cooperation of the contributors. Some of them sympathetically considered our suggestions and met our requirements unstinctingly, others infused fresh insights into our project to enhance its importance. We are grateful to all of them. We are beholden to Mrs Nirmala Parashar for allowing us to look into the portfolio of S.L. Parashar (1904-90) and borrow his sketches for the jacket design. Our appreciation to the publishers for the immense pain they have taken and for the patience they have shown in producing these volumes. We thank the authorities of the ICHR for encouraging this venture.

Needless to say the views expressed in these volumes are those of the contributors and not of either the editors or the ICHR.

4 February 2000

S. Settar
Indira Baptista Gupta

Lord Mountbatten and the Punjab Boundary Commission Award

V. N. DATTA

The Punjab Boundary Commission Award (known as the Radcliffe Award) has provoked a long and bitter controversy among historians, civil servants and public men, particularly in Pakistan.[1] The focus of controversy is Lord Mountbatten, the Viceroy, who is accused of collusion with Sir Cyril Radcliffe, Chairman of the Boundary Commission, in altering the Punjab boundary at the last stage, to the disadvantage of Pakistan. It is alleged that Mountbatten had exerted pressure on Radcliffe to allot Ferozepur, Zira and also a large portion of Gurdaspur district to India, giving it thereby a link with the state of Jammu & Kashmir. In other words, the allegation is that Mountbatten hatched a conspiracy to favour India against Pakistan. For this betrayal of trust reposed in him, Mountbatten is castigated by his critics as the villain of the piece, and his villainy is attributed to Jinnah's refusal to appoint him as the Governor-General of Pakistan on the eve of his departure from India.[2] In addition to this foul play of changing the boundary line, Mountbatten is reproached for adopting dilatory tactics in announcing the Radcliffe Award, which is presumed to have caused half a million casualties and 13 million migrations. For such horrible consequences, according to a British historian, Mountbatten 'deserved to be court-marshalled on his return to England'.[3] A Pakistani commentator has declared the Radcliffe Award 'a territorial murder'.[4] That Radcliffe allowed himself to be duped, becoming thereby a 'scapegoat of a classic kind' is a challenge to his integrity as Chairman of the Boundary Commission.[5] In response Mountbatten said that these allegations were cooked up to malign him and Radcliffe as 'crooks', tricking Pakistan in an underhand fashion.[6]

*This article is a revised version of the Inaugural Lecture delivered for the National Institute of Punjab Studies at India International Centre, New Delhi, on 19 February 1999. Originally it was presented at the Indian History Congress, Patiala, on 29 December 1998, focusing within a narrow range on the boundary question.

The animosity against Mountbatten has lingered in Pakistan. In March 1956 Mountbatten was denied passage over the Pakistan territory, *en route* to India, for a visit to naval establishments in his capacity as First Sea Lord of the Royal Navy.[7] Zafarullah Khan, Foreign Minister of Pakistan, complained to Noel Barker, Secretary for Commonwealth Relations, about Mountbatten's notorious role.[8] In March 1948, Begum Liaquat Ali Khan, wife of the Pakistan Prime Minister, repeated the same charge to Gorden Walker, Under-Secretary for Commonwealth Relations, at a dinner party hosted for the British delegation visiting Pakistan.[9] The Pakistan Prime Minister, Liaquat Ali Khan also brought up the matter in the Joint Defence Council, New Delhi, on 19 March 1948.[10]

According to Phillip Barker, Secretary of State for Commonwealth Relations, Radcliffe had indeed 'altered his award at the last minute but we have no knowledge that this was done on the advice of Mountbatten'.[11] Radcliffe's Secretary, Christopher Beaumont, in an interview to the *Daily Telegraph,* on 24 February 1992, said that 'Mountbatten interfered and Radcliffe allowed himself to be overcome. Grave discredit to both.'[12] Mohammad Ali Jinnah condemned the Radcliffe Award as 'unjust, incomprehensible and even perverse'.[13] He added 'It may be wrong, unjust, perverse, it may not be judicial but a political award, but we had agreed to abide by it and it is binding on us. An honourable people, we must abide by it.'[14] Mountbatten never repudiated the charge in public. He considered it beneath his dignity to issue any formal denial. In an interview, he assured that Jinnah had told a trusted friend that he had not done anything wrong or dishonourable and that Liaquat Ali Khan never doubted his integrity.[15]

The documentary evidence cited for Mountbatten's gerrymandering was his Secretary Sir George Abell's letter of 8 August 1947 addressed to the Punjab governor, Sir E. Jenkin's Secretary, S.E. Abbott.[16] Attached to this letter was a printed sketch map showing Ferozepur and Zira *tehsils* as a part of Pakistan. A note indicating the inclusion of Ferozepur and Zira *tehsils* in Pakistan was prepared by Radcliffe's Secretary, Christopher Beaumont. However, the sketch map was drawn by Abell according to Beaumont's instructions. Jenkins, recalled that on 'about the 10th or 11th (August) he received a secraphone message from the Viceroy's House, "Eliminate salient" '. This direction meant making Ferozepur and Zira *tehsils* a part of India.[17] In Radcliffe's Award signed on 12 August 1947, these two *tehsils* were allotted to India. In this manner the boundary line was changed between 8 and 12 August 1947.

Why did the Viceroy's Personal Secretary Abell dispatch the letter and sketch map to Jenkins? Realizing that the Punjab situation was critical, which he characterized as 'revolutionary', Jenkins had asked for an advance boundary forecast to concentrate his limited forces in key areas where violence was most likely to break out. Abell provided the requisite information. Later Abell's letter and sketch map, which were left in the safe of the Punjab Government House, Lahore, fell into the hands of Jenkins's successor, Sir Francis Mudie (Governor of West Punjab on 15 August 1947) who passed them on to the Pakistan Prime Minister, Liaquat Ali Khan.[18]

About Abell's letter, Mountbatten said that it had been sent without his knowledge and that the 'information between the Viceroy's Secretary and Abbott, the Governor's Secretary, was of a Private Secretary level'.[19] Later in an interview he stated that what Abell had sent was a 'rough draft which was undergoing formal adjustment'.[20] When confronted with the issue of alteration in the boundary line, Radcliffe recalled on 23 July 1964 that he might have prepared two or three drafts but nothing was conclusive until the final draft.[21] He added that there was nothing wrong in giving advance information as he had done so previously in the case of Bengal and Assam.[22] When the Pakistan government raised the Kashmir issue in the Security Council, the British government wanted to arm itself with a planted Parliamentary question, and Radcliffe was called to the Commonwealth Relations Office to assist in the matter. In his letter to Sir Archibald Carter, Permanent Under-Secretary of State for India, dated 13 April 1948, Radcliffe wrote:

> There could be no award until I had decided to make a report to the Viceroy and only the document which contained the report could be called an award. All the earlier drafts, and there were quite a few, were drafts and no more.[23]

The statement attached to the planted question emphasizes that the award of the Punjab boundary was the result of Radcliffe's 'own unfettered judgement' and that 'at no stage was any attempt of any kind made by the Governor-General to influence his decision'.[24]

The Radcliffe Award allotted a substantial portion of the Muslim majority Gurdaspur district to India. On 9 August 1947 a stern message from Liaquat Ali Khan to Lord Ismay, Chief of the Viceroy's staff, was delivered by Chaudhri Mohammad Ali, Cabinet Secretary of Pakistan, warning that 'if a large part of Gurdaspur were given to India, it was bound to imperil further relations between Pakistan and Britain'.[25]

II

This paper examines the accusation whether Mountbatten altered the boundary in collusion with Radcliffe, and if so, then under what compulsion, and if not, then why the accusation continues to persist. The question is whether the boundary line was altered between 8 and 12 August 1947 when Radcliffe signed the Award and sent it off to Mountbatten on 13 August. Was this contentious issue a logical outcome of an inherently incongruous arrangement aggravated by personal factors or fortuitous circumstances? To settle this question it is necessary to set out the terms of our discussion. We have to widen the scope of our enquiry and examine (a) the working of the Boundary Commission; (b) the claims of political parties (the Congress, the Muslim League and other groups representing the minorities); and (c) the Radcliffe Award and the reasoning behind it, in addition to the role Mountbatten and Radcliffe had in the settlement of the boundary question.

A statement made by the Prime Minister Clement Attlee in the House of Commons on 3 June 1947 announced that for a detailed investigation of the boundary question relating to the partition of Punjab:

> A boundary commission will be set up by the Governor-General, the membership and terms of reference will be settled in consultation with those concerned. It will also be instructed to demarcate the boundaries of the two parts of the Punjab on the basis of ascertaining the contiguous majority areas of Muslims and non-Muslims. It will also be instructed to take into account other factors.[26]

The terms of reference of the Boundary Commission had been put up by the Congress and were in line with the statement of 3 June, mentioned earlier. The *Gazettee of India* issued a notification, dated 30 June 1947, which laid down the following terms of reference for the partition of Punjab:

> The Boundary Commission is instructed to demarcate the boundaries of the two parts of the Punjab on the basis of ascertaining the contiguous majority areas of Muslims and non-Muslims. In doing so it will take into account other factors.[27]

In the same notification the following were appointed as members of the Punjab Boundary Commission:

1. Mr Justice Din Mohammed,
2. Mr Justice Muhammad Munir,
3. Mr Justice Mehr Chand Mahajan, and
4. Mr Justice Teja Singh.

The first two were Muslim League nominees, and the other two were the nominees of the Congress.

For determining the boundary line, a proposal to seek the assistance of the United Nations for the nomination of three members for each Commission, Punjab or Bengal, to sit with expert assessors had been made but Jawaharlal Nehru, member, Interim Government (External Affairs and Commonwealth Relations), thought that such a course would involve a cumbersome procedure and delay matters.[28] At the first meeting of the Partition Council held on 27 June 1947, Jinnah's proposal of appointing Sir Cyril Radcliffe (whom he knew personally), as Chairman of both the Punjab and Bengal Commissions was accepted.[29] The Chairman was given a casting vote, which was considered the only way in which the boundary question could be settled. Thus the Chairman was required to act as umpire while giving the Award.[30] Originally, the Lord Chancellor Jowett had suggested Radcliffe as Chairman of the Arbitral Tribunal but with his appointment as Chairman of the Boundary Commission, Sir Patrick Spens, the last Chief Justice of British India, was appointed as Chairman of the Arbitral Tribunal that was to resolve disputes over the assets of the old British Empire between the successor regimes.

Radcliffe was perhaps the most brilliant lawyer at the Bar. Born in 1899, he was educated at Haileybury College and New College, Oxford. A Fellow of All Souls, Oxford, he was called to the Bar of the Inner Temple in 1924 and was King's Counsellor (1935) and Bencher of the Inner Temple (1943). During the war he served as Director General of Information and Broadcasting. Strictly an establishment man, he extolled the virtues of censorship and secrecy in the conduct of public affairs. He took prompt action to curb the anti-British campaign carried on, by Nehru's sister Vijayalaxmi Pandit, in the United States in 1944. He believed that the 'Press is all right so long as it does not interfere with the plans of the Government.'[31] After the war in 1945 Radcliffe returned to the Bar and practiced in the Judicial Committee of the Privy Council. He was Vice-Chairman, General Council of the Bar (1946). He subsequently chaired a number of commissions and committees including the Royal Commission on the Taxation of Profits and Income and the Royal Commission on the Monetary System as well as enquiries dealing with the highly sensitive matters of espionage and suppression of information, such as the Vassall spy case, the *Daily Express* dispute and the D. Notice case. Both the Labour and Conservative governments sought his legal opinion on matters relating to nationalization of coal industries.[32] He was created a Viscount in 1972, and he died in 1977.

Radcliffe arrived in New Delhi on 8 July 1947 and the same evening met the Viceroy and Indian political leaders, Nehru, Jinnah, Baldev Singh and Liaquat Ali Khan. After staying with the Viceroy for two days, he was lodged in the Comptroller's house within the compound of the Viceroy's estate. Christopher Beaumont of the Indian Political Service was appointed the Secretary of the Boundary Commission to assist Radcliffe. V.D. Iyer was to act as Assistant Secretary to the Joint Chairman. Like the Kauravas and Pandavas of the *Mahabharat*, Nehru and Jinnah were to have the 'future of their kingdom decided on the cast of the dice'.[33]

The 3 June statement in its appendix had specified the provincial boundaries of the Muslim majority districts of Punjab according to the 1941 census figures that were to be used until the report of a Boundary Commission became available. The Muslim majority areas comprised the whole of Rawalpindi and Multan divisions, and the districts of Gujranwala, Gurdaspur, Lahore, Sheikhupura and Sialkot of Lahore Division.[34] In his broadcast of 3 June 1947, Mountbatten made it clear that 'the ultimate boundary will be settled by the Boundary Commission and will certainly not be identical with those which have been provisionally adopted'.[35] In his letters to Sir E. Jenkins and Sir F. Burrows, on 5 June 1947, he reiterated that the 'Boundary Commission will obviously not consider the matter prejudged by fixing of these arbitrary boundaries but will go into the merits.'[36]

The public sittings of the Commission took place in the Lahore High Court building from 21 to 31 July 1947 inclusive, with the exception of Sunday the 27 July. The Commission sat from 10 a.m. to 1 p.m. and 2 p.m. to 4 p.m. each day. In the absence of the Chairman, public sittings were presided over by the senior member of the Commission, Justice Din Mohammed, Chief Judge of the High Court, Bahawalpur, at the suggestion of Justice Mehr Chand Mahajan.

M.C. Setalvad presented the Congress case before the Commission. He was assisted by a dozen or more lawyers and public men including Bakshi Tek Chand, Jivan Lal Kapur, Harnam Singh, Shiv Shastri, Thakurdas Bhargava and R.B. Badri Das.[37] The Muslim League was represented by Sir Muhammad Zafarullah Khan who was assisted by Sir Firoz Khan Noon. A number of memoranda from political parties and the Bikaner and Bahawalpur states were received by the Commission for consideration.

Besides the 17 districts listed in the national division in the appendix to the 3 June statement (minus a non-Muslim majority area of the Pathankot *tehsil*), the Muslim League claimed the following areas for inclusion in West Punjab:

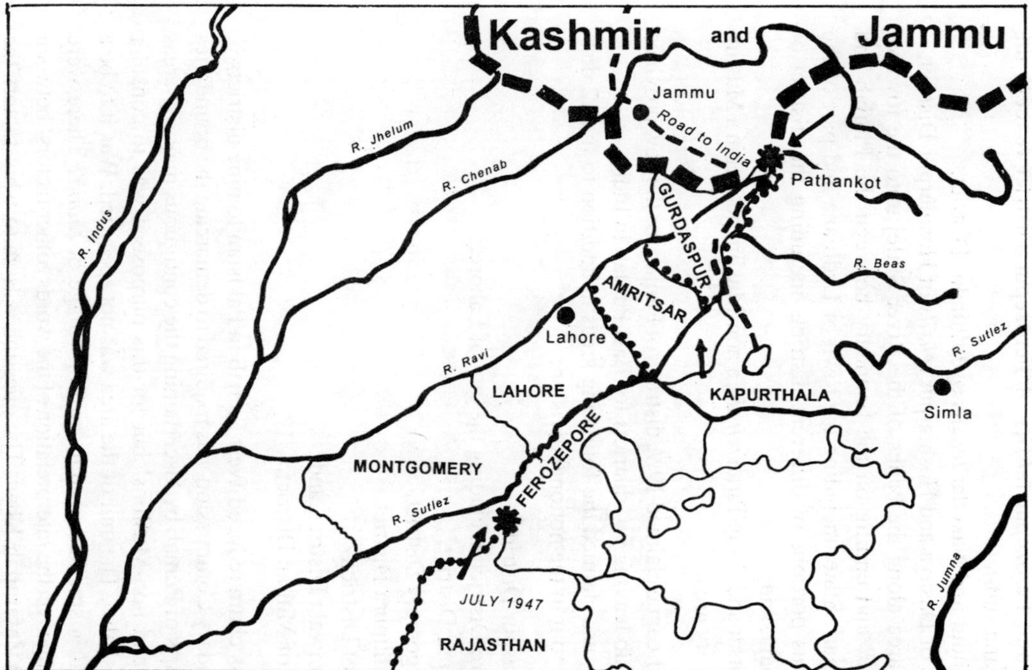

Source: Alastair Lamb, *Kashmir A Disputed Legacy, 1846-1990* (Karachi, 1992), p. xiv a.

MAP 1: PARTITION BOUNDARIES IN PUNJAB
Notional boundary between India and Pakistan in
the Punjab as implied by the Indian Independence Act, 18 July 1947

(a) Ajnala *tehsil* of Amritsar District,
(b) Majitha *zail* of Amritsar *tehsil* in the same district,
(c) Portions of Fazilka and Muktsar *tehsils* of Ferozepur District,
(d) Zira and Ferozepur *tehsils* of Ferozepur District (except the Nathana sub-*tehsil*),
(e) Jullundur and Nakodar *tehsils* of Jullundur District,
(f) Parts of Dasuya and Hoshiarpur *tehsils* of Hoshiarpur District,
(g) The area along the banks of the River Sutlej upto the town of Ropar, and ending on the boundary between the Punjab and Nalagarh State, including the town of Ludhiana and part of the various portions of different districts including the district of Ambala, and
(h) Amritsar and Taran Taran *tehsils*, a non-Muslim pocket in a Muslim majority area.

The Muslim League claimed 19 $^1/_2$ districts of Punjab for the new province of West Punjab leaving $9^1/_2$ districts for East Punjab in India.

The Congress claimed the following areas in addition to the 12 districts allotted to it in the notional division:

(a) Gurdaspur District,
(b) Lahore District, including the city of Lahore,
(c) Lyallpur District,
(d) Montgomery District,
(e) Sheikhupura District,
(f) Sialkot District,
(g) Gujranwala District, and
(h) Parts of Multan District.

The Congress claim reduced West Punjab in Pakistan to nine districts.[38]

The Boundary Commission was required to demarcate the boundaries of the two parts of Punjab by 'ascertaining the contiguous majority areas of Muslims and non-Muslims' but for this purpose it was to consider 'other factors' also. The unit of the area was not specified. Was it to be a district, *tehsil*, a smaller sub-unit, *zail* or village or *thana*? There were heated exchanges on the interpretation of the words 'other factors' between Setalvad and Zafarullah Khan. The question was as to what factors the Commission was required to consider for demarcating the boundary. The words 'in doing so' in the text of the terms of reference also generated much controversy among the Counsels, who interpreted them in ways that suited their interests. The legal battle centred on the terms 'contiguous majority areas', 'in doing so' and 'other factors'.

Setalvad argued that the expression 'in doing so' qualified the word 'demarcate', and was related to the actual process of partition or to any general or wider consideration on the future viability of India and Pakistan, both as a polity and an economy. He emphasized that the primary task for demarcating the boundary was undoubtedly to ascertain the contiguous majority areas of Muslims and non-Muslims, but other factors such as administrative and economic necessity, physical features, communications, water or irrigation systems and historical considerations, such as the protection of the religious and cultural life of the Sikhs, were not subsidiary, but equally important. Thus, according to Setalvad, the delimitation of the boundary was not limited to majority population considerations. On the contrary, Zafarullah Khan attached little importance to 'other factors', which meant to him only local factors, just minor territorial adjustments after ascertaining the Hindu and Muslim contiguous majority areas to make the boundary practical. He argued his case on the basis of the numerical majority of Muslims in the *tehsils*.

Setalvad claimed for the East Punjab the boundary along the River Chenab including Lahore, Sheikhupura and the Canal Colonies of Lyallpur and Montgomery District. Zafarullah Khan demanded for West Punjab the boundary extending to the River Sutlej and the Shivalik Hills. The area was to include the complete Divisions of Rawalpindi, Multan and Lahore and also a number of *tehsils* in the Jullundur and Ambala Divisions. Harnam Singh pleaded for a Sikh homeland in the area between the Beas and Chenab including the Canal Colonies, which the Sikhs through hard labour and determination had turned from a desert into a land of prosperity. The Bikaner and Bahawalpur states made claims for the retention of Ferozepur headworks in East and West Punjab, respectively.

Like the Counsels who had argued the case for their parties, the members of the Boundary Commission were also divided on party lines. Treating the *tehsil* as the determining factor of the boundary, Justice Din Mohammed claimed for West Punjab all the districts assigned in the notional division plus Amritsar, Zira, Ferozepur and that part of Pathankot, which controlled the irrigation of Upper Bari Doab. Justice Munir repudiated the Sikh case and ridiculed the Sikh position on the ground that by joining hands with the Hindus, they had forfeited their right to ask for separate claims as a community.[39] He supported the Muslim League demand. Justice Mahajan's boundary line approximated to that of the Congress. According to him, India and Pakistan should be demarcated to the west of the Ravi and its neighbourhood including Sheikhupura, Nankana Sahib, Lyallpur and Montgomery.[40] Justice Teja Singh wanted

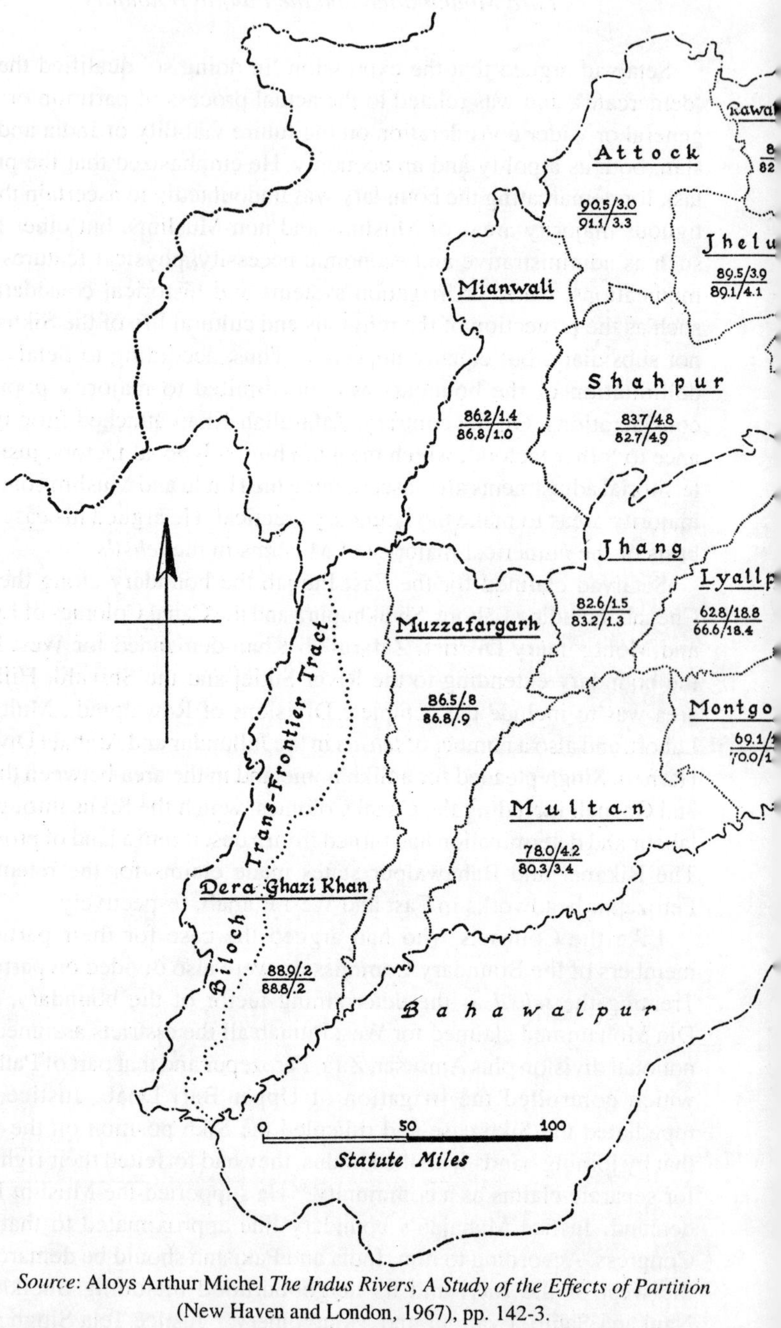

Source: Aloys Arthur Michel *The Indus Rivers, A Study of the Effects of Partition* (New Haven and London, 1967), pp. 142-3.

MAP 2: PERCENTAGES OF MUSLIMS AND SIKHS IN THE DISTRICTS OF THE BRITISH PUNJAB ACCORDING TO THE CENSUSES OF 1941 AND 1931

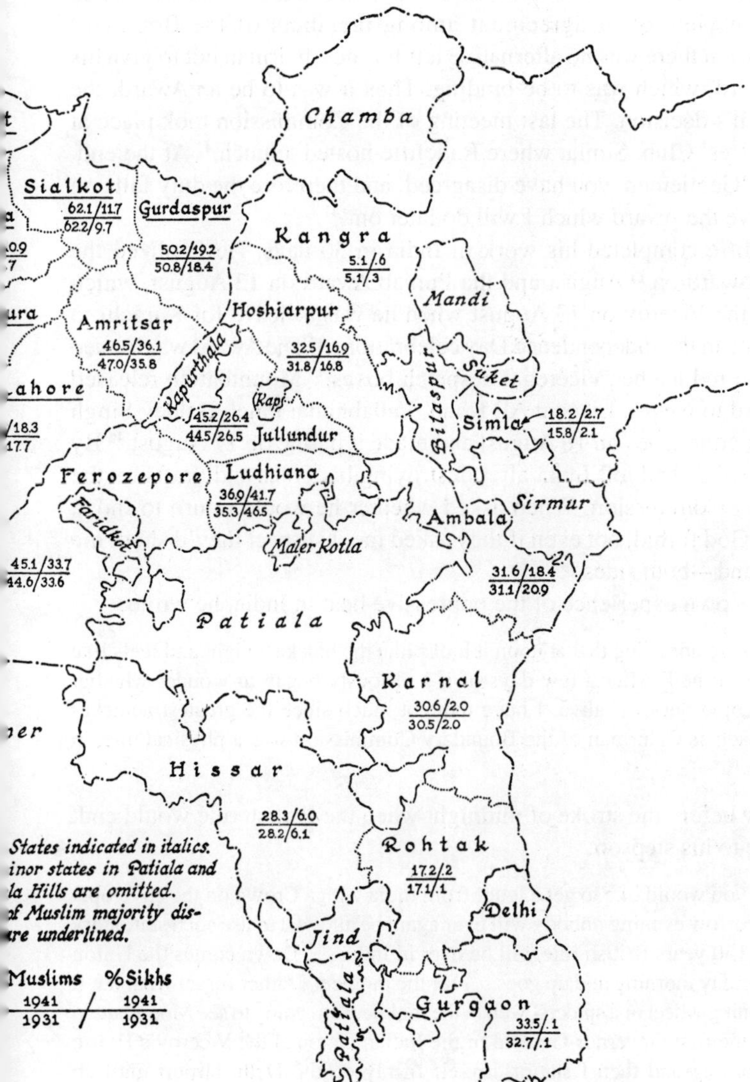
Chamba
Sialkot
62.1/11.7
62.2/9.7
Gurdaspur
50.2/19.2
50.8/18.4
Kangra
5.1/.6
5.1/.3
Mandi
Hoshiarpur
32.5/16.9
31.8/16.8
Amritsar
46.5/36.1
47.0/35.8
Kapurthala
Kap
Suket
Bilaspur
Lahore
45.2/26.4
44.5/26.5
Jullundur
Simla
18.2/2.7
15.8/2.1
Ferozepore
Ludhiana
36.9/41.7
35.3/46.5
Faridkot
Sirmur
Ambala
Maler Kotla
45.1/33.7
44.6/33.6
31.6/18.4
31.1/20.9
Patiala
Karnal
30.6/2.0
30.5/2.0
Hissar
28.3/6.0
28.2/6.1
Rohtak
17.2/2
17.1/1
Delhi
Jind
Patiala
Gurgaon
33.5/.1
32.7/.1
States indicated in italics.
inor states in Patiala and
la Hills are omitted.
of Muslim majority dis-
are underlined.
Muslims %Sikhs
1941 / 1941
1931 / 1931

the East Punjab boundary to be fixed at the Chenab. He was willing to make Qadian a neutral territory if Nankana Sahib was similarly treated.[41]

The Commission moved on to Simla in the first week of August and was lodged in Cecil Hotel where Radcliffe joined in to finalize the Punjab report. In view of disagreement among members of the Boundary Commission there was no alternative left for the Chairman but to give his own Award, which was to be binding. Thus it was to be an Award, the Chairman's decision. The last meeting of the Commission took place at the Services' Club, Simla, where Radcliffe hosted a lunch.[42] At the end, he said, 'Gentlemen, you have disagreed, and therefore the duty falls on me to give the Award which I will do later on.'[43]

Radcliffe completed his work in India in 36 days. He finalized the Bengal Award on 9 August and the Punjab Award on 12 August, which reached the Viceroy on 13 August when he was to leave for Karachi to participate in the Independence Day celebrations.[44] The Award was locked inside the red leather Viceregal despatch boxes.[45] Mountbatten released the Award to Nehru, Liaquat Ali Khan, Vallabhbhai Patel, Baldev Singh and their colleagues on 16 August and made it public on 17 August.[46] By then Radcliffe had left India after destroying his notes and drafts on the Boundary Commission. When asked whether he would return to India, he said 'God forbid, not even if they asked me. I suspect they'd shoot me out of hand—both sides.'[47]

On his own experience of the oppressive heat in India, he wrote:

> The heat is so appalling that at noon it looks like the blackest night and feels like the mouth of hell. After a few days of it I seriously began to wonder whether I would come out of it alive. I have thought much since the greatest achievement I made as Chairman of the Boundary Commission was a physical one, in surviving.[48]

A day before the stroke of midnight when the British rule would end, he wrote to his stepson:

> I thought you would like to get a letter from India with a Crown on the envelope. After tomorrow evening nobody will ever again be allowed to use such stationery and after 150 years British rule will be over in India . . . Down comes the Union Jack on Friday morning and up goes . . . for the moment I rather forget what but it has a spinning wheel or a spiders' web in the middle. I am going to see Mountbatten sworn as the first Governor-General of the Indian Union at the Viceroy's House in the morning and then I station myself firmly on the Delhi airport until an aeroplane from England comes along. Nobody in India will love me for the Award about the Punjab and Bengal and there will be roughly 80 million people with a grievance who will begin looking for me. I did not want them to find me. I have worked, travelled, and sweated . . . oh I have sweated the whole time.[49]

Radcliffe was not considered by his critics the right sort of man for the job he undertook. He knew neither the country, the language nor the inhabitants of the areas. He never saw the land he was supposed to partition. He was supposedly to fly to see the terrain in the middle of July when he went to Lahore but the flight had to be cancelled due to a storm. Sir Patrick Spens, the last Chief Justice of British India, remarked that Radcliffe knew nothing of the problem he was asked to resolve, and quipped, 'What do judges know about the demarcation of boundaries?'[50]

Curiously enough, Radcliffe attended only the second and third procedural meetings of the Commission on 14 and 15 July but did not attend the public sittings of the Commission when the Counsels representing the parties argued their case. The judges heard the case without the Chairman of the Commission being present. Some parts of the proceedings of the Bench, or at best, their summaries were flown daily from Lahore to Delhi for the Chairman by a special plane. Setalvad considered the whole procedure 'strange and almost farcical'.[51] He wrote, 'the person whose decision was to be the award was not to hear the counsel putting forward arguments on different sides, but he was to decide on a record of these arguments at a place far away from actual scene of the hearing'.[52] When Setalvad pointed out to Radcliffe the 'procedural ridiculousness' of the course he had adopted, Radcliffe replied that 'as the Award was to be completed before 15 August, he had no time to hear the parties'. Setalvad said that he would have preferred to appear as a Counsel before him than the judges.[53] Justice Munir's disappointment was equally evident in his comment, 'The members of the Commission were reduced to the position of the Advocates. Our reports were waste paper while the report of the Chairman was the report of the Commission.'[54]

In his poem on 'Partition' composed in May 1966, W.H. Auden mocks Sir Cyril Radcliffe and rouses emotions of disgust at his cutting, carving and transforming the boundary between India and Pakistan. Auden wrote:

Unbiased at least he was when he arrived on his mission,
Having never set eyes on this land he was called to partition.
Between two peoples fanatically at odds,
With their different diets and incompatible gods.
'Time', they had briefed him in London, 'is short'. It's too late
For mutual reconciliation or rational debate:
The only solution now lies in separation.

The Viceroy thinks, as you will see from his letter,
That the less you are seen in his company the better,
So we've arranged to provide you with other accommodation.

We can give you four judges, two Moslem and two Hindu,
To consult with, but the final decision must rest with you.

Shut up in a lonely mansion, with police night and day
Patrolling the gardens to keep assassins away,
He got down to work, to the task of settling the fate
Of millions. The maps at his disposal were out of date
And the Census Returns almost certainly incorrect,
But there was no time to check them, no time to inspect
Contested areas. The weather was frightfully hot,
And a bout of dysentery kept him constantly on the trot,
But in seven weeks it was done, the frontiers decided,
A continent for better or worse divided.
The next day he sailed for England, where he quickly forgot
The case, as a good lawyer must. Return he would not,
Afraid, as he told his Club, that he might get shot.[55]

Radcliffe was expected to complete his work by 15 August 1947. He knew that he would have to rush to finish his work. He complained that the task allotted to him was incredibly complex. He found the Indians out of touch with the real issues facing them. He said:

> Amazing people. They had absolutely no conception. They asked me to come in and do their sticky business for them and when I had done it they hated it. But what could they expect in the circumstances? Surely they must have realized what was coming once they had decided on Partition. But they had made absolutely no plans for coping with the situation. Strange chaps. Just did not do homework.[56]

Later Radcliffe was to express the view that he could have done the job properly had he been given two years.[57]

Endowed with a sharp intellect, Radcliffe grasped the essentials of the boundary question. He realized the difficulty of demarcating a boundary in the Punjab because of the existence of elaborate canal systems, a single administration and a network of road and rail communications. He also recognized the 'stubborn geographical fact of the respective situations of Lahore and Amritsar'.[58] He had suggested earlier that Punjab waters should remain 'a joint venture run by both the countries but his suggestion was rejected and he was asked to proceed with his work'.[59] In the light of discussions with his colleagues on the Commission and British officials and by the study of maps and other official and non-official material placed at his disposal, he realized that the disputed area lay between the Beas and Sutlej rivers on the one hand and the Ravi on the other. The area broadly covered the districts of Gurdaspur, Amritsar, Lahore and Ferozepur and a portion of Multan Division.

III

Surprisingly, the Radcliffe Award (barring an area in the Kasur *tehsil*), corresponds with the demarcation of the boundary made by Lord Wavell on 7 February 1946, which he had sent to the Secretary of State, Pethick Lawrence.[60] Wavell had three sketch maps prepared indicating the boundary.[61] The Secretary of State commended Wavell's recommendation on 18 February 1946 with his comment, 'I do not think that any better division than the one that Wavell proposed is likely to be found.'[62] Wavell's boundary line actually had been drawn up by V.P. Menon, Reforms Commissioner and Secretary to Governor-General (Public), 1945-6, and B.N. Rau who was serving on special duty in the Governor-General's Secretariat (Reforms). V.P. Menon had sent a detailed note on the demarcation of Punjab boundary to the Viceroy's Secretary, Sir George Abell, which excluded the districts of Amritsar and Gurdaspur from Pakistan as he thought them to form a 'complete block, . . . which will meet the serious Sikh objections'.[63]

The matter does not rest there. The provocation of the Menon-Rau proposal was a note, 'The next step in India', from Guy Wint, the journalist attached to the External Affairs Department, Government of India, to Jenkins, dated 15 October 1945. The proposal recommended the adjustment of boundaries in the Punjab and Bengal, and the appointment of an international tribunal to settle the boundary question with experts drawn from Canada and Australia. In fact Mrs Guy Wint's proposal was drafted by K.M. Panikkar who had the ambition of being appointed the constitutional adviser to the Viceroy.[64]

The notional boundary laid down in the second schedule of the Indian Independence Act of 18 July 1947 corresponds exactly to Wavell's line except that it places the Muslim majority district of Gurdaspur in Pakistan. Wavell had emphasized in his letter to the Secretary of State dated 7 February 1946, that in the Punjab, 'the only Muslim majority district that would not go into Pakistan under demarcation was Gurdaspur, which must go with Amritsar for geographical reasons, and Amritsar, being a sacred city of Sikhs, must stay out of Pakistan'.[65]

Mountbatten was deeply concerned about the Sikhs whom he called 'the valiant community'. He was astonished to find that the 'Sikhs were almost equally divided in two parts of the Punjab' and he dilated on it in his broadcast of 3 June 1947 and at the Press Conference on 4 June 1947.[66] In his letter dated 4 July 1947, he wrote to Nehru, 'Unless major alterations were made by the Boundary Commission, the Sikh community will be so divided that almost half will remain in the Muslim provinces of West Punjab.'[67]

Mountbatten emphasized that the Sikhs had asked for the partition of Punjab. Though the Sikh leadership was divided on political issues, it was united on the partition of Punjab. During 1946-7, Baldev Singh, Giani Kartar Singh, Ujjal Singh, Swaran Singh and Tara Singh urged the British authorities on several occasions to partition Punjab in a manner so as to safeguard their legitimate interests.[68] In this connection they met the Punjab governor, Jenkins; the Viceroys, Wavell and Mountbatten; the Secretary of State, Pethick Lawrence; and also sent a delegation to England to meet Attlee and R.A. Butler, the Conservative leader. The key mediators who consistently supported their case were Billy Short, E.P. Moon and Jenkins.

On 30 April 1947, Giani Kartar Singh, Harnam Singh and Ujjal Singh met Lord Ismay, Chief of the Viceroy's Staff.[69] Their main focus was on the Lahore Division, particularly Lahore city. They emphasized that in no case would they like the Lahore Division to be included even as an interim arrangement in Pakistan territory. 'It was a matter of life and death for the Sikhs and they would far sooner all die fighting', they said.[70] This claim was later discussed in the Viceroy's staff meetings.

The controversy hinged on the allotment of a larger portion of Gurdaspur District and the *tehsils* of Ferozepur and Zira to India. There is no difficulty in understanding the compulsions that made Radcliffe allot the Gurdaspur area to India. Gurdaspur was a Muslim majority district. Much controversy arose in the Boundary Commission about the accuracy of its census, but finally the figure of 51.14 as its Muslim percentage was accepted. Of the four *tehsils* only in Pathankot did the Muslim constitute a minority (38.8 per cent) while in Gurdaspur their percentage was 59.16, in Batala 55.01 and in Shakargarh 51.32.

Gurdaspur was contiguous to the Muslim majority Sialkot District (66.10 per cent), the state of Jammu & Kashmir (about 77 per cent) and the Kapurthala State under Sikh rule (56.35 per cent). The Upper Bari Doab canal irrigated a larger area of Lahore District than either or both Amritsar and Gurdaspur Districts, and almost two-thirds of the area was served by the system. With its population of 6,32,131 as compared with Amritsar's 3,89,581, the city of Lahore was deriving much of its municipal water supply from the Lahore branch.[71] Thus the control of Upper Bari Doab canal was more vital to Lahore District than to any area within its range. From the point of view of population, contiguity and irrigation, Radcliffe would have been amply justified in allotting Gurdaspur District

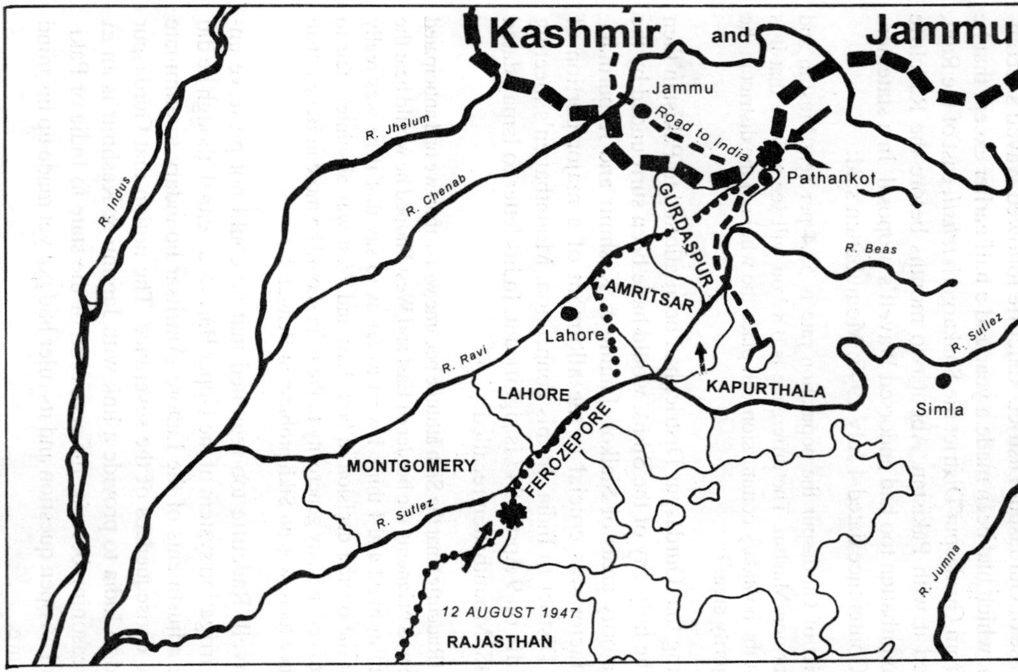

Source: Alastair Lamb, *Kashmir A Disputed Legacy, 1846-1990* (Karachi, 1992) p. xiv c.

MAP 3: PARTITION BOUNDARIES IN PUNJAB
Final Award of the Radcliff Commission arrived at on 12 August 1947
but not published until 16 August 1947

to Pakistan. In awarding Gurdaspur to India, Radcliffe disregarded population, contiguity and irrigation as determining factors in the delimitation of the boundary.

In the case of Gurdaspur District, Radcliffe followed Wavell's recommendation, which had been made a year and a half earlier except that he detached from Gurdaspur District the Shakargarh *tehsil*, east of the Ravi, and clubbed it with Pakistan. About two months before the Radcliffe Award, Mountbatten too had endorsed Wavell's proposal. In a statement at a Press Conference dated 4 July 1947, Mountbatten said:

> In the district of Gurdaspur the population rate is 50.4 per cent Muslim and 49.6 per cent non-Muslim. The difference is 0.8 You will see at once that it is unlikely that the boundary commission will place the whole of the district in the Muslim majority area.[72]

Supposing that Gurdaspur District had been allotted to Pakistan then Amritsar, the holy city of the Sikhs, would have been surrounded by the Muslim majority areas of Sialkot, Jammu & Kashmir and Kapurthala. The Sikh factor was crucial in the allotment of a major portion of Gurdaspur District to India. In this connection, Mountbatten's meeting with Radcliffe on 9 April 1947 is significant. In his letter to Ismay dated 2 April 1948, Mountbatten recalled:

> I said to him (Radcliffe) that the Sikh attitude became worse than we had anticipated and when he was balancing the border of East and West I hoped he would bear the Sikh problem in mind and I think I went as far as to say that if he was really satisfied that the overall decision in both East and West was absolutely fair to both then I trusted that any generosity to Pakistan should be more in Bengal than in Punjab since there was no Sikh problem in Bengal.[73]

Like Wavell, Radcliffe too regretted that he could not preserve undivided the irrigation system of the Upper Bari Doab canal, though he did make some adjustments of the Lahore–Amritsar boundary to eliminate some of the consequences of the severance. The notion that Gurdaspur was allotted to India to provide a link with Jammu & Kashmir is an *ex post facto* reasoning because the accession of the state to India or Pakistan was still an open question and its ruler had not yet made up his mind about its future.

Surprisingly, the boundary line in respect of Ferozepur and Zira *tehsil* was changed on 10 or 11 August 1947. This is evident from a letter dated 8 August 1947 addressed by the Private Secretary to the Viceroy, George Abell to S.E. Abbott, Secretary to the Punjab governor, Jenkins.[74] Later the Mountbatten-Jenkins correspondence also deals with the same

controversial issue.[75] The Ferozepur District was predominantly non-Muslim with 54.92 per cent in the 1941 census; the two northern *tehsils* Ferozepur and Zira were Muslim majority areas with 55.25 per cent and 56.22 per cent. The third *tehsil* Fazilka was non-Muslim (56.72 per cent).

Mountbatten is accused of pressurizing Radcliffe to allot Ferozepur and Zira *tehsils* to India. Radcliffe's Personal Secretary, Christopher Beaumont confirms it.[76] Walter Henry John Christie, Joint Private Secretary to the Viceroy, records in his Diary dated 9 August 1947 that the Viceroy 'is a tired flap, and is having to be dissuaded from asking Radcliffe to alter the boundary'.[77] It is rather curious that V.P. Menon, Mountbatten's Constitutional Adviser and confidant, gives only bare facts on the boundary question and is silent on the controversies raised.[78]

Much pressure was brought on Mountbatten about Ferozepur and Zira by Nehru and Maharaja Sadul Singh, the ruler of Bikaner. Sadul Singh had known Mountbatten since childhood.[79] He and Mountbatten had served together on the staff of the Prince of Wales, later King Edward VIII, when he visited India in 1922. Mountbatten called the Maharaja Hiru and the Maharaja referred to Mountbatten as 'Dickie'. Nehru sent a note to Mountbatten from A.N. Khosla (Chairman, Central Waterways, Irrigation and Navigation Commission), warning that the allotment of Ferozepur to Pakistan would be a 'disaster' to India from the irrigation and strategic point of view. Mountbatten had visited Bikaner a few weeks earlier, and enjoyed the Maharaja's hospitality.[80] Later he was to invest the Maharaja with a title. K.M. Panikkar, Prime Minister of Bikaner and Kanwar Sain, Chief Engineer (Irrigation), met Mountbatten on 11 August at 11 a.m. about Ferozepur and Zira, but Mountbatten refused to intervene. To this Panikkar responded by saying that their ruler wanted it to be conveyed that if Ferozepur headworks and the Ganga water, on which Bikaner depended for its economic existence, were allotted to Pakistan, then Bikaner would have no option but to join Pakistan.[81] Mountbatten did not record Panikkar's meeting with him but Kanwar Sain did about two decades later, but how far one can rely on his account is difficult to say because it is a reconstruction in retrospect.

It seems that in lieu of the Gurdaspur area and a small portion of Lahore District, which had been allotted to India, Radcliffe wanted to compensate Pakistan by giving it Ferozepur and Zira *tehsils*. After partitioning Gurdaspur District, he wanted to partition Ferozepur District and to assign its headworks to Pakistan to balance the Madhopur headworks which went to India. Mountbatten met Radcliffe on 9 August 1947 over a drink hosted by Ismay and urged him to adopt a preferential treatment to the

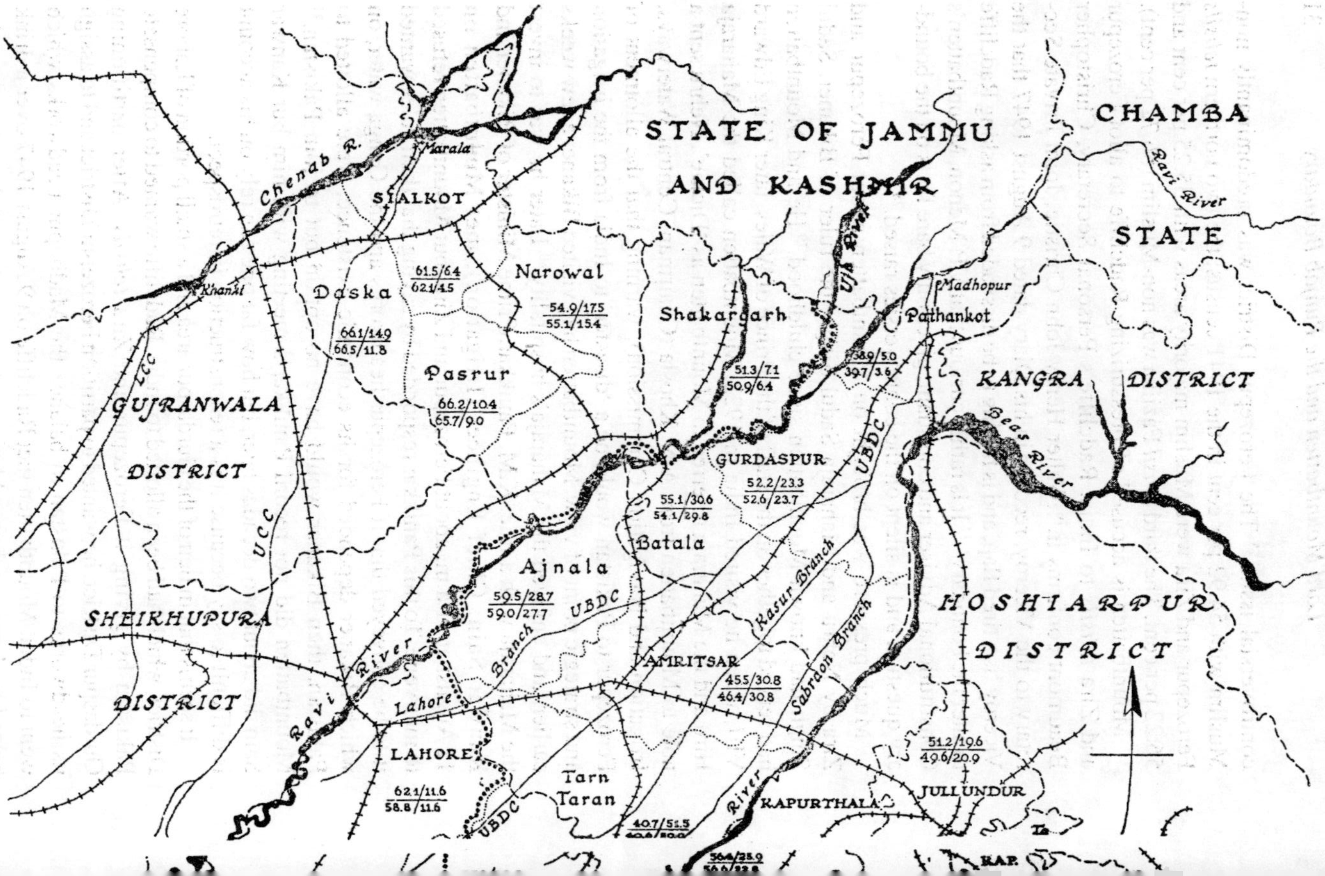

STATE OF JAMMU AND KASHMIR
CHAMBA STATE
Ravi River
Chenab R.
Marala
SIALKOT
Khanki
LCC
Daska
61.5/6.4
62.1/4.5
Narowal
54.9/17.5
55.1/15.4
Shakargarh
Ujh River
Madhopur
Pathankot
66.1/14.9
66.5/11.8
Pasrur
66.2/10.4
65.7/9.0
51.3/7.1
50.9/6.4
38.9/5.0
39.7/3.6
KANGRA DISTRICT
GUJRANWALA DISTRICT
UCC
UBDC
Beas River
GURDASPUR
52.2/23.3
52.6/23.7
55.1/30.6
54.1/29.8
Batala
Ajnala
59.5/28.7
59.0/27.7
Kasur Branch
Sabraon Branch
HOSHIARPUR DISTRICT
SHEIKHUPURA DISTRICT
Ravi River
Branch
Lahore
AMRITSAR
45.5/30.8
46.4/30.8
LAHORE
62.1/11.6
58.8/11.6
Tarn Taran
River
KAPURTHALA
JULLUNDUR
51.2/19.6
49.6/20.9
40.7/51.5
KAP.

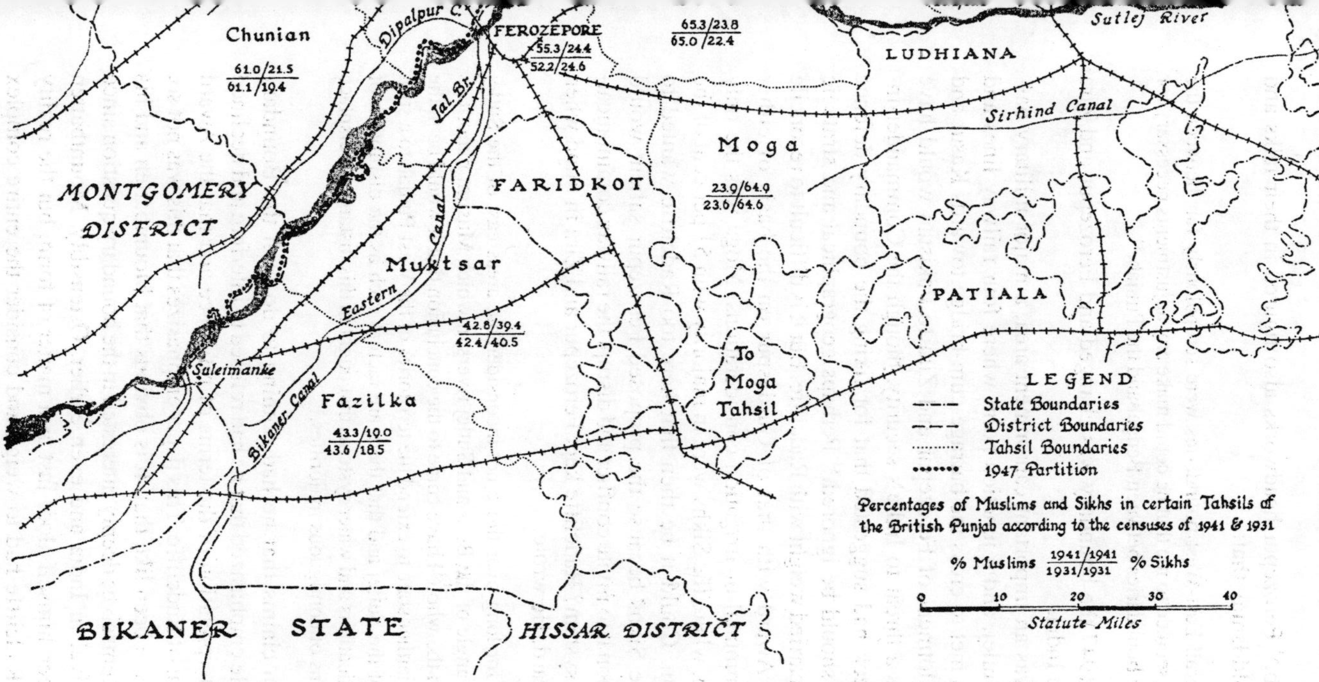

Source: Aloys Arthur Michel, *The Indus Rivers, A Study of the Effects of Partition* (New Haven and London, 1967), pp. 150-1.

MAP 4: THE CENTRAL PUNJAB, SHOWING THE RELATION OF THE PARTITION LINE TO THE MUSLIM AND SIKH POPULATION BY *TEHSIL* AND TO THE IRRIGATION AND RAILWAY SYSTEMS

Sikhs in Punjab.[82] Ferozepur headworks also figured in their talks and Mountbatten told Ismay that:

> provided the overall East-West boundaries were scrupulously fair between the two dominions it seemed to me that he could make any adjustments necessary for balancing out the boundaries between Bengal and the Punjab.[83]

By 11 August 1947 the boundary was changed and Ferozepur and Zira were allotted to India.

Ferozepur was an important cantonment area, a major military bastion south of Sutlej, and a junction point where four railway lines and three highways met to cross the barrage-cum-bridge towards Kasur and Lahore. The allotment of Ferozepur and Zira to Pakistan would have been viewed as a threat to India's security, though the Commander-in-Chief Auchinleck had suggested that for fixing the boundary defence considerations should be ignored.[84] Perhaps geographical and strategic considerations carried weight with Radcliffe. But it is difficult to reconcile the Ferozepur Award with that of Gurdaspur on the basis of either contiguous communal or irrigation considerations. Moga was the only *tehsil* in Punjab, where the Sikhs were in majority with 51 per cent of the total population. Could it be then that here too Radcliffe wanted to compensate the Sikhs because the proposed Ferozepur salient would have abutted upon it to invite conflict and disrupt the railway communications and water system? Radcliffe kept Ferozepur and Zira in mind when he gave his Award. He wrote:

> I have hesitated for long over those not inconsiderable areas east of the Sutlej River and in the angle of the Beas and Sutlej rivers in which Muslim majorities are found. But on the whole I have come to the conclusion that it would be in the true interests of neither state to extend the territories of the West Punjab to a strip on the far side of the Sutlej and that there are factors such as the disruption of railway communications and water systems that ought in this instance to displace the primary claims of contiguous majorities.[85]

Mountbatten claims that he had nothing to do with the Boundary Commission. He emphasized that he had refused to interfere and declined to offer any interpretation of the terms of reference and that the Award was entirely that of Radcliffe. This paper emphasizes that this was not so, nor should it have been like that. It is obvious that Mountbatten and his officials kept themselves deeply interested in the boundary question since Radcliffe's arrival in India and even earlier. Ostensibly, Mountbatten professed to keep himself aloof just as a matter of form, but the reality was different. Radcliffe had to weigh and consider the entire complex problem in its details, and the Viceroy as head of the government, was to ensure that the boundary should be drawn in a manner as to eschew all possible friction and conflict between the rival parties.

Radcliffe was not expected to work in solitude, cultivating his own garden. He had to seek information, he had to exchange views and get his doubts clarified. All this required scrutiny and examination by way of discussion on vital issues particularly for a man who did not know the country. Jinnah knew that Gurdaspur had been allotted to India. That is why he sent Chaudhri Mohammad Ali to meet Ismay on 9 August in this connection. Nehru knew the fate of Ferozepur and Zira, and wrote about it to the Viceroy on 9 August. Panikkar too met Mountbatten on 11 August for this purpose. Radcliffe had sought the Viceroy's opinion on 2 August 1947 about the interpretation of the contiguous majority areas of the adjoining districts of Assam.[86]

IV

The conclusion is that the Radcliffe Award corresponds to the border line specified by Wavell in 1946, and Wavell's boundary line was actually drawn by V.P. Menon and Sir B.N. Rau; the provocation for this was the note prepared by K.M. Panikkar for which he used his friend Guy Wint's name. A Muslim majority district of Gurdaspur was allotted to East Punjab because of its geographical contiguity to Amritsar and for the purpose of giving protection to it. Radcliffe was not the progenitor of the demarcation of the boundary, but was an accessory to give the Award a semblance of impartiality and a seal of authority. Mountbatten was adept at using Radcliffe as a conduit for his schemes and ideas. Further, it is a myth that Mountbatten kept himself out of the boundary question—he was very much there, and adopted a posture of non-involvement to evade criticism from those likely to be dissatisfied with the Award. The boundary line was changed between 9 and 12 August 1947 at the last stage in respect of Ferozepur and Zira, but for want of material evidence, one can only speculate as to why it was done. It is difficult to fathom motives and there could be multiple reasons. But one is struck by the fact that both the Gurdaspur and Ferozepur Award were inconsistent. In the realm of politics, consistency is perhaps not a virtue. With his usual perception, Bismarck had said, 'Politics is the art of the possible, and of the relative.'

Mountbatten delayed the announcement of the Award until 16 August. He tried to persuade Radcliffe to postpone its dispatch to him beyond

13 August, but he declined.[87] Mountbatten gave out to his close associates that his object in delaying the announcement was not to mar the Independence Day celebrations as he feared that there might be strong reactions against the Award in the country.[88] V.P. Menon had advised Mountbatten to postpone the announcement as he feared that Nehru and Patel might boycott the Constituent Assembly meeting in case of adverse recommendations on the boundary question. Mountbatten was shrewd enough to realize that after 15 August the British were not to bear the responsibility for the disturbances, which might inevitably follow the Award.[89] The two countries became free when their boundaries were not defined. There was utter confusion followed by blood, toil and tears, rapine, pillage and slaughter, arson, death and destruction. The poet Faiz has captured the anguish of blasted hopes and suffering in the following lines:

Yeh dag dag ujala yeh shab guzida-e-sahar
Woh intzar tha jis ka woh sihar to nahin
Yeh woh sihar to nahin jis ki arzoo leyker
Chaley thay yar key mil jayengi kahin na kahin
Falaq key dasht main taron ki akhri manzil
Kahin to rookey ga safina-e-gamey dil.

(This is not the long-looked for break-of-day!
Not that clear dawn in quest of which those comrades
Set out, believing that in heaven's wide void,
Somewhere must be the stars' last halting place,
Somewhere the verge of night's slow-washing tide,
Somewhere an anchorage for the ship of heartache!)[90]

NOTES

1. For Mountbatten's critics who accused him of changing the boundary line, see Alastair Lamb, *Birth of a Tragedy in Kashmir* (London, 1964), pp. 31-8; Chaudhri Mohammad Ali, *The Emergence of Pakistan* (Lahore, 1985), pp. 178 and 213-25; M.A.H. Ispahani, *Qaid-e-Azam Jinnah As I Knew Him* (Karachi, 1967), p. 248; and Sir Francis Mudie in Kirpal Singh, ed., *Selected Documents on Partition of Punjab, India and Pakistan, 1947* (Delhi, 1991), Appendix II, p. 734.

   For Mountbatten's defenders on the boundary question, see the autobiography of Mehr Chand Mahajan, *Looking Back* (New Delhi, 1963), p. 115; Michael Brecher, *Nehru, A Political Biography* (London, 1959), pp. 360-1; Leonard Mosley, *The Last Days of the British Raj* (London, 1961), pp. 230-1; Alan Campbell-Johnson, *Mission with Mountbatten* (London, 1951), pp. 230-1, Philip Ziegler, *Mountbatten: The Official Biography* (London, 1985), pp. 421-2; and H.V. Hodson, *The Great Divide, Britain, India and Pakistan* (Karachi, 1985), pp. 354-5.

   Lamb revised his earlier views and wrote that the Award was in no way related to the Kashmir question but was based on considerations arising from the division of waters from certain canals. See Alastair Lamb, *Crisis in Kashmir* (London, 1966), p. 42.

2. Brecher, op.cit., p. 360.
3. Andrew Roberts, *Eminent Churchillians* (London, 1994), p. 112.
4. S. Hasham Raza, ed., *Mountbatten and the Partition of India* (New Delhi, 1989), p. 112.
5. Lamb, op.cit., p. 38.
6. Kirpal Singh, ed., op.cit., Document (hereafter Doc.) 227, Mountbatten to Lord Ismay, 2 April 1948.
7. Brecher, op.cit., p. 352.
8. Kirpal Singh, ed., op.cit., Doc. 235.
9. Ibid.
10. Ibid.
11. Ziegler, op.cit., p. 421.
12. *Daily Telegraph* (London), 24 February 1992.
13. M. Rafique Afzal, *Speeches and Statements of the Quaid-i-Azam, Mohammed Ali Jinnah* (Lahore, 1966), p. 432.
14. Ibid.
15. Brecher, op.cit., p. 361.
16. Nicholas Mansergh, editor-in-chief, *Transfer of Power 1942-7*, Vol. XII (London, 1983), Doc. 377.
17. Ibid., fn. I.
18. Kirpal Singh, ed., op.cit., Doc. 238; see Hodson, op.cit., p. 253; see P.T. Mansfield, Box LXI, p. 108, South Asian Centre, Cambridge; see Robert Rhodes James, 'Churchill, the Man', in Raymond A. Callaham, ed., *Churchill, Retreat from Europe* (London, 1984), p. 108.
19. Mansergh, op.cit., Doc. 377.
20. Brecher, op.cit., p. 361.
21. Kirpal Singh, ed., op.cit., p. 744.
22. Ibid.
23. Hugh Tinker, 'Persuasion, Decision, Factors and the Partition of Punjab', in *Journal of Asian Studies,* Vol. XXVI (Utah, August 1977), p. 704.
24. Ibid.
25. Mansergh, op.cit., Doc. 486, Viceroys' Personal Record.
26. Ibid., Vol. XI (London, 1982), Doc. 45.
27. Ibid., Doc. 415.
28. Ibid., Doc. 128.
29. Ispahani, op.cit., p. 27.
30. Mansergh, op.cit., Vol. XII, Docs 164 and 367-8.
31. Patrick French, *Liberty or Death, India's Journey to Independence* (London, 1997), p. 321.
32. Ibid., p. 324, Mian Muhammad Sadullah, *The Partition of the Punjab, A Compilation of Official Documents*, Vol. I (Lahore, 1987), p. 99.
33. French, op.cit., p. 324.
34. Mansergh, op.cit.,Vol. XII, Doc. 45.
35. Ibid., Doc. 44.
36. Ibid.
37. Motilal Setalvad, *My Life, Law and Other Things* (Bombay, 1971), p. 108.
38. Justice Mehr Chand Mahajan has summed up succinctly the Muslim League and

Congress claims. See Mian Muhammad Sadullah, *The Partition of the Punjab, Compilation of Official Documents*, Vol. III (Lahore, 1987), pp. 160-1.

39. Ibid., pp. 509-12.
40. Ibid., p. 182.
41. Ibid., p. 115.
42. Mehr Chand Mahajan, op.cit., p. 115.
43. Ibid.
44. Mosley, op.cit., p. 200; H.V. Hodson, op.cit., p. 315.
45. Larry Collins and Dominique Lapierre, *Freedom at Midnight* (London, 1976), p. 282.
46. Mansergh, op.cit., Vol. XII, Doc. 377, fn. I.
47. Mosley, op.cit., p. 200.
48. Ibid., p. 197.
49. Quoted in Sunil Khilnani, *The Idea of India* (London, 1997), p. 201.
50. Kirpal Singh, ed., op.cit., p. 749.
51. Setalvad, op.cit., p. 111.
52. Ibid.
53. Ibid.
54. Ispahani, op.cit., p. 251.
55. W.H. Auden, *Collected Poems,* ed., Edward Mendelson (London, 1976), p. 604.
56. Mosley, op.cit., p. 200.
57. Roberts, op.cit., p. 91.
58. Mansergh, op.cit., Vol. XII, Appendix to Doc. 488, Radcliffe to Mountbatten, 12 August 1947.
59. Mosley, op.cit., p. 185.
60. Mansergh, op.cit., Vol. VI (London, 1976), Doc. 406.
61. Ibid., Doc. 428. The maps referred to are facing, p. 966.
62. Ibid., Doc. 440.
63. Z.H. Zaidi, ed., *Quaid-I-Azam Muhammad Ali Jinnah Papers, Prelude to Pakistan (20 February-2 June 1947)*, Vol. I, Part 2 (1st series, Karachi, 1993), Appendix XII.37.
64. Mansergh, op.cit., Vol. VI, Doc. 350, note by Mrs Guy Wint. See also Z.H. Zaidi, ed., op.cit., Vol. I, Part 2, Appendix XII.20. Note by E. Jenkins to V.P. Menon, 18 October 1945, ibid., Appendix XII.21.
65. Mansergh, op.cit., Vol. VI, Doc. 406.
66. Ibid., Vol. XI, Docs 44 and 59-60.
67. Ibid., Doc. 497.
68. Ibid., Vol. VII, Docs 56-7 and 445; ibid., Vol. X (London, 1981), Docs 115 and 240.
69. Ibid., Doc. 258.
70. Ibid.
71. Aloys Arthur Michel, *The Indus Rivers, A Study of the Effect of Partition* (New Haven and London, 1967), p. 189. This is a valuable study of Punjab from the irrigation and water system standpoint.
72. Kirpal Singh, ed., op.cit., Doc. 329.
73. Ibid., Doc. 237, also p. xxvi; see S. Hasham Raza, ed., op.cit., p. 42.
74. Mansergh, op.cit., Vol. XII,Doc. 377.
75. Ibid., fn. I.
76. *Daily Telegraph* (London), 24 February 1992.
77. Mansergh, op.cit., Vol. XII, Christie's Diary, Doc. 389, fn. 3.

78. V.P. Menon, *The Story of the Integration of the Indian State* (Delhi, 1956), p. 122; idem, *The Transfer of Power in India* (Bombay, 1957), p. 112.
79. Lord Mountbatten, *The Second Jawaharlal Nehru Lecture* (London, 1968), p. 27. See also Karni Singh, *The Relations of the House of Bikaner with the Central Powers* (New Delhi, 1974), p. 321.
80. Kanwar Sain, *Reminiscences of an Engineer* (New Delhi, 1978), p. 118; see also Mansergh, op.cit., Vol. XII, Doc. 402.
81. Ibid., Doc. 405 fn. See Rima Hooja, *Prince, Patriot, Parliamentarian: Biography of Dr. Karni Singh* (New Delhi, 1997), p. 103. The Maharaja is reported to have told Paul Ramsay Brown who was working in the Bikaner Railways till 1949 that if Ferozepur had been allotted to Pakistan then he would have been forced to join Pakistan. In his autobiography, K.M. Panikkar makes no mention of his meeting with Mountbatten. See K.M. Panikkar, *An Autobiography,* trans. from Malayalam by K. Krishnamurthy (Delhi, 1977).
82. Kirpal Singh, ed., op.cit., Doc. 237; see Raza, ed., op.cit., p. 43; also see Hodson, op.cit., p. 351.
83. Ibid.
84. Mansergh, op.cit., Vol. XII, Doc. 52.
85. Ibid., Appendix I to Doc. 488.
86. Ibid., Doc. 318.
87. Ibid., Doc. 389.
88. Ibid.
89. Ibid.
90. Khalid Hasan, ed., *Kalam-e-Faiz: the Unicorn and the Dancing Girl* (New Delhi, 1988), pp. 19-20.

Tragedy and Triumph: The Last Days of Mahatma Gandhi

B.R. NANDA

The last two years of Gandhi's life were the saddest and the most heroic. He was shocked and bewildered by the drift towards the Partition of India and the explosion of violence, which preceded and followed it. He first saw its ravages when he visited Calcutta in October 1946, after what the *Statesman* described as 'the Great Calcutta Killing'. He confessed to 'a sinking feeling at the mass madness which can turn a man into a brute'. He was on his way to eastern Bengal, where in the Muslim-majority district of Noakhali local hooligans, exploiting poor communications and encouraged by fanatical mullahs and ambitious politicians, had burnt properties of the Hindus, looted their crops, desecrated their temples, abducted their women and made forcible conversions. Thousands of Hindus had fled from their homes.

Gandhi found the atmosphere in East Bengal charged with suspicion and fear. He embarked on a village-to-village tour, not to apportion blame for the riots, but to create conditions in which the two communities could again live together peacefully. He confided his strategy to his secretary, Professor N.K. Bose:

> The first thing is that politics has divided India today into Hindus and Muslims. I want to rescue people from this quagmire and make them work on solid ground where people are people. Therefore, my appeal here is not to the Muslims as Muslims nor to the Hindus as Hindus, but to ordinary human beings who have to keep their villages clean, build schools for their children, and take many other steps so that they can make life better.[1]

He lifted the question of communal peace from the plane of politics to the plane of humanity. 'Everyone of us,' he said, 'is equally guilty of what anyone of us has done.' He deprecated the habit of providing a moral alibi by blaming the riots on *goondas* (hooligans). 'Who are the *goondas*?' he asked and answered, 'We are responsible for their creation as well as encouragement.' When the Hindus pleaded for Hindu pockets in Muslim areas and for police and military reinforcements for their safety, he told them that the only protection which any minority could really count on was that given by neighbours to neighbours. Nor did he accept the specious pleas of Muslim politicians that the accounts of the riots in East Bengal had been fabricated by the Hindu press to discredit the Muslim League ministry. 'Thousands of people,' Gandhi said, 'were hardly likely to become homeless and penniless simply to spite the ministers in Calcutta.'

While Gandhi was busy with his pilgrimage for peace in East Bengal, the peasantry of Bihar wreaked terrible vengeance on their Muslim neighbours for the crimes committed on the Hindu minority in East Bengal. He moved over to Bihar, where his refrain was the same as it had been in Bengal: the majority must repent and make amends; the minority must forgive and forget and make a fresh start. In Bihar, however, he was in a position to pull up the Congress ministry, and call upon Nehru and Patel, who were in the Interim Government, to take the sternest measures. While he was agonizing over the violence in Bihar, news arrived of serious riots in the Muslim-majority districts of West Punjab.

Gandhi was dismayed by this prairie fire of religious frenzy and barbaric violence, which was rapidly spreading across the subcontinent. All his life he had laboured for the day when India would attain freedom and set an example to the world in non-violence. The chasm between what he had cherished in his heart and what he saw was so great that he could not help feeling a deep sense of failure. His first impulse was to blame himself. Had he been unobservant, careless, indifferent, impatient? Had he failed to detect in time that while people on the whole had been overtly non-violent in the struggle against foreign rule, they had not really imbibed his message of non-violence?

With hindsight, we can see that Gandhi was exaggerating his own responsibility and the failure of his method. The violence which erupted in 1946-7 was in its scale and intensity entirely in a category different from the sporadic communal riots of the inter-war years on such issues as cow slaughter and music before the mosques. It had its origin in the hatred and tensions, which the Muslim League's seven-year campaign for Pakistan had aroused in its champions as well as in its opponents. The basic plank in this campaign was that Hindus and Muslims had nothing in common in the past or the present. While the negotiations on the new constitution for India after the British departure dragged on in the summer of 1946, the masses were seized with vague hopes and fears. No one could say with any degree of certainty whether India would survive as one country or would be cut up into two or more states, whether Punjab and Bengal would be divided, whether the princely states would be integrated into the Indian federation or become independent kingdoms. The Adivasis of central India and the Nagas of Assam suddenly found champions for independence, which they had never claimed before; there was talk of 'Dravidastan' in the south (which Jinnah applauded), and a thousand-mile corridor to link the two wings of a future Pakistan. The Nizam of Hyderabad was intriguing with the Portuguese to secure access to the port of Goa so as to be able to set himself up as an independent sultan. The rulers of several other states, such as Travancore and Bhopal, entertained similar grandiose ambitions. All this could not but excite popular fantasy; the turbulent elements in the country began to see in the coming transfer of power a period of power vacuum such as had occurred in the twilight of the Mughal Empire.

In the winter of 1946-7, Gandhi considered the restoration of peace as the most important and urgent task for the country. He sought to purge fear, hatred and violence from the hearts of the people and to instil mutual trust and tolerance. His walking tours, his prayer meetings and speeches acted as a soothing balm on the hapless victims of the riots. But what dismayed him was the way mass madness was escalating from Calcutta to East Bengal, from East Bengal to Bihar and the West Punjab.

Gandhi steeled himself to visit the riot-torn areas until the flames of hatred and violence had been quenched. His colleagues and followers in the Indian National Congress appreciated the loftiness of his mission, but were sceptical of its success. As Nehru told Mountbatten, the Mahatma was 'going round with ointment trying to heal one more spot after another on the body of India, instead of diagnosing (its) cause and participating in the treatment of the body as a whole'. This assessment would have been endorsed by Vallabhbhai Patel, Rajagopalachari, Rajendra Prasad and other leaders who perceived the riots as the fallout of the gravest political crisis which the country had ever faced, a crisis which in fact seemed to be the culmination of the 60 years' triangular contest between British imperialism, Congress nationalism and Muslim separatism.

To the historian, it seems surprising that Gandhi should have been so shocked by the acceptance of the Partition of the country by the Congress leadership. Since March 1940, when Jinnah first propounded his two-nation theory and demanded the secession of the Muslim-majority areas in the east and the west, the Congress had been continually softening its stand under the impact of the League's strident propaganda and the confrontation with the British rulers. Soon after the Lahore session of the Muslim League in 1940, while rejecting the two-nation theory,

Gandhi wrote in the *Harijan* that he knew 'no non-violent method of compelling the obedience of eight crore Muslims to the will of rest of India. . . . The Muslims must have the same right to self-determination that the rest of India has. We are at present a joint family. Any member may claim a division.'[2]

Two years later, the Congress Working Committee in its resolution on the Cripps Proposals declared that it 'cannot think in terms of compelling the people of any territorial unit in the Indian Union against their declared and established will'. In 1944, in his protracted talks with Jinnah, Gandhi not only accepted the possibility of the Partition of the country, but discussed the mechanism for effecting it. And finally, in the summer of 1946, the Congress accepted, of course after much heart-searching, the Cabinet Mission Plan with its loose three-tier structure and a central government limited to three subjects: foreign affairs, defence and communications. The durability of this was however open to doubt. When such a federal government was suggested for the two wings of Pakistan in 1970, Z.A. Bhutto compared the lot of such a government to 'a widow without a pension'.

The Cabinet Mission Plan proved stillborn. The Congress accepted the Plan, but with its own interpretation of the 'Grouping Clause', which differed from that of the Muslim League. The Muslim League withdrew its acceptance of the Plan and refused to join the Constituent Assembly. When the Viceroy, Lord Wavell formed an Interim Government headed by Jawaharlal Nehru, the League announced Direct Action on 16 August 1946. Rattled by the holocaust which followed in Calcutta and East Bengal, Lord Wavell inducted the Muslim League into the Interim Government, but with results which were just the opposite of what he had hoped for. The Interim Government, instead of becoming more representative and effective, was paralysed by the conflict between its Congress and League members. The Viceroy did not have a clue as to what he should do, and proposed a 'Breakdown Plan' for British military evacuation of the subcontinent, province by province. Prime Minister Attlee considered it a counsel of despair, and decided to appoint a new Viceroy to devise and implement a scheme for a more orderly termination of British rule in India.

On 20 February 1947 the British government came out with a momentous statement announcing 'their definite intention to take the necessary steps to effect the transfer of power into responsible Indian hands by a date not later than June 1948'. This statement could well have acted as a 'shock therapy' to bring the contending parties together. It had just the opposite effect because of the provision in it that if on 'the appointed date' there was no single government for the whole of British India, power might be transferred 'in some areas to the existing provincial governments or in such other ways as may seem most reasonable'. The Muslim League, which had ministries only in Bengal and Sind, took this to mean that it just had 15 months to capture the provincial governments in the remaining provinces which it claimed for Pakistan: Punjab, NWFP and Assam. It unleashed a campaign of Direct Action in the form of demonstrations, which resulted in widespread communal disturbances in West Punjab in March 1947. The response of the Congress Working Committee came in a resolution demanding the partition of the Punjab; it was a signal to the Muslim League that it would not be allowed to get away with the Hindu-majority areas in the east and the west. The logic which the League applied for the Partition of India could well justify the partition of these two provinces.

By the time Lord Mountbatten arrived in India towards the end of March 1947, the Congress leadership was trying to reconcile itself to Pakistan as 'the lesser evil'; the choice was narrowing down to Partition or civil war. While the new Viceroy was hammering out a scheme acceptable to the Congress, the League and the British government, Gandhi, a helpless spectator, was watching the course of events. It hurt him to see that he was unable to carry conviction with his closest colleagues and even with the rank and file of the Congress. It has been suggested that he was isolated and even betrayed by Nehru and Patel who were 'avid for power'. As for Gandhi's isolation, it was largely self-inflicted; he chose to carry on with his humanitarian mission in Bengal and Bihar instead of returning to Delhi, where fateful decisions were being taken. More importantly, his views seemed utopian and impracticable not only to Nehru and Patel, but to almost all members of the Congress Working Committee on whom the burden of decision rested. They knew that they were not the only players in the making of events. For a quarter of a century, the Congress had been calling for the end of foreign rule. The British withdrawal had now been decided and dated. Partition could only be avoided, if a viable alternative was devised with the concurrence of all the three parties, the British government, the Congress and the Muslim League. This alternative was not in sight.

Gandhi was thinking hard how to pull the country back from the precipice of Partition. In his second meeting with Lord Mountbatten on 1 April 1947 he proposed that Jinnah should be invited to form a government of his own choice to which the Congress would extend its support. The proposal 'astounded' the Viceroy, but it was also rejected out of hand by Patel and Nehru, who had been driven to despair by their experience of working with the League representatives in the Interim Government; in any case, they were certain that such unilateral gestures would not melt Jinnah's heart. Mountbatten did not convey Gandhi's proposal to Jinnah, but it is doubtful if the League leader's reaction would have been different from what he had said about a similar proposal made by the Mahatma in August 1942:

> If they [the Congress] are sincere I should welcome it. If the British Government accepted the solemn declaration of Mr. Gandhi and by an arrangement hands over the government of the country to the Muslim League, I am sure that under Muslim rule non-Muslims would be treated fairly justly, nay, generously; and further the British will be making full amends to the Muslims by restoring the Government of India to those from whom they have taken it.[3]

When Gandhi's proposal to hand over power to Jinnah did not find favour, he put forward a basic proposition: there should be no surrender to threats of violence; there must be peace before there was Pakistan. He argued that the communal polarization in the country was not a permanent phenomenon, that the British had in any case no moral right to impose Partition on an 'India temporarily gone mad'. The British, he said, could depart from India, but they had no right to divide it.

In the first half of 1947 most political observers would have agreed with Gandhi on the urgency of ending communal violence, but they believed its root cause was political. It was the problem of unity *versus* partition, which had unhinged the minds of the people and this problem had to be resolved in Delhi and London. Gandhi's approach was different. He sought to work upon the people at the grassroots, and convince them that they could live together as good neighbours as they had done for centuries. His tours of Bengal and Bihar had met with a measure of success, but he was handicapped by the fact that his voice did not carry weight with the Muslim community as it had once done. If his efforts at restoring amity had been supplemented by someone who commanded the allegiance of the Muslim community, his task would not have been half as difficult. If Jinnah had toured East Bengal or West Punjab, he might have helped in stopping the riots. Such an idea would simply have been laughed out of court by the League leader. 'In politics', Jinnah said, 'one has to play one's game as on the chess-board'.[4] However deplorable communal violence was, it became the strongest argument in his brief for Pakistan. The Quaid-i-Azam's reiteration of 'Congress tyranny' and

'Hindu Raj' for a decade had succeeded in producing in his followers and even in his colleagues a strange blend of paranoia, combativeness and bravado.[5] The League leaders were wont to ridicule Gandhi's non-violence; whether or not they believed in violence, they seemed to believe in the threats of violence. Jinnah himself had inaugurated his Direct Action campaign in August 1946 with the remark: 'Today we have forged a pistol and are in a position to use it.'[6] Insofar as these threats were designed to rouse the Muslims, frighten the Congress and impress the British, they succeeded; both the Congress and the British in the end were driven to the conclusion that Partition was the only alternative to chaos. When riots broke out, the League leaders were reluctant to condemn the misdeeds of their co-religionists, and heaped all the blame on the Hindus, the Congress and the British. In November 1946, George Abell, the Private Secretary of the Viceroy, wrote after a meeting with Jinnah's deputy, Nawabzada Liaquat Ali Khan, that he 'got the clear impression that the League could not afford to let the communal feeling in the country to die down'.[7] The restoration of peace thus became an intractable problem. The Interim Government at the Centre was a house divided against itself; in the provinces the British governors and senior ICS officers, conscious of their imminent departure, had neither the will nor the ability to cope with large-scale disorders. There was a real danger of the police and the army being infected with the communal virus.[8] It was the stark choice between a partition and civil war, which drove the Congress leaders to accept Partition.

Later-day commentators have been asking why Gandhi did not fast to prevent Partition. Fasting was certainly one of the ultimate weapons in Gandhi's armoury of satyagraha; he had used it on certain occasions to exercise moral pressure. This pressure was, as a rule, directed not against those who differed with him, but against those who loved and believed in him; he sought to prick the conscience of the latter and to convey to them something of his inner anguish when things went wrong. A fast dramatized the issues at stake; ostensibly it suppressed reason, but in fact it was designed to free reason from inertia and prejudice which hindered the meeting of minds. Gandhi did in fact have recourse to fasting at Calcutta in September 1947 and at Delhi in January 1948. These two fasts have been rightly reckoned among the greatest miracles of modern times; they had a magical effect in quenching the flames of hatred and violence. These fasts were, however, undertaken *after* independence and were in reality directed by Gandhi against his own co-religionists. To prevent Partition, there was no point in Gandhi's fasting or starting civil disobedience against the British, who were not susceptible to such moral pressure, and were in any case leaving the country. Nor would there have been any point in his undertaking a fast in West Punjab or East Bengal where he had been painted for years as an enemy of Islam. The leaders of the Muslim League were proof against the nuances of satyagraha; they would have at once denounced Gandhi's fast as a trick to cheat them of the prize of Pakistan, which lay within their grasp.

Gandhi's proposition that the British had no right to partition India, but should leave India to her fate was acceptable neither to the Muslim League nor to the British. It had been an unalterable strategy of Jinnah since 1937 to seek the realization of his objectives with the help of the British;[9] for him the correct sequence was: 'Partition first and independence afterwards.' In 1946-7 the Labour government had decided not to let Jinnah exercise a veto on the freedom of India, but it could not ignore him either. After all, he had obtained a decisive mandate in the general election of 1946 in which he had won—on the issue of Pakistan—all the Muslim seats in the Central Assembly and 90 per cent of the Muslim seats in the provincial legislatures. Prime Minister Attlee advised Jinnah to 'enter the Constituent Assembly and try to resolve the problem through mutual negotiations by argument and compromise'.[10] But Jinnah insisted on Partition, undaunted even by the prospect of the division of the Punjab, Bengal and Assam. With the looming threat of civil war, the Labour government could not afford to leave India, as Gandhi said, 'to its fate'. Such a momentous decision, as the liquidation of British Empire in India, needed the support of public opinion and approval of both Houses of Parliament in Britain. Churchill and the Conservative Party would never have allowed any solution, which was not acceptable to Jinnah and the Muslim League.

On 1 June 1947, a day before Mountbatten formally presented his Partition plan to the Indian leaders, Gandhi's secretary Pyarelal heard him murmuring to himself:

> I find myself all alone. Even the Sardar and Jawaharlal think my reading of the situation is wrong and peace is sure to return if partition is agreed upon. . . . They wonder if I have not deteriorated with age. I can see clearly that the future of independence gained at this price is going to be dark. Everybody is today impatient for independence. Therefore, there is no alternative.[11]

Nehru, Patel, Rajagopalachari, Rajendra Prasad and other Congress leaders were not the only ones who were persuaded that though the Partition was an exorbitant price, it was worth paying for a lasting peace on the subcontinent. The Muslim League was congratulating itself on its victory against heavy odds in achieving 'homelands for the Muslim nation'. The British government was relieved at the prospect of an orderly transfer of power. Gandhi alone was troubled by feelings of disillusionment, despair and deep foreboding. Two years before, in a flash of self-revelation he had told an American editor: 'I am not a man who sits down and thinks out problems syllogistically. I am a man of action. I react to a situation intuitively. Logic comes afterwards.'[12] In the summer of 1947, the Mahatma's intuition clashed with the logic of politicians and administrators; hence the 'communication gap' between them. Strangely enough, his intuition had brought him instantly to the same conclusion eight years earlier, when the then Viceroy, Lord Linlithgow had first broached the subject of Pakistan with him. The Viceroy wrote after a meeting with the Mahatma in March 1939:

> Before we concluded, I thought it well to mention the Pakistan project to him, and to ask him whether he thought it had any life in it. He said, he understood, not, but that might come . . . he doubted if it (the Pakistan project) would stand any detailed examination, though it had no doubt wide possibilities. I asked whether by that he meant that it might represent an upsurge running back into the depths of the Muslim world. He said that might indeed be the case in certain circumstances, but even if Pakistan admitted of realization, it would never settle the communal question in India or represent more than a sharp division which might in due course give rise to a major calamity.[13]

Gandhi was once asked what he would do after India attained freedom. 'If India becomes free in my lifetime', he replied, 'and I have energy still left in me, I will take due share, though outside the official world, in building up the nation on a strictly non-violent basis.' In 1947 just when the bloodless revolution against British rule, which he had led for a quarter of a century, was succeeding, the country was torn by internecine strife. Sad at heart, he did not participate in the celebrations at Delhi on 15 August; he spent that day in Calcutta, fasting and praying. His presence provided an immediate healing touch to Calcutta, which had been tense since 'the Great Calcutta Killing' of the previous year, but he remained apprehensive. His worst fears were confirmed when a fortnight later a Hindu mob, inflamed by the news of massacres and migration from West Pakistan, went on a rampage. Gandhi himself escaped a murderous assault, while he was trying to pacify the rioters. He immediately went on a fast, which he broke only when the representatives of both communities gave a solemn pledge that they would see that Calcutta remained peaceful. The fast had a magical effect in restoring sanity in Bengal. The 'One-

Man Boundary Force', as Mountbatten described Gandhi, succeeded in achieving in Bengal what 50,000 troops under Major-General Rees could not achieve in Punjab. Suhrawardy, the former League Premier of Bengal who had ridiculed and obstructed Gandhi's peace mission in Noakhali in the winter months of 1946, was a chastened man after 15 August 1947 and begged Gandhi not to go to East Bengal but to work for communal harmony between Hindus and Muslims in Calcutta. In his memoirs, he explained why he joined Gandhi's peace mission:

> If the Muslims of Calcutta and environs were massacred or driven away, there would be repercussions in East Bengal and that the Hindus would be similarly treated. There were almost four times as many Hindus in East Bengal as Muslims in West Bengal. . . . The result could be that the Muslims of Bihar, Assam and United Provinces certainly and elsewhere probably would be slaughtered or driven out to make room for refugees. There would be a terrible holocaust all over the country.[14]

Gandhi saved West Bengal and East Pakistan from a holocaust. He could not accomplish a similar feat in the west because by the time he reached Delhi in September 1947, the worst had already happened in West Pakistan and East Punjab both of which had nearly completed, what is now called, 'ethnic cleansing'. Nevertheless, Gandhi's presence in Delhi from September 1947 to January 1948, helped to stem the tide of violence. During these months hundreds of thousands of Hindu and Sikh refugees from West Pakistan were fleeing and seeking refuge in Delhi, UP, Bihar and other provinces. If the Nehru government had not taken the firm steps it did, and if Gandhi had not quenched the flames of hatred and revenge through his endless vigil, his fasts and, finally, through his martyrdom, a Hindu backlash of the type, which Suhrawardy had feared for East Pakistan, might have created a new stream of refugees which would have overwhelmed West Pakistan. Gandhi could not prevent the division of the country, but he had done all he could to mitigate its ravages.

NOTES

1. N.K. Bose and P.H. Patwardhan, *Gandhi in Indian Politics* (Bombay, 1967), p. 7.
2. *Harijan*, 6 April 1940.
3. Jamil-ud-din Ahmad, ed., *Some Recent Speeches and Writings of Mr Jinnah* (Lahore, 1952), p. 447.
4. Ibid., p. 87.

5. Several speakers at the Convention of Muslim League legislators in April 1946 had adopted a menacing posture. Sir Firoz Khan Noon said, 'If we find that we have to fight Great Britain for placing us under one Central Government or Hindu Raj, then the havoc which the Muslims will play will put to shame what Chengiz Khan and Halaku did', *Dawn*, 11 April 1946. Abdur Rab Nishtar, who was to become a member of the Indian government later in the year, said: 'The real fact is that Mussalmans belong to a martial race and are no believers of non-violent principles of Mr Gandhi', *Dawn*, 26 March 1946.
6. Asked if the proposed Direct Action would be violent or non-violent, Jinnah said, 'I am not going to discuss ethics', *Dawn*, 1 August 1940.
7. George Abell to Wavell, 18 November 1946, in Nicholas Mansergh, editor-in-chief, *The Transfer of Power 1942-7*, Vol. IX (London, 1980), Doc. 49.
8. On 30 June, General Auchinleck asked Cariappa, the seniormost Indian officer, to get the views of the officers on the question of the defence problems of politically divided India. Cariappa reported: 'Officers representing Pakistan collectively said one army for India was desirable, but was not practicable in the present circumstances,' Cariappa to Auchinleck, 15 July 1947, quoted by Partha Sarathi Gupta, 'Imperial Strategy and the Transfer of Power 1939-51', in Amit Kumar Gupta, ed., *Myth and Reality: The Struggle for Freedom in India, 1945-47* (Delhi, 1987), p. 22.
9. Jinnah told the annual session of the Muslim League in 1943: 'Pakistan we want—and that commodity is available not in the Congress market, but in the British market.'
10. Attlee to Jinnah, 23 July 1946, Mansergh, op.cit., Vol. VIII (London, 1979), pp. 110-11.
11. Pyarelal, *Mahatma Gandhi, The Last Phase*, Vol. II (Ahmedabad, 1958), pp. 210-11
12. Idem, *Mahatma Gandhi: The Early Phase*, Vol. I (Ahmedabad, 1956), p. 120.
13. Lord Linlithgow's minute of 15 March 1939, Linlithgow Papers.
14. M.H.R. Talukdar, ed., *Memoirs of Husain Shaheed Suhrawardy* (Bangladesh, 1987), p. 108.

Mahatma Gandhi and the Partition of India

CHITTABRATA PALIT

INTRODUCTION

In the historiography of modern India, Gandhiji has been the most controversial figure. He has been viewed as the father of Hindu nationalism and, therefore, militating against the Muslims. The Hindu fundamentalists, on the other hand, look upon him as a betrayer of the Hindu cause and a promoter of Muslims. Both hold him ultimately responsible for the Partition of India. He was finally assassinated by a Hindu fanatic on 30 January 1948.

On the question of political mobilization, he is held responsible for imperfect mobilization of workers and peasants in the freedom struggle, while the other school gives him the sole credit for providing the Indian National Congress its sorely needed mass base for the first time. In the economic field, he is criticized for his obscurantist advocacy of the primitive economy of *charkha* and the village community. On the other hand, Marxists pin him down as a spokesman of the bourgeoisie for his concept of trusteeship of big business.

This is an attempt to review the positive aspects of Gandhiji's satyagraha and his final role in the Partition of India. Communal tension in India had its inception when Sir Syed Ahmad Khan decided to launch the Aligarh movement by reconciling the Muslims to British rule after the Revolt of 1857 and inspiring them to go for Western education. Theodore Beck, as the Principal of the Anglo-Oriental Mohammedan College, instigated Muslim youth to tread a separatist path. The Anglo-Mohammedan Defence Association was another platform to cement Muslim loyalty to the British and foment separation from the Hindus. Thus a communitarian movement launched by Sir Syed turned communal by and by. The National Mohammedan Association (1877), founded by Ameer Ali, similarly convinced Abdul Latif's Mohammedan Literary and Scientific Society (1864) to also join the separatist fold. In 1887, Badruddin Tyabji, the third president of the Indian National Congress exhorted Sir Syed to join the Congress, but he refused on the ground that the Muslims were a separate nation. This was the first utterance of the two-nation theory and it was repeated later by the Aga Khan Deputation (1907), soon after the formation of the Muslim League in 1906, which swore loyalty to the British in the days of the swadeshi movement. Mohammad Iqbal, who was known to be a secular Urdu poet but was later completely sold to the idea of a separate Pakistan, became the other prophet of the two-nation theory by the 1930s. The Cambridge-bred Choudhury Rahmat Ali and Khaliquzzaman had already mooted it in the 1930s. Mohammad Ali Jinnah by then had captured the Muslim League as his political platform and made the two-nation theory its main plank in 1940. At the other end Hindu retaliation led to the birth of the Hindu Mahasabha (1937). And fundamental-ism begot fundamentalism.

Gandhiji sought to reconcile the two warring communities throughout his life. His greatest effort was to support even a fundamentalist pan-Islamic Khilafat movement to win the Muslims over to the Congress platform and the result was the Lucknow Pact (1916). But after the fall of the Khilafat in 1920, the Ali brothers backed out. As we shall see later, Gandhiji continued to play his role as a mediator between the two communities, during the years of the transfer of power. Gandhiji has also been accused by both contemporaries and some historians of being the prophet of Hindu nationalism. But Gandhiji himself declares in his autobiography that his god was an ethical god. His idiom was Hindu as was practical for a politician trying to rally a Hindu majority. But when in Peshawar, he spoke of Khudai raj and among the Christian communities in Kerala, the kingdom of Christ. To him Ishwar was the same as Allah or Ram, and Rahim was the refrain of his most favourite song, which began with the praise of Raghupati Ram. His Ram Rajya was similarly a moral utopia and had nothing to do with the kingdom of Ayodhya. A similar stand was taken by Sukarno, the father of Indonesian nationalism, following Gandhiji, who spoke in the Hindu idiom among the Hindus, in Muslim terms among the Muslims and in Marxist jargon amongst the secular intellectuals.

PRELUDE TO PARTITION

On the specific question of Partition, there is again a wide divergence of views. Michael Edwards quotes from the letters of Prime Minister Attlee to Admiral Mountbatten, the Viceroy-designate, who landed in Delhi on 22 March 1947:

It is the definite objective of His Majesty's Government to obtain a unitary government for British India and the Indian States, if possible within the British Commonwealth, through the medium of a Constituent Assembly set up and run in accordance with the Cabinet Mission Plan and you should do the utmost in your power to persuade all parties to work together to this end and advise His Majesty's Government in the light of developments as to the steps that will have to be taken. Since, however, this plan can only become operative in respect of British India by agreement between the major parties, there can be no question of compelling either major party to accept it.[1]

Mountbatten retained a number of Lord Wavell's subordinates to assist him in the transfer of power. Among them were George Abell, who was believed by Congress to be pro-Muslim and V.P. Menon, a Hindu, who had been a close friend and adviser of the Congress leader, Sardar Patel. Edwards writes:

As soon as the charade of the installation was over, Mountbatten and his staff went to work on reconnaissance and intelligence. The effect of Lord Mountbatten's charm and Lady Mountbatten's too upon Nehru was profound. . . . Gandhi, now relegated to the position of the Congress's private saint was also to receive the full blast of the Mountbatten charm. But there was really no point of contact between these two men. . . . At the Viceroy's invitation, Gandhi returned from a pilgrimage to the riot-torn areas of Bihar to meet him. When they met, Gandhi suggested a plan to the Viceroy. . . . The Viceroy said that Gandhi should call upon Mr. Jinnah to form a government leaving it to Jinnah to decide whether there should be Hindu ministers or not. . . . The idea though spectacular enough, had even less chance of being accepted by Congress in 1947—regardless of Gandhi's support. . . . Inevitably Congress threw out this suggestion and Gandhi returned to Bihar. . . . The Mahatma no longer spoke for the Congress and it is very doubtful whether he could have reimposed his influence *even if he had wanted to* ... he was slowly coming to the conclusion that partition might be the only way to avoid huge violence, and he was later to throw his influence as he still possessed on the side of those who were prepared to accept Pakistan.[2]

Edwards candidly says that Gandhi had never yearned for political power. He only desired that those in power should be favourable to his ideas of reform. In 1947, he was 77 years of age and before he died he wanted to put an end to the sufferings of the innocent. He returned to Bihar because for him the petty wranglings and intrigues at Delhi were of little importance in the face of the greater menace which stalked India and 'who, after a little thought', Edwards solemnly notes, 'would deny that he was right?'[3]

Jinnah was more or less convinced that Mountbatten was pro-

Congress and was not to be trusted. Edwards rightly diagnoses the situation:

> Mountbatten's blandishment seemed only a variation on the old attempts to force him to accept a Congress-dominated central government. . . . Jinnah was now as unapproachable and as unamenable to reason as Hitler at Berchtsgaden and it was not long before Mountbatten realised that the chances of handing over power to a united India were remote at least within this present time limit of June 1948.[4]

On 15 April, Mountbatten invited Gandhi and Jinnah to issue a joint statement condemning the use of force for political ends appealing to all communities to refrain from all acts of violence. It was rather like telling a fire to stop burning. Edwards observes that Jinnah had no intention of calling off the agitation at the end of April. The Interim Government was also hopelessly divided between the two blocks already promoting separatist Indian and Pakistani interests. The finance minister, Liaquat Ali's socialist tax of 25 per cent affected the Hindu big business, which supported the Congress. Mountbatten had now decided on Partition and Nehru was slowly veering towards it. 'The Muslim League can have Pakistan', he said, 'but on the condition that they do not take away other parts of India which do not wish to join Pakistan'. There were however more profound reasons than Gandhi and Nehru's exasperation, as Sardar Patel reported that the Congress machine was falling apart under the strain of communal disorder and the failure of its leaders to achieve independence quickly. Edwards wrote:

> Powerful capitalist interests in Congress were now preparing for the possibility of disowning Nehru just as they had disposed of Gandhi, and Patel was their spokesman. It was also Patel who had put forward the resolution calling for the partition of the Punjab and Bengal. Now he was to put forward the partition of India not to satisfy Jinnah but to save Congress from collapse.[5]

The Department of Information and Broadcasting, Delhi, headed by Patel circulated stories, which led inevitably to further violence. The Muslim League did not sit idle either. It was set on dividing the assets of British India as if Partition was a matter of time. Liaquat Ali already proposed the division of the Indian Army on communal lines.

Partition was in sight, but Gandhi suddenly as a last ditch measure, came out strongly against the partition of the Punjab and Bengal. After a brief talk with Jinnah arranged by the Viceroy, Gandhi declared that he did not accept the principle of division and renewed his gospel of unity. But as Edwards shrewdly observes: 'Now when the prizes of freedom were within grasp, he was no longer needed at the helm and saints are out of place when there is hard bargaining to be done between businessmen.'[6]

Jinnah was also opposed to the partition of Punjab and Bengal. Perhaps he wanted the full cake of the two provinces having a Muslim majority. Violence was on the rise in these two provinces and a large-scale migration from unsafe to safe areas was already taking place. Mountbatten was also getting impatient and restless. Events overtook Gandhi, Jinnah, Nehru, Patel and the Viceroy. Mountbatten was now convinced that Partition was inevitable. So also were the Congress and Muslim League leaders. They were all eager to achieve a smooth transfer of power without further bloodbath. V.P. Menon, Mountbatten's aide, had already prepared the plan for Dominion Status for the two partitioned states of India and Pakistan. He had already taken Patel's concurrence. Now it was the turn of Nehru to accept it, as he arrived at the Viceroy's Lodge, Simla, on 8 May 1947. Nehru found the scheme appealing and was determined that even Dominion Status should not stand in the way of India's freedom. After the 9 May discussion with Nehru, Mountbatten announced that 'there would be a meeting on 17 May of all important Indian leaders, Nehru, Patel, Jinnah, Liaquat Ali and Baldev Singh so that the Viceroy might present to them a new plan for the transfer of power'. But parleys went on till the draft plan was finally acceptable to all parties. The hardest bottleneck was over Jinnah's demand for a corridor connecting what would be the two halves of Pakistan. It was just a spanner to keep the issue of Partition alive.

Gandhi was not in the picture, but at a prayer meeting on 31 May he exclaimed, 'even if the whole of India burns, we shall not concede Pakistan, even if the Muslim demanded it at the point of the sword'.[7] Edwards asks why Gandhi uttered such inflammatory sentiments at such a late date, especially when he had already agreed to Pakistan at a meeting of the Congress Working Committee where Patel and Nehru announced their own acceptance. In fact, in that meeting, Gandhi had complained that he had been bypassed in such a decision—made when he was away to Noakhali to contain communal violence in the riot-torn district.[8] Edwards comments:

> There is no simple clear-cut answer. Gandhi was an extremely complicated personality and his thoughts and actions displayed the emotional characteristics of the fanatic mind. He was mild yet ruthless when he thought it necessary to attain his ends. Like so many religious reformers he loved Mankind but was not above hating men who stood in his way. . . . Was he now hoping in some way to discredit those Congress leaders who had rejected him in their hour of triumph? Or was he attempting to dissociate himself in advance from any responsibility for

Congress' decision to accept Partition which would certainly come as a shock when it was made public?[9]

Edwards concludes that 'after independence, the orthodox Hindu political parties were to attack Gandhi violently for having played a double game and it was such attacks which led finally, though indirectly, to his assassination by a Hindu extremist in January 1948'.[10] This is obviously the view of a prejudiced mind, who failed to gauge the sentiments that ran high in Gandhi's innermost mind, which sometimes came out in the form of rejection and dejection when he knew that his point would not be carried by his own disciples. He used no wiles and guiles for retaining his way or leadership. It was the agony of a soul which strove hard to keep India united and failed in the end. He had composed his own epitaph when he said: 'Let the country be divided over my dead body.' This was carried out by Nathuram Godse.

GODSE AND GANDHI

It is surprising that Edwards calls Gandhi a Hindu fanatic, who began supporting the Muslim cause and Pakistan out of his frustration at being bypassed by Patel and Nehru who opted for Partition against his scheme of a Hindu undivided state. Nathuram Godse, who assassinated Gandhi on 30 January 1948, held the opposite view. He thought that Gandhi was pro-Muslim and wanted to give away the free Indian states to the Muslims. In his *Testament* of 1977, Godse says that he started hating Gandhi for his doctrine of ahimsa or non-violence, because that would make the Hindus imbecile, as against the virile Muslims. The Hindu community would be unable to protect themselves against the riotous offensive of the Muslims.[11] This was his reason for entering politics and he first brought out a daily paper *Agrani* to challenge Gandhi's defence of Muslim rights, whenever it appeared in any of Gandhi's speeches and writings. He was more opposed to Gandhi's patronage of the Muslims, rather than to his doctrine of non-violence itself. In his more militant paper *Hindu Rashtra,* he even criticized Gandhi's tactics of fasting to bring the Congress in line with his views which, according to him, were mainly to pander to the Muslim demands. Godse foresaw the Partition of India in Gandhi's scheme of things. He did not like Gandhi's lionizing of Suhrawardy's government in Bengal even when there were repeated atrocities on the Hindus there. He says that Gandhi even called him (Suhrawardy) an apostle of religion in one of his prayer meetings. He quotes from Mosley, *The Last Days of the British*

Raj,[12] which said that it was 'only when Hindus and Sikhs had come out in retaliation that the chief ministers had called for military aid'.[13]

Born and brought up in a Chitpavan Brahmin family, Godse was steeped in Hindu history and culture and his thoughts were shaped by Naoroji, Vivekananda, Tilak and Gokhale. He felt that as a patriot he must protect the Hindu community from ruin and Gandhi's policies worried him because Godse felt that he might barter Hindu India for a Muslim government to retain his position as the king-maker. He criticized several of Gandhi's actions. Gandhi read the Koran in a Hindu temple in a *bhangi* colony and preached tolerance, soon after his visit to riot-torn Bengal and the edification of Suhrawardy. But, according to Godse, Gandhi would not dare reading the *Gita* in a mosque. Another crucial incident that worried Godse was Gandhi's fast for Hindu-Muslim amity, but this really, according to Godse, was to allow Pakistan to draw 54 crores from the Indian treasury as its share soon after Partition. Finally, the Hindu Mahasabhaites were not reconciled to the idea that the Congress would rule as a single party in free India after the Partition. This was not the national government of its choice. For all these developments, Godse held Gandhi responsible who, according to him, wanted to protect his personal saintliness, if not leadership, at the cost of the country. These were his justifications for assassinating Gandhi.[14]

Godse's views were his own construct of Gandhi's 'diabolical' role at that crucial time. Gandhi's vacillations were mostly a sentimental response to political vicissitudes, but basically he would have liked to keep India undivided even at the cost of losing his own and Congress leadership. This will be clarified when we go into the actual transfer of power where Patel, Azad and Nehru played vital roles.

MAULANA AZAD AND GANDHI

Maulana Azad described the transfer of power as a prelude to Partition. The Congress leadership under the presidentship of Azad had already agreed with Lord Wavell to accept the Cabinet Mission Plan for an Interim Government to keep India undivided. Azad had been president for seven years, from 1939 to 1946, but he chose to retire at this crucial stage of negotiation. He concluded that the election of Sardar Patel would not be desirable in the existing circumstances. He decided to propose the name of Jawaharlal Nehru as the next president on 26 April 1946. He later wrote:

I acted according to my best judgement but the way things have shaped since then had made me realize that this was perhaps the greatest blunder of my political life. I have regretted no action of mine so much as the decision to withdraw from the Presidentship of the Congress at this critical juncture. It was a mistake which I can describe in Gandhiji's words as one of Himalayan dimension. My second mistake was that when I decided not to stand myself, I did not support Sardar Patel. We differed on many issues but I am convinced that if he had succeeded me as Congress president, he would have seen that the Cabinet Mission Plan was successfully implemented. He would have never committed the mistake of Jawaharlal which gave Mr. Jinnah the opportunity of sabotaging the plan. I can never forgive myself when I think if I had not committed these mistakes, perhaps the history of the last ten years would have been different. . . . One factor which gave greater strength to my decision was Gandhiji's view. He agreed with me that I should not continue as President but he was not wholly pleased that I had proposed that Jawaharlal should succeed me. Perhaps he was somewhat inclined towards Sardar Patel. But once I had proposed Jawaharlal's name, he gave no public indication of his views.[15]

This gives us an inkling of Gandhi's reaction to the other decisions. He would submit to them but without approving them from his heart. The Muslim League Council and the Congress Working Committee accepted the Cabinet Mission Plan. It only needed the approval of the AICC. Jawaharlal Nehru took over as Congress president when the AICC met and Azad moved the resolution on the Cabinet Mission Plan and briefly spoke about its main features. The Leftists opposed it with great vehemence. The Congress Socialists took the leading part in the opposition. Maulana Azad strongly pleaded that the Congress had stood for the freedom and unity of India and opposed all fissiparous tendencies. He could not understand how people like the Congress Socialists could regard this victory as a defeat.[16] His speech had a decisive influence on the audience. When the vote was taken, the resolutions were passed with an overwhelming majority. Thus the seal of approval was put on the Working Committee's resolutions accepting the Cabinet Mission Plan. In the words of Azad:

Now happened one of those unfortunate events which changed the course of history. On 10th July, Jawaharlal held a press conference in Bombay in which he made an astonishing statement. Some press representative asked him whether with the passing of the resolution by AICC, the Congress had accepted the plan *in toto* including the composition of the Interim Government. Jawaharlal in reply stated that Congress would enter the Constituent Assembly completely unfettered by agreements and free to meet all situations as they rise. Mr. Jinnah was . . . not at all happy about the outcome of the negotiation with the Cabinet Mission.

Jawaharlal's statement came to him as a bombshell. He immediately issued a statement that this declaration by the Congress President demanded a review of the whole situation. The Muslim League Council met him at Bombay on 27th July. Mr. Jinnah in his opening speech reiterated the demand for Pakistan as the only course left open to the Muslim League. After three days discussion, the Council passed a resolution rejecting the Cabinet Mission Plan. It also decided to resort to direct action for the achievement of Pakistan.[17]

Azad further wrote:

Jawaharlal argued that he had no objection if the Working Committee wanted to reiterate that the Cabinet Mission's Plan has been accepted by the Congress, but felt that it would be embarrassing to the organization and also to him personally if the Working Committee passed a resolution that the statement of the Congress President did not represent the policy of the Congress.[18]

Though the Congress Working Committee framed a fresh resolution in support of the Cabinet Mission Plan without reference to Nehru's statement, it was too late to stop Jinnah. In Azad's words:

When the League Council met at the end of July and decided to resort to direct action, it also authorized Mr. Jinnah to take any action he liked in pursuance of the programme. Mr. Jinnah declared 16 August, the 'Direct Action Day', but he did not make it clear what the programme would be . . . 16 August was a black day in the history of India. Unprecedented mob violence . . . plunged the great city of Calcutta into an orgy of bloodshed, murder and terror. Hundreds were injured and property worth crores of rupees was destroyed. Processions were taken out by the League which began to loot and commit acts of arson. Soon the whole city was in the grip of *goondas* of both the communities.... Jawaharlal is one of my dearest friends and his contribution to India's national life is second to none. . . . I have nevertheless to say with regret that he is at times apt to be carried away by his feelings. Not only so but sometimes he is so impressed by theoretical considerations that he is apt to underestimate the realities of a situation.[19]

Azad blames Gandhi for acceding to Nehru's plan to exclude the Muslim League from joining the Ministry in UP in 1937 and his silent endorsement of Partition in 1946 was contrary to the beliefs of Nehru and Patel. Gandhi did not protest against this decision, which he did not approve from his heart. He was, in any case, sure that his opinion would be brushed aside. This was evident as Gandhi expressed his opinion outside the party circles. Azad wrote:

When I became aware that Lord Mountbatten was thinking in terms of dividing India and had persuaded Jawaharlal and Patel, I was deeply distressed. I realized that the country was moving towards a great danger. The partition of India would be harmful not only to Muslims but to the whole country. I was and am still convinced that the Cabinet Mission Plan was the best solution from every point of view. It preserved the unity of India and gave every community an opportunity to function with freedom and honour.[20]

Azad approached Patel and then Nehru to uphold the Plan but both were already convinced that Muslims and Hindus could not be united into one nation and there was no alternative to Partition. Azad then turned to Gandhiji:

Gandhiji remained my only hope. During this period Gandhiji was staying at Patna. He had earlier spent some months in Noakhali, where he made a great impression on local Muslims and created a new atmosphere of Hindu-Muslim unity. We expected that he would come to Delhi to meet Mountbatten and he actually arrived on 31 March. I went to see him at once and his very first remark was, 'Partition has now become a threat. It seems Vallabhbhai and even Jawaharlal have surrendered. What will you do now? Will you stand by me or have you also changed'? I replied 'I have been and am against partition. . . .' Gandhiji said 'If the Congress wishes to accept partition it would be over my dead body. So long as I am alive I will never agree to the partition of India. Nor will I, if I can help it allow Congress to accept it.'

Azad further narrates that Gandhiji met Lord Mountbatten for three consecutive days and was closeted with Sardar Patel after the first meet. When Azad met him afterwards, he found that Gandhiji had also changed. He wrote:

In despondency I at last said, 'if even you have now adopted these views, I see no hope of saving India from catastrophe'. Gandhiji did not reply to my comment but said that he had already made the suggestion that we should ask Jinnah to form the Government and choose the members of the Cabinet. He said that he had mentioned this idea to Lord Mountbatten and he was greatly impressed by this idea. I knew this was so. When I met Mountbatten the day after Gandhiji talked to him; he told me that if the Congress accepted Gandhiji's suggestion, Partition could still be avoided. . . . Unfortunately this move could make no progress as both Sardar Patel and Jawaharlal opposed it vehemently. In fact, they forced Gandhiji to withdraw his suggestion. Gandhiji reminded me of this and said that the situation now was such that Partition appeared inevitable.[21]

But the Partition came through with violence and bloodshed. During the whole of this period Gandhiji was living in terrible mental anguish. He strained every nerve to restore good feelings between the communities and secure the life and property of the Muslims. Gandhiji's distress was increasing every day. Formerly the whole nation had responded to his slightest wish. Now it seemed that his fervent appeals were falling on deaf ears.

PATEL AND GANDHI

Here a profile of Sardar Patel would not be out of place. Mosley describes him:

> Patel was well aware that he was regarded by the Left Wing of the Congress Party as a die-hard capitalist whose constant attention to the practical side of Congress administration was the typical activity of *a non-idealist* and *non-intellectual*. . . . Nonetheless it was Patel . . . who kept the Party going with regular infusions of money from the big Hindu millionaires, and with frequent purgings and oilings of the political machine of a nature with which Nehru would never have been asked to soil his hands.[22]

His assessment of Patel in other contexts also rings true:

> Patel was the iron fist of Congress which rarely even bothered to wear a velvet glove. He believed in hammering out agreements by sheer force and weight of numbers. At this moment, Azad believed he would be the wrong man to face the crises looming ahead; and he decided to back Nehru, a subtle man like himself (or so he thought) instead.
>
> It was not necessarily a *fait accompli*. . . . Until this moment Patel had been sure that Gandhi favoured his election, for when they had talked of it previously, the Mahatma had indicated that he would welcome it. Now, like the rest of the Congress delegates, he waited for Gandhi to give a sign; and he was sufficiently confident that the sign would be against Nehru and for him that he made no overt move himself to secure it.
>
> But the day of the Congress election came, and Gandhi made no sign. Mortified, well aware that at his age, the chance would never come again, Patel had to sit back and watch his rival once more take the presidency from him—and this time at the most important moment of all. He never forgave Azad for the events of 1946. He moved away from Gandhi whose devoted disciple he had always been.[23]

Gandhi gave the nod in favour of Nehru, perhaps because of his fatal weakness for Nehru, who he thought would tread his path more obediently as a middle of the roader. But both Azad and Gandhi were swayed by Nehru and Patel, in rejecting the Wavell Plan and opting for Partition.

In the end, Gandhi was forlorn. To retain his foothold in the Congress and fatherhood of the nation, he even argued with both Nehru and Patel to accept Partition inside the Congress. His last mission to Mountbatten was to suggest the name of Jinnah as the Prime Minister of undivided India. But as Mosley observes:

He found his plan rudely rebuffed by Congress, and the Viceroy wrote to him to point out that there had been a 'misunderstanding' about his own reception of it. What happened in fact, was that immediately after the meeting Mountbatten and his staff set to work to sabotage the plan which they [and many Congress leaders] considered unworkable. The sabotage was so effective that Gandhi shortly afterwards informed Congress that he would take no further part in the discussions with the Viceroy or play other than a minor advisory role in Congress affairs and departed once more for his healing mission in Bihar.[24]

Within a fortnight of his arrival, the Viceroy eliminated him from the negotiation for Indian independence. It was an elimination of enormous importance and gravity for India. For Gandhi was one of the only two members of the Congress party against the Partition of India into Pakistan and Hindustan. Mosley repeats with conviction that 'Gandhi had never left anyone least of all Patel in doubt of his objection to any form of Partition. But he knew that even fasting would not mend it.' As B.R. Nanda sums up:

Gandhi opposed the two-nation theory and the division of India but he had written as early as April 1940: 'I know no non-violent method of compelling the obedience of eight crores of Muslims to the will of the rest of India, however, powerful a majority, the rest may represent. The Muslims must have the same right of self-determination that the rest of India has. We are at present a joint family. Any member may claim a division.' This was a perfectly logical position for a leader, who was committed to non-violence to adopt, but another leader following the example of Abraham Lincoln may have insisted that there could be no compromise on the unity of the country.[25]

Gandhiji was making too many concessions to the Muslim League and Jinnah, which the Congress High Command did not approve. Gandhi was by then stepping out of his inner circle.

EPILOGUE

Gandhi had become a lonely figure left with his secondary role as a messiah of peace in the riot-torn Bihar, Calcutta, Noakhali and Delhi. He had gone out of the way to placate H.S. Suhrawardy when following the Muslim League's directive of Direct Action on 16 August 1946, the League government declared it a holiday and communal riots broke out on an unprecedented scale in the city of Calcutta. N.K. Bose, companion of Gandhi in those days, wrote:

The offensive began from the side of Muslim mobs, but within a few hours, the Hindus who rightly or wrongly felt that the government was entirely apathetic or had abdicated in favour of the rowdy elements also struck back. The resistance stiffened in the course of the next three days, and in the meanwhile, Calcutta saw the murder of several thousand men, women and children. The mutual slaughter continued for some weeks.[26]

In Noakhali, the riots were one-sided, a carnage of Hindu killings. Suhrawardy wanted to put off Gandhi's visit by saying that the reports were exaggerated. But Gandhiji said for himself that the efficacy of non-violence had miserably failed. Bose further wrote :

There was a prevailing feeling of helplessness before the magnitude of the forces of evil which were stalking the land and perhaps all this left Gandhiji in a lonely, and, may be, also in a slightly disturbed frame of mind.[27]

When independence came, Gandhiji was in Calcutta and is recorded to have said, 'It is not for me to rejoice. Leave me alone to shed my tears.' Maulana Azad has not a word for Muslim atrocities in Bengal though he condemns Hindu attacks on Muslims in Delhi in no uncertain terms. Azad squarely blames Patel for mishandling the riots in Delhi. But Durga Das wrote:

Partition and transfer of power were accompanied by the tragedy and turmoil of wholesale uprooting of population, mass murder and looting and other acts of barbarity. The entire socio-economic structure of the affected provinces seemed on the verge of collapse.[28]

How the problem of restoring peace and sanity and resettling the uprooted and depressed victims of the trauma of Partition was handled primarily by Patel, with courage and firmness, is revealed in the correspondence of Patel. Gandhi appeared critical of Patel and over-solicitous towards the Muslims. A political discard of the Congress, he was becoming a stepfather of Pakistan, according to men like Godse. At least this was the defence put up by Godse during his trial for the assassination of Mahatma Gandhi. Gandhi's role in Indian politics had ended before his death. But his doctrine of non-violence as a solution for political issues earned him his martyrdom.

Mosley, pays high tribute to Gandhi in his final analysis:

In many ways, Gandhi was a saint. The three great aims of his life were Indian freedom, the unity of his people, Hindus and Muslims, and the betterment of the lot of the Untouchables. For these three goals, he was willing to suffer and die.[29]

In this broader sense he remains the Father of the Nation.

NOTES

1. Michael Edwards, *The Last Years of British India* (Calcutta, 1963), p. 145.
2. Ibid., p. 148-9.
3. Ibid., p. 150.
4. Ibid.
5. Ibid., p. 152.
6. Ibid., p. 155.
7. Ibid., p. 165.
8. Ibid., p. 166.
9. Ibid.
10. Ibid., p. 167.
11. Nathuram Godse, *Testament* (1977), trans. into Bengali by Nirodbaran Hazra (repr., Calcutta, 1989), p. 53.
12. Leonard Mosley, *The Last Days of the British Raj* (London, 1961).
13. Godse, op.cit., p. 66.
14. Ibid., pp. 66-7.
15. Maulana Abul Kalam Azad, *India Wins Freedom* (New York, 1960; New Delhi, repr., 1989), pp. 162-3.
16. Ibid., pp. 164-5.
17. Ibid., pp. 165-6.
18. Ibid., p. 166.
19. Ibid., pp. 168-70.
20. Ibid., p. 172.
21. Ibid., pp. 202-4.
22. Mosley, op.cit., p. 81
23. Ibid., p. 78.
24. Ibid., pp. 95-6.
25. B.R. Nanda, *Gandhi and His Critics* (New Delhi, 1993), p. 94.
26. N.K. Bose, *My Days with Gandhi* (Calcutta, 1953), p. 37.
27. Ibid
28. Durga Das, *Sardar Patel's Correspondence*, Vol. IV, 1949-50 (Bombay, 1961), Introduction.
29. Mosley, op.cit., p. 72.

Congress and Partition

SUCHETA MAHAJAN

It has become commonplace to describe our freedom as a flawed or a blemished dawn—because of the attendant horrors of Partition. The paradox that 15 August 1947 was both a day of celebration and mourning is generally noted but its complexity is not understood. While independence is seen as the culmination of the anti-imperialist struggle or the devolution of power by the colonial rulers, Partition is seen as the final act of the divide and rule drama or the inevitable outcome of the age-old Hindu-Muslim rift or as the betrayal by the compromising, bourgeois nationalist leadership—depending on the ideological predilections of the author. Such explanations fail to comprehend the complex, contradictory reality that freedom came with Partition, because they do not recognize independence and Partition as parts of an integral whole, as twin, contingent phenomena. In our view, the paradox of independence-Partition reflects another paradox, that the national movement was both a success and a failure. The task of the national movement was twofold—structuring classes, communities and regions into a nation and securing independence from colonial rule for this emerging nation. While the national movement succeeded in building up a national consciousness sufficient to wrest freedom, the process of the nation-in-the-making remained incomplete and the Congress, the party of the national movement, failed to keep the country united.

The need was to integrate a strategy to combat communalism with the strategy of anti-imperialism. This would have brought complete success, freedom *and* unity. However, the Congress devoted little attention to this task, in the belief that the communal question could wait or would get

*The argument of this paper was fleshed out in discussions with Sarvepalli Gopal and Bipan Chandra. I am grateful to them for their comments on earlier drafts. This paper draws on Chapters 12 and 13 of my book, *Independence and Pakistan: the Erosion of Colonial Power in India* (New Delhi, 2000). The research for this paper was funded by the University Grants Commission, New Delhi, the Indian Council of Social Science Research, New Delhi, and the Charles Wallace (India) Trust, United Kingdom.

resolved in the course of the anti-imperialist struggle. There was little intellectual recognition or effort to understand communalism in order to combat it, as was done in the case of colonialism, by generations of nationalists. Nehru's generation tried to come to terms with the phenomenon but failed to appreciate its intractability in its extremist stage. The well-tried method of concession did not work once minority communalism had entered the extreme, mass and fascist phase—it was akin to building sand dykes at high tide.

The acceptance of Partition in 1947 was thus only the final act of a process of step by step concession to the League's intransigent championing of a sovereign Muslim state. The autonomy of Muslim majority provinces was accepted in 1942 at the time of the Cripps Mission. Gandhi went a step further and accepted the right of self-determination of the Muslim majority provinces in his talks with Jinnah in 1944. In June 1946, the Congress conceded the possibility of the Muslim majority provinces (which formed Groups B and C of the Cabinet Mission Plan) setting up a separate Constituent Assembly but opposed compulsory grouping and upheld the right of NWFP and Assam not to join their groups, if they so wished. By the end of the year, Nehru said he would accept the ruling of the Federal Court on whether grouping was compulsory or optional. The Congress accepted, without demur, the clarification by the Cabinet, in December 1946, that grouping was compulsory. The Congress officially referred to the Partition in early March 1947 when a resolution was passed in the Congress Working Committee that Punjab (and by implication Bengal) must be partitioned, if the country was divided. The final concession to the League's demands was in June 1947 when the Congress accepted the Partition under the 3 June Plan.

The Congress' denial of the legitimacy of the League's claim weakened in the face of the League's incessant demand for Pakistan, backed by mass action. The League used to good effect against the Congress the strategy that the Congress had applied to undermine colonial authority. The conviction that India must be free backed by mass pressure had broken the spring of empire. Akin to the process of decline in the morale of the Indian Civil Service officials was the one that took place in the morale of the Congress leadership. The brave words of the leaders contrasted starkly with the tragic retreat of the Congress. While loudly asserting the sovereignty of the Constituent Assembly, the Congress quietly accepted compulsory grouping and abandoned NWFP to Pakistan. Similarly, the Congress leaders finally accepted the Partition most of all because they could not stop communal riots, but their words were all about not surrendering to the blackmail of violence. Nehru asserted on 22 August 1946 that 'we are not going to shake hands with murder or allow it to determine the country's policy'.[1]

What was involved here was a refusal to accept the reality that their words or actions in the present could not reverse the logic of the failure in the past. It is often forgotten that the acceptance of Partition by the Congress in the summer of 1947 was a consequence of the long-term failure of the Congress to draw in the Muslim masses into the national movement and stem the surging waves of Muslim communalism which, especially since 1937, had been beating with increasing fury. This failure was revealed with stark clarity by the 1946 elections, in which the League won 90 per cent of the Muslim seats. Though the war against the League was lost by early 1946, defeat was conceded only after the final battle was mercilessly waged in the streets of Calcutta and Rawalpindi and the village lanes of Noakhali and Bihar. By early 1947, the Congress leaders felt that only an immediate transfer of power could forestall the spread of Direct Action and communal disturbances.

The virtual collapse of the Interim Government also made Pakistan appear to be an unavoidable reality. Patel argued, in the All India Congress Committee meeting on 14 June 1947, that the Congress has to face up to the fact that Pakistan was functioning in Punjab, Bengal and in the Interim Government. Nehru was dismayed at the turning of the Interim Government into an arena of struggle. Ministers wrangled, met separately to reach decisions and Liaquat Ali Khan as Finance Member hamstrung the functioning of other ministries. In the face of the Interim Government's powerlessness to check governors from abetting the League and the Bengal provincial ministry's inaction and even complicity in riots, Nehru often wondered whether there was any point in continuing in the Interim Government while people were being butchered. Immediate transfer of power would at least mean having the authority the Congress was now expected to wield, but was powerless to exercise.

In April 1947, the Congress leaders, J.B. Kripalani, C. Rajagopalachari, Rajendra Prasad and Sardar Patel met Mountbatten and told him that they had come around to the view that there was no alternative but to accept Partition.[2] By 1 May 1947, the Working Committee accepted Partition, not as the League demand, but as the 'principle of Partition based on self-determination as applied to definitely ascertained areas'. Mid to end April seems to be the period when Congress reconciled itself to the Partition of the country.[3]

The Congress leaders offered diverse arguments for accepting the

Partition. First of all, there were the arguments given by the leaders that Partition reflected popular will and it was the only 'way to be free'. Then there were the hopes expressed that it would not be a final settlement but a temporary measure and that it would end communal violence. They believed they were avoiding the worse alternatives of balkanization and civil war. They finally conceded that there was no other option—those explored had reached a dead end. This left the alternatives of a mass movement and anti-communal struggle by the party and imposition of unity by force. It was too late for the former and the party did not have state power. The two proved to be non-options.

PARTITION AS THE 'POPULAR' WILL

The Congress leadership was at pains to stress that they had accepted Partition because that was the people's choice. Gandhiji was most forthright:

> The demand has been granted because you asked for it. The Congress never asked for it. . . . But the Congress can feel the pulse of the people. It realised that the Khalsa as also the Hindu desires it. . . . They have taken this course because they realised that it was not possible to get around the Muslim League in any other way. . . . We do not wish to force anyone. We tried hard. We tried to reason with them but they refused to come into the Constituent Assembly.[4]

Gandhiji's rejoinder to N.K. Bose's suggestion that he was protecting Congress leaders by supporting the Working Committee on Partition is particularly illuminating: 'Don't you realise that, as a result of one year of communal riots, the people of India have all become communal. They can see nothing beyond the communal question. They are tired and frightened. The Congress has only represented this feeling of the whole nation. How can I then oppose it?'[5]

Nehru, similarly, alluded to pressures from both quarters in his explanation of the 'various reasons that had forced the Congress to accept the division of India'. The first pertained to the Bengali and Punjabi Hindu pressure to divide the two provinces.[6] The second referred to the unwillingness of Muslims to be part of India: 'The Congress has to face the fact that certain sections of the people do not want to remain with the rest of India.'[7] Since 1942, Nehru's stand, and that of the Congress,[8] had been that while they opposed the League's demand for Pakistan, 'if the Muslims wish to have Pakistan, it will not deny it to them'.[9]

Nehru repeated it more firmly in May 1947 when he interpreted it as

Gandhiji's view.[10] Gandhiji held the opinion that any arrangement for the division of India or the provinces should not take place through the British agency. If the people of the areas concerned desired a division, there would be nothing to stop them. In the CWC meeting of 1 June 1947, Patel and Nehru said that their stand flowed out of the resolutions passed by the AICC itself since 1942, namely, that no part of India could be coerced into accepting a constitution against its will.[11] Again, when the AICC finally accepted Partition on 15 June 1947, it justified its decision by referring to the same clause in the CWC resolution on the Cripps Plan, drafted by Nehru and accepted by Gandhiji and the Congress.[12]

The Congress had thus always maintained that it would accept Pakistan if that were the popular demand of the Muslims. It said this with the confidence of years of moulding popular opinion in the anti-imperialist struggle wherein the Congress anticipated popular will and was one step ahead of it, hence had led the people into movements and out of them. On the communal front the Congress, however, not only reflected popular will, but it was led by popular opinion as well. This was tantamount to surrendering all initiative to the people by letting them believe that their writ alone would run. In practice there were qualifications to this stand. For one, popular opinion was very much influenced by the stands taken by the Congress; it was not only that the Congress reflected popular opinion. Sarat Bose had made this clarification earlier in the context of the controversy over the partition of Bengal. He had argued that the Congress should not take cover behind public opinion but take a firm stand against the partition of Bengal. That would strengthen the hands of all those who were for a united Bengal and erode the Hindu Mahasabha's new-found strength, which, in his view, was largely the making of the Congress.[13]

There was another qualification to the notion of the popular will. Since it was not quantifiable or easily demonstrable, it was open to diverse interpretation and conflicting uses. The controversy over the partition of Bengal again revealed this problem, with Nehru and Patel arguing for partition and Sarat Bose opposing it and upholding unity. Both camps on the ground that people wanted it.[14] Naturally, then, with both sides claiming popular support, it was unlikely that public opinion could be interpreted as an impartial tribunal. Nehru suggested this two way process between popular opinion and the acceptance of Partition in his broadcast over All India Radio, on 3 June 1947. He accepted that the 'future of India can only be decided by the people' but stressed that 'decisions cannot await the normal course of events. So while we must necessarily abide by what the people finally decide, we have to come to certain decisions ourselves, and to recommend them to the people for acceptance.'[15] This, of course, begged the question: Was Partition recommended by the people or dictated by popular opinion?

PARTITION AS A FINAL SETTLEMENT

One of the beliefs nurtured by the Congress leaders was that the 3 June Plan would effect a settlement. Its terms were unfortunate, that is a division of the country, but its finality seemed to offset its sad part. The letter sent by the Congress president to the Viceroy on 2 June 1947, drafted by Nehru, made explicit that the Congress accepted the proposals 'in order to achieve a final settlement'.[16] Nehru's letter to Mountbatten, written 20 days later, emphasized this aspect of popular acceptance: 'Whether people like the decisions or not they accept them and have a general feeling that a settlement has been arrived at.'[17] Patel echoed the sentiment: 'I also feel happy that the announcement of 3 June at least settles things one way or the other. There is no further uncertainty.'[18] As Nehru pointed out, settlement involved the League: 'This is dependent on the acceptance of the proposals by the Muslim League and a clear understanding that no further claims will be put forward.'[19]

It was soon clear that the League would as usual dodge acceptance. Jenkins, the Punjab governor, had cautioned an already pessimistic Nehru that Liaquat Ali Khan had said that HMG would have to enforce Partition, the League would not accept it.[20] Jinnah's broadcast on All India Radio 'accepting' the proposal was in contrast to Nehru's eloquent appeal.[21] Jinnah made a fairly blatant communal speech, which brought forth the now ritualistic protest from Patel[22] and the equally ritualistic Viceregal response. The League's Council did accept the 3 June Plan, but Patel maintained that the League's 'resolution is contradictory and there is studied evasion of straightforward acceptance . . . the Pakistan of the statement of June would merely be a springboard for action against Hindustan, and . . . there is no possibility of a settlement on this basis.'[23]

What emerged was the League's half-hearted acquiescence. There was little of the cooperation and willingness to agree that the Congress expected of the League, now that its demand for Pakistan was met: 'We agreed to accept the Plan in the hope that the Muslim League, having got what it wanted, will cease its hymn of communal hate and co-operate in the reconstruction of society and economic structure of the two states.'[24] Gandhiji expressed a similar hope but added a qualification: 'I would ask you to rely upon the plighted word of Muslim leaders. They have got their Pakistan. They have no quarrel with anyone in India—at least they should have none.'[25]

The Congress leaders drew their expectations from the Congress' experience with its opponents, the British regime, over the last few years. Once the British announced that they were quitting India, the Congress leaders changed their confrontationist posture *vis-à-vis* the Raj. Their main demand had been met and they were willing to forsake the minor ones in the belief that the severing of the colonial connection should be as painless as possible and future relations cordial. They went more than halfway to meet the British point of view on controversial issues, such as the future of the INA prisoners and the punishment of officials guilty of excesses in 1942. It seems the Congress expected the League to do the same—respond to the Congress acceptance of Partition with a gesture of cooperation that would make the separation easy and bloodless. But this was not to be.

Nehru had said in another context: 'Mutual consent involves a settlement, imposition involves carrying on the dispute.'[26] This doomed the 3 June Plan to discord, for though the two parties agreed to the imposition, it remained an award imposed by the British, and not a settlement between the Congress and the League. Girija Shankar Bajpai summed up the matter neatly: 'The so-called settlement which is to be made public tonight will, I fear, leave many things unsettled.'[27]

UNITY THROUGH PARTITION?

One of the reactions to Partition was to see it as a temporary measure. Most people were unable to accept that Pakistan was forever. They continued to believe that a united India would be forged and that the two countries would be reunited. Congress leaders were no exception; they too 'nursed the hope that one day Pakistan will come back to us'.[28] Hope in an eventual united India reconciled them to the present reality of division.

The possibility of reunion after Partition had seemed a pipe dream to Nehru in 1945. In 1947 he extended the possibility into a likelihood and argued that unity would not only follow Partition, it would flow from it. This would happen because no coercion was involved. Nehru propounded this view in his All India Radio broadcast on 3 June 1947 appealing to the people to accept the Plan: 'The united India that we laboured for was not one of compulsion and coercion, but free and willing association of a free people. It may be that in this way we shall reach that united India sooner than otherwise and that she will have a stronger and more secure foundation.'[29] Partition thus signified the contemporary desire of some parts of the country to lead a separate existence. The hope was that once passions subsided, common interest would draw those parts and the rest of India together and a united India would result.[30]

However, when Nehru found that the expression of the hope that India and Pakistan would be one was misinterpreted by Pakistan to imply India's designs on Pakistan, he gave up talking of a united India[31] and spoke instead of the united action of the two countries, though he flinched from using the words India and Pakistan.[32] Others were to echo Nehru's hopes, including Rajendra Prasad and P. Subbaroyan.[33] However, it was not Subbaroyan, but another of Sapru's correspondents, Girija Shankar Bajpai, who proved prophetic: 'Two Indias will in reality be foes not friends for a long time to come.'[34]

Nehru's interpretation made the inevitable seem desirable. Gandhiji strove to make the desirable real. He saw that the first step was to ensure that the Partition decision remained reversible: 'The Viceroy has already stated in his speech and he has also assured me that when we approach him united this decision would be revoked.'[35] When Gandhiji saw that few came forward to oppose Partition vocally, he exhorted people not to accept it in their hearts. That would be a way of opposing Partition and it would limit the decision to being a mere geographical divide:

> We may take it that the physical division of the country is now certain. Since the Congress has accepted the plan, we must now look for another way. That way I have been showing. Just as land or other property can be partitioned so also can men's hearts. If therefore our hearts are true we can behave as if they had not been partitioned.[36]

His faith in the indivisible unity of the country found eloquent expression:

> How long can a thing over which the two are not agreed last? Geographically we have been divided. But so long as hearts too have not been divided, we must not weep, for all will be well so long as our hearts remain whole. The country may well be divided today into Pakistan and Hindustan. In the end we have to become one.[37]

If Gandhiji was eloquent, Nehru was poetic: 'But of one thing I am convinced that ultimately there will be a strong and united India. We have often to go through the valley of the shadow before we reach the sunlit mountain tops.'[38]

Equally necessary in Gandhiji's view was that the Partition decision should not be reinforced by other actions that would tend to cement it. That was why he opposed the partition of the army, [39] migrations across the border and most of all, the India Independence Bill, because it 'created' two 'nations', India and Pakistan, to whom Britain would transfer power. He wrote to Patel: 'The news today is the limit. Look at the Reuters cable. The Bill provides for two nations. What then is the point of the big talks going on here . . . if there has been no tacit acceptance on our part you people can prevent this crime.'[40] Gandhi realized that the British actions one by one made the Partition decision more difficult to reverse. Each step was another nail in the coffin of united India and there were many such steps. Arthur Moore assured Gandhiji that Patel and others felt that the Pakistan area had to be taken back. Gandhiji was forthright in his denial: 'There you are greatly mistaken. Personally I feel Pakistan has come to stay. They realise it.'[41]

PARTITION AS AN END TO VIOLENCE?

Another hope vested in the 3 June Plan was that it would end communal violence and put a stop to murder and arson. The Congress leaders acutely felt their powerlessness in stemming the tide. They came round to the view that as only Partition would satisfy League ambitions, it must be accepted in the interests of a final settlement. Once the political impasse was broken, communal tension would ease.[42] It was the same belief that violence would cease with the Partition, which lay behind Nehru's statement that Hindus and Sikhs would be safe in Pakistan.[43] Patel explained why they would be safe: 'It is possible the Pakistan Government may find the presence of Hindus and Sikhs indispensable . . . and now that the Muslims have secured a homeland for which they have agitated in season, and out of season, they may find that it is in their interest to ensure protection and justice to the minorities.'[44] He explained that 'we may also be able to afford some protection on the basis of reciprocity in regard to treatment of minorities'.[45] Patel felt that Pakistan would take a sympathetic stance towards minorities for fear that the Indian government would be harsh on Muslims if they ill-treated the Hindus and Sikhs.[46] Nehru was optimistic that 'the sobering and calming effect' of the announcement of 3 June would continue.[47] Patel was somewhat more cautious: 'Whether these disturbances will continue after Partition is difficult to prophesy and still remains to be seen.'[48] Sachidananda Sinha apprehended very serious troubles: 'The chances are that before long we shall be thrown back into the conditions which prevailed in India in the early eighteenth century after the death of Aurangzeb in 1707.'[49] In April 1947, the Governor of the Punjab, Evan Jenkins, had warned the authorities that he anticipated worsening of the communal situation after the announcement of the Partition.[50] The Viceroy told Jenkins in May that 'no more troops were available for the Punjab as the British expected disorder in other parts of India following an official announcement in June'.[51]

Sadly, events proved right not Nehru, but Jenkins, Mountbatten and Sinha. Partition was effected, but violence continued, in fact got intensified. By August 1947, 'Punjab had become worse than all the hells we ever heard of', commented Rajagopalachari.[52] What happened was far from what the leaders had expected. In fact, the situation was pointing the other way, towards the persecution of minorities in the Punjab. Gandhiji spoke out, 'so that what I say may reach the ears of the Muslims': 'the Muslims are on the rampage. They say that now that they have Pakistan, they will make slaves of everyone else. . . . If after Pakistan has come into being the conflict is further sharpened then it will only mean that we have been made fools of.'[53] Migration was so extensive that transfers of population, though opposed earlier, were subsequently arranged by the two governments. Nehru, who had declared that he was 'opposed to the principle of population transfers' [54] and Patel, who had proudly said that he could 'never be guilty of such . . . cowardly advice' as asking Hindus to migrate,[55] were at the helm of the government that effected these transfers. From Patel's hope that 'minorities may not have anything to fear' to Rajendra Prasad's brutally truthful admission was a long way: 'It seem[ed] West Punjab and the Frontier Province will have no Hindu or Sikh and similarly East Punjab will have no Muslim.'[56] Nehru explained his change of stand at a press conference on 12 October 1947. In Sheikhupura he came across:

> old friends and colleagues of mine. They came up and charged me with having deluded them. They were referring to a broadcast I had made ten days previously from All India Radio in which I had appealed to the people not to migrate but to stay on. They told me they had followed my advice and this was the consequence: their families were all dead and they were the sole representatives left. After that it became impossible for us to talk in terms of asking them to stay on in spite of those consequences and face greater dangers.[57]

Thus, though the Congress accepted Partition as a last measure, when all else failed to stop the violence, this tactic was as incapable of containing violence as the earlier ones. The irony was cruel: 'The Partition of India was agreed to by the Congress leaders in the hope of averting [as Nehru himself declared in his radio talk on 3 June] a civil war between Hindus and Muslims, but a civil war did result, perhaps in acuter form.'[58] If they had anticipated that Partition would unleash greater furies of violence, rather than stemming the existing tide, perhaps the Congress leaders may not have accepted Partition.[59] According to B.R. Nanda, 'somehow their dread of civil war was greater than Gandhi's, who believed that after the British departure a few days of blood letting were likely to bring the parties back to sanity'.[60]

Gandhiji was willing to risk anarchy, which Congress was not: 'They thought it was better to Partition the country so that both the parts could live happily and peacefully rather than let the whole country go to pieces. About this I did hold a different view. My view was that no one could take an inch of land by resorting to violence and murder. Let the whole country be reduced to ashes.'[61] He told the British repeatedly that they should leave India, to anarchy, if need be: 'He [the Englishman] was self-deceived in that he believed that he could not leave India to possible anarchy if such was to be India's lot. He was quite content to leave India a cockpit between two organised armies.'[62] In a question and answer session with D. Campbell, Reuter's correspondent in Delhi, Gandhiji said: 'It would be a good thing if the British were to go today. Thirteen months mean mischief to India. The British will have to take the risk of leaving India to chaos or anarchy. This is so because their rule has been imposed on the people. And when you remove that rule there might be no rule in the initial state.'[63] Gandhiji's willingness to risk anarchy rings truer in retrospect than the Congress leaders' obsession with peace.

PARTITION AND STRONG CENTRE *vs.* UNITY AND WEAK CENTRE

There was a silver lining to the cloud. The limitations of sections, grouping and, most of all, a weak centre, imposed by the Cabinet Mission Plan, could be bypassed. Nehru had seen this to be an advantage earlier, too, when commenting on the implications of the 20 February 1947 statement.[64] He had appreciated that the Constituent Assembly could be 'much freer to do what it likes for the part of India it represents'.[65] With time his conviction and his tone became more emphatic:

> I want that those who stand as an obstacle in our way should go their way. I wish that at least 80 or 90 per cent of India should move forward according to the map

of India which I have in my mind . . . if unity is not possible, we shall have to concentrate our efforts in some parts of the country where we can develop things in an ideal form.[66]

The 'map of India', added Radhakrishnan, should have two salient contours—a democratic socialist state and a strong centre.[67] Patel stressed the latter:

We are now free to develop about 80 per cent of our country in our own way. If we can consolidate our forces, have a strong Central Government and a strong army, we can, during the course of five years, make considerable progress. If we can only make substantial progress in the development schemes that are pending, it would give great hope to the country.[68]

PARTITION NOT BALKANIZATION

The 3 June Plan, envisaging transfer of power to two dominions, was preceded by the 10 May 1947 'bombshell' at Simla. Mountbatten claims that the draft proposals, which he showed Nehru on a 'hunch', produced a dismayed reaction from Nehru: 'the picture of India that emerged frightened me . . . a picture of fragmentation and conflict and disorder, and, unhappily also, of a worsening of relations between India and Britain'.[69] Nehru feared the proposals would 'invite balkanisation . . . provoke certain conflict and . . . create many "Ulsters" in India'. The crucial problem, in Nehru's view, was that 'The proposals start with the rejection of an Indian Union as successor to power and invite the claims of large numbers of successor states who are permitted to unite if they wish in two or more states.' The previous process had begun with a request for unity and then given an option to the provinces to secede—now separation would be followed by a request to join up again.'[70]

Mountbatten quickly clarified in his draft to HMG that only two successor states were permissible. This was what Mountbatten had initially argued at the Governors' Conference in mid April 1947—that provinces be given a choice to join either the Indian or the Pakistan Constituent Assembly.[71] There would then be no possibility of their becoming independent and India becoming balkanized as a result. Most governors agreed, though they wished to give the provinces the option to contract out later. But Mountbatten's adviser, Pug Ismay, stressed that HMG would not agree unless provinces were given a free choice and Conrad Corfield, who headed the Political Department, supported him, pointing out that free choice was being given to the states. Ismay's opinion seems to have been accepted and Nehru was dismayed by the wide freedom that the draft proposals vested with the provinces and states.

The earlier formulation was already aimed at placating the princes, many of whom were demanding the right to stand apart from any union, India or Pakistan. Jalal has argued that the threat of balkanization was unreal in practice [72] and there could have been little difference between the draft proposals and the final 3 June Plan as far as the future of the princes goes (provinces were another matter), for realpolitik would have ensured their integration with one union or another, administratively or otherwise. Was the danger of balkanization then apparent or real? It is likely that it was real, though one cannot prove a hypothetical theorem. Be as that may, there appeared to Nehru to be a vast difference in black and white between the 3 June Plan and the earlier proposals. The former was better than the latter. That must have aided Nehru's acceptance of the final plan, for after the possibility of balkanization—a Partition must have seemed its relatively harmless cousin. Princely states standing out would have meant a graver blow to Indian unity than Pakistan was.

UNITY BY FORCE?

Nehru posed the options before the Congress: 'I would like to draw your attention to the Muslim League's demand for Pakistan. There are only two ways to resolve this—either through mutual discussions and negotiations or through a fight!'[73] The limits of discussion were soon reached—Jinnah's favourite expression being 'No' and his favourite action, stalling. That left the option of fighting the League on its own terms. Hindu communal opinion, both within and outside the Congress, was in favour of this option and pressed the Congress to boldly declare that it would never agree to the formation of Pakistan and would fight those who wanted it every inch of the way. Purshottamdas Tandon, Congress leader and Speaker of the UP Legislative Assembly, appealed to the 'Congress and the manhood of the country' to 'even at this stage prevent this betrayal'.[74] Ram Ratan Gupta, a Congressman from Kanpur, called upon members of the Constituent Assembly to oppose this needless gift to Jinnah as it was 'a sheer repudiation and negation of our avowed principles and a gross betrayal of the pledge we have given to the electorate on whose strength is based the edifice of our organization'.[75] M.R. Jayakar, the Liberal leader with Mahasabha sympathies, bemoaned:

> We have no Benjamin Franklin who could tell the Muslims 'we will not allow you to secede and, if you wish to fight, we shall meet you on your own ground'.

From the very beginning the process of appeasement went on and a year ago the appeasement took the form of concessions surrendered at the sight of violence. This will go on until Congress makes up its mind to stand firm and meet violence on its own ground.[76]

Gandhiji's objection was fundamental, as it was to the very use of force for any end. On two occasions, when the League refused to come into the Constituent Assembly and when he visited Noakhali, where Muslim communalists had spread terror in the countryside, Gandhiji made it clear that, whatever the provocation may be, his way could never be that of force or compulsion, even if the alternative was Pakistan.[77] Nehru's approach was pragmatic rather than principled: 'We could have checked them by resorting to the sword and the *lathi* but would that solve the problem?'[78] In fact, violence could have intensified the problem: 'The use of violence at this time to maintain Indian unity will have disastrous results. Civil war will check the progress of India for a long time to come.'[79]

In their meetings with Mountbatten in early April 1947, Kripalani, Rajagopalachari and Rajendra Prasad ruled out imposing unity by force. Kripalani, who was then the Congress president, said: 'Rather than have a battle we shall let them have their Pakistan.'[80] Rajagopalachari admitted, 'the ideal of a united India could not be imposed by force', [81] while Rajendra Prasad echoed Nehru's fears of a civil war.[82] Elsewhere, Rajendra Prasad maintained that the Congress could not have done otherwise: 'We must be prepared either to prevent it [Partition] by force or to consent to it. . . . The Congress from the very beginning has held that it cannot contemplate coercing any part of India.'[83]

The problem with maintaining unity by force was that it went against the democratic grain of the Congress. The Congress was constrained by the lack of state power at the national level, despite the presence of Congress members in the Interim Government and its powerlessness to control developments in the crucial provinces of Punjab and Bengal. The instruments at the command of the Congress to impose unity were not the armed forces of the state, which were controlled by the British, but the cadres of the party. The option of unity by force then meant matching the League hooligans with the Congress *goondas* and raising volunteer bodies, which could counter the Muslim National Guards—in short, the turning of the Congress into a Hindu communal organization, and a fascist one at that. If the Congress chose to concede Partition rather than attempt to prevent it by force, it was a choice that could hardly be faulted.

The situation would have been completely different had the Congress been in power and in a position to use state force to suppress communalism. Though the Congress leaders were in the Interim Government, they were powerless because of the non-cooperation by the League. In practice, the Interim Government's powers in the sphere of law and order were limited to protest to the Viceroy, backed by threats to resign or demand that the League resign, as the case may be. The British, of course, were not powerless; they could 'keep law and order if they wanted to'.[84] Mountbatten was duly pressed to assert his powers to stop the bloodshed and end the trend of the weakening of the Centre that Wavell had introduced.[85] Nehru asked the Governor of Punjab to use troops as they inspired more confidence than the police.[86] Gandhiji's outlook was different. He pointed out that looking to the British was wrong, a sign of weakness, and for military help doubly so.[87] This had been his view in mid 1946, when he had warned that senseless violence, by warranting the use of bayonets, would prolong British rule.[88] Bloodshed and the rash of riots did not shake Gandhiji's conviction that the British should leave India forthwith, they only strengthened it.

If state force alone could ultimately subdue fascist communalism, why did the British not use it? Why did communal fires blaze and British officers stand idly by? Nehru's view was that British officials were incapable of and disinterested in containing the communal virus: 'They feel that they have to go anyhow pretty soon, so why should they bother?' He added, 'there is often also a secret satisfaction that India is going to pieces'.[89] The main reason for their indifference and even callousness was that they no longer had any stake in India. Their future was not linked with India any more.[90] If their future made them callous, their past made them vengeful. Having been pushed into the corner by the Congress movements, as recently as 1942, they were not unhappy to see Congressmen in a tight spot.[91] The senior officials indignantly denied Nehru's charge that trouble was maximum where there were British officials in charge.[92] There was another dimension, that of the gradual collapse of the structure of the civilian regime, which the Congress leaders were unwilling to concede.[93]

Two processes linked up here, not unseen by Nehru. The decline of authority, which made the continuance of British rule impossible, also made the communal violence difficult to suppress. The consensual answer to the first dilemma was independence, to the second, partition. Mountbatten's answer was a 'quick decision'; failure to make which 'would be tantamount to failure to take the responsibility of civil war off the Viceroy's shoulders. The only alternative he could recommend, it should be made clear, was immediate evacuation.'[94] Gandhiji's answer was that the British should leave India, to anarchy if need be, but they should leave immediately. The Congress took ingredients from both Mountbatten and Gandhiji in equal measure to concoct their answer—British should leave immediately but to agreement, not anarchy.[95] The mixture was explosive.

If British officials had 'ceased to care', some Indian officials cared only for their community. As the communal conflict in national politics grew, it seeped into the bureaucracy, the police and the army.[96] Often communal sentiment remained at the stage of sympathy and bias, felt but not blatantly expressed. At certain times it took the form of complicity, active or passive, in riots. As riots spread, and more important, migrations began, the sympathies of officials were often blatant. How did one meet communal violence with a partially communalized police and even army? Or rebuild a hate-free atmosphere with the aid of a communalized administration? It seemed as impossible a task in some ways as launching a mass movement to achieve unity with communalized cadres and people.

UNITY THROUGH STRUGGLE?

It has been argued that the alternative to Partition lay along the path of anti-British mass struggle, whose fallout would be Hindu-Muslim unity.[97] Even a close associate of Gandhiji, S.N. Aggarwal, argued that a mass struggle was the answer: 'if we could compel the Britishers to quit India, we can also tell them plainly but firmly: "No, India shall not be divided". And if Pakistan is forced on us, even then the nation must resist it with all the strength at its command by starting a countrywide mass rebellion.'[98]

Gandhiji's understanding was different. He pointed out to Louis Fischer that the existing violence negated any possibility of a mass movement: 'I cannot think of civil disobedience when there is so much violence in the air.'[99] A year later and this time in the context of communal violence, Gandhi explained to his associate, N.K. Bose, that the situation was surcharged with communalism and not at all favourable for a struggle.[100] Gandhi was speaking on the basis of his own experience, when he had stumbled on communal sentiments in the lonely furrow he ploughed in Noakhali.[101] The trouble was that Gandhi was the accepted practitioner par excellence of the art of successful mass movement and there was a tendency to see the mass movements he led as conjured by him from nothing, with the magic wand of his charisma, perhaps. Few realized that deciding the moment when to commence satyagraha was based on a careful reading of the popular strength and a persistent checking of the pulse of the people. What could even a mass leader do when the mass of people had succumbed to the plague? Gandhiji said: 'You say that if I give you the lead you will follow me. Have you ever thought against whom and to whom I can give the lead?'[102]

N.K. Bose naively suggested to Gandhiji to create a situation by his efforts he had done earlier. Gandhiji's answer encapsulated in a handful of words the essence of the relationship between a leader and his people:

> I have never created a situation in my life. I have one qualification which many of you do not possess. I can almost instinctively feel what is stirring in the heart of the masses. And when I feel that the forces of good are dimly stirring within, I seize upon them and build up a programme. And they respond. People say that I had created a situation, but I had done nothing except giving a shape to what was already there. Today I see no sign of such a healthy feeling. And therefore I shall have to wait until the time comes.[103]

The extent of communalization of society can be estimated from the fact that it affected the party cadres, who had traditionally been propagators of staunch secularism. Such Congressmen were, to be fair, not completely communal either, in the sense of being active purveyors of communal ideology. They mirrored the frailties and strengths of the rest of the society. Many Congressmen were unable to stand up to the test imposed by the heightened communal tension and riots and developed sympathy for the communal standpoint. As early as 14 July 1945, Nehru admitted to the Viceroy, Lord Wavell, that 'some of the Congress Hindus were anti-Muslim'.[104] A year later, he proposed that the AICC office set up a minorities department, one of whose urgent tasks would be to 'suggest ways of preventing the growth of communal and sectarian feeling among Congressmen'.[105]

This tendency was aggravated after independence. Partition and the holocaust that attended it communalized politics further. Communal forces not only grew in strength but began to make steady inroads into nationalist bastions. B.G. Kher, the Chief Minister of Bombay, commented on this trend to Patel on 26 May 1948: 'Hindu-Muslim relations last year made the Hindu preaching more popular and many Congressmen also got affected by the communal virus.'[106] The AICC session in November 1947 revealed sharp differences among Congressmen over the question of what attitude was to be adopted towards communal elements. The final resolutions adopted were a reiteration of the secular position of the Congress: 'They make clear that we cannot compromise our ideals because communal organizations are shouting a great deal.'[107] The debate had showed up the ambiguity among Congressmen and this itself was disturbing to Nehru. He lamented to his Chief Ministers: 'Even many Congressmen have given way to this mental turmoil and confusion.'[108] The ambiguity, said Nehru, arose from a shared affinity with the outlook of bodies such as the RSS and Hindu Mahasabha: 'Unfortunately a number of Congressmen without thinking are attracted to this development of Fascist and Nazi modes of thought and practice.'[109] This undoubtedly made the task of suppressing the communal forces difficult, but also made it more urgent. The enemy was within, it was not a distant threat, and Nehru warned his Chief Ministers that if this was ignored they would do so 'at our peril'.[110]

Communalism was not the only malady plaguing the party. It was disorganized and undisciplined. After the battering of the war years, the task of welding the Congress, planned in 1945, had been interrupted by other pressing concerns—fighting elections, forming ministries, running the Interim Government, and not least of all, participating in the negotiations and the Constituent Assembly.[111] Party reorganization took a back seat, despite awareness among the leaders, including Nehru, that it needed to be done.[112] Congressmen scrambling for seats in the provincial legislatures and the Constituent Assembly upset Gandhiji, as, in his view, these forums were only one possible arena of political work and not the most important one.[113] Nehru assumed the presidency of the Congress with the objective of reviving the party, but gave up the office to head the Interim Government. In subsequent months he often spoke of losing touch with the party and even the people, because of the cares of office, but did little to correct the situation.

Hopes, beliefs, rationalization and justification apart, the truth of the matter was that the Congress accepted the Partition because there was little else it could do. 'But the Congress has to agree to it because there is no other alternative.'[114] This was Nehru's public admission to AICC members after two months of denying Partition, calling it secession, believing it would pave the way for reunion, laying responsibility at the door of the people, etc. Patel had made a private confession earlier: 'Frankly speaking, we all hate it, but at the same time see no way out of it.'[115] Amrit Kaur explained the Congress stand to Sudhir Ghosh in London: 'The Congress had seemingly no option left.'[116] For once, even Gandhiji did not have an answer. The master strategist had not been able to adapt satyagraha and *ahimsa* to serve the end of communal unity. In his concluding speech to the momentous session of the All India Congress Committee on 14 June 1947, at which Partition was accepted, Kripalani, then President of the Congress, said: 'Why then am I not with him (Gandhiji)? It is because I feel he has yet found no way of tackling the problem on the mass basis. When he taught us non-violent non-cooperation, he showed us a definite method, which we had at least mechanically followed, but today he himself is in the dark.'[117] The rapidly unfolding events, however, did not slow their pace for an old man groping to light a path for his countrymen.

NOTES

1. S. Gopal, ed., *Selected Works of Jawaharlal Nehru*, (hereafter *SWJN*), Vols XIV-XV (New Delhi, 1981-2), and Second Series, Vols I-IV (New Delhi, 1984-6), Vol. XV, pp. 306-7.
2. Nicholas Mansergh, editor-in-chief, *Transfer of Power, 1942-7* (hereafter *TP*), Vols I-XII (London, 1970-83), Vol. X, pp. 308-9, 194-6, 179-80 and 213-15 *passim*.
3. Congress had despaired of a united India by February 1947 in the view of Anita Inder Singh, *The Origins of the Partition of India, 1936-1947* (Delhi, 1987), p. 226. By March 1947, Congress had reconciled to the partition of Punjab and Bengal, S. Gopal, *Jawaharlal Nehru, A Biography*, Vol. I, *1889-1947* (New Delhi, 1976), p. 343. This was in the event that the country would be partitioned.
4. Gandhi's address to the prayer meeting, 11 June 1947, Mahatma Gandhi, *Collected Works of Mahatma Gandhi* (hereafter *CWMG*), Vols LXXVIII-XC (New Delhi, 1979-84), Vol. LXXXVIII, pp. 73-5.
5. N.K. Bose, 'My Experiences as a Gandhian-II', in M.P. Sinha, *Contemporary Relevance of Gandhism* (Bombay, 1970), p. 52.
6. See Sucheta Mahajan, 'Pressures on a Colonial Regime and Working of Imperial Policy, Transfer of Power in India, 1945-47', Ph.D. thesis, Jawaharlal Nehru University (New Delhi, 1993), Chapter 10, section on partition of Punjab and Bengal.
7. Nehru's speech at Liberty Week meeting, 9 August 1947, *SWJN*, Second Series, Vol. III, p. 134.
8. This contradiction existed even in Gandhiji, who, on the one hand, challenged anyone to create Pakistan over his dead body and, on the other, conceded that no one could prevent Partition if the Muslims wanted it.
9. 10 March 1946, *SWJN*, Vol. XV, p. 34.
10. Interview to Norman Cliff, 25 May 1947, ibid., Second Series, Vol. II, p. 180.
11. All India Congress Committee Papers (hereafter AICC Papers), G-30, 1946-8, cited in Anita Inder Singh, op.cit., p. 230. Singh wrongly refers to an AICC meeting on 1 and 2 June 1947.
12. A.M. Zaidi, ed., *The Encyclopaedia of the Indian National Congress*, Vol. VI (New Delhi, 1981), pp. 110-14.
13. 'The Congress stand regarding Partition has been taken advantage of by the sections mentioned above to inflame communal passions further. . . . As regards West Bengal,

the agitation for Partition has gained ground because the Congress came to the aid of the Hindu Mahasabha and also because communal passions have been roused among the Hindus on account of the happenings since August last,' Sarat Bose to Patel, 27 May 1947, Durga Das, ed., *Sardar Patel Correspondence* (hereafter *SPC*), Vols I-X (Ahmedabad, 1971-4), Vol. IV, pp. 45-6.

14. Sarat Bose told Patel that having been in close touch with public opinion both in West and East Bengal, 'I can say that it is not a fact that Bengali Hindus unanimously demand partition.' Contrast this with Syama Prasad Mookerjee's dismissal of Sarat Bose: 'He has no support whatsoever from the Hindus and he does not address one single public meeting', 27 and 11 May 1947, ibid., pp. 45 and 40, respectively.
15. 3 June 1947, *SWJN*, Second Series, Vol. III, p. 99.
16. Ibid. p. 91. Jalal completely inverts reality and argues that the Congress insisted that Partition be final and absolute because it wanted to exercise full power. She blames the Congress for wanting a divorce, not a limited separation, Ayesha Jalal, *The Sole Spokesman, Jinnah, the Muslim League and the Demand for Pakistan* (Cambridge, 1985), p. 280.
17. 22 June 1947, *SWJN*, Second Series, Vol. III, p. 181.
18. Patel to B.M. Birla, 10 June 1947, *SPC*, Vol. IV, p. 56.
19. Congress president to Viceroy, 2 June 1947, drafted by Nehru, *SWJN*, Second Series, Vol. III, p. 91.
20. Jenkins' record of interview with Nehru, 30 May 1947, ibid., Vol. II, p. 311.
21. See *SPC*, Vol. IV, pp. 121-4, for both speeches
22. 3 June 1947, ibid., p. 125.
23. Patel to Mountbatten, 10 June 1947, ibid., p. 147.
24. Kripalani's speech at the AICC session, 14 June 1947, AICC Papers, G-71, 46/7, Nehru Memorial Museum & Library, New Delhi (hereafter NMML).
25. Speech at Gurudwara Panja Sahib (5 August 1947), *CWMG*, Vol. LXXXIX, p. 5.
26. Interview to Norman Cliff, *News Chronicle* correspondent, 25 May 1947, *SWJN*, Second Series, Vol. II, p. 180.
27. Girija Shankar Bajpai to Tej Bahadur Sapru, 3 June 1947, Sapru Papers, S-1, Roll 1, B-39, National Archives of India, New Delhi (hereafter NAI). Rajendra Prasad enumerated the 'many difficult and intricate problems', still to be solved—'the division of assets and liabilities, of services, of armed forces and settlement or agreement regarding transport and communication, coinage and tariffs, legation and other international organizations in foreign countries and this country [and] the settlement of boundaries', to S. Sinha, 5 June 1947, Rajendra Prasad Papers (hereafter R.P. Papers), 6-I/45-6-7, S. No. 51, NAI.
28. Patel to Bozman, 11 July 1947, *SPC*, Vol. IV, p. 469. Rajendra Prasad expressed the same sentiment in a letter to S. Radhakrishnan, 'We do not yet know what is going to happen but we are not without hope that after sometime reunion may become possible,' 6 May 1947, R.P. Papers, 19-P /47, Col. 1, Part 2, S.No. 1.
29. *SWJN*, Second Series, Vol. III, p. 99. Such an unconventional slogan, 'unity through partition', surprisingly found a taker in Mudie, the pro-League, Governor of Sind. He argued, at the Governors' Conference on 15 April 1947, that once Pakistan was got on paper both parties would be talking of unity, *TP*, Vol. X, pp. 242-5.
30. Nehru to Sultan Sjahrir, 17 June 1947, *SWJN*, Second Series, Vol. III, p. 197.
31. 5 January 1948, ibid., Vol. V, p. 177.
32. Nehru to Sultan Sjahrir, 17 June 1947, ibid., Vol. III, p. 157. Jinnah did not share these

hopes for 'closer relations'. On 17 April 1947 he had told the Viceroy: 'You must carry out a surgical operation; cut India and its Army firmly in half and give me the half that belongs to the Muslim League', Viceroy's personal report, *TP*, Vol. X, pp. 298-301.

33. Rajendra Prasad wrote to Sinha, 'I am feeling [*sic*] that Pakistan will soon discover the utility of a union with India and will reconsider its position, and when that happens, we shall be happy, but whether that comes about or not, we have to go ahead with the present plan', 5 June 1947, R.P. Papers, 6-I/45-6-7, S.No. 51. Subbaroyan wrote to Sapru: 'However I am hoping that once the division has been made and the constitutions get working it may be possible for the two parts at least to act in unison by means of agreements for purposes of defence and foreign relations', 27 June 1947, Sapru Papers, S-2, Roll 5, S-613.
34. Girija Shankar Bajpai to Sapru, 3 June 1947, Sapru Papers, S-1, B-39. The Governor of UP, Wylie, concurred: 'The moment India is partitioned all sorts of vested interests in the two separate states will arise and you cannot ever bring them together again.' Quoted by Horace Alexander, Oral History Transcript (hereafter OHT), No. 12, NMML.
35. Gandhiji's prayer meeting speech, 4 June 1947, *CWMG*, Vol. LXXXVIII, p. 75. Mountbatten had, in fact, wanted ratification of the Partition after a year so that Indians could see what it 'implied and involved' and, if possible, evolve a different outlook. But Ismay ruled out an 'escape clause' as wrong and avoiding finality. This was at the Viceroy's 18th staff meeting on 21 April 1947, *TP*, Vol. X, pp. 347-9.
36. Gandhiji to Munnalal Shah, 11 June 1947, *CWMG*, Vol. LXXXVIII, p. 130.
37. Prayer meeting speech, 12 June 1947, ibid., pp. 138-9. Nehru, Patel and Kripalani, all three spoke in Gandhiji's language. In Patel's words, 'What nature and God had intended to be one can on no account be split in two for all times', *Hindustan Times* (hereafter *HT*), 12 August 1947. Kripalani echoed him: 'Sooner or later the basic unity will assert itself and those who are anxious to break away now will be equally anxious to return to the common lap', ibid., 20 June 1947.
38. Nehru to Brigadier Cariappa, 29 April 1947, *SWJN*, Second Series, Vol. II, p. 377. Nehru continued to speak in this refrain after independence: 'Ultimately both the Dominions will unite into one country. India cannot and will not remain divided. That is my conviction no matter how much I am personally criticized for having accepted partition', 28 November 1947, Reception by Sikh Seva Dal, ibid., Vol. IV, pp. 189-90.
39. 'The Partition was indeed an error. . . . The Partition of Army, however, is a terrible mistake we are making', 15 July 1947, *CWMG*, Vol. LXXXVIII, p. 341. Also see ibid., p. 335.
40. 23 June 1947, ibid., p. 196. Rajendra Prasad's reaction was a study in contrast. He did not see the deeper implications of the Act, that it legalized division. He only saw that it legalized the position of the two governments and did away with the need for a temporary constitution. 'By passing an Act, giving it the status of a dominion and thus legalising and placing on a statutory basis the position of the Government in each of the two dominions, the British Parliament will be in a sense providing for the interim period until our constitution is framed. I was at one time thinking whether it would be necessary for us to pass a sort of a temporary constitution, taking as our basis the Government of India Act 1935 with appropriate amendments to enable us to run the administration until our permanent constitution is framed. Along with that we would be also working on the permanent constitution so that even if the permanent constitution were not ready when power will be transferred in June 1948, we would have a

temporary constitution to go by. But it seems they have relieved us of that burden and we shall have power transferred to us by August next, some 10 months before the date they had fixed for it, but also a statute, by which we could go on until a permanent constitution is framed', Rajendra Prasad to Sachidananda Sinha, 5 June 1947, R.P. Papers, 6-I/45-6-7, S. No. 51.

41. Interview to Arthur Moore, 10 July 1947, *CWMG*, Vol. LXXXVIII, p. 311. Subbaroyan conveyed Gandhi's pessimism to Sapru: 'He felt', to use his own words, 'that the Hindus were being wound up' (and he instanced Pandit Shukla's speech), 'and it is going to be hard for the two communities to be reconciled in the future', 27 June 1947, Sapru Papers, S-2, Roll 5, S-613.
42. Nehru argued that Partition is better than murder of innocent citizens while Rajendra Prasad explained to S. Sinha: 'Considering all that was happening and viewing the future we felt that there was no escape from division unless we were determined to have a long period not only of uncertainty and instability but of strife, conflict and even bloodshed spread over large tracts of the country. We hope however that we shall be able to carry on the great constructive work of nation building in an atmosphere of peace, if not goodwill', 5 June 1947, R.P. Papers, 6-1/45-6-7, S. No. 51. Kripalani's speech to the AICC, on 14 June 1947, first referred to Partition as the only way to get freedom from Britain. 'Secondly, the plan seemed to open a way out of this tangle, chaos and frustration resulting from the deteriorating communal situation in the Punjab, Bengal, Bihar and the Frontier Province. The provincial governments were unable to cope with the riots', AICC Papers, G-71/46-7.
43. Nehru to AICC delegates, 15 June 1947, *SWJN*, Second Series, Vol. III, p. 112.
44. Patel to Secretary, Shiromani Committee Jain Biradari, Rawalpindi, 22 June 1947, *SPC*, Vol. V, p. 287.
45. Ibid.
46. Patel to Parmanand Trehan, 16 June 1947, ibid., Vol. V, p. 289.
47. Nehru to Mountbatten, 22 June 1947, *SWJN*, Second Series, Vol. III, p. 181.
48. Patel to Secretary, Shiromani Committee Jain Biradari, Rawalpindi, 22 June 1947, *SPC*, Vol. V, p. 287.
49. S. Sinha to Rajendra Prasad, 9 July 1947, R.P. Papers, 5-D/96-7.
50. Jenkins warned Ismay on 14 April 1947 that the announcement of Partition would be 'followed by an immediate blow up. There was therefore a military problem of considerable magnitude', *TP*, Vol. X, pp. 231-4. Jenkins wrote to Mountbatten on 4 August 1947, 'Nor can all the King's horses and all the King's men prevent—though they may be able to punish—conflict between communities interlocked in villages over wide areas of the country', ibid., Vol. XII, p. 516.
51. Cited in Anita Inder Singh, op.cit., p. 224.
52. Rajaji to Rajendra Prasad, 30 August 1947, R.P. Papers, 23-C/46-7.
53. Prayer meeting address, 14 June 1947, *CWMG*, Vol. LXXXVIII, p. 152.
54. Interview with Mountbatten, 10 June 1947, *SWJN*, Second Series, Vol. III, p. 212.
55. Patel to R.K. Sidhwa, MLA, Sind, 23 May 1947, *SPC*, Vol. V, p. 317.
56. Rajendra Prasad to S. Sinha, 23 September 1947, R.P. Papers, 5-D/46-7.
57. *SWJN*, Second Series, Vol. III, p. 147.
58. S. Sinha's comment must have seemed painfully true to Rajendra Prasad, 16 September 1947, R.P. Papers, 5-D/46-7. 'Even though the Congress agreed to a division of the country in the hope, which had thus far proved vain, that thereby internal conflicts might cease, it has never accepted the theory that there are two or more nations in

India', AICC resolution, 15 November 1947, *SWJN*, Second Series, Vol. IV, p. 180. In Abdul Majid Khan's view the Congress got scared after the March riots and made the 'tactical blunder' of preponing the date of withdrawal from June 1948 to 15 August 1947. If they had not done so, 'the riots would have come to an end after two or three months. 'Of course, there would have been mass killing among the three communities, but the country could remain united', OHT, 348, NMML. H.K. Mahtab argued that it would have been better to have fought it out as happened in Nigeria: 'Some party would have been defeated and then some compromise would have been arrived at, but unfortunately what happened in India was that partition was done by agreement. There was no fighting. Both sides agreed to part', OHT, 306, NMML.

59. 'Our calculations were evidently wrong as events have proved. Yet oddly enough on the 15th August and after there was such tremendous popular rejoicing all over the country that we felt that we had done rightly. But the poison was there and it came out and spread with amazing rapidity', Nehru to Sheikh Abdullah, 10 October 1947, *SWJN*, Second Series, Vol. IV, p. 269. S. Gopal adds: 'as Nehru acknowledged, had the leaders of the Congress anticipated this, they might well have preferred to keep India united and distraught', S. Gopal, *Jawahar Lal Nehru, A Biography* (Delhi, 1979), Vol. II, p. 1.
60. B.R. Nanda, *Mahatma Gandhi: A Biography* (New Delhi, 1958), p. 489. Gandhi believed that communal violence under British aegis was pernicious—once the British left, the people and the country would go through the fire, none the less, but it would be purifying. For further elaboration, see *CWMG*, Vols LXXXVI, LXXXVII and LXXXVIII, pp. 83, 152 and 416 and 14, respectively.
61. Talk with visitors from Punjab, 17 July 1947, ibid., Vol. LXXXVIII, p. 356.
62. *Harijan*, 20 July 1947, NMML.
63. Ibid., 18 May 1947. 'He [Mountbatten] could have allowed the carnage to go on, if it had to go on, and said that he would not bow before the sword', prayer meeting address, 14 June 1947, *CWMG*, Vol. LXXXVIII, p. 153.
64. Nehru to Asaf Ali, 24 February 1947, *SWJN*, Second Series, Vol. II, p. 51.
65. Nehru to Krishna Menon, 23 February 1947, ibid., p. 45.
66. Speech at Jallianwala Bagh Day meeting, 13 April 1947, ibid., pp. 89-90. With a common centre, the League would constantly be threatening to leave the government. Viceroy's 6th misc. meeting, 22 April 1947, *TP*, Vol. X, pp. 363-4. Brecher is of the view that a larger India would have had disintegrating pulls, Michael Brecher, *Nehru: A Political Biography* (London, 1961), p. 77.
67. 'If predominantly Muslim zones are getting out both in the N. and in the N.E., there is no reason why we should not have a strong socialist state', S. Radhakrishnan to Rajendra Prasad, 29 April 1947, R.P. Papers, 1-B/47, S. No. 2.
68. Patel to Neogy, 18 June 1947, *SPC*, Vol. V, p. 72. Neogy had written, 'Though every patriotic Indian must grieve over the partition of India, the scheme, as now announced, is the best that could be devised in the present circumstances. From one point of view Hindustan will have some chance of planning for future development, now that the obstructive elements in the Central Government will have to leave', Neogy to Patel, 7 June 1947, ibid., p. 71.
69. Nehru to Mountbatten, 11 May 1947, *SWJN*, Second Series, Vol. II, pp. 131-3. He complained that Mieville had shown him a rough draft of one and a half pages but the latter insisted he had been shown the full draft. Actually Mountbatten had modified them later, but Nehru believed that HMG had imparted 'an ominous meaning' to the proposals. He dashed off a letter of protest immediately to Mountbatten and followed

it up with a long discursive note on the proposals. Notably Hugh Tinker, Morris Jones, S. Gopal and R.J. Moore have offered various interpretations of the 'incident at Simla'. See R.J. Moore, *Escape from Empire, The Attlee Government and the Indian Problem*, (Oxford, 1983), pp. 272-80, for a summary.

70. Viceroy's meeting with his staff attended by Nehru, 11 May 1947, *SWJN*, Second Series, Vol. II, p. 142.

71. Mountbatten's insistence with HMG that the proposals be modified to meet Nehru's objections has helped historians to erroneously argue that Partition was being conceded in deference to Nehru's wishes—that Partition was the Congress demand. For instance, Jalal argues that Mountbatten gave in to Congress on this point because if he fell foul of Congress it would be impossible to continue to run the country, Jalal, op.cit., p. 262. Actually it was no volte-face for Mountbatten, made under pressure from Nehru, but return to a position he shared with Nehru and had been persuaded to abandon by HMG and the Ismay-Corfield lobby. Sumit Sarkar seems to have accepted the impression Mountbatten sought to give, in taking Mountbatten's revision of HMG's proposals (in response to Nehru's objections) as 'proof' of the pressure the Congress could but chose not to wield over the British authorities because of their desire for a quick transfer of power, Sumit Sarkar, *Modern India, 1885-1945* (Delhi, 1983), pp. 448-9. In our view the real proof of the Congress strength would lie in its ability to get reversed a decision whose revoking would go against British interests and against the inclinations of the Viceroy.

72. In Jalal's view the 'apparent' threat to balkanize India was bandied to induce the Congress to offer to be in the Commonwealth. The Congress bait to Mountbatten was their offer of Commonwealth membership and Mountbatten's reciprocal gift was the transfer of power to the Union. Mountbatten duly modified Plan Balkan to suit the Congress requirements, denying independence to the provinces, Jalal, op.cit., p. 249. In sharp contrast to Jalal is Moore's view of the likely alternative scenario (had the Simla Agreement on dual dominionhood not come through): 'a rash of unstable regimes', police actions and foreign intervention perhaps (as in Afghanistan in 1979). 'The Simla deal averted the fragmentation of British India, drawing the limits of unity by restricting the options of Muslim majority areas to membership of India or Pakistan. . . . Probably the main attraction of the deal to Congress was that it promised to banish the spectre of princely Ulsters. It is likely that the primary significance of the deal will come to be seen as its preparation for the integration of the 562 princely states within the two dominions and that the Mountbatten viceroyalty will be assessed mainly in terms of his contribution to that process. . . . Mountbatten, Nehru, Patel and V.P. Menon had found the solution to the problem of British India's fragmentation in the dual dominion deal. . . . A negotiated settlement consonant with political realities emerged, maximizing unity without the deployment of force', Ayesha Jalal, op.cit., pp. 180 and 200. In Bimal Prasad's view, the Mountbatten Plan should really be called the Mountbatten-Nehru Plan as 'it nipped a serious mischief in the bud' by preventing many partitions: 'This was no mean achievement', Bimal Prasad, *Gandhi, Nehru and J.P.: Studies in Leadership* (Delhi, 1984), p. 120. B.R. Nanda is of the view that the independence of the princes would have been worse than Partition, B.R. Nanda, 'Nehru and the Partition of India', in Philips and Wainwright, eds, *The Partition of India, Policies and Perspectives* (London, 1970). See also H. Brasted and C. Bridge, '15 August 1947: Labour's Parting Gift to India', in J. Masselos, ed., *India: Creating a Modern Nation* (New Delhi, 1990), for the argument that limited fragmentation was Labour's achievement.

73. Jallianwala Bagh Day meeting, 13 April 1947, *SWJN*, Second Series, Vol. II, pp. 88-9.
74. Typed note, 4 June 1947, P.D. Tandon Papers, Group 13, S.No. 361. A correspondent of Tandon's commented: 'Pakistan is the "Munich" of India and the Congress', R.N. Dhar to Tandon, 19 July 1947, ibid., Part II, File No. 231.
75. 19 July 1947, ibid.
76. 21 May 1947, Sapru Papers, S-I, Roll 3, J-100.
77. *CWMG*, Vols LXXXVIII and LXXXVI, pp. 73 and 106.
78. Speech at AICC meeting, 15 June 1947, *SWJN*, Second Series, Vol. III, p. 112.
79. Speech at Liberty Week meeting, 9 August 1947, ibid., p. 134.
80. 17 April 1947, *TP*, Vol. X, pp. 308-9.
81. 11 April 1947, ibid., pp. 194-6.
82. 10 April 1947, ibid., pp. 179-80.
83. To Radhakrishnan, 6 May 1947, R.P. Papers, File No. 19-P/47, Col. 1.
84. Viceroy's interview with Kripalani, 17 April 1947, *TP*, Vol. X, pp. 308-9.
85. Viceroy's interview with Patel, 12 April 1947, ibid., pp. 213-15.
86. Nehru to Jenkins, Interview, 30 May 1947, *SWJN*, Second Series, Vol. II, p. 309. Jenkins ruled it out. He saw the problem as lack of information and wrong tactics. So Nehru appealed to Mountbatten, adding a personal plea to save Lahore: 'My mother came from Lahore and part of my childhood was spent there.' He wanted Mountbatten to declare martial law and give orders to the troops to be ruthless in suppressing trouble. Mountbatten simply agreed that 'something must be done', Nehru to Mountbatten, 22 June 1947, ibid., Vol. III p. 139.
87. Gandhiji's statement to the director of an influential British daily, *Harijan*, 10 November 1946. Also see his reply to Shankarrao Deo, ibid., 15 September 1946.
88. 'What senseless violence does is to prolong the lease of life of British or foreign rule. I believe that the authors of the State paper issued by the Cabinet Mission desire peaceful transfer of power to representative Indian hands. But if we need the use of the British gun and bayonet, the British will not go or, if they do, some other foreign power will take their place', ibid., 25 August 1946.
89. Nehru to Agatha Harrison, 22 May 1947, *SWJN*, Second Series, Vol. II, p. 337. Also see Sudhir Ghosh to Patel, 26 August 1947, Sudhir Ghosh Papers, NMML, and see Viceroy's interview with Kripalani, 17 April 1947, *TP*, Vol. X, pp. 308-9.
90. According to Jayaprakash Narayan, Indians were told by British officials to go to their future rulers, 21 March 1947, statement cited in Anita Inder Singh, op.cit., p. 219. Mountbatten reported to his governors that a member of the Interim Government had told him that a British official, when informed on the phone, that houses in an outlying district were on fire, replied, 'We are leaving anyhow—what do we care?' Governors' Conference, 15 April 1947, *TP*, Vol. X, pp. 242-5.
91. The Sind governor, Mudie, made the counter accusation that Congressmen were angry with him and accused him of being partisan to the League, because he was Chief Secretary, UP, during the 1942 movement, and had rounded up Congress leaders, Nehru's interview with Mudie, 15 April 1947, ibid., pp. 259-80
92. Nehru's speech at AICC, 15 June 1947, *SWJN*, Second Series, Vol. III, p. 110. Moon is reported to have walked up to an armed sepoy who was in the process of looting and given him a hard kick on the bottom, IOR Mss Eur C 601, Oriental and India Office Collections, British Library, London. Jenkins disagreed with the allegation that officials did not do their duty: 'The senior officials employed in Rawalpindi and Attock are all British, and I am satisfied that the official outlook is quite impartial', Jenkins to Amrit Kaur, 24 April 1947, Rajkumari Amrit Kaur Papers, File No. 3, NMML. Gandhiji put

the onus on the services: 'They have to see to it that the suspicion that they are behind the riots is not true', prayer meeting, 10 April 1947, *CWMG*, Vol. LXXXVII, p. 252.

93. Kripalani was not willing to concede Mountbatten's argument that British governors could not overrule their Ministers in the changed conditions. He held to the view that the prestige of the British governor was still so high that any man worth his salt could make his government keep law and order, Mountbatten's interview with Kripalani, 17 April 1947, *TP*, Vol. X, p. 309. The Governor of NWFP was also of the view that the 'situation . . . is being held by what remains of the prestige of the Government of the days that are gone', Caroe to the Viceroy, 23 November 1946, Caroe Collection, Mss Eur F 203/1&2, Accession No. 4780, NAI.
94. Mountbatten was blatantly manipulative as usual. He sent Ismay to London with a draft statement backed by the above threat, Viceroy's staff meeting, 14 April 1947, *TP*, Vol. X, p. 223.
95. 'I am sure than ever of the rightness of what Bapu said last year that the first thing to be done is an immediate transfer of power to some Indian authority', Nehru to Agatha Harrison, 22 May 1947, *SWJN*, Second Series, Vol. II, p. 337 (Gandhiji had actually said hand over to anarchy if need be).
96. 'The feelings between the communities are much the same as though a civil war was going on. An official, if he tries to be impartial is merely suspected on both sides, so he tends to take shelter with one side or the other, according to his community', Note by Abell, 26 March 1947, *TP*, Vol. X, pp. 26-7. In the Commander-in-Chief's opinion, the overall situation had deteriorated rapidly over the last three months, interview with Mountbatten, 14 April 1947, ibid., pp. 223-6. For communalism in the army, see ibid., pp. 60 and 1033. Also see Hunt and Harrison, *The District Officer in India, 1930-1947* (London, 1980), p. 243.
97. Kamaladevi Chattopadhyay contends that the only alternative to the Partition was a mass movement because the British were willing to quit only on the basis of the Partition. Gandhiji's leadership was crucial, for the Socialists could not have launched a movement on their own, with Gandhiji neutral and Congress against it, OHT, 388, NMML. 'The only real alternative lay along the path of united militant mass struggle against imperialism and its Indian allies, the only thing which, as we have repeatedly seen, the British really dreaded', Sarkar, op. cit., p. 438.
98. *Harijan*, 1 June 1947
99. Louis Fischer, *The Life of Mahatma Gandhi* (New York, 1983), p. 435.
100. Bose, op.cit., p. 52. It is worth noting that the All India Forward Bloc faced the same constraint— 'a suggestion that a movement against the Government should be launched to remedy this was rejected, owing to the communal situation', see report of the Working Committee meeting, November 1946, I.B. note dated 20 February 1947, Indian Political Intelligence Records, IOR L/P&J/12/648, Oriental and India Office Collection, British Library, London.
101. N.K. Bose and Gandhi's biographer, B.R. Nanda, concur that despite Gandhi's staking all, his efforts in Noakhali and Calcutta (August-September 1947) had only a short-lived success. Calcutta witnessed the miracle of peace on Independence Day, but 31 August 1947 saw a Hindu mob attack Gandhi's house and bricks and lathi blows just missing him, Bose, op.cit., pp. 255 and 275 and Nanda, op.cit., p. 506.
102. To visitors from Punjab, 17 July 1947, *CWMG*, Vol. LXXXVIII, p. 356.
103. N.K. Bose, op.cit., p. 53.

104. *SWJN*, Vol. XIV, p. 46.
105. 6 August 1946, ibid., Vol. XV, p. 488.
106. *SPC*, Vol. VI, p. 78.
107. Nehru to Chief Ministers, 22 November 1947; *SWJN*, Second Series, Vol. IV, p. 453.
108. Ibid.
109. Nehru to Chief Ministers, 7 December 1947, ibid., p. 461.
110. Ibid.
111. Since mid-1945, the Congress leaders had realised the necessity of revitalizing the party but 'involvement in the negotiations took its toll of organisational work and in August 1946, Nehru reiterated that the Congress had lost its vitality. Nehru hoped that the Interim Government would open an opportunity to carry out Congress programmes, but this was not to be', Anita Inder Singh, op.cit., pp. 230-1.
112. Nehru's notes for AICC, 6 August 1946, AICC Papers, 69 (Part 2), 1946. Also see File Nos G-39 (KW-1) 1946 (Part 3), 1946-8, G-6 (KW-1) 1947, 27/1947 and 6/1947, AICC Papers, NMML.
113. D.G. Tendulkar, *The Mahatma*, Vols I to VIII (Delhi, 1960-3), Vol. VII, p. 186. If Prasad's correspondent from Calcutta is to be believed, what was worse was that some of the scramblers were bribable. He feared that Bengal MLAs could be bought over by the League to support independent Bengal, see R.P. Papers, 6-1/45-6-7.
114. Nehru's speech to AICC, 9 August 1947, *SWJN*, Second Series, Vol. III, p. 134.
115. Patel to Bozman, 11 July 1947, *SPC*, Vol. IV, p. 469.
116. Amrit Kaur to Sudhir Ghosh, 9 July 1947, Sudhir Ghosh Papers, p. 1.
117. Tendulkar, op.cit., Vol. VIII, p. 22.

The Last Straw that Broke the Nation's Back: The Formation of the Constituent Assembly of India

S.K. CHAUBE

CAUSALITY, CHANCE AND INEVITABILITY

E.H. Carr, in his seminal lecture on *What is History*, joined issue with Karl Popper, on historicism, and Sir Isaiah Berlin, on his postulate that 'failure comes from resisting that which works best . . . in favour of some systematic method or principle claiming universal validity'.[1] The statement had been made by the latter in course of a BBC lecture on 'Political Judgements' in which he had called Bismarck a genius as he had understood the material with which he was working when others were led away by abstract theories. Beyond finding Berlin's admiration for Bismarck 'odd',[2] Carr raised the questions:

> Did the eventual disaster occur because of some hidden flaws in the structure of the Reich? Or because something in the internal conditions which brought it to birth destined it to become self-assertive and aggressive? Or because, when the Reich was created, the European and the world scene was already so crowded, and expansive tendencies among the existing Great Powers already so strong, that the emergence of another expansive Great Power was sufficient to cause a major collision and bring down the whole system in ruins? On the last hypothesis, it may be wrong to hold Bismarck or the German people responsible, or solely responsible, for the disaster. You cannot really blame the last straw. But an objective judgement on Bismarck's achievement and how it worked awaits an answer from the historians to these questions.[3]

While replying to Popper, Carr comments that historians admit of chance and accident but do not think that accidents cannot be causally explained. Carr's citation of Montesquieu's comment—'If a particular cause, like the accidental result of a battle, has ruined a state, there was a general cause which made the downfall of this state ensue from a single battle'[4]—however, gives the impression that, like Montesquieu, Carr did not adequately distinguish between a particular cause and an accidental cause or, by stretching this argument, between a particular event and an accidental event.

The central thesis of Carr is, however, that no history is value free. A historian chooses his facts according to his own view of the present and the future and orders them accordingly. Value-wise, the historically significant point about Partition is that no one owns it, at least publicly. All the three major actors, the Congress, the Muslim League and, even the British government, argue that there was no alternative—due to the arrogance of the two other parties. That is because, like a war, Partition was an unmitigated disaster for an overwhelming majority of the concerned people. Yet, like a war, Partition did benefit a section of the people. It is possible to argue that a section of the beneficiaries had actually anticipated the benefits and worked towards their attainment or, at least, did not try to resist such efforts. The exercise of identifying such guilty men may, however, become difficult if the alternatives available are found to be both unsatisfactory as, for instance, in the case of Chamberlain's dilemma over the Munich Pact. In the case of the Partition there was in fact such an alternative—the grouping plan—which might have saved the territorial unity of India but would have sacrificed a strong central government. Let it be admitted at this stage that there was, and is, a view across the communities that the Partition of India was necessary, if not good.

Notwithstanding the imaginary fight between Karl Popper and his 'historicists', no historian can accept the thesis of inevitability that denies the role of purposive human intervention into the course of events. But once the inevitability thesis is rejected the 'ordering of facts' becomes important and every particular event becomes significant in the chain of causation. Such a particular event may or may not be *causally* connected with the subsequent occurrence. If they are not *causally* connected with an occurrence we can call the antecedent facts external and subsequent occurrence accidental. But even if they are causally connected with the subsequent occurrence the causality need not be inevitable.

THE DECISIVE CAUSE

Within this theoretical framework, in a chain of antecedent facts (causes) there can be something like a decisive cause in the sense that, had it not been there, the incident might not have taken place at all or, at least, at the moment that it took place. Thus the Russo-German non-aggression pact of 7 August 1939 might not be the cause of World War II but it was the decisive cause of the war in the sense that it prompted Hitler to attack Poland on 1 September. Had Hitler not attacked Poland on that day there was a sporting chance that Britain and France might not have swung into action against Germany. There was also a remote chance of the Second World War not happening at all.

Chronologically, a decisive cause is also the ultimate cause—the proverbial 'last straw'. It will be argued that, had the Constituent Assembly of India not been summoned and allowed to work in the way it did, Partition might not have happened in August 1947 and, even, not at all.

When, however, one speaks of a 'chain of causes', one assumes a relative independence of each cause. On the other hand, an antecedent event may not necessarily be a cause. By the same logic a decisive event may not be a decisive cause. The former is usually a part of the latter. I am not considering the concepts of 'decisive factor' and 'decisive circumstance' because they do not lay sufficient stress on human action and are partly fatalistic or deterministic. Politics is the art of human intervention, organized and purposive. Its focus is on parties, groups and leaders.

THE BACKGROUND

It will be useful to organize our 'facts' in the following order:

1. The British occupied India—two-thirds of it directly and one-third indirectly—and told the Indians that they were not a nation. Therefore, they were unfit to rule themselves.
2. The metropolitan leaders of India found out the means by which the British were draining India and founded the Indian National Congress (hereafter INC).
3. The Indian 'nation', to them was not a cultural/religious/sectarian nation but an assemblage of the entire population in the sense that the French saw themselves as a nation in 1789. Like the Continental Congress of the 13 north American colonies of Britain, the INC saw itself as the platform of the people of India.
4. For several years the INC declined to consider any 'local issue'. It never passed any resolution on a religious issue. Even its Khilafat programme related to the sultanate of Turkey and not to its religious implications.
5. Sir Syed Ahmad advised the Muslims to collaborate with the British Raj but stressed the need for unity of the two communities (Hindu and Muslim) on the social plane.

6. The first time the British introduced elections in India—at the local government level—in 1883, they created a separate electorate for the Muslims. Elections were introduced in the provincial and the central councils in 1909 along with separate electorate for the Muslims. Subsequently separate electorates were introduced for other interests and communities.
7. The INC and the Muslim League collaborated at Lucknow in 1916 but fell out at the All-Parties Conference in 1929—over the question of separate electorates. It was there, however, that the idea of a federation was floated.
8. The INC and the Muslim League collaborated even in the 1937 Provincial Assembly elections but later fell out over power-sharing. The result was the Pakistan resolution of 1940.
9. During the Second World War the INC-Muslim League split was complete. The Cripps Mission and the Cabinet Mission both worked with reference to the Pakistan plan, though in different ways. The Constituent Assembly was sanctioned under the Cabinet Mission Plan.

THE CONSTITUENT ASSEMBLY OF INDIA

The Constituent Assembly of India was indirectly elected on the basis of three separate electorates—General, Muslim and Sikh. Though separate electorates were a major plank of the Muslim League from 1906 and were strongly disliked by the INC, the latter had acquiesced in them in 1916 (the Lucknow Pact). In 1927 'Jinnah persuaded a number of Muslim leaders' on a joint electorate with reservation of seats for minorities, one-third reservation for Muslims in the Central Legislative Assembly, representation in proportion to population in Punjab, Bengal and the proposed provinces of Sind, Baluchistan and the North West Frontier Province. In May 1927 the AICC accepted the Jinnah offer but, in February 1928, retracted under the pressure of the Hindu Mahasabha. In 1928 Jinnah gave a fresh proposal: immediate separation of Sind, a federation with residual powers to the provinces, one-third of the Central Legislative Assembly seats for Muslims and reservation of seats for the minorities in Punjab and Bengal 'till adult franchise was established', franchise for the time being was based on property and was iniquitous for the Muslims.[5]

As the INC was committed to the principle of universal adult franchise it was not difficult for it to see the strength of Jinnah's argument. But M.R. Jayakar, the Hindu Mahasabha leader, brushed aside the proposal as well as other such compromise formulae. The Nehru Committee conceded only reservation at the central legislature and the Muslim-minority provinces.[6] The result was Jinnah's opposition to the Nehru Committee Report. Yet the INC neither accepted nor rejected the Communal Award of Ramsay MacDonald. Separate electorate, therefore, was not a point of irreconcilable difference between the Congress and the League. In the Central Legislative Assembly the Congress accepted an amendment of Jinnah, to its resolution on the 1934 White Paper, accepting the Communal Award 'as far as it goes' until a solution was arrived at by the concerned communities.[7]

It is a different matter that after the Partition decision, the Congress leadership decided to do away with the separate electorate altogether and provided for reservation for Scheduled Castes and the Scheduled Tribes in the legislature, as a temporary measure. The Nehru Report would concede the creation of Sind as a separate province, only after the grant of Dominion Status, with weightage for the Hindu minority there. Sind was separated from Bombay as a province along with the introduction of the 1935 reforms and the Congress party took part in the election in Sind.

It was on the nature of the federation that the ultimate difference between the Congress and the League boiled down to. The INC refused to co-operate with the federal part of the Government of India Act 1935, because of excessive control of the Governor-General and the virtual freedom of the princely states to flout the federal norm. The Muslim League did the same for the federation envisaged by the Act which was not loose enough. The League wanted the residual powers with the provinces—in the spirit of a loose federation—while the Nehru Committee had envisaged a tighter union with residual powers to be with the centre. The 1935 Act was quite unitary in spirit but the Governor-General's overwhelming authority was unacceptable to the Congress.

However, the Muslim League's Lahore resolution (1940) went beyond the concept of a loose federation with autonomous provinces when it demanded the creation of 'independent states of Pakistan'. Several historians have attributed this hardening of the League's attitude to the Congress refusal to admit the League into its coalitions, particularly in UP, after the elections of 1936-7.

The demand for 'independent states' was not spelt out in detail and could fall short of the demand for secession as the resolution did not speak of 'soverignty' or of one state of Pakistan. There is reason to believe that the Muslim League was thinking in terms of Dominion Status within the framework of the British Commonwealth of Nations—probably of the Canadian variety. In fact, Pakistan remained an independent dominion long after India became a sovereign republic. The political vocabulary of the subcontinent did not include the term 'sovereign' until India framed its new constitution.

THE IDEA OF A CONSTITUENT ASSEMBLY

In the history of the world the birth of a constituent assembly is associated with a bourgeois democratic revolution such as the Philadelphia Constitutional Convention of 1787 and the French National Assembly of 1789. In the first case it was the end of the British imperial rule, in the second the end of the monarchical *ancien regime*. The second condition of a constituent assembly is a democratic assertion of the people's rights behind it. In Britain such a constituent assembly was never brought into being because the two conditions were never jointly met. The Instrument of Government issued by the Lord Protector, Oliver Cromwell, in 1649 was not produced by a democratic assembly. Cromwell established a dictatorship. In 1689 Britain got the Declaration of Rights without ending monarchy. Lenin saw a constituent assembly as the product of a bourgeois democratic revolution. Instead, he established a dictatorship of the working class, in the process disbanding the constituent assembly created after the February Revolution.

In the British imperial system a constituent assembly was unknown. The Charlottetown Conference (Canada) of 1 September 1864 was a consultative body summoned by the Governor-General as were the Adelaide Convention (Australia) in March 1897 and the Durban Conference (South Africa) of 1908. On the other hand, when the Sinn Fein members of the British Parliament met at Dublin on 21 February 1919 as the Dail Eireann in order to establish a republican Ireland, there started a civil war that led to the partition of Ireland and that is not completely over yet. Ireland was partitioned in 1920 and an election was ordered in the southern part in 1921. The Irish National Parliament began to work independently but decided to participate in the election. Lloyd George worked out a treaty between the representatives of Great Britain and Ireland and got the Irish Free State Act amended separating the southern Irish Dail from the British Parliament. Eamon de Valera's Republican Party opposed the treaty but was defeated by Michael Collins's pro-treaty party at the election of 1922. 'The Constitution of the Irish Free State Act' that the Dail passed on 22 October 1932 reflected a compromise with the British Parliament and led to a second civil war. Southern Ireland became independent in 1932 but a sovereign republic in 1948. The experience of the Indian Constituent Assembly was somewhat similar to that of Ireland.

THE DEMAND FOR A CONSTITUENT ASSEMBLY FOR INDIA

Although the demand for a constituent assembly was first raised by the Swarajist Congressmen, who did not see eye to eye with either Gandhi or the Left, the Congress Left came out with full-throated support to the idea at Lucknow (1936). Stressing that the Government of India Act, 1935 was thoroughly unsatisfactory the INC demanded a constituent assembly elected on the basis of a universal adult franchise or as near to it as could be. While it stressed that any constitutional scheme for the future of India must take into account the vital interests of the Muslims, on the other hand, the League called for talks with the Congress. Soon this initial hesitation of the League turned into open hostility. In October 1937 it strongly attacked the idea.[8]

The League's preference for direct Congress-League talks was undoubtedly élitist while the Congress demand was democratic. But the League thought that the constituent assembly idea was an instrument for circumventing the issue of minority safeguard. In essence, the rival positions reflected the contradiction between individual rights and group rights. The League claimed itself to be the sole representative of Muslim interests—a claim which had not been substantiated by the elections of 1937. But the developments between the Lahore session of the League (1940), where it rallied several non-League parties, and the elections of winter 1945-6 when it made an impressive showing changed the Congress-League balance with regard to minority support.

The Congress made two mistakes in this flux. It counted chickens before they were hatched: it wanted the British to summon a constituent assembly over the League's objection. Why the British would oblige the Congress was never explained. The second mistake lay in the Congress approach to the non-League Muslim parties. It not only rejected the idea of a coalition with the Muslim League in UP, it rejected all possibilities of collaboration with the non-League parties in other provinces. Although it was the largest party in the Bengal Assembly, without an absolute majority, it chose not to join a coalition with the Krishak Praja Party of A.K. Fazlul Haq. If the Congress wanted to crush the Muslim League, its strategy of alienating all the other Muslim parties was grievously wrong.

The August 1940 offer of Linlithgow was the first British acknowledgement of the claim that constitution-making for India was an Indian responsibility. But by no means could it be interpreted as an agreement to convene a constituent assembly. Linlithgow actually suggested talks among all the major Indian parties for arriving at a consensus on the constitution on the familiar dominion model which fitted in with Jinnah's formula. Jinnah's support to British war efforts in India, contrasted with the Congress attitude, endeared him further with the British government. The British may legitimately be seen, after the war, to be paying him back, for his valuable services, through the grouping plan.

THE CABINET MISSION PLAN

A constituent assembly was formally suggested by the British first through the Cripps Mission, which also recognized the possibility of non-accession of provinces to it—after the war was over. After the war the Cabinet Mission Plan, slightly varying from the Cripps Mission Plan, was handed out to the Indians. Briefly, the Cabinet Mission acknowledged the Indians' right to frame their constitution. But the constitution that the Indians would frame would actually be a draft constitution—in the form of a bill—which HMG would recommend to the British Parliament for passing. The constituent assembly, to be summoned by the Governor-General, would be elected by the existing provincial legislatures, with the addition of a few members from the Chief Commissioners' provinces. The constituent assembly would negotiate with the rulers of the princely states on the terms of their participation in it with a view to setting up an all-India federation with maximum autonomy for its units.

Then came the twist: first, by overstretching the principle of autonomy and then by making a mockery of it. The Cabinet Mission felt that if a group of provinces desired to have an intermediate layer of government—between themselves and the federal union—they should be allowed to do so. Therefore, the Cabinet Mission laid down three sections: Section A comprising the representatives of Madras, Bombay, UP, Bihar, CP and Orissa; Section B comprising the representatives of Punjab, Sind and the North West Frontier Province; and Section C comprising the representatives of Bengal and Assam.

Sections B and C would be, as a whole, Muslim-majority though Assam was not a Muslim-majority province. Section A would be Hindu-majority. Thus the Cabinet Mission proposed three communal zones but refused to concede Assam the freedom to stay out of Section C. Joining the sections was compulsory. After the Constituent Assembly formally met, it would split into sections, which would first decide if they would constitute groups and draw their constitutions. After the groups had done substantive work they would reassemble as the Constituent Assembly to draw the provincial and the union constitutions. The group constitutions could be reviewed after 10 years and a province would be free to walk out of a group only after a general election was held under the new constitution.

Political observers were puzzled at the ingenuity of the grouping scheme. On 6 May 1946 Azad, as Congress president, wrote to Pethick Lawrence complaining that the grouping scheme had not been discussed in the meetings of the Congress with the Cabinet Mission and that the Congress delegates to the talks 'were feeling mystified and disturbed at the vagueness of the talks and some of the assumptions underlying them'. On 24 May the Congress Working Committee, in a resolution, demanded that the provinces should in the first instance have the right to make their own choice 'whether or not to belong to the section in which they are placed. On 25 May the cat was out of the bag. The Cabinet Mission said that the Congress interpretation did not accord with the Cabinet Mission's intentions: 'The reasons for the grouping of the provinces are well known, and this is an essential feature of the scheme and can only be modified by agreement between the parties.'[9] The only other party, in this case, was the Muslim League. Thus the grouping scheme, in the Congress party's view, and rightly so, encapsulated the substance of Pakistan.

The only explanation to this puzzle is that the Cabinet Mission Plan was an Award, a condition attached to the transfer of power. The Constituent Assembly of India was to be summoned by the Governor-General and would have to function within the perimeter of the Cabinet Mission Plan. Provincial autonomy, if not a ruse, was merely a formula for solving the communal problem.

On 15 June, Wavell sought to assuage the Congress apprehensions through a letter to Azad. Sitting in the sections did not automatically mean being a part of a group for, after all, a section would have to first decide on setting it up. The central question was, however, whether or not the provinces in a section would severally or jointly decide the issue. The Cabinet Mission ordained it to be a joint decision. Given the political scenario in 1946 the result of such joint decisions was a foregone conclusion. Groups B and C would vote for some version of Pakistan and Assam, if not the NWFP, would be trapped into it. The Congress further suspected that these groups would frame electoral rules in such a way as to make the withdrawal of any province from a group after the election impossible. The Congress did not want the provinces to sit in groups against their wishes.

INCONSISTENCIES IN THE CABINET MISSION PLAN

The greatest inconsistency in the Cabinet Mission Plan was that, though it swore by provincial autonomy, it granted the provinces nothing of it. The provinces had no right to frame their constitution; they would be framed by the sections. They had no choice in joining or leaving a section. They had no veto, as provinces, on a decision of a section. In the central Constituent Assembly, too, they had no voice as provinces. The other inconsistency was that, while decisions in the central Constituent Assembly were subject to communal veto, decisions in the sections were to be made by a simple majority of the entire membership, that is, without a communal veto.[10] It may be noted that the Cripps Mission had said that it was inconceivable that the British government would impose a constitution on any unwilling province. But this was precisely what the British did in 1946.

Between the Cripps Mission and the Cabinet Mission the political configuration of India had changed. In 1937 the Muslim League hegemony in the Muslim-majority provinces had not been established. In 1946 the League became dominant in Bengal and Punjab to the extent that it could secure absolute majority in both Section B and Section C (19 out of 35 and 35 out of 70, respectively). A.K. Fazlul Haq's association with the Lahore Resolution of the Muslim League would naturally place him in the League camp, in Section C, raising the League's strength to 36.

The Congress, therefore, had strong reason to object to the idea of sections. On 26 June 1946 the Congress Working Committee declared it unjust to the (Congress-following) provinces of Assam and the North-West Frontier and to the Sikh minority in Punjab.[11] The second part of this objection, however, showed the Congress in poor light and went against the logic of provincial autonomy. This was the first instance of the Congress putting forward a communal cause.

But the really objectionable part in the whole episode was the Congress decision to join the Constituent Assembly before sorting out the question of the sections. On the other hand, between 27 and 30 July 1946 the Muslim League Council meeting refused to participate in the Constituent Assembly until the Congress had accepted the Cabinet Mission Plan in its entirety.[12] This is not to suggest that the Muslim League was a paragon of virtue for the League Council called for Direct Action on 16 August 1946 that led to a blood bath in Calcutta and other parts of the country. The League was merely more consistent.

When the Muslim League joined the Interim Government of the Governor-General, on 13 October 1946, without joining the Constituent

Assembly, the Congress raised objection as the Muslim League had not accepted the Cabinet Mission Plan *in toto*. The League retorted that the Congress had not accepted the Cabinet Mission Plan *in toto* either. Interestingly the Governor-General glossed over the inconsistencies. He had convened the Constituent Assembly and constituted the Interim Government and left it to the concerned members to join them at their pleasure. There are indications that he took enough initiative to persuade the League to join the government but chose to be passive in respect of its joining the Constituent Assembly. Though the Cabinet Mission Plan had laid down the schemes for both the Constituent Assembly and the Interim Government, there was no logical connection between the two. The Interim Government was envisaged, according to the Cabinet Mission, so that 'while constitution-making was in progress', the administration of the country could go on.

The Congress and the League did not meet in the Constituent Assembly before the decision on Partition was taken. They met daily in the Interim Government where the *decisive event* occurred in the form of the Liaquat Ali budget in February 1947, which the Congress thought was meant for creating a rift between it and its capitalist patrons.[13] Meanwhile, on 20 February, Attlee had explicitly announced the possibility of Partition if an agreement on the Constituent Assembly was not reached soon. The Congress did not make an attempt to salvage the Constituent Assembly.

THE DECISIVE CAUSE

We have called the February 1947 budget of Liaquat Ali the decisive event for it demonstrated the irreconcilability between the postures of the Congress and the League that could not be overcome subsequently. At least Mountbatten, after his arrival in March 1947, did not have the patience to attempt it. The modalities of Partition and transfer of power were decided by the middle of May turning down Nehru's plea for the Partition following, instead of preceding, the transfer of power.[14] Until that time Partition was not a settled fact. The announcement was made on 3 June 1947.

Yet neither the 16 August 1946 Direct Action of the Muslim League, nor the Liaquat Ali budget of February 1947, could be called the decisive cause of Partition. Direct Action was the result of the Muslim League's frustration at not being included in the Interim Government initially and the Liaquat Ali budget was a game of one-upmanship in the context of the rivalry generated over the Constituent Assembly's work. Politically, it was rather insignificant because the League refused to work as a part of a cabinet with collective responsibility. In fact there was no responsibility at all of the Interim Government, which legally was a version of the Governor-General's Executive Council and the League was absent in the Constituent Assembly.

It was the League's refusal to join the Constituent Assembly which proved to be the decisive cause of Partition. The Congress response to this intransigence was somewhat confusing or deliberately misleading. While the Muslim League joined the Interim Government after the Congress had done so, the Congress insisted that the League could not do so without joining the Constituent Assembly. The Congress, on its part, had accepted the Constituent Assembly with a qualification, namely, without compulsory grouping. The 'controversial' press conference of Nehru, on 10 July 1946,[15] stating that the Congress had no intention to abide by grouping and would be free to change the Cabinet Mission Plan after joining the Constituent Assembly, was perfectly in accord with the Congress Working Committee position but not within the ambit of the Cabinet Mission Plan. Both the Cabinet Mission and the Governor-General had made it clear that the Constituent Assembly was not a sovereign body. On 7 September 1946 Nehru, in a broadcast, said that the Congress was perfectly prepared to sit in sections, which would consider the formation of the groups and that 'we do not look upon the Constituent Assembly as an arena for conflict or for forcible imposition of one viewpoint over another'.[16] This did not change the position a bit as the Congress would not concede the right of the provinces to veto a group constitution and/or walk away from it at any moment.

The nuances of the second part of Nehru's statement became salient when, on the second day of the Constituent Assembly's work (10 December), J.B. Kripalani moved for the constitution of a Committee on Rules of Procedure of the Constituent Assembly. Kripalani said that the original draft of the resolution had provided for the Committee's power to frame rules for sections and committees of the Assembly but he dropped the words 'sections and committees' as they were superfluous. The Assembly rules *included* the rules for sections and committees thereof. The delightful vagueness of the statement was at once challenged by two members from Bengal, Suresh Chandra Banerjee of the Congress and Syama Prasad Mookerjee of the Hindu Mahasabha who had come on a Congress ticket. Mookerjee demanded the restoration of the words and argued:

When the sectional assemblies will meet each may frame its own rules of procedure. The question may then arise whether the Constituent Assembly as such had the authority to frame rules of procedure for the sections at all. Reference will then have been made to the resolution which gave the authority to the Rules Committee to frame rules and then the only mention that will be found will be that this committee was appointed to frame the Rules of Procedure of the Assembly. . . . If your intention is that the Rules Committee will also frame rules for the sections, why not say specifically 'including sections and committees', so that there may not be any ambiguity or doubt whatsoever when sections start doing their work?[17]

Interestingly, when, in view of the general support of the House to the amendment, Nehru advised Kripalani to accept it, M.R. Jayakar, another leader of the Hindu Mahasabha from Maharashtra who had come on a Congress ticket, opposed the amendment. 'Remember the word "sections",' he said and added:

You are asked by express terms to legislate for them in advance of their future formation. Remember 'sections' include 'B' and 'C' sections. Remember further that in 'B' and 'C' sections there is likely to be—almost certainly to be—a preponderance of a certain group of men who are not present here today and who may be present at the date when these sections begin to function. That group of men are not present here today under a feeling of suspicion, if not hostility. . . . Remember that this group of men is not present here today and is, besides, watching these proceedings with jealousy and suspicion to discover whether you are taking anything out of their hands and deciding it finally in advance of their future arrival. If you do so may it not interfere with their future arrival here in a friendly and trustful atmosphere?[18]

Jayakar's sympathy with the Muslim League at this stage may appear odd and definitely at variance with Mookerjee's attitude if we remember his role at the All Parties Conference in opposing the Muslim League demand for a limited period of separate electorate. The explanation may be found in Mookerjee's direct involvement with the Group C and his past connection with the Bengal Provincial Congress Committee as against Jayakar's past connection with Liberal politics. Jayakar, in fact, opposed the adoption of the Objectives Resolution during the first session of the Constituent Assembly, on 19 December, through an amendment seeking an adjournment of the consideration of that resolution. His argument was similar:

Within the limits of the power which the Cabinet Mission's statement of 16 May accords to this preliminary meeting, it cannot validly lay down any fundamentals, however sketchy they may be, of the Constitution. That must wait until we meet in the sections and the provincial constitutions have been prepared. At this stage, the two other parties, the Muslim League and the Indian states, are expected to be present. . . . We are no doubt a sovereign body as you, sir, very rightly remarked but we are sovereign within the limitations of the Paper by which we have been created. We cannot go outside those limitations except by agreement and the two other parties being absent no agreement can be thought of.[19]

Jayakar had failed to get the formation of the Rules Committee postponed but succeeded in getting the passage of the Objectives Resolution deferred. At the beginning of the second session, on 21 January 1947, Jayakar withdrew his objection to the passage of the Objectives Resolution as the Muslim League had shown no intention to join the Assembly. He regretted the delay but thought that it was justified. Earlier he had got a rebuff from Patel on this issue.[20] Jayakar resigned, one suspects, as a reaction. (His place was later taken by B.R. Ambedkar, who lost his seat from Bengal after the Partition.)

Immediately thereafter, on 31 January/1 February 1947, the League Working Committee objected to the passing of the Objectives Resolution in its absence as it had laid down several fundamental principles including a republican structure and the appointment of the various committees, particularly the Advisory Committee on the Minorities, etc., referred to in paragraph 20 of the Cabinet Mission's statement, and the passing of the Rules of Procedure of the Constituent Assembly, particularly Rule 63, through which the work of the Sections were sought to be controlled. It was clear to the Muslim League that 'By taking these decisions in the Constituent Assembly and by appointing a packed committee consisting of individuals chosen by the Congress, the Congress has already converted that truncated Assembly into a rump and something totally different from what the Cabinet Mission's statement has provided for.'[21] Nehru's speech at the States Peoples' Conferençe on 18-20 April 1947 was the last official invitation to the Muslim League, from the Congress, to join the Constituent Assembly. While submitting the first report of the Committee on Union Powers, on 25 April, N.G. Ayyangar said:

The coming of the Muslim League is not yet officially ruled out. There is still a possibility of their coming in though the probability is perhaps very small. . . . Whether they will come in or not will be definitely known before the June-July session of this Assembly.[22]

ARROGANCE OF THE PARTIES CONCERNED

If the Muslim League was arrogantly opposed to proceedings of the Constituent Assembly outside the framework of the Cabinet Mission Plan, except for the singular instance of postponement of the passage of the

Objectives Resolution by about a month, the Congress showed no inclination to accommodate the League demand. Even in his address to the States Peoples' Conference in April 1947 Nehru said that the work of the Constituent Assembly would go on notwithstanding the League's absence. In April itself demands were raised by the Hindu Mahasabha and the Congress for the partition of Bengal and Punjab driving the nail into the coffin of provincial autonomy.

But the height of this arrogance, on the part of the Congress, was reached on 14 July when K.M. Munshi, while presenting the report of the Order of Business Committee in the Constituent Assembly, called the 16 May Plan 'the parricides's bag which was invented by the Roman law'. He said:

> We have no sections and groups to go into, no elaborate procedure as was envisaged by it, no double majority clause, no more provinces with residuary powers, no opting out, no revision after ten years and no longer only four categories of power for the centre. We, therefore, feel free to form a federation of our choice, a federation with a centre as strong as we can make it subject of course to this that the Indian states have to be associated in this great task on a footing of the four categories of power and such further powers as they choose by agreement to cede to the centre. Therefore, Sir, I personally am not at all sorry that this change has taken place.[23]

Munshi's high ranking in the Congress leadership in the Constituent Assembly, his association with numerous vital committees of the Constituent Assembly, his political roots in Bombay and his proximity to the Indian big business are too well known to need documentation. Yet the speech reflected more than arrogance on the part of Munshi. It suggests that the Congress (and the Indian big business) never liked the idea of provincial autonomy except as a means of devolution of power from the British to Indian hands mixed with the need for communal adjustment. For a strong centralized government—which is the need of a national big bourgeois—the Congress could, and did, sacrifice the territorial unity of the country.

CONCLUDING OBSERVATIONS

It was a perfectly legitimate aspiration on the part of the Congress to get a sovereign constituent assembly. The pitiable part of it was that it believed that the Constituent Assembly which the Governor-General had convened was actually a sovereign body or at least could be turned into one. It fell to Jinnah to point out the fallacy. He said 'It is no use imagining things', and further added:

The Constituent Assembly is not a sovereign body. Either we accept the view or not. If we accept that it is not a sovereign body, the only honourable course open to us is to treat it for what it is. It is an assembly summoned by the Viceroy, who has been appointed by the British government. It is not going to be sovereign by a statement or show of bravado.[24]

Jinnah was in very good company. Gandhi, who had welcomed the idea of a constituent assembly, on 19 November 1939, as providing 'the easiest method of arriving at a just solution to the communal problem',[25] wrote to Sardar Patel on 4 December 1946:

1. I am quite clear that if there is a boycott by the Muslim League of the Constituent Assembly, it should not meet under the Cabinet Mission's statement of 16th May. It clearly contemplates the cooperation of the major parties, viz., the Congress and the League.... If the government convenes the Constituent Assembly inspite of the boycott, they can legitimately do so only under some other statement which they can draw up in consultation with the Congress. It should not be forgotten that, however powerful the Congress has become, a constituent assembly, as contemplated today can only meet by action of the British government.

2. Even if the Constituent Assembly meets inspite of the boycott but with the willing cooperation of the British government, it will be under the visible or invisible protection of the British forces, whether Indian or European. In my opinion we shall never reach a satisfactory constitution under these circumstances.[26]

Herein lies the objectionable part of the whole episode. There is no reason to think that the Congress leaders did not understand what Gandhi understood. It is, therefore, reasonable to assume that they were hoping for 'willing cooperation of the British government' in the undertaking of bulldozing the Muslim League's opposition. At the end of the Second World War the Congress was correctly convinced that the days of British rule in India were numbered. In such a situation an honest and bold policy would have been to directly challenge the Raj with an agitational programme after rejecting the Cabinet Mission scheme. A shrewd policy of bargain, on the other hand, would dictate the prolongation of the talks perhaps backed by an agitational programme. In the middle of 1946, however, the Congress was ready neither for an agitation nor for a delay. Instead, it chose to shift the focus of its attention from the British to the Muslim League, ignoring the potential for harm that the departing British could cause to India.

NOTES

1. E.H. Carr, *What is History* (Harmondsworth, 1964), pp. 91-2 and 127.
2. Ibid., p. 127.
3. Ibid., pp. 129-30.
4. Ibid., p. 101.
5. Sumit Sarkar, *Modern India 1885-1947* (Delhi, 1983), pp. 262-3.
6. Ibid., p. 263.
7. N.N. Mitra, *The Indian Annual Register* (hereafter *IAR*), *1935*, Vol. I (repr., Delhi, 1990), p. 287.
8. See Shibanikinkar Chaube, *Constituent Assembly of India: Springboard of Revolution* (New Delhi, 1973), pp. 19-23.
9. Ibid., p. 263.
10. Ibid., pp. 54-5.
11. *IAR*, *1946*, Vol. I, op.cit., pp. 175-6.
12. Anil Chandra Banerjee, *Indian Constitutional Documents* Vol. IV (Calcutta, 1961, 3rd rev. edn), pp. 241-4.
13. See V.P. Menon, *The Transfer of Power* (Calcutta, 1957), p. 348; and C.D. Deshmukh, *Economic Developments in India* (Bombay, 1957), p. 46.
14. Nicholas Mansergh, editor-in-chief, *Transfer of Power 1942-7*, Vol. X (London, 1981).
15. See Abul Kalam Azad, *India Wins Freedom* (Calcutta, 1957), p. 155.
16. See P. Sitaramayya, *History of the Indian National Congress*, Vol. II (Bombay, 1947), p. ccliv.
17. *Constituent Assembly Debates* (hereafter *CAD*), Vol. I, pp. 22-3.
18. Ibid., p. 27.
19. Ibid., p.57.
20. See Chaube, op.cit., pp. 67-8.
21. *CAD*, Vol. III, p. 381.
22. *CAD*, Vol. IV, pp. 544-5.
23. *IAR*, *1946*, Vol. II, op.cit., p. 167.
24. *Harijan*, 19 November 1939.
25. Banerjee, op.cit., p. 118.
26. M.K. Gandhi, *Letters to Sardar Vallabhbhai Patel* (Ahmedabad, 1957), pp. 197-8.

Genesis of Partition

KHWAJA A. KHALIQUE

The demand for the creation of independent states for Muslims, concentrated in the north-western and north-eastern parts of the country, made in March 1940, was the logical culmination of a long standing communal divide. It is, therefore, essential to get at the root of this communal divide and find out what made the Muslims demand a separate state for themselves. To get an answer, we have to dissect the social milieu, the cultural orientation, the mindset, the thought process and the formulation of attitudes of the two communities. This requires tracing the interaction of various forces at work since the advent of Islam in India, particularly after the Muslims lost political power.

Religion, which has an overwhelming influence on peoples' lives in this country, played a major part in shaping the attitudes of the two communities towards each other. Hinduism's great quality of absorbing new groups and peoples within its fold filled Muslims with apprehension, particularly after they had lost political power as they wanted to maintain their identity. Another characteristic of Hinduism was its exclusiveness in daily life, which forbade interdining and intermarriage with the people of other castes and religions. So it was not surprising that Hindus and Muslims, having lived as neighbours for centuries, remained distinct and separate.

Though racially, it had a substantial percentage of Hindu converts to Islam, the Muslim population of the subcontinent had absorbed layer upon layer of Arabs, Turks, Afghans, Iranians, and others. The admixture of so many racial stocks, in course of time, resulted in the emergence of a new group that transcended racial barriers. This was made possible because Islam does not permit social barriers or restrictions on interracial marriages among Muslims. The same was true for Hindu converts to Islam, who were admitted not only to a new faith but to a new society. Thus there developed a community whose religion, dress, cuisine and many daily chores of life were distinct from the rest of the local population with whom it could not eat together or intermarry. This new community also developed a new language, Urdu, written in the Persian script, which though it had a common Prakritic syntax with Hindustani has a large percentage of Arabic, Persian and Turkish words. Also its poetry borrowed its form and imagery from Iran and Central Asia. Most of the literature produced by Muslims since the later Mughal period is in Urdu and is considered by the community as its precious heritage.

Another important characteristic of the Muslim community, which was a source of friction with Hindus, was its trans-Indian world perspective, as against nationalism. Islam, which makes a distinction only between believers and non-believers, does not permit any differentiation between human beings on the basis of race, colour or nationality. Muslims were, therefore, always inclined to look beyond national boundaries. This was also the *raison d'être* of the institution of the Caliphate from the early days of Islam and of the pan-Islamic movement later.

This background, mindset and perspective of the Muslims of the subcontinent explains their attitudes and responses, policies and reactions to all socio-political developments in the country from the time of the break-up of the Mughal Empire up to the Partition of the country in 1947. These may be briefly recounted here. Muslim sufis, saints, scholars, thinkers, poets, artists, artisans and traders, who came to India, as well as those who were born in India, gave a new vigour and richness to Indian life in thought, culture and civilization. But after the fall of the Mughals, Muslims in India ceased to be a dynamic force, they became inactive and decadent. Nor did they have anything creative to offer except with regard to the development of the Urdu language. The whole community took a back seat with the decline of the Mughal Empire. This degeneration began during the second half of the eighteenth century, and continued for about a century.

During this period the vacuum in Muslim leadership was sought to be filled by religious leaders like Shah Waliullah. The ulama worked hard to halt the decay of Muslims in India and rejuvenate them. To achieve this end, Shah Waliullah translated the Koran to make it easily understandable, and gave a fresh interpretation of Islam, so as to reconcile the differences between its various sects and schools. He even tried to persuade the regional Muslim powers to wage a jihad (holy war) against the Marathas and Jats. His explanation for the decay of the empire and the degradation of Muslims was that the Indian Muslim, because of Hindu influences, had become indifferent to Islam and his remedy was that Indian Muslims should forsake Hindu practices and customs. Shah Waliullah was thus unconsciously instrumental in distancing Muslims from Hindus and harming the common culture, which had been evolving at the mass level.

The strong fight put up by the ulama against the British for the restoration of the Muslim power not only failed but, in the process, also worsened the fate of Muslims. After the capture of Delhi by the British in 1803, the ulama declared a holy war against them. Shah Abdul Aziz advised Muslims not to learn the English language and not to serve under the British. The unsuccessful fight of the ulama had earned for the Muslims the hatred and hostility of the British who now embarked on a policy of depriving Muslims of high positions in administration and also by striking them economically.

The first big changes in the administration were introduced in 1793 by Lord Cornwallis. He reserved most of the higher executive appointments exclusively for Europeans and transferred the control of the entire administration into British hands. Under the Permanent Settlement, which introduced a new revenue system, old Muslim revenue officers were replaced by European officers and the tax collectors, majority of whom were Hindus, were made hereditary zamindars. Further, in the days of Lord William Bentinck during 'resumption operations', a very large number of Muslim families, who failed to establish their full title to the grants from the Mughals lost their lands and property and became paupers. The abolition of Persian as the court language in 1837 and the replacement of the Muslim criminal law by the Indian Penal Code threw many Muslims out of employment.

The cumulative effect of all these steps was the replacement of Muslims from most government jobs by Hindus who had, in the matter of learn-ing English and acquiring modern education, stolen a march of more than 50 years over Muslims. This resulted not only in loss of power and prosperity among Muslims but a corresponding gain for the Hindus. The shift of administrative power and wealth from Muslims to Hindus naturally bred illwill and heart burning among Muslims against Hindus. This was further aggravated by the British government, which openly sided with the Hindus against the Muslims. An instance of this was provided in 1842, when the Governor-General, Lord Ellenborough, while restoring the gates of the Somnath temple said 'the insult of 800 years is at last avenged'.[1] He believed that the best way of restoring 'equilibrium between the two religions was to bring the Muhamaddans to their senses'.[2] Such an outburst by a Viceroy could only have been motivated by the British desire to create discord between Hindus and Muslims and to play one against the other.

The Muslims after 1857 could not organize themselves into any political agitation against the British. They had already paid a very heavy price for their participation in the revolt of 1857. Muslims were by then too poor and frightened to run any further risks. The loss of governmental power and the change in the court language, the failure of all their efforts to regain political power, the hostility of the new rulers, the lack of modern education and rampant poverty—all these had created for them a situation, which demanded a basic change in their political thinking as well as leadership. This change did come about. A few Muslims like Sir Syed Ahmad Khan, accepted the challenge of modernity and stood up against the ulama. The Muslims were goaded to take to English education and change their entire attitude towards the British. The lead in this direction came from members of the Muslim aristocracy called *ashraf*, who strengthened their position by taking to English education and by making loyal overtures to the British.

It is one of the many paradoxes of modern Indian history that, while almost during the entire rule of the Company the Muslims led in battles against the British, the new middle class élite, comprising mainly Hindu traders, stood solidly behind the Company. After the revolt of 1857, the roles of Muslims and Hindus *vis-à-vis* the British government were reversed: the Hindu élite started gradually turning away from the path of loyalty to the British and the Muslim leadership became the chief pillar of British rule. A parallel development was that the Muslim leadership got estranged from the new Hindu élite, which had, under the British dispensation, attained wealth as well as a position of authority that had been the earlier preserve of the Muslims.

While tracing the history of the communal divide that finally culminated in the Partition of the country, it is worth noting that the social and cultural organizations of the nineteenth century, starting from Raja Rammohun Roy's Brahmo Samaj in 1830, had a common feature. Though the aims and objects were catholic and broad-based, yet in practice they mostly tended to be either Hindu or Muslim, depending on the religious faith of their founders and organizers. For instance, the Landholders' Association and the British India Association had very little to do with Muslim landholders and Muslims. In the same way, Sir Syed's Translation Society catered mostly to Muslims.

The nineteenth century also witnessed the Hindu revivalist movements, the most notable of which was the Arya Samaj, founded by Swami Dayanand, who gave a call to the Hindus to go back to the Vedas, as the Wahabis had earlier given a call to the Muslims to go back to the Koran. There ensued a long exchange of polemics between the Arya Samaj leaders and the ulama. Cow protection societies appeared in the 1880s, which led to a number of Hindu-Muslim riots.

In 1885, the Indian National Congress was founded and the subsequent political history of India was shaped by the multilateral interaction between the forces of British imperialism, the Congress and Hindu and Muslim communalism. Henceforth, there was to be a continuous tug of war between the Congress, which had brought together people from the entire country on a common platform with common aims and grievances, on the one hand, and a Muslim leadership which wanted to chart a separate course, on the other. This was coupled with Hindu and Muslim communal forces playing their own role in driving Muslims towards separatism. The British government in this scenario played one community against the other.

The basic issue between the Congress and the Muslim leadership until Partition was that the latter considered the Congress to be a Hindu body and denied its claim to represent Muslims. The Congress, on the other hand, always tried to attract and enlist the support of Muslims. We shall examine how this struggle between the Congress and the Muslim leadership, first under Sir Syed Ahmad and then under the Muslim League (which shaped the political course of events from 1885 to 1947), was finally won by the Muslim League, resulting in the Partition.

The birth of the Congress was the culmination of the sustained work done for decades by public organizations like the Brahmo Samaj, the Prarthna Samaj and the British India Association.[3] But most of these organizations and their leaders were Hindu and their work was confined to Hindus. It was however, not deliberate but the result of circumstances that made the Hindus stand almost alone in the vanguard of education and progress at that time. From its inception, therefore, the Congress assumed a Hindu bearing, though fundamentally it was broad based. The Congress leaders, however, always denied the charge of any such communalism.[4]

Also the loyalist Hindu zamindar class in Bengal, represented by Nabgopal and Akchoy Chandra Sarkar, had advocated that Hinduism was the basis of unity in India and, therefore, the foundation of Indian nationalism. Sarkar further held that Islam was a stumbling block in national unity.[5] Nationalism as propounded by the Bengali Hindu zamindars was thus complementary to the two-nation theory, which the Muslim aristocracy under the leadership of Sir Syed had developed in the 1880s.

The charge that the Congress was a communal body, was levelled at its very first session.[6] It was, however, countered by the arguments that it had Muslims, Christians and Parsis among its delegates and that its demands were for the political advancement of all sections of Indians. It was also a fact that out of the 72 delegates at the first Congress session only two were Muslims, and the foremost Muslim leader of the time, Sir Syed, was not among them. The Muslim contention was that when Muslims were not present at the session, the Congress could not claim to speak on their behalf. Before its second session at Calcutta, the Congress invited the two premier Muslim organizations of the country—the Central National Mohammedan Association and the Mohammedan Literary Society—to send delegates but both refused to do so. The second session was attended by 27 Muslim delegates, out of a total of 413 delegates. In order to woo Muslims the Congress chose Badruddin Tyabji, who had not attended the first two Congress sessions, to preside over its third session at Madras.

TWO-NATION THEORY

The Congress efforts to attract Muslims made Sir Syed come out with his famous Lucknow outburst against it, before a representative gathering of Muslims, on 28 December 1887, when he declared that Hindus and Muslims were two separate nations. He said that representative institutions were unsuited to Indian conditions, as the number of Hindu voters being four times that of Muslim voters, Hindu candidates would always win and the system of representative government would thus only lead to the perpetual subjugation of the Muslims by the Hindus.[7] Sir Syed's speech was described by one British newspapers, as 'one of the most remarkable discourses ever delivered by a native of India'.[8]

After Sir Syed's Lucknow speech, Muslims hailed him as their political leader. Meetings were held at important centres where resolutions were passed, endorsing Sir Syed's views. Muslim associations in the country accorded their approval to his stand. The Muslim press, too, with some notable exceptions, supported Sir Syed. For instance, the *Muslim Herald* wrote:

> We proudly accept Sir Syed as our leader and exponent, the summit and crown of Islam, a faith that binds together . . . the five crore Indian Mussalmans. His speech sounds the keynote of our policy.[9]

On the other hand, the *Ahmadi* of Bengal wrote:

> They [Mussalman] never think for a moment whether there is an atom of reason in all that Sir Syed has said. And they never care to know what the Congress is and what grand objects it seeks to achieve.[10]

Sir Syed and his colleagues also maintained that a few Muslim delegates at the Congress were not the genuine representatives of the Muslims. The same insinuation was made later against Congress Muslims by the Muslim League, during its campaign for Pakistan in the 1940s when Maulana Abul Kalam Azad was called the 'Showboy' of the Congress and Jinnah refused to accept him as a representative of the Muslims.

To the charge that the Muslims were not with them, the Congress reply was that the comparative small number of Muslim delegates was the natural result of the lack of higher education among them. But not many were convinced by this explanation. The Congress, however, remained undaunted and continued with its wooing of Muslims.[11] Accordingly, at its fourth session in 1888, a resolution was passed that it would not take up any subject for discussion to which Hindu or Muslim delegates as a body objected, and thus conceded, the principle of 'communal veto' which was to become at a later date a strong demand of the Muslim League. The Muslims responded to this favourably and at the Bombay Congress session in 1889, of the nearly 2,000 delegates, 254 were Muslims, the largest Muslim attendance that any Congress session had had so far.

With the eruption of Hindu-Muslim riots and the Hindi-Urdu controversy, the tenth Congress at Madras in 1894 resulted in the Muslim representation falling to a barely 24 in a total of about 1,200 delegates. Of these delegates, 18 were from places near Madras. The position at the eleventh Congress at Poona in 1895, was even worse. There were only 19 Muslims out of 1,584 delegates, and of these, the residents of Poona or places nearby numbered 17. However, in yet another effort to attract Muslims, the Congress, chose a Muslim, Rahmatullah Sayani to preside over its twelfth session at Calcutta in 1896. Sayani's presidential address led to a debate among Muslims, mainly carried in the *Muslim Chronicle* and later covered by other Muslim press. However, a majority of the participants in the debate agreed with the Muslim policy of non-cooperation with the Congress.

To add to the Hindu-Muslim differences, which were getting more and more embittered by the 'cow killing' riots and quarrels over government jobs at the time, a section of the Hindu press—the *Advocate* of Lucknow and the *Indian Nation* of Patna—took a blatantly anti-Muslim stand, in the Graeco-Turkish War, which made the Muslims believe that the Hindus would always grudge the victory of Islam and rejoice at its defeat, irrespective of where it took place.

The death of Sir Syed made politically conscious Muslims feel orphaned, particularly because he had left behind no proper political organization which could carry on his work. The existing organizations, the Central National Mohammedan Association and the Mohammedan Literary Society were unable to cope with the new situation. Muslims were also disillusioned at the way the cause of Urdu was betrayed in UP. After the death of Sir Syed, Muslim leaders meekly gave in to a mild threat from the governor, Sir Anthony McDonald in 1901. Thus at the beginning of the twentieth century, educated Muslims felt the need to have a political organization like that of the Congress, which could take up their cause.

PARTITION OF BENGAL

The partition of Bengal on 16 October 1905 not only gave a boost to political consciousness among Muslims but also a blow to Hindu-Muslim amity. The event was depicted by the British government as a boon to Muslims, because in the new province of East Bengal they would number 60 per cent and thus have a greater share in its administration than they could ever have hoped for in a united Bengal. Lord Curzon had told Muslim gatherings that his object in partitioning Bengal was not only to relieve the Bengal administration but also to create a Muslim province where the followers of Islam could be predominant.[12] For instance, on 18 February 1904, in a speech at Dacca, Curzon tried to woo Muslims thus: 'The proposed Partition would invest the Mohammedans in East Bengal with a unity which they have not enjoyed since the days of Musalman Viceroys and kings.'[13] Not all the Muslim leaders were, however, taken in by these arguments. Some strongly condemned the scheme of partition. The whole of Bengal seemed to have risen against the government on this issue. But the large-scale participation by Muslims in the anti-partition movement caused much anxiety to the government, which outlined a strategy of winning over Bengali Muslims by exploiting the conflict of interests between Muslim peasants and Hindu zamindars, resulting in a few communal riots in Bengal. Coming as it did, soon after the Hindi-Urdu controversy in the UP, it further estranged Hindu-Muslim relations. Moreover, Tilak's activities in giving an aggressive colour to Hinduism frightened many Muslim leaders, who were now convinced that Muslims must have their own separate political organization, which would safeguard their political interests adequately.

The number of Muslim delegates, which was a barometer of Hindu-Muslim relations, was again reduced at successive Congress sessions in the beginning of the twentieth century. For instance, in 1903, there were not even 10 Muslim delegates out of 538; in 1904 there were 30 Muslim delegates out of 1010; and in 1905, at Banaras, there were only 20 Muslim delegates out of 757.[14] But the 1906 Congress session at Calcutta had 50 Muslim delegates, including M.A. Jinnah. This was, however, in no way, a reflection of the prevailing trend among Muslim leaders who were increasingly wanting a political organization exclusively for the community.

BIRTH OF MUSLIM LEAGUE

On 1 October 1906 at Simla, about 50 Muslim leaders from all over India met Lord Minto and presented him with their special demands, which were appreciated by the Viceroy. Within three days, they decided to form a central political organization. On 31 December 1906, at the conclusion of the Muslim Educational Conference at Dacca, a special meeting of all delegates and prominent Muslims from all over India unanimously passed a resolution deciding to form a political association called All India Muslim League, with a view to protect and advance the political interests of the Muslims of India and to promote among them feelings of loyalty to the British government. It is ironic that the resolution proposing the formation of the Muslim League should have been seconded by Hakim Ajmal Khan, who later became the Congress president. Ironically, again, at the same time, Jinnah was elected as the Vice President of the Indian Mussalman Association at Calcutta, which was formed with the objective 'to work with other communities in all political and economic matters because the interest of Muslims were in no way different from those of others'.

The Muslim League, in its first six successive annual sessions, demanded among other things:

(i) Separate denominational representation in all elective bodies from the Imperial Council down to municipal, district and local boards;
(ii) Separate representation for Muslims in public services on the basis of their population and their political importance, that Muslim candidates instead of competing with the candidates of other communities, should be appointed only on the basis of the minimum qualifications required for each post; and
(iii) Recognition of Urdu as the lingua franca of the country.

The special Aligarh session of the League in March 1908 demanded adequate representation of Muslims in all councils with separate electorates and weightages at all stages and also 50 per cent representation in the Viceroy's Executive Council.

The Muslim League demand for separate electorates and weightages generated a rival communalism. Aurobindo Ghosh who had pleaded for nationalism in 1908 felt that there was no hope unless nationalism was given a Hindu colour and confirmed the two-nation theory. Addressing the Society for Protection of Religions, he declared:

> I say no longer that nationalism is a creed, a religion, a faith. I say it is *Sanatan Dharma* which for us is nationalism. This Hindu nation was born with *Sanatan Dharma*, with it, it moves, with it, it grows. When the *Sanatan Dharma* declines, then the nation declines.[15]

Yet another development that alienated Muslims was the use of Hindu symbols for mass mobilization in the cause of national freedom. The historical literature produced during the period often referred to the Hindu struggle against Muslim imperialism. Maharana Pratap and Shivaji gradually became national heroes. With the advent of the twentieth century, the Arya Samaj movement had become militant. In 1907, an association was founded for the reconversion of non-Hindus to Hinduism, known as Shuddhi Sabha or Arya Pratinidhi Sabha. This resulted in widespread communal tension in north India.

On the other hand, a great change took place in the course of Muslim politics. The annulment of the partition of Bengal and the pre-war international situation were mainly responsible for this change. In December 1912, the Muslim League Council sought to work, in cooperation with other communities, for a system of self-government suitable to India. Thereafter for over a decade, the League steadily pursued a policy of cooperation with the Congress and opposition to the government. At its Lucknow session in March 1913, the League president, Muhammad Shafi, severely attacked Britain for rejoicing over Muslim reverses in the Balkan, Tripoli and Iran. For the first time many Congress leaders were invited to address the Muslim League session and were lustily cheered. Jinnah who had opposed denominational electorates started attending Muslim League sessions from 1912. Muslim leaders changed their opinion about Tilak, who was for over two decades dubbed as, bent on establishing Brahmanical rule in the country. Meanwhile, the Congress opposition to separate electorates had withered away and its leaders continued their efforts for a Congress-League rapprochement.

After eight months of deliberations, a joint reforms scheme was finalized, which was ratified by the Congress and the League sessions held separately at Lucknow in December 1916, which came to be know as the Lucknow Pact. The Congress conceded the demand for separate electorates and substantial weightages in the provinces where Muslims were in a minority. Muslim representation was restricted to 50 per cent of the elected representatives in Punjab and 40 per cent in Bengal. In the Imperial Legislative Council, Muslim representation was fixed at 33 per cent of the elected members. Muslims of the minority provinces were given weightage in both the provincial councils and the Imperial Legislative Council. Each community was also given a communal veto.

At the end of the First World War, the Khilafat movement of the Muslims, supported by Gandhiji and his Non-Cooperation movement, had electrified the whole political atmosphere of the country and brought a sea change in Hindu-Muslim relations. Many Hindu leaders were asked to address mosque meetings and many Khilafatists addressed temple assemblies. But this cordiality between the two communities was not to last for long. The Moplah outbreak in August 1921 had a devastating effect on the future course of politics and the communal situation. The government gave wide publicity to the riots and, holding the Moplah outbreak to be the direct result of the Khilafat movement, exploited the riots to spearhead a propaganda offensive against the Khilafat and Non-Cooperation movements.

By the end of 1921, the Khilafat movement had run its course and Gandhiji had also expressed his helplessness in controlling and disciplining the course of the Non-Cooperation movement.[16] The Khilafat movement got a big setback with Britain and Afghanistan signing a Friendship Treaty on 22 November 1921. The abolition of the Khilafat as an institution by the Turks themselves, in February 1924, gave a final death blow to the Khilafat movement. Though it ostensibly achieved nothing, the movement created considerable political consciousness among the Muslim masses.

TOWARDS RESPONSIBLE GOVERNMENT

Muslims had reacted favourably to the Government of India Act of 1919, which was a step towards the establishment of a constitutional government in the country. But the Congress rejected the Constitution and did not take part in the elections held in 1920 under this Act. The Muslim League went radical and identified itself with the Congress. It did not meet as a separate body between 1919 and 1924. And, when it did meet in 1924 under Jinnah's presidentship, it insisted on immediate and far-reaching constitutional advances. Its resolution on swaraj contained six principles.

The first four dealt with the old demands of separate electorates and minority safeguards. But it introduced two new demands: (1) India must be a federal polity; and (2) any territorial redistribution must not affect the Muslim majority in Punjab, Bengal and the NWFP. The Muslim League foresaw that even in a federal India, the centre was bound to be Hindu-dominated. It, therefore, demanded full provincial autonomy.

The period from 1913 to 1924 saw the Congress and the Muslim League come closer, an exceptional phenomenon, which can be explained by two factors: (1) the repeal of the partition of Bengal had made Muslims bitter against the British; and (2) the British animosity towards Turkey had aggravated this feeling. The thaw in the Hindu-Muslim relations did not mean that the fundamental differences had disappeared. What had happened was that because of anti-British emotions, the Muslims felt a desire to reach at some understanding with the Congress. Gandhi saw in this a fine opportunity to bring Muslims closer to the Congress and threw himself on the side of the Khilafat movement. The Muslims naturally welcomed this. However, the Congress-Muslim League rapprochement proved to be unproductive. The Khilafat and Non-Cooperation movements did provide opportunity for Hindu-Muslim unity for a short while, but it soon evaporated and the country witnessed the worst Hindu-Muslim riots in its history. Within a year of the ending of the Congress-League honeymoon, in December 1925, the Muslim League attacked the concept of nationalism as an ideology, asserted that Hindus and Muslims were not just two distinct religious sects but two distinct nations. The December 1925 session of the Congress was marked by the virtual absence of Muslim delegates. The only Muslim leaders present at the session were the Ali brothers and Maulana Azad. Madan Mohan Malaviya pointed out that Muslims had deserted the Congress.

The entire country witnessed communal outbursts during this period—Bihar riots in 1917, Moplah riots in August 1921, riots in Punjab, UP, Ajmer and Sindh in 1923 and the Kohat riots in September 1924. This vitiated the atmosphere in the early 1920s so much that Hindu revivalists found an excellent opportunity to resurrect the religious conversion (*shuddhi*) movement, which had been started by the Arya Samaj. The Hindu Mahasabha movement also received a great fillip. The *sangathan* movement spread and Hindu youth organized themselves as a volunteer force, later known as the Rashtriya Swayamsevak Sangh (RSS). The Hindu communal mobilization was, in turn, followed by a corresponding Muslim mobilization in the form of the *tabligh* and *tanzim* movements, which were counterparts to those of the *shuddhi* and *sangathan*. The Jamiyat and Khilafat leaders took enthusiastic part in these movements. The *shuddhi* movement was also taken up with such vigour in parts of UP that in the first half of 1923, more than 18,000 Malkana Rajput, Gujjars and Banias were reconverted to Hinduism. Both Hindu and Muslim fanatics, of this time, carried out the most provocative propaganda against each other through the press, pamphlets and abusive speeches.

The communal warfare stunned Gandhiji, who went on a 21-day fast at Delhi after the Kohat riots in September 1924. Prominent leaders from most of the parties hurriedly called a Unity Conference, which unanimously agreed upon a code of conduct. *Shuddhi*, *sangathan*, *tabligh* and *tanzim* movements were abandoned, but only for a while. After three months, they were revived and communalism returned with a vengeance. Fazlul Haq of Bengal, once a great supporter of the Khilafat and non-cooperation movements, raised the cry of 'Islam in danger' in 1925, allegedly on account of the growing power of the Hindus.

After the boycott of the Simon Commission, the All Parties Conference convened by the Congress had appointed a Committee with Motilal Nehru as Chairman to prepare a constitution for India. The report of this committee, known as the Nehru Report, rejected federation as a possible solution to the communal problem and envisaged a unitary government at the centre. It also did not provide for separate electorates or any weightages. Reservation of seats for Muslims was allowed only at the centre and in the Muslim minority provinces. The Report was rejected by all shades of Muslim opinion. An All India Muslim Conference met at Delhi in 1929 under the chairmanship of the Aga Khan and laid down Muslim demands, which were, so to say, the Muslim reply to the Nehru Report. These were:

(i) The Central government was to be a truly federal government with complete provincial autonomy and the residual powers were to be vested in the provinces;
(ii) Separate electorates should continue;
(iii) Existing weightage for Muslims in the Hindu majority provinces should continue;
(iv) Muslims should be given their due share in the central and provincial cabinets;
(v) A due proportion of seats should be given to Muslims in the public services and on all statutory self-governing bodies; and
(vi) There must be safeguards for the protection and promotion of Muslim education, language, religion, personal laws and charitable institutions.

In March 1929, Jinnah drew up his famous 14 Points, which were a reiteration of all the earlier Muslim demands and which greatly influenced Muslim thinking for the better part of the next decade.

The Simon Commission, after visiting India in 1928 and 1929, published its report in May 1930, which recommended a federal framework for India. The Congress rejected the report while the Muslim League reserved its judgement knowing that the matter would be finally decided at the Round Table Conference.

The three sessions of the Round Table Conference at London in 1930 and 1931, could not produce any settlement of the communal problem. So the British government came out with its own Communal Award in August 1932, which retained separate electorates for Muslims and all other minorities. The Muslim majorities in Punjab and Bengal were reduced to minorities. The Award was, however, not popular with any party. The recommendations of the Round Table Conference were incorporated in the Government of India Act, 1935, which came into operation on 1 April 1937. Part II of the Act, dealing with the All India Federation, however, never came into operation.

After the general elections in 1937, the Congress formed its governments in six provinces—UP, CP, Bihar, Orissa, Bombay and Madras, but only after getting embroiled in two controversies with the Muslim League. First, the Congress had obtained an assurance from the Viceroy that the provincial governors would not use the 'special powers' given to them by the Act for safeguarding the interests of the minorities, which was greatly resented by the Muslim League. Second, the Congress refusal to form a coalition government with the League in UP unless it ceased to function as a separate group, also angered the League.

The Congress rule in the six provinces from July 1937 to October 1939, was held out by the Muslim League to have been a nightmare for the Muslims. The *Pirpur Report*, the *Shareef Report* and Fazlul Haq's pamphlet *Muslim Sufferings Under Congress Rule* gave details of the alleged excesses of the Congress governments against Muslims, such as the ban on beef, the forbidding of *azan* (call to prayer), noisy processions before mosques at prayer time, attacks on worshippers in mosques and the boycott of Muslim shops. The Muslim League also took strong exception to the Congress education policy. A committee appointed by the All India Muslim Education Conference to go into this matter criticized the Wardha scheme of education and the scheme of Vidya Mandirs. The Muslim complaint was that it was intended to wean Muslims away from their culture, religion and traditions, to superimpose Hindu culture on the education system, as well as introduce highly objectionable textbooks and sanskritized Hindi at the cost of Urdu.

THE MOVEMENT FOR PAKISTAN

The Congress rule in the six provinces from 1937 to 1939 led to a significant change in the attitude of the Muslim League towards constitutional issues. At its 1938 annual session at Patna, the League authorized Jinnah 'to explore the possibility of a suitable alternative which would completely safeguard the interests of Musalmans'. And in March 1939, the League Working Committee appointed a body to examine various schemes already propounded and those that might be submitted thereafter. Thus, by the beginning of 1940, Muslim politics had decidedly taken a significant turn. The Muslim League, which had all through wanted an Indian federation with limited powers, now no longer wanted a federation. As the Congress travelled towards the idea of a united India, the League turned towards 'Muslim independence'. The political unity of India, which had been taken for granted by the Muslim League before 1937, was no longer looked upon as an axiom. The Indian political situation had undergone a fundamental change.

Before the All India Muslim League passed its historic Lahore (or Pakistan) Resolution in March 1940, the establishment of a separate Muslim state or states in the subcontinent had been advocated by some public figures like Saiyid Jamaluddin Afghani, Abdul Jabbar Khaire and Abdus Sattar Khaire, the latter two known as the Khaire brothers. In 1928, at the Calcutta meeting of the All Parties Convention, the Aga Khan had advocated independence for each province.[17] However, Sir Mohammad Iqbal was the first important public figure to propound the idea of Pakistan from the platform of the Muslim League. In his presidential address to the League's annual session at Allahabad in 1930, he said:

> I would like to see Punjab, North-West Frontier Province, Sindh and Baluchistan amalgamated into a single state. Self-government within the British empire or without it, the formation of a consolidated North-West Indian Muslim state appears to me to be the final destiny of the Muslims, at least of North-West India.[18]

At the third Round Table Conference, Iqbal had pleaded that there should be no central government in the subcontinent and that the provinces should be autonomous and independent dominions.[19]

Iqbal did not give a name to his projected Muslim state. That was the work of Rahmat Ali at Cambridge, who issued a pamphlet *Now or Never*, in January 1933, pleading the idea of Partition. He wanted Pakistan to comprise Punjab, the NWFP, Kashmir, Sind and Baluchistan. Bengal and Assam would form another Muslim state of *Bang-i-Islam.* The Nizam's dominions in the south would be named Usmanistan. These three states should then form a triple alliance.[20]

In September 1939, the Working Committee of the All India Muslim League resolved that it was irrevocably opposed to any federal scheme in which a permanent majority ruled over a permanent minority, thereby reducing a democratic and parliamentary system of government to a farce. This was described as totally unsuited to the genius of the peoples of India who were composed of various nationalities and did not constitute a national state.[21]

It was, however, the Lahore Muslim League session of March 1940 that adopted the establishment of independent Muslim states as its final goal. Jinnah, in his presidential address said that the Muslims were a nation by any definition. The problem of India could not be solved if it was treated merely as an inter-communal question. It was an international issue and must be dealt with as such. He further said that the Hindus and Muslims had two different social philosophies and social customs. They neither intermarried nor interdined together. They belonged to two different civilizations, which were based mainly on conflicting ideas and concepts. Hindus and Muslims derived their inspiration from different sources of history. They had different epics and different heroes. Very often, the hero of one was the foe of the other, and likewise their victories and defeats overlapped. To yoke together two such nations under a single state, he said, must lead to growing discontent and final destruction of any fabric that may be built up for the governance of a state. Therefore, Muslim India could not accept any constitution which would necessarily result in the permanent rule of a permanent majority. The only course open to all, Jinnah said, was to permit the major nations to establish separate homelands by dividing India into sovereign states.[22]

The Muslim League resolution proposing the Partition of the country said:

> No constitutional plan would be workable in this country or acceptable to Muslims unless it is designed on the following basic principles, namely, that geographically contingguous units are demacated into regions which should be so constituted . . . that the areas in which Muslims are numerically in a majority as in the north-western or eastern zones of India, should be grouped to constitute independent

states in which the constituent units shall be autonomous and sovereign.[23]

After the adoption of the Lahore Resolution, Jinnah explained to the Muslims of the Hindu majority provinces that whether India was partitioned or not, they would always remain minorities. By opposing the division of India, they could not improve their position but they would obstruct the freedom of a majority of Muslims in the subcontinent. Jinnah held that India was already divided and partitioned by nature, Muslim India and Hindu India existed on the physical map. There was neither a country, nor a nation, nor a central national government in existence that was being divided or violated.[24] Jinnah pointed out that autonomous provinces were already in existence under the 1935 constitution. In some of them Muslims predominated, while others were mainly Hindu dominated. Their reconstitution into a 'geographical, contiguous, homogenous independent zone' was, therefore, the most feasible and practicable scheme.[25]

The Muslims, as Jinnah stated, did not want to harm or injure any other community or interest. They asked for bare justice. They wanted to live an honourable life as free men. They stood for free Islam and free India.[26] Jinnah continued that Muslims were not demanding Pakistan from Hindus because they did not possess the whole of India. It was the British who took India from the Muslims and the Muslim demand was addressed to the British. It was 'utter nonsense' to say that Hindustan belonged to Hindus because if larger habitation were the criterion, India was the motherland not only of the Dravidians, but also of the aborigines.[27]

For the protagonists of Pakistan, the biggest proof of the correctness of their case was that a non-Muslim observer like B.R. Ambedkar was convinced that the Pakistan scheme, despite all its disadvantages, offered a feasible way out of the political impasse in India. In his book, *Thoughts on Pakistan*, he saw no substance in the Hindu objections to the Pakistan scheme and shared the Muslim fears of domination by caste Hindus.[28]

After the outbreak of the Second World War, the British government in its 8 August 1940 offer, promised Dominion Status and a constituent assembly for India at the end of the war. It also assured that full weight would be given to the views of the minorities in any revision of the constitution and that no further political development which did not satisfy the minorities would be approved by His Majesty's Government. The Muslim League had thus extracted an unequivocal declaration from the British government that Muslim satisfaction would be sought in any future constitutional arrangement.

The Cripps Proposals, published on 30 March 1942, apart from reiterating Dominion Status and a constituent assembly for India at the end of the war said that any constitution made would be acceptable to the British government subject to the condition, that any province would be free to keep itself out of the proposed Indian Union. And, if such non-acceding provinces so desired, they could have their own separate union analogous to the proposed Indian Union. The Congress opposed the non-accession clause of the proposals because it contained the seeds of India's disintegration. The Muslim League was also not satisfied with the non-accession clause, as according to it, this did not ensure the creation of Pakistan as envisaged by it and, therefore, it too rejected the Cripps Proposals, though the possibility of a Muslim state was implicit in it.

The general elections to the Central and provincial legislatures were held in the winter of 1945-6 on very clear issues. The Muslim League went into the fray to vindicate its claim of speaking for Muslim India and to prove the popular backing for the demand of Pakistan among Muslims. The Congress manifesto was that the Congress represented all Indians, and India was to remain one undivided country.

In the elections for the Central Legislative Assembly held in December 1945, the Muslim League won every single Muslim seat, the Nationalist Muslims forfeiting their deposits in many instances. The Congress success in non-Muslim constituencies was equally spectacular. The League won 86.6 per cent of the total Muslim vote and the Congress 91.3 per cent of the total general vote. In the provincial elections, held in early 1946, again the two main parties swept their respective constituencies. The Congress won a total of 930 seats, gaining an absolute majority in eight provinces. The Muslim League captured 428 out of 492 Muslim seats. The results of the general elections, by establishing beyond doubt that the Muslim League represented Muslim India and that the Congress represented the rest of India, showed the Hindu-Muslim problem in its stark reality.

An important landmark in the evolution of Pakistan was the convention of the Muslim League legislators at Delhi on 7-9 April 1946, which modified the original Lahore Resolution of March 1940 and declared that there should be only one Pakistan instead of two, as contemplated in the original resolution.

After the British government's announcement on 29 February 1946 to send 'a special mission of Cabinet Ministers' to solve the Indian constitutional tangle, Prime Minister Attlee declared on 15 March:

> We are mindful of the rights of minorities and the minorities should be able to live

free from fear; on the other hand, we cannot allow a minority to place their veto on the advance of the majority.[29]

On this Jinnah reiterated that the Muslims of India were not a minority but a nation and self-determination was their birthright.

After a conference with the Congress and the League representatives at Simla from 5 to 12 May, which could not throw up any agreement, the Cabinet Mission published its own Plan on 16 May. The Plan was:

There would be a Union of India comprising British India and the Indian States, which should deal with Defence, Foreign Affairs and Communications. All residual powers would belong to the provinces which would be free to form groups with their own Executives and Legislatures. Each group could determine the provincial subjects to be taken in common. Any province could by a majority vote of its Legislative Assembly call for a reconsideration of the terms of the Constitution after every ten years. A constituent assembly elected by Provincial Assemblies on the basis of population, shall frame the future constitution for India.

The Congress, which accepted the Plan on 6 July with the provisos, held that it was open to the Constituent Assembly to vary the Plan, and that no province could be compelled to belong to a group against its will. The Muslim League had accepted the Plan on 6 June because the grouping of provinces provided the foundation for Pakistan. But after the Congress stand that it had only agreed to go to the Constituent Assembly and nothing else, coupled with the silence of the authors of the Plan on this Congress policy, the Muslim League withdrew its acceptance of the Plan on 27 July.

By the end of July 1946, British India had elected its 296 representatives to the Constituent Assembly. The Congress had won all the general seats except nine, and the Muslim League all the Muslim seats except five. The first meeting of the Assembly had been called for 9 December. But the League refused to participate in the Assembly proceedings or even to recognize it as a valid body, unless the Congress accepted the grouping clause of the Cabinet Mission Plan as the authors of the Plan had interpreted it. The British government, after its failure to patch up the differences between the Congress and the League by inviting the leaders of the two parties to London on 2 December 1946, made a statement on 6 December:

Should a constitution come to be framed by a Constituent Assembly in which a large section of the Indian population had not been represented, His Majesty's Government could not of course contemplate forcing such a constitution upon any unwilling parts of the country.[30]

The Muslim League demanded the dissolution of the Constituent Assembly on 31 December 1946.

It was in this atmosphere of mutual recrimination that the British government made its historic announcement of 20 February1947, which said:

> It is a definite intention . . . to effect the transfer of power to responsible Indian hands by a date not later than June 1948. If an agreed constitution was not worked out by a fully representative assembly by that date, the government would have to consider to whom the power of the central government in British India should be handed over on the due date, whether as a whole to some form of central government for British India, or in some areas to the existing provincial governments, or in such other way as may seem most reasonable and in the best interest of the Indian people.[31]

In the same statement, it was announced that Wavell was being recalled and replaced by Viscount Mountbatten. As the Cabinet Mission Plan was for all practical purposes dead, Mountbatten had to prepare another plan, according to the British government statement of 20 February. This plan was:

> The provincial legislative assemblies of Punjab and Bengal would each meet in two parts, one representing the Muslim majority districts and the other the rest of the province. The members of the two parts of each legislative assembly sitting separately would vote whether or not the province should be partitioned. If a simple majority of either part decided in favour of partition, division would take place. Each part of the assembly would also decide whether to join the existing constituent assembly or a new constituent assembly. A soon as this was decided, the Governor–General would appoint a Boundary Commission to demarcate the boundaries of the two parts of each province on the basis of contiguous majority areas of Muslims and non-Muslims and also other factors. The Legislative Assembly of Sindh would decide between joining the existing assembly or the new constituent assembly. In the NWFP, the electors of the existing Legislative Assembly would decide by means of a referendum which constituent assembly they would like to join. Baluchistan would also be given an opportunity to express its opinion on the issue. If Bengal decided in favour of partition, a referendum would be held in the Sylhet district of Assam to decide whether it would continue to form part of Assam or be amalgamated with the new province of East Bengal.

On 2 June, the Viceroy put the Plan before a meeting of the Congress and the League leaders and Baldev Singh, the representative of the Sikhs, and it was approved. On 3 June the Plan was published. On 4 June Mountbatten held a Press Conference and mentioned 15 August 1947 as the tentative date for the transfer of power. On 10 June the Muslim League

Council gave full authority to Jinnah to accept the fundamental principles of the Plan as a compromise. On 14 June, the AICC accepted the Plan.[32]

Members of the Bengal and Punjab legislative assemblies representing the Muslim and non-Muslim majority districts met separately. In both the provinces, members from Muslim majority districts decided by a majority vote that their respective provinces should not be partitioned and that they should join a new constituent assembly, while members from non-Muslim majority districts decided by a majority vote that their provinces should be partitioned and that they should join the existing Constituent Assembly. The Sind Legislative Assembly decided by a majority vote to join a new Constituent Assembly. In Baluchistan, the *shahi jirga* and the non-official members of the Quetta Municipality met and unanimously decided to join a new Constituent Assembly. In the referendum in Sylhet, a majority voted in favour of separation from Assam and joining with East Bengal. In the referendum in the NWFP, held from 6 to 17 June, an overwhelming vote was in favour of joining a new Constituent Assembly. The Congress had boycotted the referendum because the people had not been given a third choice of voting for an independent Pakhtoonistan, besides the two choices of either joining the existing or a new constituent assembly.

Thus it was decided that the new state, Pakistan, would comprise the Muslim majority districts of Bengal and Punjab (which constituted the major area and population of these two provinces), the district of Sylhet and the whole of the NWFP, Sind and Baluchistan.

In the backdrop of the holocaust, unprecedented in India's history, and the largest ever transfer of population in recorded history, that immediately followed Partition, as well as the continuously strained relations between the two successor states, the big question arises—Whom has Partition benefitted? The most striking fact about Pakistan is how it has failed to satisfy the interests of the very Muslims who demanded its creation. The main centres of Muslim population in undivided India were Punjab and Bengal where Muslims had dominated the political scene. But both the provinces ended up by being sliced into two. Muslim Punjab lost its fertile eastern districts. Muslim Bengal, which lost Calcutta, its economic heart, and the hinterland of West Bengal, was reduced to the status of an overpopulated rural slum. As for Muslims in India, who numbered 35 million at the time, they were left high and dry at the mercy of the very people they had antagonized in their struggle for Pakistan.[33]

As to the question whether Partition could have been avoided the answer is that the Cabinet Mission Plan of 16 May 1946 had provided a way out and at one stage both the Congress and the Muslim League had accepted it, but the destiny of India had willed otherwise. The grouping clause of the Plan, the main attraction for the League, was too much for the Congress to digest. It also thought that there was no way to stop the prevailing chaos in the country but to accept the Partition Plan. The Congress Working Committee accepted it with only one dissenting voice—that of Khan Abdul Ghaffar Khan.[34] As Gandhiji observed, 'Everybody is today impatient for India's independence. Therefore, there is no other help.'[35]

NOTES

1. Thomson and Garrett, *Rise and Fulfilment of British Rule in India* (2nd edn, London, 1935), p. 353; cited in Rafiq Zakaria, *Rise of Muslims in Indian Politics* (Bombay, 1970), p. 4.
2. Alagnon Law, ed., *India under Lord Ellenborough*, p. 65, cited in Zakaria, op.cit., p. 4.
3. Pattabhi Sitaramayya, *History of Indian National Congress* (Bombay, 1946), pp. 17-22.
4. Zakaria, op.cit., p. 48.
5. B.B. Majumdar, *History of Indian Social and Political Ideas from Rammohan to Dayanand* (Calcutta, 1967), pp. 116 and 120, cited in V.V. Nagarkar, *Genesis of Pakistan* (Bombay, 1975), p. 27.
6. *Indian Mirror*, 2 December 1887.
7. *Pioneer*, 11 and 12 January 1888.
8. *Times* (London), 16 January 1888.
9. Quoted in *Pioneer*, 2 February 1888.
10. Quoted in *Indian Mirror*, 7 October 1888.
11. Zakaria, op.cit., p. 61.
12. A.C. Mazumdar, *Indian National Evolution* (New Delhi, 1915), p. 207; H.W. Nevinson, *The New Spirit in India* (Delhi, 1975), pp. 11 and 168; S.N. Bannerji, *A Nation in Making* (Calcutta, 1925), pp. 185, 188 and 191, cited in Zakaria, op.cit., p.100. fn.
13. *Muslim Chronicle*, 11 November 1905.
14. *Annual Congress Reports*, 1903, 1904 and 1905, Appendices I and A, respectively.
15. Nagarkar, op.cit., p. 93.
16. Ibid., p. 116.
17. Sitaramayya, op.cit., p. 334.
18. Shamloo, *Speeches and Statements of Iqbal* (Lahore, 1948), pp. 11-12, cited in Ishtiaq Husain Qureshi, *Struggle for Pakistan* (Karachi, 1965, 2nd edn, 1969), pp. 118-19.
19. B.R. Ambedkar, *Thoughts on Pakistan* (Bombay, 1941), p. 336.
20. C. Rahmat Ali, *The Millat and the Menace of Indianism* (Cambridge, 1940), cited in Qureshi, op.cit., p. 120.
21. *Resolutions of the All India Muslim League from December 1939 to March 1940*, pp. 25-8, cited in Qureshi, op.cit., p.124.
22. Jamil-ud-din Ahmad, *Some Recent Speeches and Writings of Mr. Jinnah* (Lahore, 1952), pp. 159-81.

23. Qureshi, op.cit., p. 12 and Appendix C, p. 324.
24. Ahmad, op.cit., pp.189-90.
25. Ibid., pp.190-2.
26. Ibid., p. 193.
27. Ibid., pp. 183-7 and 252-3.
28. Ambedkar, op.cit.
29. Qureshi, op.cit., p. 245.
30. Ibid., p. 284.
31. Ibid., p. 285.
32. N.N. Mitra, *The Indian Annual Register 1947*, Vol. 1 (repr., Delhi, 1990), pp. 143-6.
33. Ayesha Jalal, *The Sole Spokesman—Jinnah, The Muslim League and the Demand for Pakistan* (Cambridge, 1985), pp. 1-2.
34. J.B. Kripalani, *Gandhi—His Life and Thought* (Publication Division, GOI, New Delhi, 1976), p. 286.
35. Ibid.

Explaining Partition: Congress-Muslim League Coalition in UP

SALIL MISHRA

Among the many explanations that are offered for the Partition of India, there is one which has been particularly popular among the historians of modern India. Unlike most explanations it has nothing to do with either Punjab or Bengal, the provinces which were actually partitioned. It is also not located in the 1940s, the decade when the forces for Partition gathered momentum. This explanation belongs to UP, and to 1937 to be exact. Having been in existence since the 1930s, it actually centres around an event, or rather a non-event. If there had been a coalition government of Congress and Muslim League in UP in 1937, the Partition of India may well not have occurred. This, though crudely and simplistically put, is the crux of the 'coalition argument'. The debate on whether or not the absence of a Congress-Muslim League coalition can be seen as having contributed to the Partition, has grown with years and has found, staunch supporters among the historians, on the one hand, and vehement opponents, on the other.[1]

Before going into the details of the debate, it is important to get a brief idea of the background to the crucial developments in UP in 1937. The Government of India Act, 1935 had granted provincial autonomy with a significantly enlarged franchise and separate electorates for Muslims. Elections to 228 constituencies took place in UP in early 1937. Of these constituencies, 66 (including two for women) were reserved for Muslims. There were three major forces competing for Muslim seats—the Muslim League, which contested 37 seats, the Congress, which contested 11 seats and the National Agricultural Parties of Oudh and Agra (hereafter NAPs) formed in 1934 by the big landlords under British protection, which contested 23 seats. Of these 66 seats, the Muslim League won 27 and NAPs 11. The Congress drew a blank losing all the Muslim seats it contested. The only Muslim legislator returned on a Congress ticket was Husain Zaheer who won from the university seat. The rest of the Muslim seats were won by Independent candidates.[2] The Congress however won a majority of seats (133) and was in a position to form a government on its own.

The period between February and July saw a tug of war between the Congress and the British government on the question of acceptance of office. The Congress High Command insisted on certain assurances from the governors as a precondition for accepting office and the government seemed reluctant to comply with the demand. Finally the issue was resolved and the Congress, under the leadership of Govind Ballabh Pant, took charge of the ministry in July. In a ministry of six, there were two Muslims—Hafiz Mohammad Ibrahim and Rafi Ahmad Kidwai, both Congressmen. Hafiz Ibrahim had won on a Muslim League ticket but subsequently left the Muslim League to join the Congress. After he became a minister, he resigned his seat, contested on a Congress ticket and won the election. Rafi Ahmad Kidwai had lost in the general elections, but was returned unopposed in a bye-election held in April 1937. The Muslim League sat in the opposition in the UP Assembly.

The information provided above would encounter no serious disagreement either from the advocates or the opponents of the 'coalition theory'. Indeed the contentious issues have not been touched so far. The major contention revolves round the possibility of the Congress and the Muslim League forming together a coalition government. Around July, before the Congress formed the government, there was indeed some talk of this. Newspapers hinted at this possibility. The *Leader*, a daily from Allahabad, gave details of a meeting being held in Lucknow between Congress and Muslim League leaders in mid-July and wrote:

> Special significance is attached to the discussion between Choudhary Khaliquzzaman, leader of the Muslim League party, Pt. Govind Ballabh Pant and Maulana Abul Kalam Azad on the eve of the formation of the Congress cabinet in UP and none should be surprised if two Muslim leaders, most likely Nawab Mohammad Ismail, president of the Muslim League Parliamentary Board and Choudhary Khaliquzzaman are taken in the Congress fold.[3]

'Negotiations with the Muslim League fail',[4] declared the same paper, three days later.

It was precisely this event which developed into a controversy among historians. Many historians argued that the Partition of the subcontinent was the product of a process, which had been unleashed in 1937 in UP. If there had been a coalition between Congress and Muslim League, the argument went, the Partition might possibly have been averted. The Muslim League might have been co-opted into constitutional politics; Jinnah might not have been pushed towards extremism from where he had no choice but to ask for Pakistan; Muslims might not have rallied behind the League; and it might not have been communalized to the extent that it was. And so, 1937 was a 'landmark in the course of communal politics in UP',[5] because it was the breakdown of Congress-League negotiations that witnessed the 'sudden growth of Muslim opinion, in favour of the League, as opposed to the Congress. The evidence places the immediate responsibility on the Congress *alone*',[6] because 'if the Congress party had adhered to its *pre-election intention* of forming a coalition ministry, the Hindu-Muslim problem might not have assumed formidable proportions'.[7] (emphasis added)

The attempts to comprehend and explain the reality of 1947 by focusing on the developments of the preceding years in UP in 1937, therefore, offers a convenient beginning. The argument that the failure of a coalition to materialize let loose an onslaught of communalism leading to Partition, has exercised such an influence on many historians that it needs to be examined in detail.

Briefly put, the argument runs like this: there was an informal electoral understanding between the UP Congress and the UP Muslim League Parliamentary Boards.[8] The Congress had virtually agreed to a coalition with the League before the elections. Their election manifestos had much in common, though there were minor differences.[9] During the elections, they avoided confrontation with each other and the Congress even delegated to the Muslim League the task of winning the Muslim seats.[10] A proof of cooperation between the two was that the Muslim League did not put up a candidate against Rafi Ahmad Kidwai in the Bahraich bye-election and he was returned unopposed.[11]

After the elections the attitude of Congressmen changed. 'Its leaders, jubilant over the recent success, assumed a dictatorial attitude.'[12] Although Jinnah 'pleaded' for cooperation to form a 'united front' of the Congress and the League, Nehru ridiculed the suggestion because in Nehru's intention 'no party other than the Congress was to be tolerated'.[13] And so, when the League leadership in UP approached the Congress for a coalition in the Legislative Assembly, the Congress leadership spurned the offer. This infuriated Jinnah. He then launched a massive campaign against the Congress. Muslims rallied behind the League because in their perception the Congress government, without the participation of the Muslim League, meant a 'Hindu Raj'. What logically followed was an increase in communalism, Hindu-Muslim conflict and bitterness, Congress-League hostility, increasing popularity of the League and the Partition of the subcontinent.

This, briefly, is the coalition story. Constructed logically, it sounds convincing and appears credible, but leaves a lot to be desired as far as empirical backing and political reality are concerned. Certain factual inaccuracies are glaringly obvious. There is, for instance, no direct evidence anywhere—in the newspapers, Congress records and prominent leaders' correspondence—of any prior agreement amounting to an alliance between the Congress and the League.[14] In fact as early as 9 January 1937, the *Leader* quoting the *Tribune* made this point absolutely clear:

> *In the absence of an understanding between the Congress and the League*, is not the Congress fully entitled to put up its candidates for Muslims as for general territorial seats? As a matter of fact, if the Congress is to blame at all, it is not because it has put up a few candidates for Muslim seats—but because it has not put up at least as many candidates for Muslim and other communal seats as it has put up for general territorial seats.[15] (emphasis added)

Also, the Congress did *not* leave the Muslim seats to be won by Muslim League. The Congress contested 11 Muslim seats as against 37 contested by the League. Should it, therefore, be assumed that both of them, put together, left the remaining 18 Muslim seats for some other party, presumably the NAPs? What is more, for as many as three constituencies, Sitapur rural, Sultanpur rural and Lucknow urban, the Congress and the League actually clashed with each other.[16] The important thing to remember is that Congress actually contested very few Muslim seats all over the country—only 58 out of 482, thereby necessarily leaving out most of the Muslim seats for other parties. It might have been for the Unionist Party in the Punjab and Krishak Praja Party in Bengal. Moreover, Jinnah could not possibly be 'pleading' with Nehru. They had already clashed with each other during their election campaigns. Nehru had made his famous and controversial statement—about there being only two parties in India—the Congress and the British government[17] and Jinnah had retaliated with his equally famous reference to the third factor—Muslim India. And this was again as early as January 1937. The verbal duel between the two leaders had started. Jinnah had asked Nehru to leave the Muslims alone, and Nehru had declared that this was communalism raised to its highest power.[18]

Commenting on what had already come to be known as the Nehru-Jinnah controversy, Shaukat Ali informed Nehru, through a statement to the press in January 1937, that he (Nehru) was not in touch with the Muslims of India, like Jinnah was. Shaukat Ali called the Congress a 'great Hindu organization' and the League the 'representative of the overwhelming majority and better minds of Muslims'. 'Muslims had no confidence in the Congress.' Shaukat Ali appealed to Nehru to end this controversy as 'the Nehru Report controversy was bad enough and it will only aggravate things'.[19] These confrontations had all taken place before the elections.

Even Kidwai's unopposed election cannot be taken to be an indication of cooperation between the two organizations for many reasons. The Muslim League had originally planned to put up a candidate against him for the Bahraich bye-election.[20] Jinnah issued a statement: 'We have decided to contest the seat which was won by the Muslim League at Bahraich. . . . The Congress, I believe, is going to contest this seat. It will be a great mistake on the part of the Congress to do so. . . .'[21] The working committee of the Muslim League Parliamentary Board was to meet in the third week of March to decide the candidate against Kidwai and applications were invited from the candidates wanting to contest the Bahraich seat on a Muslim League ticket.[22] No one applied. S. Ali Zaheer, a possible League candidate, backed out, two other independents withdrew and Kidwai was returned unopposed.[23]

Why was there such a lack of enthusiasm in contesting elections? This was the time when Congress had decided not to form the ministries and the constitutional deadlock created thus, had made the dissolution of the legislatures imminent. Completely baffled by this attitude of the Congress, the prospective aspirants for a seat in the Assembly would have certainly wondered whether there was any point in contesting the elections, when, in all probability, the provincial assemblies with a Congress majority were not going to function at all! It was precisely for this reason that all the bye-elections during those weeks of uncertainty were being decided uncontested in favour of the Congress. Apart from Kidwai's election, Congressmen were also returned unopposed from NWFP, Assam and the Madras Presidency.[24] Interestingly, once the ambiguity regarding acceptance of office cleared up in favour of acceptance by the Congress, the Muslim League did put up a candidate against it for the Jhansi-Jalon-Hamirpur bye-election and Khaliquzzaman, supposedly the architect of Congress-League unity in UP and a likely minister in the hypothetical coalition ministry, campaigned vigorously against the Congress candidate and made appeals 'in the name of Allah':

> By electing the League nominee, you will serve the country and the cause of Islam. Allah has placed the key of success in your hands. You must not lose this opportunity by sheer mistake or misunderstanding. You will combat successfully the organization having a dual policy and will thus keep the dignity and prestige of Islam intact.[25]

And this was barely seven days before the official coalition talks were to begin!

In fact, the rumour about a possible coalition between the Congress and the League had started spreading only after the declaration of the election results in which the Congress had not won a single Muslim seat. The sole Muslim elected on the Congress ticket was Husain Zaheer from the university seat.[26] It was thus felt that the Muslim component of the ministry would have to be provided by the Muslim League. Kidwai's election on the Congress ticket was important in so much as it put to rest all such speculations.

The historiographic assertion that the Congress and the League manifestos were similar with common programmes and demands also needs to be put to rest. The Congress manifesto, drafted by Nehru, bore his stamp all the way.[27] Being Nehru's brainchild, it was not likely to resemble the League's manifesto in any essential details.[28] It spoke of 'the nationalist urge of the Indian people . . . to put an end to exploitation by British Imperialism' by attaining independence. The League wanted 'full responsible government for India' which it had been wanting ever since 1912. The Congress rejected 'in its entirety the new constitution' and was contesting the elections 'to combat and end' the new Act. The League manifesto advocated the utilizing of the provincial scheme 'for what it was worth' and it accepted the Communal Award till a substitute was agreed upon. The Congress denunciation of the Communal Award in the manifesto was undoubtedly the strongest ever made by it—'the rejection, in its entirety of the new Act by the Congress inevitably involves the rejection of the communal decision'. The Congress manifesto advocated 'a reform of the systems of land tenure and revenue and rent and an equitable adjustment of the burden on agricultural land, giving immediate relief to the smaller peasantry by a substantial reduction of agricultural rent and revenue now paid by them and exempting uneconomic holdings from payment of rent and revenue'. The League manifesto, on the other hand, was 'opposed to any movement that aims at expropriation of private property'. On the question of indebtedness, the Congress manifesto recommended 'scaling down of debt', debt relief and 'cheap credit facilities by the state'. The League manifesto would not go further than to 'sponsor measures for the relief of rural indebtedness'. The Congress laid down a policy for industrial workers, removal of sex disabilities by providing equal opportunities for women and the release of political prisoners. The League manifesto did not say a word about any of them.

It is indeed surprising that with dissimilarities as stark and obvious as these, many historians should look for, and also find, commonalities between the two programmes.[29] In fact Anita Inder Singh has rightly pointed out that the 'election manifesto of the League resembled not the Congress manifesto, but the manifestos of the National Agricultural Parties of Agra and Oudh'.[30]

THE COALITION THEORY: ORIGINAL PROPONENTS

How was it then that with an empirical base as fragile as this, the coalition theory came to be so popular with some historians? What were its origins? How could it have come about? We give below the views of Harry Haig, Reginald Coupland, Maulana Abul Kalam Azad and Khaliquzzaman to answer these questions.

Harry Haig, the Governor of UP, was convinced before the elections were held, that there would be an alliance between the Congress and the Left wing of the Muslim League. This prediction was based not on the existence of any prior understanding between the Congress and the League (because there was none) but on Haig's reading of the possible election results. He was sure that the Congress would not be able to form a government on its own and would need the support of the Muslim League. His own estimate was that the Congress would get about 70 to 80 seats with about 15 sympathizers.[31] This estimate was partly based on talks with Tej Bahadur Sapru and Chintamani, editor of the *Leader*. The total number of Congress seats, thought Haig, might increase a little, 'but still no one seems to anticipate an actual majority for Congress'.[32]

A fortnight later, he admitted that the Congress prospects were improving, but not to the extent of getting a majority and that the margin between the Congress and its opponents 'may be so narrow so as to cause a good deal of embarrassment'.[33] In Haig's perception, thus, there was a certain inevitability about coalition. The government could be formed by the Congress *only* in an alliance. Such an alliance, Haig imagined, would only be with a *section* of Muslim League, ruling out the liberals and the NAPs. Khaliquzzaman, representing a section in the Muslim League that was sympathetic to Congress, seemed to Haig the obvious choice for such an alliance. He called this the Left wing of the League and estimated its possible strength in the Assembly to be about 15.

There was also a certain constitutional obligation. Section 52.1(A) of Government of India Act, 1935, stated that it was the governor's special responsibility to safeguard the 'legitimate interests of the minorities'.[34]

This was generally taken to mean that the minorities (read Muslims) should form one–third of the ministers in the cabinet, and it was the governor's job to see to that.

The election results far exceeded Haig's predictions. He now admitted that Congress would have a clear majority: 'In addition, they will presumably have some understanding with the Left wing of the Muslim League, from which no doubt they will take two ministers, and they might have in this way some 15 Muslim supporters.'[35] That Haig had ruled out even a theoretical probability of all the Muslim League legislators joining the Congress even after the coalition, becomes clear from his composition of the opposition:

> The opposition, so far as I can judge at present, will consist of about 50 Muslims, some of them returned as National Agriculturist candidates, some as Independents, *some as Muslim League*, but I think likely to coalesce into a definite Muslim party, very vigilant about Muslim interests. In addition, there will be perhaps 20 Hindus, five or six scheduled castes and about six Indian Christians, Europeans and Anglo-Indians.[36] (emphasis added)

Haig made it quite clear in his analysis that the UP Muslim League was far from being a monolithic organization. This seems a fairly obvious point, but has somehow not been taken serious note of by those historians who have argued about the Congress-League cooperation during the election. There were obviously diverse elements within the UP League with only one section with pro-Congress proclivities. S.R. Mehrotra has pointed out that there were three dominant strands within the UP Muslim League Parliamentary Board: one, which favoured an alliance with the NAPs; the second which consisted of Jinnah's followers pursuing a policy of non-alliance with any other political group; and the third that favoured cooperation with Congress. The last strand consisted of men like Khaliquzzaman, Hafiz Mohammad Ibrahim, Ali Zaheer, Saiduddin Khan and Suleiman Ansari.[37] These were the people who, Haig thought, would join the Congress, and it was with these people that coalition talks were to be held. Others in the League were clearly against it, and were trying to push it in different directions. And all these people, with the exception of Khaliquzzaman, ended up joining the Congress, coalition or no coalition. This will be discussed slightly later in this article.

To return to Haig, he had been proved both wrong and right. The Left wing of the Muslim League did join the Congress and one of them, Hafiz Ibrahim, was taken into the ministry. But all this happened without any coalition. The absence of a coalition became Haig's favourite reason to explain subsequent political developments in the Assembly. He witnessed the deteriorating Congress-League relations, the League's growing hostility towards the Congress and the series of accusations hurled against the Congress ministry by the Muslim League both inside and outside the Assembly. He examined these accusations and concluded that there was 'very little substance in them'; that they did not 'really merit any elaborate answer'; and that the League's criticism of the Congress ministry 'was a stock in the trade of Opposition', which was being 'made freely by the communalists on both the sides'.[38] Haig could see clearly that the Muslim League's charges, devoid of any basis, were politically motivated and would not have been made 'if the Muslim League had a share in the government'.[39] This, to Haig, was a case of 'opportunity lost'. A coalition made in 1937 would have led to cooperation between the arch enemies. Questions like coalition on whose terms, at what cost and the long term implications, would not have occurred to Haig. He was only trying to account for the growing hostility of the Muslim League towards the Congress and the absence of a coalition seemed a ready-made explanation. Tracing the history of Congress-League relations, Haig wrote to the Viceroy:

> The Congress had, since the general elections, been flirting with the Muslim League and suggesting some form of coalition. These conversations, resulted in the Muslim League holding aloof from my minority ministry. But when the Congress took office, they decided to reject the idea of a coalition with the Muslim League and to pursue instead a policy of direct approach to the Muslim masses. Had they entered into a coalition, I cannot help feeling that the Muslim solidarity would soon have been undermined. There are bound to be differences between the Muslims on the main agrarian and economic issues. The Muslims in office would have to make themselves responsible for definite policies in regard to these matters, they would have received the support of some Muslims and aroused the opposition of others. Nothing seems to be so effective in disintegrating a party as the taking of office.[40]

Haig's point was clear: the Muslim League in opposition could easily 'work up strong Muslim communal feelings'.

Haig's retrospection, though perfectly logical, misses out a central point. A coalition between Congress and the *whole* of the Muslim League was just not possible. It could take place only with a *section* of the League and, as has already been pointed out, this section (except Khaliquzzaman, of course) ended up joining the Congress. Haig himself had estimated in 1937 that the Congress would be joined only by a section of the Muslim League, the rest would be in Opposition.[41]

It should have been clear to Haig that Jinnah's influence on the League would ensure the impossibility of a coalition. In fact, as early as August 1936, he had narrated an incident to Linlithgow, hinting at a possible League-NAP connection.[42] There is no reference to any Congress-League coalition in Haig's pre-election analysis. Strangely enough, his obsession with the coalition as a solution to the communal problems continued till as late as October 1939, hardly three weeks before the Congress ministries resigned. Perhaps not fully aware of the direction in which the Muslim League had rapidly developed and continued to develop, Haig suggested to Kidwai, the acting premier, to expand the ministry and take two of Muslim League's representatives 'for I am convinced that we shall have no prospect of communal peace until this is done'.[43] Kidwai, while agreeing with Haig, pointed out to him 'the opposition of Jinnah who was not prepared to allow Muslim League to take office in Congress provinces unless it was done on an all India basis'.[44] Underestimating Jinnah's influence in the UP Muslim League, Haig also seemed attracted to the wisdom of this untried option. Thus three different situations—of Haig's prediction before the elections, there being no coalition, and the worsening communal situation—were being tied together in a cause-effect relationship.

Reginald Coupland, the unofficial British historian, believed that for the purpose of elections an understanding had developed between the League and the Congress, particularly in UP where a 'common platform' had been agreed upon. He said that 'the subsequent course of Hindu-Muslim relations and of the whole constitutional controversy would have been different if the Congress leaders had accepted the offer' made by Muslim League.[45] Such an understanding by Coupland seems to have been prompted by two considerations. Firstly, writing at an all India level, Coupland might have been unfamiliar with the complex nature of the Muslim League in UP as discussed above. Secondly, as a part of his general approach, he would have equated a Congress-League unity with Hindu-Muslim unity, with the two organizations representing the two religious communities. He understood the fissures in Indian society as reflecting a 'deep rooted antagonism' between the Hindus and the Muslims. The constitutional manifestation of this 'antagonism' lay, according to Coupland, in an unanimous rejection by the Muslims of 'majority rule in principle and of joint electorates in particular' ever since the beginning of elected representation. He classified the Congress as 'prominently Hindu in fact, though non-communal in principle'.[46] Little wonder, then, that he considered the Congress as essentially incapable of representing the Muslims. A coalition between the two organizations would, thus, appear to be the *only* way in which both Hindus and Muslims could be represented in the government.

Maulana Abul Kalam Azad, narrating the story of India's freedom in his autobiography written in post-Partition India, apparently wondered where things went wrong. Partition, to him, was a negation of his long cherished dream of a united India. In trying to explain this failure with hindsight and perhaps fading memory, 1937 appeared to him the turning point: 'Jawaharlal's action (of not agreeing to a coalition) gave the Muslim League in UP a new lease of life. All students of Indian politics know that it was from the UP that the League was reorganized. Mr. Jinnah took full advantage of the situation and started an offensive which ultimately led to Pakistan.'[47]

Interestingly, this was not how he looked at things in 1937 as one of the prominent actors. Replying to a query regarding a Congress-League coalition, Nehru thought that Azad was 'definitely' opposed to it.[48] Azad himself said, in an interview to the press, that there was no question of communal representation in the UP Assembly. When asked if the Congress would be ready to take one of the Muslim Leaguers, Maulana said: 'one man cannot serve two masters'. If any party wanted to join the Congress, 'it must give up its separate identity and identify itself with the Congress'.[49]

Khaliquzzaman's own version on the coalition might be considered authentic as coming straight from the horse's mouth, or alternatively, it might be taken with a pinch of salt because of his direct involvement in the coalition talks.[50] He had a personal stake in the coalition and would certainly have become a minister if the coalition had materialized. Haig had found Khaliquzzaman to be 'a man very anxious for office'[51] with 'personal ambitions and adroit manoeuverings'.[52] He was caught in a dilemma of negotiating a ministership with the Congress without wanting to abandon his base in the Muslim League. He refused to join Chhatari's ministry[53] for the reason that the 'new ministry could not last more than four months and that any one who joined it, would be politically discredited'.[54] It would have meant sinking his boat completely as far as the Congress was concerned. Knowing that his position in the Muslim League was precarious,[55] he started reaching out to Congress leaders, mainly Nehru and Pant,[56] at the risk of antagonizing other 'non-Congress Muslims'.[57] Haig's impression was that Khaliquzzaman's 'personal reception by Jawaharlal Nehru was not very cordial'.[58]

Khaliquzzaman's colleague in the Muslim League, Ali Zaheer, who resigned from it in the late 1930s, recalled in an interview, many years later, about how during the individual satyagraha of 1932, Khaliquzzaman had been nominated the 'dictator' of the Congress in Meerut and his job as a 'dictator' was to court arrest. But Khaliquzzaman escaped arrest and thereby let down the Congress 'and the whole movement practically came to a standstill (in Meerut) because of that'.[59] It is worth speculating whether this had anything to do with the 'cold reception' that he may have received from Nehru!

Khaliquzzaman failed to bring the League and the Congress together. He failed to obtain a minister's post in the Congress government, which went to Hafiz Mohammad Ibrahim who had joined the Congress after resigning from the League. He also ran the risk of losing his credibility within the League though this risk was overcome by his total and unconditional return to the League. But the failure of the coalition was also a personal failure for him, in more ways than one.

The origins of the coalition story, thus, lay in the political judgement of a governor, the paradigm of a contemporary historian, the hindsight of a nationalist leader and the personal experiences of a man who was trying to bring it about. The one thing that was common to their perception was that all of them emphasized the *desirability* of the coalition, completely overlooking its feasibility or otherwise. In other words: Was there coalition on the political agenda in UP in early 1937? And if it was, on whose agenda? Were the political forces moving towards an alliance between the Congress and the League in UP?

MEN 'FOR' AND 'AGAINST' THE COALITION IN THE CONGRESS AND THE LEAGUE

The complex nature of UP elections in 1937 still remains unfolded. The idea of coalition does not have any adequate empirical backing. Alliance finds no mention in the records of the two parties. But the various facets of the relationship between the two organizations remain unexplored. If cooperation was not the dominant theme, neither was hostility. The Muslim League's election campaign in UP centred around anti-imperialism and its rhetoric was, therefore, the same as that of the Congress.[60] At the local level certain instances of working with a common purpose are clearly visible. In Allahabad, Rafi Ahmad Kidwai raised Rs. 5,000 for Abdur Rahman, an activist of the Ahrar Party and the Muslim League candidate, to contest election against the NAP candidate.[61] Abdur Rahman eventually lost this election to a much stronger candidate, Nawab Mohammad Yusuf of NAP, who got nearly 73 per cent of total votes polled as against a mere

27 per cent for Abdur Rahman.[62] Shaukat Ali, while campaigning for the Muslim League candidate at Jhansi, asked Muslims to be sympathetic to the Congress and hinted at the possibility of an agreement between Jinnah and Nehru after the elections.[63] According to the CID report on Nehru's election tour, he regretted in his speeches the lack of Muslim Congress candidates and asked his audience to vote for a Muslim League candidate if he was either anti-government or if there was no Congress candidate contesting from a particular constituency.[64] This was later confirmed by Nehru himself.[65] In his note on the state of political parties at the end of 1936, Haig also mentioned that in western UP 'some propaganda [was] done for the League by the Congress [press]'.[66] The election campaign of the two organizations in UP generally avoided making hostile remarks against each other.[67]

There were many reasons for this. The active presence of the NAPs supported by the government had changed the complexion of the situation and had necessitated a fight between pro-government and anti-government candidates. 'As we looked upon the election campaign it was a tussle with the Agriculturist Party which was a wholly government party of big zamindars. The League was also opposing them and so inevitably our opposition to the League weakened. We did not want to split the forces opposed to pure reaction,' Nehru recalled.[68] This, it seems, was also the official Congress policy in UP. A circular issued to all the District Congress Committees stated that in the constituencies where there was no Congress candidate and if any candidate of the NAPs was contesting, Congressmen should lend support to his opponent.[69]

Vis-à-vis the League there was no clear-cut policy or any arrangement between the two, 'but a kind of convention developed'.[70] This observation of Nehru was substantiated by Ali Zaheer in an interview 30 years later. He recalled a kind of tacit understanding that the progressive elements among Muslims and Hindus would fight the elections on Muslim League and Congress tickets, respectively.[71] A coalition government was generally being anticipated because no one expected that any one party would get a clear majority in the legislatures.[72]

The election results proved them wrong, yet it was not an unblemished victory for the Congress; it had not won a single Muslim seat. 'Quite a piquant situation has arisen owing to Congressmen securing an absolute majority . . . coupled with Congress Muslim nominees' crushing defeat,' noted the *Leader*. 'The Muslim communalists would now vilify the Congress as a Hindu body of the province, if it decides to accept ministry.' However, it added: 'The trend of the talk is that the Congress will not enter a coalition, but if the inclusion of any strong member seems expedient, the Congress will insist on him, according to parliamentary procedure, to disown his former allegiance and to seek re-election on the Congress ticket.'[73]

Rajendra Prasad too ruled out the possibility of coalition with parties not accepting the Congress policy and programme.[74] Later he reiterated the same point specifically in relation to the Muslim League on the ground that the two were fundamentally different in their objectives and no coalition government could therefore be formed, if the Congress decided to accept office.[75] Nehru called it a 'discredited policy' and saw no reason why the Congress should go for it.[76] It had been a mistake, acknowledged Congress leaders even before the election results were out,[77] not to set up more Muslim candidates. This discrepancy had to be compensated for, in ways other than through a coalition with the Muslim League.

During the elections, the League had not been the main enemy. That position belonged to NAPs. The League's status in the eyes of Congress leadership was that of an enemy's enemy. But did that make the League an ally of Congress?

Certainly the Congress leadership did not think so. Any kind of coalition with the League was clearly not on their agenda. Some Muslims within the Congress were alarmed, for the rumours of a coalition which began spreading soon after the elections, would undermine their position within the Congress. Regarding a 'scheme that was being hatched . . . to bring about a coalition between Congress and League parties in the Assembly', Abdul Wali, an old Congressman from Lucknow, wrote to Nehru:

> To tell you the truth, I am deadly against it. My conviction is that the Congress will not be doing its duty to the Mussalmans of India if it ever thought of making pacts and coalitions with the Muslim League. The Congress belongs as much to the Mussalmans as to Hindus. It can very well make coalitions or enter into pacts with socialist groups—but it cannot do any such thing with any of the communal groups. That would mean that the Congress disowns that particular community. . . . My idea is that once the Congress enters into pact with the Muslim League, it loses the right to ask the Muslims to join it.[78]

Nehru replied in his characteristic way, expressing his firm opposition to all such pacts and compromises.[79] Since Pant, as alleged by Abdul Wali, was involved in the coalition talks, Nehru also conveyed to Pant his 'conviction' that any pact with the Muslim League would be 'highly injurious'.[80] Pant, in his reply, ruled out the possibility of any such talk of a pact.[81]

This was not all. There were other sections within the Congress, which looked upon the idea of a coalition with disfavour. Notable among them were the Socialists. The Congress Socialists resented any dealing with the Muslim League for a pact. Upon hearing of a move being made in that direction, they made a representation to Pant 'strongly urging him to drop the idea'.[82] If the version of the *Leader* is to be believed, the absence of a Congress-League alliance may have been a precondition behind the decision of the Socialists to accept office and join the ministry.[83]

The reasons for this aversion of the Left wingers to a Congress-League coalition should not be difficult to conjecture. To them, one very definite advantage of ministry making lay in the implementation of the agrarian tenancy legislation. It was unlikely that the Muslim League, with a strong landlord presence in it, would have gone along with the Congress in getting the tenancy bill passed. Sajjad Zaheer, a young Left wing Congressman closely associated with Nehru, pointed out this aspect in an article written many years later. The UP Muslim League in 1937 'was jaded with Muslim landlords and Nawabs'. Nehru's decision, supported by the Left forces to reject the compromise with the Muslim League was, therefore, 'correct'.[84]

But this was the Congress side of the story. What about the Muslim League? Forces in the Muslim League were moving in diverse directions. Those interested in entering office, hoped for an understanding with the Congress. Khaliquzzaman's early efforts were geared towards gaining the approval of the Congress. And so, when Chhatari convened a meeting exclusively of Muslim legislators, the Muslim Leaguers, under Khaliquzzaman's leadership, stayed away from it.[85] They also refused to join Chhatari's ministry.[86] The interim government was not going to last long and joining it would have destroyed all chances of an understanding with the Congress. Khaliquzzaman, therefore, kept in close touch with Pant, and tried hard for a 'close understanding between the Muslim League and Congress, in the hope that if the Congress came into power, they would have to take a Muslim minister from the Muslim League'.[87] Till as late as July 1937 he expressed the hope that the Congress would serve the country better by being in office.[88]

Khaliquzzaman's efforts and priorities came into direct conflict with the all India perspectives of Jinnah. Jinnah, at this stage, had started working towards the development of the Muslim League as an authoritative body of Indian Muslims. The Muslim League, under Jinnah's leadership, had not been very successful in utilizing the opportunities offered by provincial autonomy. Bengal and Punjab, the two most important Muslim majority provinces had thrown up inter-communal political formations, and the leaders there, Fazlul Haq of the Krishak Praja Party in Bengal and Sikander Hayat Khan of the Unionist Party in the Punjab, had shown little inclination towards the exclusively communal politics of the Jinnah variety, though retaining focus on Muslim seats.

The compulsions of the electoral politics containing separate electorates was that the Muslim League could not form a government in any province, on the basis of Muslim seats only. Herein lay the paradox—the practice of separate electorates, which activated and provided an incentive to communal politics, prevented its further advance into formal structures of power, which required a majority status. The problem was even more acute in a Muslim minority province like UP where the Muslim League, even if it won all Muslim seats (66 in a house of 228), would have to remain a party in opposition, or at best play a subordinate role to the party in power, depending on the goodwill of the majority party. Keeping these limitations in mind, learning the right lessons from the elections of 1937 and having been rebuffed by the leaders representing Muslims of the Muslim majority provinces, Jinnah proceeded to build his alternative politics of developing an all India political structure of Muslims. The politics of safeguards and concessions had been rendered obsolete and must then give way to a politics of seeking parity with the other all India structures. An inkling of Jinnah's renewed priorities could be seen in his election campaigns, particularly his reference to the 'Muslim India', as constituting a third force.

With this perspective, Jinnah decided to intervene in UP politics and take on Khaliquzzaman. He started with a statement barely days after the rumour regarding a coalition had got off the ground: 'I shall be glad if the Muslim League is not included in ministries in provinces where the majority does not want to seek itself [*sic*]. I hope Independent Muslims will refuse to sign the pledge of another party for the sake of ministries.'[89] If the Muslim League wanted a coalition, Jinnah said, it could be made with Chhatari's party. He initiated a talk of coalition with Chhatari[90] and drew satisfaction from the possibility of the Muslim members of the NAPs merging in the League.[91] Sensing the mood of a section of Muslim Leaguers in UP, he did not press for it, as it might have led to a split in his party. He asked the Congress to leave Muslim seats alone and called the Congress decision to contest the Bahraich Muslim seat 'a great mistake'.

The rift in the Muslim League in UP became sharper. Khaliquzzaman held important consultations with Nehru, and Nawab Ismail Khan told the Press that the majority of the Muslim Leaguers in UP were prepared to join the Congress.[92] Syed Mohammad Husain, Jinnah's representative in the UP Muslim League reacted strongly, criticizing the politics of the Left wing in the Muslim League of trying to follow the Congress line and betraying Jinnah. He warned the Muslims not to fall in the Congress trap and rally behind Jinnah instead.[93]

The battle continued without either side giving in. Which way the League's politics would go in UP depended on who was shaping it—Jinnah with his man, or Khaliquzzaman and his team. Jinnah declared that it would be useless for any individual to arrive at a settlement with a particular group and showed his disapproval of such a settlement with a direct warning to Khaliquzzaman:

> It is no use dealing with those men who are in and out of the Congress and in and out of the League, at one time with one and another time with the other, as it suits them. I am sure the Muslims of UP won't betray the Mussalmans of India and, therefore, any effort to settle by individuals which may be advantageous to them for the time being won't carry us anywhere. I have been promised by Mr. Khaliquzzaman . . . that he would let me know what the situation is in UP. I have sent him reminders and I am waiting to hear from him for the last three weeks, and I can't understand the mystery of his silence. I only trust he won't enter into any commitments which may be repudiated not only by Muslims of his province but by the Muslims of all India.[94]

Khaliquzzaman, did not yield, at least not at this stage. He retaliated:

> Mr. Jinnah has been carried away by half truths that were conveyed to him from interested quarters. When he will know the exact situation, I am sure that he will be sorry for having made some exaggerated statements. . . . My political efforts have always been directed and shall continue to be directed towards an honourable settlement with the majority community, with a view to make the freedom of the country easy of attainment. Mr. Jinnah should know that what I strive for is a settlement with a community and not with me personally.[95]

The expression 'freedom of the country' was a direct rebellion against Jinnah's leadership and a reminder to him that Khaliquzzaman, after all, was a Congressman inside the League, and therefore most suited to the task of carrying on negotiations with the Congress.

More threats to Jinnah followed. A subcommittee of the All India Muslim League under the presidentship of Nawab Ismail Khan recommended a change in the creed of the Muslim League to the 'attainment of the status of a free and independent country by India'. The committee also recommended the abolition of the office of permanent president and a complete reorganization of the League 'in order to make it truly representative of the Muslim masses'.[96] Jinnah dismissed the recommendations, called them 'entirely incorrect and misleading' and reiterated the old creed of the Muslim League (the attainment of full responsible government in India). He also denied that the office of the president was a permanent one.[97]

It was the Left wing of the UP League which was rising in rebellion. Jinnah had to put it down by asserting his all India authority. And so, a meeting of the Bombay Presidency Muslim League committee passed a resolution in the first week of May appealing to all the Muslim League legislators in UP not to act in such a way as to cause disunity among the Muslims of India by arranging sectional and provincial settlements with the Congress.[98]

Both the sides were heading for a showdown. Lucknow was to be the venue and the occasion was the meeting of the UP Muslim League Parliamentary Board to be held on 8 May and a general meeting of all the legislators convened by the Congress the next day. The Muslim League had, under Khaliquzzaman's leadership, given its consent for attending the Congress meeting.[99] Jinnah was now to use all his influence to prevent this from happening. Having arrived in Lucknow well before the League meeting, he declared: 'If I am not afraid of reactionaries, I am not afraid of the left wing opposition as well.' Criticizing Ahrars and Jamiyat al-ulama-i Hind for supporting the Congress, Jinnah made it clear that he would join hands neither with the Congress nor with British government. The *Leader* reported that Jinnah spoke in the vein of a Hitler or a Mussolini.[100] Jinnah's campaign looked likely to be successful. 'Mr. Jinnah's presence had its effect and none (from the League) now talks of joining the Congress. None should be surprised if the UPML Parliamentary Board decides on non-participation in the meeting of May 9th convened by Mr. Pant,' noted the *Leader*.[101]

This was what actually happened. The League Parliamentary Board decided that 'it cannot and should not join the Congress in its policy and programme of wrecking the constitution' and added that cooperation in other fields, excluding separate electorates and Communal Award, could be explored on the basis of work in the legislature. This ruled out the possibility of Muslim League legislators attending the Congress meeting the next day. The League board placed on record 'its complete confidence in the policy initiated and pursued by Mr. Jinnah and assures him of its loyal and unqualified support'.[102]

This was Jinnah's victory—absolute and complete. Although Khaliquzzaman attended the Congress meeting in his individual capacity, he had clearly surrendered.[103] Jinnah had triumphed in imposing his all India priorities on the UP League.

Why did Khaliquzzaman surrender? Did he earlier overestimate his support base in the League? Did he fail to convert, as he was hoping to, more League legislators to his pro-Congress stand? Was it, as the *Leader* pointed out, 'Mr. Jinnah's presence and his forceful convincing speech',[104] which turned the tables on him? Was it because he did not receive the right signals from the Congress leaders to head for a confrontation with Jinnah? Or was it his fear of being left in the lurch? It is interesting to note that Khaliquzzaman did not resign from the League to join Congress as had been done by his colleague Hafiz Ibrahim two months earlier. As it happened, the ministerial seat went to Hafiz Ibrahim and not to Khaliquzzaman who had been trying very hard for it.

Whatever be the explanation for Khaliquzzaman's defeat in Lucknow during that crucial phase, the coalition story for all practical purposes ended here, even though it was to linger on till July 1937.[105]

THE CONSEQUENCE

The failure to arrive at an understanding with Khaliquzzaman on mutually accepted terms meant that the Muslim League party under his leadership would sit in opposition.[106] The Congress on its part chose Rafi Ahmad Kidwai and Hafiz Ibrahim as Muslim ministers in a cabinet of six. This arrangement continued till October 1939 when the Congress ministries resigned and walked out of the legislatures. Many developments of this period, as also the subsequent intensification of communal politics, have been attributed to the failure of a 'coalition' to materialize. For instance, some of the observations made were: 'the absence of a substantial Muslim component with the Congress legislative party made it insensitive to Muslim sensibilities' and rendered its secular image vulnerable;[107] it led to increasing communal trouble and the widening of the gulf between the two communities;[108] it was a blunder, by Congress, of the first order;[109] and 'a fatal error, the prime cause of the creation of Pakistan'.[110] Immediately after the breakdown of the coalition, signs of a rupture began to appear in the UP Muslim League. Three of its members denounced the League activities in a statement, resigned from its membership and joined Congress.[111] The *Leader* estimated that the total number of imminent defection of Muslim legislators, both Independent and Leaguers, to the Congress would be about 12.[112] Notable among these Muslim legislators were Suleiman Ansari and Saiduddin Ahmad (from Muslim League) and

Abdul Hakim and Mohammad Husain (Independent).[113] A little later, prominent Muslim Leaguers like Sir Wazir Hasan and Ali Zaheer also resigned from the League.[114] These were initial setbacks for the Muslim League.

It has been pointed out that as a result of the Congress 'high handedness', the Muslim League consolidated its position in the bye-elections.[115] But a close examination of the results of the bye-elections for Muslim seats gives interesting information. In the two bye-elections held before July, the League and the Congress had won one seat each, with the Bahraich seat going to the Congress and the Jhansi-Jalon-Hamirpur seat won by the Muslim League candidate, Rafiuddin Ahmad (2,652 votes, 58.7 per cent) defeating N.A. Sherwani of the Congress (1,915 votes, 41.93 per cent). Of the remaining six bye-elections, the Muslim League won four, the Congress one and one more seat went to an Independent supported by the Congress. The Congress had not contested any of these six seats earlier during the general elections and it improved its position considerably by getting 77.57 per cent, 45.13 per cent, 40.84 per cent, 34.19 per cent and 24.97 per cent of the votes for the five Muslim seats, the sixth seat going uncontested in favour of the Independent candidate. On the whole the Congress got 16,076 votes in these bye-elections as against 16,918 votes obtained by the Muslim League. The percentage of votes polled by the Congress in these five constituencies was 48.7 as against 51.3 polled by the Muslim League.

The scenario inside the Assembly does not appear to have been decisively influenced by the absence of Congress-League cooperation. Muslims voted both for and against the Congress motions, although the number of Muslim legislators voting for the Congress motions was much less (about 8) compared to those against them (from 37 to 40).[116] Till the end of 1939, when the Congress government resigned, Muslim League had not been able to claim the allegiance of most of the Independent Muslim legislators.

LESSONS, PRIORITIES AND OPTIONS

To sum up, the various possibilities that existed in 1937 can best be seen in the light of the political priorities of the two leading organizations in UP. The general elections of 1937 brought home different lessons to be learnt and different options to be explored by both the Congress and the Muslim League.

To the Congress a very real option was to accept or not to accept office. Once it resolved to accept office, its chief task was to maintain its cohesiveness and its all India character and also implement, as far as possible, its programme in the legislature. A major lesson to be learnt was its poor record in the Muslim constituencies. This had implications for the Congress claims of representing all groups and communities. The Muslim absence was also capable of weakening its fight against the British government. Therefore, some method of representing Muslims had to be evolved. One option was that of indirectly representing them through an alliance with a political party that claimed to represent Muslims. This avenue was open to the Congress in 1937 in UP. But major political differences between the Congress and the League did not admit of such an easy option. After the Lucknow Pact of 1916, there had not been instances of the Congress and the League working together. Differences had cropped up on the Nehru Report (1928) and the Communal Award (1932). Jinnah and Rajendra Prasad, in their capacities as the leaders of two different political organizations, had discovered in 1935 how difficult it was to arrive at mutually acceptable political positions.[117] As public organizations, the Congress and the League had marched along very different lines through the decades of the twentieth century and a mere commonality in their opposition to the Federation scheme or to the Government of India Act, 1935, was not enough to bring them together. Their differences were real and could not be brushed aside.

Also, a coalition with the Muslim League would not ensure Muslim participation in the Congress movements. The League leadership had not been very enthusiastic about anti-British agitations and was unlikely to join the Congress, in case the Congress decided to resort to agitational politics. The proposed coalition would be confined to legislative activities and by nature was bound to be short lived. To choose the option of an alliance with the Muslim League the Congress would have had to overcome the earlier mentioned constraints and also bear the burden of certain disadvantages—like antagonizing Congress Muslims and compromising their programme in the legislature. A coalition would have appeared to Congress leadership as an option, which demanded making great efforts (overcoming political differences with Muslim League) and paying too much of a price (antagonizing Congress Muslims and damaging its secular credentials) to gain a political advantage (Muslim support). This could, at best, be short lived and confined to legislative activities, and at worst, highly unlikely to materialize.

The alternative was to gain Muslim support by making a direct appeal to Muslims to bring them into the Congress fold. This was, then, the background of the agenda to start a Muslim mass contact programme. It was likely to fulfil the Congress aspirations of being truly a representative organization. But it contained the risk of antagonizing the Muslim League. It is, therefore, not surprising that the launching of the Muslim mass contact programme by Congress, more than anything else, earned the hostility of the Muslim League and motivated it to launch a massive anti-Congress campaign.

The lessons for the Muslim League were equally unambiguous. Provincial autonomy with increased franchise brought home the importance of mass politics but also the severe limitations of pursuing minority politics. Khaliquzzaman knew that the party he led in UP, could not contest more than 66 seats in a house of 228, and it could, at best, play the role of a pressure group, a subordinate ally to the party in power, or a formidable opposition. To be able to fulfil the first two options, the League would have to seek an alliance with the Congress. But a coalition was rendered unnecessary by the election results giving the Congress a clear majority, and made unattainable by Jinnah's intervention in UP. Also, a coalition with Congress would serve no purpose unless the Muslim League was acknowledged as the sole spokesman of Indian Muslims. Jinnah ridiculed the Congress for even contesting the bye-elections for Muslim seats. The Congress' response to this was the Muslim mass contact programme. Herein lay the real conflict between the two. Accepting Jinnah's condition would have meant the Congress abdicating its role of representing Muslims by conceding this position to the Muslim League and thereby reducing itself to being a Hindu organization. The Muslim mass contact programme of the Congress, on the other hand, threatened, to reduce the Muslim League into a politically insignificant élite group if it were successful. It was suicidal for both to accept each other's conditions.

The lesson, therefore, for the Congress was to go ahead with the mass contact programme to bring Muslims into its fold. The lesson for the League was to deny Congress the right to speak for Indian Muslims and create an all India political structure of Indian Muslims under the exclusive leadership of the Muslim League. A coalition government of the Congress and the League in UP in 1937, though very much on the agenda of a few individuals, was completely marginal and actually contradictory to the long-term schemes of both the organizations.

The purpose of this article is not to contest the hypothetical observation that the absence of the coalition, *along with other factors*, created conditions for the intensification of hostile communal politics, leading eventually to Partition. Perhaps it did. It is always difficult to empirically demonstrate—for or against—speculative conjectures constructed with hindsight. The central idea in this article is to argue against the view that objective forces were moving towards a Congress-League alliance and that a coalition was aborted by the Congress after the mandate it received from the election results.

The attempt in this article has been to demonstrate (a) that the argument advocating the coalition is based on faulty empirical premises; (b) that forces in the pre-election period were not moving in any one direction (to necessarily culminate in a coalition) but in a variety of directions and that there was nothing predestined about the coalition; (c) that the actors for and against the coalition in both the organizations were unevenly distributed with only one group keen on a coalition; and (d) that to form or not to form a coalition was a strategic question to be decided by the top leaders of the two organizations keeping in mind their long term goals and priorities. Seen from the vantage point of UP in 1939, the Partition of India did not seem inevitable. Even a keen observer of the UP scenario in 1939 could not have foreseen the Partition a decade later.

NOTES

1. Besides others, the notable believers in the coalition theory, are Beni Prasad, *Hindu-Muslim Questions* (Allahabad, 1941), pp. 61-2; R. Coupland, *Indian Politics, 1936-42* (Oxford, 1944), pp. 110-12; R.C. Mazumdar, *History of the Freedom Movement in India*, Vol. III (Calcutta, 1963), p. 563; Penderel Moon, *Divide and Quit* (London, 1964), p. 15; H.V. Hodson, *The Great Divide: Britain, India, Pakistan* (London, 1967), pp. 66-7; B.B. Misra, *The Indian Political Parties: An Historical Analysis of Political Behaviour upto 1947* (Delhi, 1976), pp. 420-5; Mukul Kesavan, '1937 as a Landmark in the Course of Communal Politics in UP', Occasional Paper, Second Series No. XI, 1988, Nehru Memorial Museum & Library, New Delhi (hereafter NMML), B.B.Misra, *The Unification and Division of India* (Oxford, 1990), pp. 318-22; Deepak Pandey, *The Role of the Muslim League in National Politics* (Delhi, 1991), p. 48; Sharif-al-Mujahid, *Quaid-i-Azam Jinnah, Studies in Interpretation* (Delhi, 1993), p. 167; and Mushirul Hasan, ed., *India's Partition: Process, Strategy and Mobilisation* (Delhi, 1993), pp. 9-12.

   Amongst those historians who do not attach a decisive importance to the coalition theory in the Partition of India, mention must be made of S.R.Mehrotra, 'The Congress and the Partition of India' and B.R. Nanda, 'Nehru, Indian National Congress and the Partition of India, 1937-47', in Philips and Wainwright, eds., *The Partition of India: Policies and Perspectives, 1935-47* (London, 1970), pp. 193-8 and 156-7; S. Gopal, *Jawaharlal Nehru: A Biography*, Vol. I (Delhi, 1976), pp. 223-4; Uma Kaura, *Muslims and Indian Nationalism* (New Delhi, 1977), pp. 114-16; Michael Brecher, *Nehru: A Political Biography* (London, 1959), pp. 231-2; and Bimal Prasad, 'Congress Versus the Muslim League', in Sisson and Wolpert, eds, *Congress and Indian Nationalism: The Pre-Independence Phase* (New Delhi, 1988).
2. P. D. Reeves, B.D. Graham and J.M. Goodman, *A Handbook to Elections in Uttar Pradesh* (New Delhi, 1975), pp. 246-7.

3. *Leader*, 18 July 1937.
4. Ibid., 21 July 1937.
5. Kesavan, op.cit.
6. Misra, *The Indian Political Parties*, op.cit., p. 421.
7. B. Shiva Rao, 'India, 1935-47', in Philips and Wainwright, eds, op.cit., p. 419.
8. Kesavan, op.cit., p. 5.
9. 'Between the League and the Congress, the only two organised political parties in UP, there was hardly any difference in ideas and programmes save on the communal representation. The electoral programmes of the two were also very nearly the same in all essential matters and the leaders of the two organisations fought the elections on more or less common platform', R.C. Mazumdar, op.cit., p. 465. Also see, Mushirul Hasan, op.cit., p. 9.
10. Kesavan, op.cit., p. 7.
11. Lance Brennan, 'The Illusion of Security: The Background to Muslim Separatism in the United Provinces', in *Modern Asian Studies*, Vol. XVIII, No. 2 (1984), p. 260.
12. Z.H. Zaidi, 'Aspects of the Development of the Muslim League Policy, 1934-47', in Philips and Wainwright, eds, op.cit., p. 256.
13. Ibid.
14. The evidence that comes closest to suggesting an alliance is an interview with Sampurnanand held in 1968 by Hari Dev Sharma. Sampurnanand, who joined the Congress ministry as the minister for education in 1938, recalled that 'There was an alliance certainly [which]... broke off. The Muslim League could say with some show of reason that they did not receive a fair deal,' Oral History Transcript, NMML. But interestingly Sampurnanand speaks with a lot less certainty about the supposed alliance in his autobiography: 'It has been asserted that there was some kind of understanding between the Congress and the League. In any case, the two did not oppose each other's candidates', Sampurnanand, *Memories and Reflections* (Bombay, 1962), p. 95. It is also interesting to note that the Socialist Party of which he was an active member, was completely against having anything to do with the Muslim League. 'Congress-League pact in UP—Socialists' strong opposition', noted the *Leader* of 20 July 1937. 'Congress Socialists strongly reject the intended pact between the Congress and the League. It is understood that representation has been made to Mr. Pant strongly urging him to drop the idea', ibid.
15. Ibid., 9 January 1937.
16. Reeves, et al., op.cit., pp. 303-6.
17. Statement to the press, 18 September 1936, S. Gopal, ed., *Selected Works of Jawaharlal Nehru* (hereafter *SWJN*), Vol. VII (New Delhi, 1975), p. 468.
18. For an elaboration of this argument, see Bimal Prasad, op.cit., p. 310.
19. *Leader*, 27 January 1937; and *Pioneer*, 24 January 1937.
20. *Leader*, 7 March 1937.
21. Quoted in M.A.H. Ispahani, *Qaid-i-Azam Jinnah as I Knew Him* (Karachi, 1967), p. 31.
22. *Leader*, 22 March 1937.
23. Ibid., 10 April 1937.
24. AICC Newsletter in P. N. Chopra, ed., *Towards Freedom, 1937-47, Vol. I : Experiment with Provincial Autonomy, 1 January-31 December 1937* (hereafter *TF*) (New Delhi, 1985), pp. 47-8.
25. *Leader*, 10 July 1937.

26. Reeves, et al., op.cit., p. 309. B.B. Misra is factually inaccurate when he says that Kidwai entered the legislature through the graduate constituency, B.B. Misra, *Unification and Division of India*, op.cit., p. 319.
27. For the Congress manifesto, see *SWJN*, op cit., pp. 459-64.
28. For the Muslim League's manifesto, see Sharif-al-Mujahid, op.cit., pp. 482-7.
29. R.C. Mazumdar, op.cit., p. 465; Peter Hardy, *The Muslims of British India* (Cambridge, 1972), p. 224; Mushirul Hasan, op.cit., p. 9; S. Gopal, op.cit., p. 223; Deepak Pandey, op.cit., pp. 37-8; and Kesavan, op.cit., p. 8; among others.
30. Anita Inder Singh, *The Origins of the Partition of India, 1936-47* (Delhi, 1987), p. 8.
31. Letter to Linlithgow, 6 January 1937, *TF*, p. 21.
32. Ibid., p. 18.
33. Ibid., p. 78.
34. *The Government of India Act, 1935* (Delhi, 1937), p. 36.
35. Letter to Linlithgow, 13 February 1937, Haig Papers (on microfilm), Roll No. 2, NMML.
36. Ibid.
37. S.R. Mehrotra, op.cit., p. 195.
38. Letter to Linlithgow, 10 May 1939, Haig Papers, Roll No. 2.
39. Ibid.
40. Draft letter, undated, 1939, ibid.
41. Letter to Linlithgow, 13 February 1937, ibid.
42. Jinnah had a long meeting with the Raja of Jahangirabad, 'a thorough going conservative and always ready to support Government'. Jinnah persuaded him to stand as an Independent candidate in return for the League not fielding a candidate against him. Haig to Linlithgow, 24 August 1937, ibid. Interestingly, out of the 37 seats that the League contested, it was pitched against the NAP candidates in only 10 seats.
43. Letter to Linlithgow, 8 October 1939, ibid., Roll No. 1.
44. Ibid.
45. Coupland, op.cit., p. 15.
46. Ibid., p. v.
47. Abul Kalam Azad, *India Wins Freedom* (Bombay, 1959), p. 160.
48. Letter to Abdul Wali, 30 March 1937, *SWJN*, op cit., p. 77.
49. *Leader*, 15 July 1937.
50. Choudhry Khaliquzzaman, *Pathway to Pakistan* (Lahore, 1961), pp. 160-8.
51. Letter to Linlithgow, 31 March 1937, *TF*, p. 310.
52. Letter to Linlithgow, 7 May 1937, *TF*, p. 479.
53. After Congress' refusal to form the government, the governor had invited the Nawab of Chhatari, leader of the NAPs, to form a government. Chhatari formed an interim government in April. Khaliquzzaman and his supporters refused to join Chhatari's government on the ground that the new government did not represent the will of the people. However, the Raja of Salempur, another prominent League leader in UP, did join Chhatari's government and became a minister.
54. Letter to Linlithgow, 31 March 1937, *TF*, p. 310.
55. Ibid.
56. Khaliquzzaman was a close associate of Nehru but they had drifted apart in 1936 after he had joined the League. Nehru had expressed his displeasure at Khaliquzzaman joining the 'reactionaries', Nehru's letter to Abdul Wali, 30 March 1937, *SWJN*, op.cit., p. 77.

57. Haig to Linlithgow, 22 April 1937, *TF*, p. 422.
58. Haig to Linlithgow, 7 May 1937, *TF*, p. 479.
59. Interview with S. Ali Zaheer by B.R. Nanda, Oral History Transcript, NMML.
60. For the anti-imperialist thrust of the Muslim League's election campaign, see the 'Weekly Reports' prepared by UP Intelligence, on political activities (hereafter WRPA), available at the Intelligence Headquarters, Lucknow. See specially, Nos 6 (b), 1937; 24 (c), 1937; 54 (b and c), 1937; and 37 (b), 1937.
61. Ibid., No. 19, 1937.
62. Reeves, et al., op.cit., p. 299.
63. WRPA No. 54(c), 1937.
64. Ibid., No. 65 (c), 1937.
65. 'During my tours where there was no Congress Muslim candidate, I usually supported the League candidate, if he was not an obvious reactionary as sometimes he was', letter to Rajendra Prasad, 21 July 1937, *SWJN*, op cit., p. 166.
66. Haig's note, undated, Haig Papers, Roll No. 2.
67. 'During the general elections in UP there was not much conflict between the Congress and the League. It was the desire of both parties to avoid a conflict as much as possible and to accommodate each other', Nehru to Rajendra Prasad, 21 July 1937, *SWJN*, op cit., p. 165.
68. Ibid., p. 166.
69. *Leader*, 2 February 1937.
70. Nehru to Prasad, 21 July 1937, *SWJN*, op cit., p. 166.
71. S. Ali Zaheer uses the term 'advanced sections' but it is quite clear that he refers to progressive, Oral History Transcript, NMML.
72. Ibid.
73. *Leader*, 6 March 1937.
74. Ibid., 4 March 1937.
75. Ibid., 8 March 1937.
76. 'We have thought for long in terms of pacts and compromises between communal leaders and neglected the people behind them. That is a discredited policy and I trust that we shall not revert to it', address to Congress Legislators, 19 March 1937, *SWJN*, op cit., p. 62.
77. Bhulabhai Desai on UP elections, *Leader*, 31 January 1937, and Nehru's speech at Ara, ibid., 3 February 1937.
78. Letter to Nehru, 28 March 1937, *TF*, p. 289.
79. Letter to Abdul Wali, 30 March 1937, *SWJN*, op cit., p. 77.
80. Letter to Pant, 30 March 1937, *TF*, p. 78.
81. Letter to Nehru, ibid., 2 April 1937, p. 328.
82. *Leader*, 20 July 1937.
83. Ibid., 21 July 1937.
84. 'Notes on Hindu-Muslim Unity', *Mainstream*, Vol. V (17 June 1967), pp. 28 and 29.
85. *Leader*, 4 March 1937.
86. Ibid., 6 April 1937.
87. Haig's letter to Linlithgow, 7 May 1937, *TF*, p. 479.
88. *Leader*, 10 July 1937.
89. Ibid., 15 March 1937.
90. Ibid.

91. Ibid., 22 March 1937.
92. Ibid., 23 April 1937.
93. Ibid., 21 April 1937.
94. Statement to the press, 26 April 1937, *TF*, p. 428.
95. *Leader*, 28 April 1937.
96. Ibid., 4 May 1937.
97. Ibid., 5 May 1937.
98. Ibid., 6 May 1937.
99. Ibid., 28 April 1937.
100. Ibid., 9 May 1937.
101. Ibid.
102. Ibid., 10 May 1937.
103. Surprisingly, Khaliquzzaman makes no mention of the May meeting in his book.
104. *Leader*, 10 May 1937.
105. A long letter from Nehru to Rajendra Prasad (21 July 1937, *SWJN*, op cit., pp. 165-71), gives details of the last effort made by Khaliquzzaman in July regarding a position in the ministry. It appears he was willing to give a 'blank cheque' if he and Nawab Ismail Khan were included in the ministry. Nehru 'disliked the bargaining for seats in the ministry'. This dislike, according to Nehru, was shared by others in the Congress. Yet, in spite of all the risks that it involved (pp. 168-9), they were attracted to the possibility of the UP League being wound up. So 'stringent' conditions were offered for the inclusion of two Muslim Leaguers in the ministry. The Congress policy in the legislature was to be accepted *in toto;* all the League legislators were to become members of the Congress legislative party and abide by its discipline; they were to support the Congress candidate in the bye-elections; and go along with the Congress party if it resigned from the ministry. These were difficult conditions and Khaliquzzaman had no authority to accept them. The official coalition talks thus ended.

    It should be clear from the preceding discussion that it was a complete miscalculation on Nehru's part to hope for a winding up of the League Parliamentary Board through an agreement with Khaliquzzaman. He could not possibly carry the UP League with him even in March/April when he had greater control over it. In May it had become an impossibility after Jinnah's intervention in UP and Khaliquzzaman's surrender to him. Quite obviously, he did not have much of a 'blank cheque' to offer.
106. Khaliquzzaman, op.cit., p. 161.
107. Kesavan, op.cit., pp. 29-30.
108. Coupland, op.cit., p. 184.
109. Hodson, op.cit., p. 67.
110. Penderel Moon, op.cit., p. 15.
111. *Leader*, 25 July 1937.
112. Ibid., 24 July 1937.
113. Ibid., 3 July and 11 July 1937.
114. These defections should not be attributed merely to the formation of government by the Congress. Quite the opposite happened in Bihar where a number of Muslims left the Congress to join the Muslim League, following the Congress decision to form a government, see Papiya Ghosh, 'The Making of Congress Muslim Stereotype: Bihar, 1937-39', in *IESHR*, Vol. XXVIII, No. 4 (October-December 1991), p. 424.
115. Misra, *Indian Political Parties*, op.cit., p. 432. However, his statement 'of the four

bye-elections held in UP, the League won four' is factually incorrect. Out of a total of eight bye-elections that were held for Muslim seats, the Muslim League won five (Reeves, et al., op.cit., pp. 311-14). Of these eight, two had been held before the coalition talks began.

116. *Proceedings of UP Legislative Assembly*, Vols I-XXI (Central Secretariat Library, New Delhi, 1937-9).

117. For the details of Rajendra Prasad-Jinnah talks, see G-65/ 1937, All India Congress Committee Papers, NMML.

The North-West Frontier Province and the Partition, 8 August-15 September 1947: A View from the Top

PARSHOTAM MEHRA

Contrary to popular belief that the major brunt of the Partition in terms of large scale communal riots and mass killings, arson and loot, followed by massive migrations of populations was borne by people in the Punjab and Delhi, the harsh truth is that the North-West Frontier Province too was deeply involved. Sadly though, happenings there have been largely overshadowed by greater tragedies elsewhere. This largely because being a predominantly Muslim province, its Hindu-Sikh minorities, small in numbers, were relatively ill organized and eventually provided scope for only a one-way human traffic. In the event, the still, feeble voice of the non-Pakhtun, non-Muslim adjunct of the population was drowned in the cacophony of all that was happening on both sides of the divide in the Punjab, and, nearer home, in Delhi.

There is another aspect of the Frontier scenario that deserves attention. The Congress ministry headed by the veteran Dr Khan Sahib, elder brother of the better-known Abdul Ghaffar Khan, the Frontier Gandhi, was accused by its political rivals of being pronouncedly anti-Muslim and of running a pro-Hindu outfit. All the same, the confidence it had long inspired in the miniscule Hindu-Sikh minority in the province was now (in August 1947) fast eroding. For as the days closed around it, the Congress ministry's capacity for effective governance seems to have well-nigh vanished. Thus, when it came to the crunch, the two small minority

*It is a pleasure to record my debt of deep gratitude to S.D. Bambri, Manager of the *Tribune* (Chandigarh), who made it possible for me to dig up some old issues of the paper; to the Librarian and staff of the Nehru Memorial Museum & Library, for all the help they rendered in filling up some vital gaps; and above all, to my old friend and colleague, S.R. Bakshi, who all through has been very cooperative and understanding.

communities found themselves out on a limb as it were; they were political orphans, virtually helpless.

Another source of stability and strength to the province, and not to the minorities only, had been the provincial governor. Sadly, the brief if troubled tenure of Sir Olaf Caroe (March 1946-June 1947) was mired in a raging conflict with the Khan Sahib ministry, and much else besides. He was succeeded as a *locum tenens*, by an army commander, Lt. Gen. Sir Rob Lockhart, who was later to be Commander-in-Chief of the Indian Army. His singularly brief, less than eight-week tenure (24 June-11 August 1947), was largely preoccupied with the holding of a referendum.

Sir Rob's successor, hand-picked by the Quaid-i-Azam, was an old Frontier hand, who had earlier held office for almost a decade, 1937-46. Widely respected, Sir George Cunningham had been a tower of strength to the province and its government.[1] And, no doubt, to its minorities. Apart from being an efficient administrator, Cunningham was a meticulous and dispassionate chronicler. The paragraphs that follow about all that happened on the Frontier in the week preceding the Partition and the few that followed it rest largely, if not indeed wholly, on entries in the governor's personal diary,[2] which have been supplemented, where necessary, by reports in contemporary newspapers.

Two brief footnotes may be in order. Sir George Cunningham, who retired as governor on 2 March 1946, was succeeded by Sir Olaf Caroe. The latter's brief, barely 15-month tenure was, as noticed in a preceding paragraph, riven by acute controversy. The main was the well-nigh running battle with his premier, the redoubtable Dr Khan Sahib, who enjoyed a convincing majority in the provincial legislature. Nor was that all. For Sir Olaf had also fallen foul with the head of the Interim Government in New Delhi. Jawaharlal Nehru, it may be recalled, had been sworn in on 2 September 1946 and entrusted *inter alia* with the charge of the foreign department. The latter *included* tribal affairs which, at the provincial level, fell within the purview of the governor in his capacity as Agent to the Governor-General.

In the wake of some aerial bombing of the tribal territory (August end-early September) there was an outcry that the freshly-inducted Hindu member of the Viceroy's Executive Council, was personally responsible for this barbarous act. To refute this blatant lie and, in no small measure, this adverse criticism, Nehru decided to visit the tribal areas to see things for himself. The decision evoked a powerful negative response from the provincial governor who was strongly persuaded that in the then highly surcharged sectarian feelings in the country as a whole, the visit was inopportune and would only help to stoke the fires of strong communal passions.

And so it did. For his part Nehru held Sir Olaf, and his political officers, partly, if not indeed wholly, responsible for the less-than-friendly, even hostile, reception accorded to him and his entourage during their four-day sojourn in the tribal territory.[3]

Sir Olaf's relations with his council of ministers, bad as they were, became markedly worse in the wake of Nehru's October visit. Not long thereafter, the provincial Muslim League launched its so-called civil disobedience campaign of hatred and calumny, against the incumbent Congress government. The latter on their part, felt convinced that the governor gave both overt as well as covert support to their political rivals. In the event, there was hardly any meeting of minds between the governor and his council of ministers. And, as the months rolled by, relations became considerably strained.[4]

Meanwhile all visitors to Government House in Peshawar, including the Governor-General Wavell (November 1946), Pug Ismay, Lord Mountbatten's Chief of Staff and the Viceroy himself (April 1947), carried the unmistakable impression that Caroe was at once high-strung and edgy and not truly in control of men and affairs. In the final count when, in terms of the 3 June Plan, it was decided to hold a referendum in the Frontier on the question of its joining the Indian or the Pakistani Constituent Assembly, Caroe, whom his ministers had charged with being highly partisan, was eased out of office, his place being taken by Sir Rob Lockhart in an interim arrangement.[5]

Caroe and his friends had much hoped that in the wake of the Frontier deciding to cast its lot with Pakistan, the Quaid would opt for his return to Government House in Peshawar. Sadly for them, Jinnah decided not to, and chose instead to recall Sir George Cunningham.[6] The latter took over on 12 August 1947 and after the birth of Pakistan two days later remained in the saddle for a little over seven months, until March-end 1948. Our narrative starts with his arrival in London (8 August) on his way to Peshawar via Karachi and New Delhi.

At the India Office (London), George Cunningham learnt that on Rob Lockhart's advice and the demand of the Pakistan provisional government, the governor was to dismiss the Khan Sahib ministry on the evening of 11 August or the morning of 12 August. And with George Cunningham's own taking over (12/13 August) he was 'at once' to call the Muslim League to form a government.

The governor-designate was 'horrified' by these suggestions, which he deemed 'constitutionally improper'. Moreover, local feelings could have been 'unnecessarily embittered' and 'serious trouble' probably started even before he arrived and took over. Cunningham fully endorsed the India Office stance that (a) dismissal 'without any choice of dissolution' would be unconstitutional when the Ministry still had a majority in the legislature; and (b) Section 93 rule was 'obviously not required' for law and order purposes and so was also unconstitutional. In any case, His Majesty's Government should 'hold its hand' before 15 August and leave it to the Pakistan government to decide for itself after that date.[7]

A brief digression may be in order. The recent recommendation by the Union Cabinet (September 1998) for the imposition of President's rule in Bihar by invoking Article 356 bears a mention. This article of the Indian Constitution (1950) was patterned closely on Section 93 of the Government of India Act, 1935. Here too the Cabinet's plea was the breakdown of law and order while the state government enjoyed a convincing majority in the (state) legislature. The President turned down the recommendation and asked for its reconsideration.

II

To revert to the Frontier. On 9 August 1947 news arrived that the Viceroy had suggested to the Quaid 'to discuss' the whole question of the fate of the Khan Sahib ministry with George Cunningham when he arrived in Karachi. All this while, the Inspector General (Police) and the Area Commander (Army) in Peshawar were 'very nervous' about any breaches of peace that might occur in the event of the Congress government being sacked, and expressed the view that in a couple of months after he (George Cunningham) had had time 'to exert some influence', things might look up.[8]

While in Karachi on 10 August, Cunningham had a 'two hour solid' meeting with Jinnah, who felt 'bitterly' about Mountbatten's change of stance and appeared to suggest that Cunningham might do the trick for him. For his part, the governor-designate was unfazed: 'I made it clear pretty quickly', he noted, that he would not oblige the Quaid. All the same, he was worried that 'whatever assurances' Dr Khan Sahib held out to him (George Cunningham), the Quaid 'could not trust' them.

Nor was that all. Jinnah was clear in his mind that Dr Khan Sahib 'meant to sabotage' the whole idea of Pakistan. On being repeatedly asked —'three or four times'—to spell out what he meant, the Quaid refused to elaborate and confined himself to some 'vague statements'. No wonder, Cunningham felt 'rather annoyed' at Jinnah's refusal to 'take me fully into confidence'.[9]

In Peshawar, on 13 August 1947, Cunningham repeated to Dr Khan Sahib all that had transpired between him and the Quaid, reiterating the position that the 'only grounds' on which he would consider dismissing the premier were: (a) 'If he (Dr Khan Sahib) insisted on declaring' that Pakhtunistan would be an independent state; and (b) 'If he (Dr Khan Sahib) failed to satisfy' him (Cunningham) that the premier meant generally to cooperate with the Pakistan constitution. Dr Khan Sahib's assurances on both counts were categorical: that he had 'no intention' of proclaiming an independent Paktunistan and that he would 'do nothing injurious' to the Pakistan constitution.[10]

A word here on Jinnah's thinking that Dr Khan Sahib meant 'to sabotage' the whole idea of Pakistan and the premier's categorical assertion that he had 'no intention' of proclaiming an independent Pathanistan. Whatever Dr Khan Sahib's real intent, there is no denying that newspaper reports did suggest some disturbing trends. Thus it was widely believed that with the League and the Red Shirts failing to arrive at 'some settlement', there may be 'two parallel governments' functioning in the Frontier province from 15 August, with Dr Khan Sahib who 'still commands confidence' of the overwhelming majority of the legislature and 'over 70 per cent' of the Pathan masses, both in the settled districts and the tribal belt, 'declaring independence' and refusing 'to hand over' to the new Pakistan government. The only way out, it was suggested, was to hold fresh general elections on the issue of Pakistan *versus* Pathanistan, a demand to which the Quaid was 'not likely' to agree. All the same, the Pathan movement had now gained 'sufficient ground' and the masses were wedded to it.

Meantime reports suggested that the Fakir of Ipi had held out 'open and active' support to the Khan brothers for the establishment of Pathanistan. And his call had enthused 'hundreds' of young Pathans who continued swelling the ranks of Abdul Ghani Khan's 'Zalme Pakhtoon'.[11]

To say all this is not to unsay that chinks had begun to appear in the nationalist armour. The first known defection from its ranks was that of Nawabzada Allah Nawaz Khan, Speaker of the Frontier Legislative Assembly who had been re-elected from the Muslim rural constituency of D.I. Khan South on the ticket of the Jamiyat ul-ulama, a close electoral ally of the Congress party. Explaining his action, the Nawabzada declared that owing to the division of India on 'communal lines', the place for 'nationalist independent Muslims' was in the ranks of the Muslim League. The speaker's brother, it was reported, followed in his footsteps.[12]

To revert to the new governor's arrival in Peshawar, where his long interview with the premier was followed by another with Abdul Qaiyum, the leader of the Muslim League in the NWFP Assembly. Qaiyum was sure that the Congress would do its worst to make Pakistan a failure; that its talk about disturbances, if the Khan Sahib ministry were dismissed, was a 'bluff'. In the event, the League leader did not anticipate any 'serious trouble'.[13]

Cunningham's impressions of his talks with the incumbent governor, Rob Lockhart, whom he had come to replace, left him in no doubt that he (Lockhart) had felt 'very anxious' as to the repercussions of dismissing the Khan Sahib ministry and was 'so much the better' for every day this was postponed.[14] The premier and his ministerial colleagues did not attend the Pakistan flag hoisting ceremony on 15 August even though they had been asked and had promised to attend. Dr Khan Sahib's 'alleged reason', Cunningham noted, was the fear that with the Muslim Leaguers intent on pulling down the flags on the ministers' cars, he (Dr Khan Sahib) 'could not answer' for the acts of his own followers.[15]

A footnote may be in order here. In his report of 8 September 1947 to the Quaid, Cunningham referred to the provincial CID information that there was 'a plan' to pull flags off the ministers' cars and probably to stone them. In the event, Dr Khan Sahib was persuaded by his colleagues not to run the risk of an ugly, ignominious incident. In fact, the governor concluded, they were all really glad 'to have this excuse' to abstain from the ceremony.[16]

Later that evening, Dr Khan Sahib confided in the governor that but for Caroe, he and his colleagues would have quit office as far back as April 1947. On being pressed why he would not oblige him (Cunningham) now, the premier retorted that 'things had gone so far' that it would be better 'to let Jinnah stultify himself by taking the constitutionally improper step of dismissing them'. All the same, Dr Khan Sahib 'did however promise' that 'even in the event' of his dismissal, he and Abdul Ghaffar Khan would 'try and prevent' any kind of disturbance or violence from their followers. 'Personally', the governor recorded, he trusted Dr Khan Sahib and would like to keep him in the Ministry. The real 'difficulty' though lay with Jinnah who desired Dr Khan Sahib's dismissal.[17]

The governor's talk with Mehr Chand Khanna, the Finance Minister, was revealing. The minister was 'not particularly nervous' about outbreaks of violence by Muslims against Hindus and Sikhs but feared some 'isolated instances', which must be 'immediately stamped out'. He was of the view that the Muslim League had lately lost ground and was strongly persuaded that if there were an election, the Congress would 'probably get in again'.[18] A week later, Cunningham noted that 'a good many of the more thinking members' of the Muslim League would still like a coalition of the Congress and the Muslim League—'if that were possible'. The main stumbling block here was not so much the Muslim League or the way Jinnah might view matters but the instransigence of the Congress. For Dr Khan Sahib was 'adamant against' serving with Muslim League ministers.[19]

All this while, Cunningham was getting 'rather apprehensive' about the Quaid's delay in replying to his telegrams of 15 and 20 August and wired to him for 'early orders'. The day following (21 August), the Quaid intimated that he had indeed done the needful, legalizing the dismissal of the ministry by amending the Government of India Act for the purpose.[20]

Newspaper reports indicated that the Frontier governor's 'unconstitutional action' in dismissing the Khan Sahib ministry was covered by 'a dictatorial power', which the Quaid had assumed in terms of the new sub-section 5 of Section 51 of the adapted Government of India Act, 1935. This was special to Pakistan and stipulated that 'with regard to the choosing, summoning and dismissing' of ministers the governor was to be 'under the general control of and comply with the directions' issued by the Governor-General. It was suggested that Sir George Cunningham's earlier record of installing the minority Aurangzeb Khan ministry of the Muslim League in September 1943 and keeping it in power until March 1945 by imprisoning a number of Congress MLAs had made him 'adept at this game'.

There was also speculation that the Pakistan Constituent Assembly may change the composition of the Frontier Legislative Assembly to ensure a majority for the Muslim League. And later when the (Muslim League) ministry had had time to consolidate its position, it may opt for fresh elections.[21]

The die was now cast. On 23 August, the governor asked Dr Khan Sahib to come and meet him. The premier 'in an extraordinarily friendly form' was 'rather [more] pleased' than otherwise that he was giving up the ministry. Cunningham had much hoped that Dr Khan Sahib and his colleagues might resign and avoid 'the necessity of dismissal'. Though Dr Khan Sahib would 'clearly have preferred to do this', he was overruled by Mehr Chand Khanna and Qazi Ataullah who 'want to make it appear' that Jinnah had taken 'a false step'. When the premier came back to intimate him that they had decided not to quit on their own, Cunningham 'dismissed' his ministry.[22]

Later that day, Abdul Qaiyum was sworn in as the head of a two-member ministry and took over the all-important portfolios of law and order, as well as finance, while his deputy, Mohammad Abbas Khan, was delegated revenue and local government. The new premier undertook to restore law and order as well as confidence among the people and pledged that it would be his 'foremost duty' to protect the life and property as well as 'legal rights and privileges' of the minorities.[23]

Happily, the governor noted, there had been 'no unpleasant reactions' to the change of the ministerial guard. And this despite the 'very pessimistic rumours' about the impending 'disturbances and bloodshed'. 'Each day that passes' without the clash of rival political forces, the Congress and the Muslim League, meant 'so much more chance' of peace.[24]

Interestingly enough, some of Cunningham's informants continued to hold that the Congress had 'deliberately timed to embark on a war of nerves' to frighten everyone, that once the Khan Sahib ministry was dismissed, there would be a lot of trouble. One such informant was Sheikh Mahbub Ali, for long Cunningham's confidant, who told the governor that most of their talk was 'bluff' and that the Muslim League was then 'far too strong' for the Congress.[25]

On 4 September 1947, Cunningham recorded that there had been 'a steadily increasing' number of attacks on Hindus and Sikhs—some were 'isolated incidents', while others were 'organized'. Earlier on 26 August he had talked of 'a slight epidemic of communal assaults' during the preceding four to five days. He then noted that:

> Since the Haripur incident on August 26th, there has been a massacre at Takht Bhai in Mardan district with a certain amount of arson and a very bold attack on a troop train between Kohat and Khushalgarh in which 40 Hindu troops were killed.

The governor's thinking was that 'unless the Punjab slaughters ceased at once', it would be 'impossible to hold back our people'. Even the best among the Muslims, he noted, while they 'really do condemn' the killings would not go so far as to shoot a fellow Muslim 'to stop them'. One result of the communal slaughter was that 'for the time being', the 'toughs' of the Congress and the Muslim League 'seem to have sunk' their differences![26]

Meantime, Cunnigham advised the Pakistan government about the new agreements it must 'conclude with the States in the Frontier'. Waziristan, he reasoned, was 'the only real difficulty and I have recommended (as I did two years ago about the Tuker report[27]) that we should clear troops out of Waziristan altogether and hold only up to Wana and Miran Shah with Scouts, nothing at Razmak'.[28]

Sadly, all this while discipline in the ranks was gradually loosening. For, on 7 September, even as his entourage approached the Peshawar Fort, there was a lot of commotion. Here a Sikh sentry of the 19th Lancers had 'possibly accidentally' shot a Muslim sepoy of the 3rd/8th Punjabis. And even as looting and arson spread, somebody was seen carrying off great bundles of cloth from a shop within a few feet of a section of the Frontier Constabulary. And nobody seemed to take notice. The governor was very rude to the Subedar Major of the Constabulary and the Acting Senior Superintendent of Police caught hold of a few of the looters. But the damage had already been done. Later that evening there was a spate of rumours that 'probably' 100 Hindus and Sikhs had been done to death. Which included 'a good many of our clerks and their families'.[29]

Twenty-four hours later while things were 'quieter' in the cantonment, with stray murders still going on, looting and arson had started in Peshawar city. As it got dark, the situation looked 'very menacing'. Cunningham reasoned whether the police and the constabulary and 'to a lesser extent' even Muslim troops, had 'really connived at both murdering and looting'. But, it was clear, the 'animosity' was 'primarily' against the Sikhs. For out in the countryside, people were keen to 'get at' the Sikhs; they 'don't mind about the Hindus'.[30]

A day later, Cunningham noted that fires in the city of Peshawar seemed to be 'pretty well out' while discipline and morale were 'gradually' being restored in the police and the constabulary. For bringing about some modicum of normalcy, the governor had been sending around 'some of the more respectable' Muslims to interact with people in cantonments, the city and villages, to impress upon them that 'this sort of thing' would prove 'ruinous' to both Pakistan as well as the Muslims left behind in India.[31]

Newspaper reports furnished more details about the 'serious disturbances' that had broken out at Peshawar engineered by an 'armed mob' from Kohat and the Dandikotal transborder areas. The mob had attacked 'a large number' of Hindus and Sikhs and looted their property which, alongwith a retinue of women, was carried in a convoy of motor vehicles and on donkeys. There were attacks too on a number of government officials belonging to the minority communities as also on a unit of the Indian Army's Signals Regiment. Also, the mob succeeded in stopping planes from taking off from the aerodrome—a situation remedied only when the Area Commander sent in some tanks. It was pointed out that 'exaggerated accounts of alleged happenings' in East Punjab had vitiated the atmosphere in the province and people were asked 'to retaliate'.

The NWFP government's press communique (10 September) underscored the point that the 'tragic events' of 7-8 September were the handiwork of the enemies of Pakistan; that the work of shepherding the non-Muslims to places of safety was being accomplished 'energetically'; and that more than 5,000 non-Muslims had been concentrated in zones where 'adequate' protection had been provided.[32]

With the evacuation of all Sikh troops from Peshawar on 10 September, Cunningham heaved a sigh of relief. He was keen that Hindus and Sikhs left over in the city and Sadar Bazaar be provided 'ample protection', rather than taking the 'defeatist line' of herding them together in the Peshawar Fort or in other refugee camps.

Meanwhile the governor had run into one Pir Baksh: 'the only man whom I have yet met' who admitted that it was the Muslims in Amritsar who 'really started the bad feeling' nearly three to four months earlier. There was no gainsaying though that the Sikhs had taken revenge 'out of all proportion'.

Just about that time news came from Nowshera of 'fairly serious attacks' by Muslims on the Hindus and Sikhs, 140 of whom had been killed. Troops and police 'seem to have done well to bring the situation under control'.[33] On a visit to Miran Shah (11 September), Cunningham met all the leading Waziristan Maliks who were 'professedly' pro-Pakistan. Yet, he gathered, they really had 'mental reservations' on the subject.[34] The day following he was in Bannu (12 September) where he found the atmosphere 'very good'. The Hindus and Sikhs who numbered 15,000 odd were in a pretty secure position for they had 'plenty of weapons' and did not want to leave the town. The governor was also impressed by the general smartness of the police, which was 'better than [in] any other district' he had visited. The reason, he argued, was that they had not been so constantly engaged or having to deal with 'intra-party disturbances and intrigues'.[35]

Things in Peshawar and Nowshera were 'outwardly' very normal. Estimated at 12,000 to 15,000, most of the Hindus were housed in refugee camps. And unless they were 'either moved out or re-absorbed' in the cities, the position was 'dangerous'. All talk about the Afridis taking part in the looting was, Cunningham noted, 'greatly exaggerated'; he doubted 'if they did 5 per cent' of it. He was also emphatic that 'so far' not a single Hindu or Sikh had been 'molested' in the tribal territory.[36]

III

Two Governor's Reports, of 8 and 15 September 1947, which fall within the time frame of this piece may be briefly summed up. Their purpose, as Cunningham wrote, was 'not to enter into very much detail, but rather to give you my general feeling . . . on the whole situation'. Their confidentiality was ensured by the fact that at his end these were to be seen by 'nobody except my own Secretary'.

The first report started by underlining that, on the 'internal political side', things had 'turned out better' than what most people had anticipated. When he arrived, there were 'forecasts' about clashes between supporters of the Congress and the Muslim League; 'happily' there had been, till that date, no such disturbances. This was partly because the Congress did not feel 'strong enough at present' to start mischief and partly because of the 'serious communal troubles' over the past ten days. This may not however, the governor warned, prevent 'some of the hotheads' from the two sides making trouble.

He was struck, on his return to the province after 18 months, by the growth of feeling in favour of the Muslim League. It pervaded all classes: 'our Muslim officials, our City people and the villagers'. Many of his friends who used to have 'distinct' Congress leanings earlier, were now '100 per cent Muslim League'.

The report referred to the shooting, 'probably accidentally', of a Punjabi Muslim sepoy by a Sikh sentry and to its aftermath: 'a very large number' of Hindus and Sikhs killed, 'some looting' in the city and a fire at one place. There was also reference to a feeling of 'such intense fury' against the Sikhs, a feeling of 'angry resentment' that had affected the discipline of 'our police and the Army', to the extent that 'it is difficult' for our officers to get their men 'to intervene forcibly' when murder and loot were going on. There is a mention of the alleged participation of Patiala and other State troops in the atrocities, which the Sikhs were committing in Punjab.

Finally, a reference to a lead article in the *Pakistan Times* (4 September 1947), under the caption 'Spy Ring', which was the 'grossest misrepresentation' of what Jenkin wrote in a letter. The insinuation 'running all through the article' was that the British—'and this must include all British officers serving in this country'—were 'disloyal' to Pakistan. "Would it be possible', the governor implored, to persuade the paper in some way to remove this impression about the *bona fides* of British officers serving in Pakistan?[37]

It may be of interest to note that on 6 September, the *Civil and Military*

Gazette (Lahore) wrote a brief editorial, 'A Mare's Nest?' which referred to the letter written by W.P.N. Jenkin who, till recently, had been DIG, CID, in Punjab. A photocopy of Jenkin's letter had appeared in the *Pakistan Times*, whose London correspondent claimed that it threw 'a flood of light' on British plans 'to organise a fifth column' in Pakistan. Among other things he had suggested Pakistan's inclusion—should it so desire—in the security orbit of the British Commonwealth in which the secret service played a role. The hope was that the people of Pakistan would welcome 'a link-up which [*sic*] British security would afford them'. The purpose in view, the *Pakistan Times* had argued, could only be served by people who enjoyed the confidence of the Pakistan government. By implication, Jenkin and other high-ranking British officials serving in Pakistan did not enjoy that confidence. The *Civil and Military Gazette* suggested that the revelation or the 'scoop' was likely to be 'more embarrassing' to the Pakistan than to the British government.[38]

The report of 15 September also referred to the fires and looting in Peshawar on 9 and 10 September, when about 150 Hindus and Sikhs were done to death.

The discipline in the Army and the Police affected by the 'communal virus' was, according to the Inspector General of Police, 'actually better at the end of the disturbances than at the beginning'! Meantime, the governor intimated, he was 'mobilizing' Muslim leaders of every class to throw their weight into the scale against frequent outbreaks of violence.

There is a brief reference to the situation in the city of Bannu where an estimated 15,000 Hindus and Sikhs 'wished to stay where they were', with the governor 'encouraging' this kind of feeling even in places like Peshawar and Nowshera.[39] In the meantime newspaper reports suggested that at a meeting between the Indian and Pakistani prime ministers at Lahore on 14 September both the governor and premier of the NWFP had indicated that 'only two major incidents' had occurred in the province: that 250-300 Hindus and Sikhs had been murdered in Haripur in the Hazara district and 'about the same number' killed in Peshawar. Of an estimated 45,000 Hindus and Sikhs in the province, 15,000 were said to be in Peshawar and another 15,000 in Bannu, the remaining 15,000 in an evacuee camp. The Hindus and Sikhs of Peshawar and Bannu were welcome to stay back; in any case the NWFP government 'does not want' them to leave.[40]

A word on the time frame, 8 August-15 September, may not be out of place. By the third/fourth week in September, and certainly by the first half of October, the NWF tribes, slowly but surely, got sucked into the conflict in Kashmir. In the initial stages, this was done behind Cunningham's back; certainly without his knowledge, much less his concurrence. In any case, after mid-September the scenario in the NWFP got more complex, while, with the tribal intervention, the deep and murky waters of the Jhelum, got murkier and muddier. Hence this brief narration of the events of the week preceding, and those immediately following the Partition, may draw to a close here.

NOTES

1. George Cunningham, born 1888; educated, Fettes College, Edinburgh, Magdalen College, Oxford; joined Indian Civil Service, 1911; after 1914, served mainly on the North-West Frontier; Personal Assistant to Chief Commissioner, NWFP, 1915-19; Counsellor, Political Agent, North Waziristan, 1922-3; Counsellor, British Legation, Kabul, 1925-6; Private Secretary to Viceroy (Lord Irwin), 1926-31; Member, Executive Council, NWFP, 1932-6; and Governor, NWFP, 1937-46. After Pakistan's establishment, Governor, NWFP, August 1947-March 1948.
2. Sir George (and Lady) Cunningham arrived in Peshawar on the evening of 28 February 1937 and left, on superannuation, exactly nine years later, on 2 March 1946. For all these years, while in India, Cunningham maintained a Diary which, for the most part, was dictated to his Secretary, R.H.D. Lewis. The first part of the Diary starts on 12 March 1937 and ends on 2 March 1946; the second begins on 8 August 1947 and draws to a close on 30 March 1948 (hereafter referred to as the 'Cunningham Diary' abbreviated as CD). The first part, on microfilm, is in the National Archives of India (New Delhi), bears Acc. No. 4241; the second, is in the India Office Library and Records (now India Office Records, of the Oriental and India Office Collections, of the British Library), London (hereafter IOR), Mss Eur D 670/8.
3. For more details of Nehru's visit to the tribal areas reference may be made to Parshotam Mehra, *The North-West Frontier Drama, 1945-1947: A Reassessment* (New Delhi, 1998), pp. 63-83.
4. For the mounting acerbity in relations between Caroe and his Premier, Dr Khan Sahib, see ibid., pp. 127-46.
5. For events leading to Caroe's virtual sack or dismissal, see ibid, pp. 149-60.
6. Two exchanges regarding Cunningham's reappointment may be of interest. In a letter of 4 July 1947, Cunningham acknowledged a communication from Sir A. Carter of India Office intimating him of Jinnah's offer to appoint him (Cunningham), Governor of NWFP; his response was brief: 'After full consideration and with much regret my answer must be in the negative'. Later, it would appear, he had a change of heart and accepted Jinnah's offer to resume office at Peshawar. On 21 July 1947, Sir A. Carter wrote to say that he felt 'rather badly that after the noble way in which you have behaved, J. [Jinnah] should be haggling in this way'. The obvious reference is to the fixation of Cunningham's salary and other emoluments.

   Meantime, on 20 July 1947, Mountbatten had written to the Secretary of State that he was most anxious 'that Cunningham should accept Jinnah's offer'. And 'a very early decision' was called for so that Cunningham's name 'may be submitted to the King'.

For more details, see IOR, Mss Eur D 670/9. A reference may also be made to Parshotam Mehra, op.cit., pp. 215-22.

7. CD entry for 8 August 1947.
8. Ibid., 9 August 1947.
9. Ibid., 10 August 1947.
10. Cunningham's interview with Dr Khan Sahib took place on the evening of 13 August after he (Cunningham) had taken his oath of office. The 'Notes' of the interview however were recorded on 14 August. For details, see ibid., 14 August 1947.
11. *Tribune* (Lahore), 10 August 1947. The half column report was datelined Nowshera, 8 August 1947, and emanated 'From our own correspondent'.

    A word on the Zalme Pakhtun (also Zulme Pakhtun), literally, the 'Young Pakhtun', a militant outfit founded by Badshah Khan's eldest son, Abdul Ghani. It had no linkage with the Khudai Khidmatgars or 'Red Shirts' of Badshah Khan. Designed essentially 'to defend, not offend', its main purpose was to counter the vicious Muslim League agitation propaganda against the Pakhtunistan movement. The Zalme Pakhtun did not believe in non-violence; its volunteers wore deep red uniforms and carried firearms. For more details see D.G. Tendulkar, *Abdul Ghaffar Khan: Faith is a Battle* (New Delhi, 1967), pp. 418, 439 and 450.
12. The Nawabzada had been re-elected from the same constituency defeating two independent candidates by an impressive margin: 3,368 votes against 837 and 41, respectively. For more details, see Erland Jansson, *India, Pakistan or Pakhtunistan: The Nationalist Movements in the North-West Frontier Province 1937-47* (Uppsala, 1981), Appendix III, 'The 1946 Elections', pp. 255-63. Also see the *Hindustan Times*, 22 August 1947.
13. The interview with Abdul Quaiyum took place on the morning of 14 August 1947. Cunningham noted *inter alia* that he was 'more hopeful' after seeing Abdul Quaiyum who had risen 'very much' in stature since he (Cunningham) left the province 18 months earlier, CD, 14 August 1947.
14. Ibid., 13 August 1947.
15. Cunningham was given to understand that the 'real reason' why Dr Khan Sahib and his ministerial colleagues did not attend the flag hoisting ceremony was the feeling that if they attended, and were dismissed immediately thereafter their followers would 'laugh at them' for having extended their hand of friendship and 'having had it spurned'. For more details, see ibid., 15 August 1947.
16. Governor's Report, 8 September 1947. The Cunningham Papers have 14 Governor's Reports in all, addressed to the Quaid-i-Azam: the first is dated 8 September 1947, the last 2 March 1948. Besides there are 'Minutes of a meeting on convening the Frontier Legislative Assembly', held on 10 February 1948. And there is a list of 45 members of the NWFP Legislative Assembly alongwith the names of the Speaker, Nawabzada Allah Nawaz Khan, and the Deputy Speaker, Lala Girdhari Lal Puri. All these are to be found in IOR, Mss Eur D 670/23.
17. CD, 15 August 1947.
18. *Inter alia* the minister told the governor that the financial position was 'not too good' but the principal difficulty was 'only immediate ways and means'. The Pakistan government, he told the governor, had been asked for a loan to help tide over this crisis, ibid., 16 August 1947.
19. Ibid., 23 August 1947.

20. Ibid.
21. *Hindustan Times*, 24 August 1947, under the headline, 'How Jinnah Assumed Dictatorial Powers: Dismissal of Ministry Challenge to Pathans'.
22. See note 18 above.
23. *Hindustan Times*, 25 August 1947.
24. Ibid.
25. Ibid., 28 August 1947.
26. For details, see CD, 4 September 1947. Cunningham noted *inter alia* that he had just sent 'a long summary' of the tribal and Frontier states' position along the whole Frontier and asked the Pakistan government to come to a decision about the new agreements to be drawn up.
27. A word on the Tuker report. In 1945, the Government of India appointed a five member committee under the chairmanship of Major General (later Lt. Gen.) Sir Francis Tuker to consider Frontier problems particularly the respective roles of the regular armed forces and the civil forces and the extent to which the former might be replaced by the latter. Two members, including the Chairman, held that there must be a declared policy of immediate disarmament of the tribes to be carried out in the first place in Waziristan (and the Khyber). The Commander-in-Chief was inclined to support the minority view. George Cunningham, as well as Olaf Caroe (who had the ear of the Viceroy), advised that tribal disarmament could not be considered in isolation but only in the larger context of India's relations with Afghanistan and the prevalent political situation in India. The Commander-in-Chief was in favour of withdrawing regular troops from Waziristan (and the Khyber) and to substitute Scouts and Khassadars in their place. In the final count, nothing much seems to have changed. For more details, see Nicholas Mansergh, editor-in-chief, *Transfer of Power*, Vol. VI (London, 1976), Wavell to Pethic-Lawrence, 15 November 1945, Document No. 190

    Lt. Gen. Sir Francis Tuker was General Officer Commanding, Ceylon (now Sri Lanka), 1944-5 and later, General Officer Commander-in-Chief, Eastern Command, India, 1946-7. Sir Francis Tuker's well-known book, *While Memory Serves* (London, 1950), is hypercritical of the manner in which HMG handled political developments in India leading to the transfer of power.
28. CD, 4 September 1947.
29. Ibid., 7 September 1947.
30. Ibid., 8 September 1947.
31. Ibid., 9 September 1947.
32. *Hindustan Times*, 11 September 1947.
33. CD, 10 September 1947.
34. Ibid., 11 September 1947. The governor had motored to Miran Shah and everything seemed 'perfectly normal' *en route*. At Miran Shah, the general spirit and morale among all the officers and men 'seemed excellent'.
35. Ibid., 12 September 1947,
36. Ibid., 13 September 1947.
37. Governor's Report, op.cit., 8 September 1947.
38. *Civil and Military Gazette* (Lahore), 6 September 1947.
39. Governor's Report, 15 September 1947.
40. *Hindustan Times*, 15 September 1947.

Prelude to Partition: Communal Politics in the Central Provinces and Berar, 1937-1947

KANCHANMOY MOJUMDAR

A supposition underlay the course of communal politics in India resulting in the country's Partition: Muslim minority interests were unsafe under majority Hindu rule. Both the concatenation of circumstances and deeds and misdeeds of leaders jockeying for power turned the supposition into a harsh reality. The Muslim League asserted the reality after the 1937 elections when the Indian National Congress, dubbed as a Hindu party, formed ministries in several provinces. The Congress ultimately acquiesced in the reality when it settled for the Partition of the country after futile attempts at a partnership of power with the League.

This majority-minority syndrome confirming the conflicting interests of the two constituted the focal point of communal politics in the Central Provinces and Berar. But then, while communalism in the province at the mass level grew on its own impulse, at the élitist—and decisive—level it was an act of grafting by external forces. This was more true of the Muslims in the local political élite than of the Hindus. Significantly enough, before 1937, the relations between the two were not conflictual but of close cooperation.

Muslims being a very small community and politically far more inert than the Hindus, communalism in the CP and Berar could not assume a very fearful character, and that notwithstanding the provocative functioning of some Hindu communal groups. Actions and the reactions of Hindu and Muslim communal élite groups did not create for the local authorities any grave political crisis. But then, communalism, in widening the Hindu-Muslim divide, was a factor in regional politics, which the local government made ample use of during times of political difficulty.

One more harsh reality stood out in the communal politics of the CP and Berar: personal advancement, not promotion of community interest, often motivated the local Hindu and Muslim leadership in either lining up with the government at times or falling out with it at others. A section of the leadership willingly played into the hands of the government, and thereby kept communal politics within limits, albeit unwittingly.

The genesis of communalism in the politics of the CP and Berar lay in the rivalry between the Hindu and Muslim leadership for sharing local power. The rivalry was coeval with the introduction of electoral politics in the province and was commensurate and coextensive with successive constitutional reforms, which widened the scale and scope of Indian participation in the administration. The elections of 1937 and 1946 made the rivalry acute, worsening the Congress-Muslim League relations after the former formed ministries twice. Following the 1937 elections, the League's hold on the local Muslims became both wider and firmer, and with it came about a clear polarization of local Muslim political opinion and activity.

During the elections and, more so, in the decade that followed, Hindu communal organizations such as the Hindu Mahasabha, the Arya Samaj and the Rashtriya Swayamsevak Sangh (RSS) became far more active than ever before, and so did the Khaksars, the Sirat Conference and the Muslim National Guards, all Muslim communal organizations. The rash of riots over cow killing by the Muslims and playing of music before mosques by the Hindus were both a symptom and an aggravator of the worsening Hindu-Muslim relations at the mass level.

The strong anti-Muslim prejudices of some Congress ministers were matched by most League legislators' avowed anti-Hindu bias. Communalism showed up even at the lower levels of the administration, Hindu government employees having lost the confidence of local Muslims. and Muslim government employees being distrusted by local Hindus. The deepening insecurity felt by the Muslims led to their panic exodus to Hyderabad in 1947-8. According to the 1941 and 1951 census figure the number of Muslims in the population of the province fell from 4.6 per cent to 3.8 per cent.

II

The very small Muslim political élite of the CP and Berar had, before 1937, worked hand in hand with both the government and the local Hindu leaders, not at cross purposes with either. The larger section of the élite, mostly landholders, businessmen and retired government employees, received official patronage and favours in the form of titles like Khan Bahadur and Khan Saheb. A few others, mostly professionals, were junior colleagues of liberal minded Hindus leading local political parties.

Some Hindu leaders—Sir E. Raghavendra Rao,[1] for one—used Muslim support to broaden their political base; when in power, they provided the Muslims with government jobs and more educational opportunities as a mark of favour. Muslim members in the provincial legislature, no more than seven till 1937,[2] while dealing with political issues, hardly functioned as a solid communal bloc, although elected from exclusive Muslim constituencies. They were, of course, keen to maintain Muslim cultural identity, and in this they could count on the support of their Hindu colleagues. Some Muslim MLCs' demand for exclusive denominational schools, for example, was supported by some Hindu MLCs and opposed by other Muslim MLCs, the former emphasizing the need to recognize the cultural distinctiveness of the Muslims and the latter urging that the issue of education had better not be treated on communal lines.[3] Hindu legislators also supported their Muslim colleagues' demand that the government increase the number of Muslim gazetted holidays.[4] Sometimes Muslim legislators were elected to offices in the legislature with their Hindu colleagues' support,[5] party affiliation, not religious faith, determining the choice. Many Muslims got elected to municipalities from wards predominantly Hindu. The only issue, which at times caused sparks of discord between the Hindu and Muslim political élite, was the restrictions imposed on cow killing within municipal limits for sanitary reasons, the latter concerned over the livelihood of butchers, predominantly Muslim.[6]

The frequent communal riots in the 1920s[7] no doubt got publicized in the local media and discussed in the local legislature but more as a law and order problem than as an insoluble political issue. The Hindu *sangathana* movement, which picked up from the 1920s,[8] caused Muslim reaction, but the government feared no political fallout from it. The gradual Muslim political awareness posed the government no political problem any more than it portended a challenge to the dominant position held by the Hindu élite in the local political life. There was for long none, among the local Muslims, to command the allegiance of the entire community; and there was no political party to do so either. The small interest groups among the Muslims and the small Muslim population in the province[9] no doubt received political notice under the communal electoral system, but they were too insignificant a factor for political reckoning by either the dominant Hindu political leadership or the vigilant local government.

Change came thick and fast in 1937 and the years that followed, for three developments took place at the time, which had a bearing on communalism in the political life of the province, and each development was causally related to the other: the enlargement of the general electorate and the increase in the number of reserved constituencies for the Muslims by the Government of India Act, 1935;[10] the increasing rivalry of the League and the Congress at the national level on every political and constitutional issue; and the stepped-up activities of Hindu and Muslim communal organizations, which influenced the general masses more than ever before.

Politics in the CP and Berar after 1937 became far more mass based than heretofore and political activities became far more affected by mass psychology. Pandering to mass communal ill-feelings was now looked upon as a means of protecting, promoting, preserving and projecting the political interests of the leadership, both Hindu and Muslim. In such a situation even some legislators, hitherto moderate and liberal, turned rabid communalists, viewing every political issue from a communal point of view and thereby seeking to feather their own political nests.

Then there was the impact on the public mind of the news of happenings elsewhere in the country, which the local press, also divided on communal lines, reported quite often with considerable distortions. But, the key to the communalized local politics lay in the growing bitterness between the Congress and the League after the 1937 elections followed by the formation of a Congress ministry. The Congress won the elections as impressively as the Muslim League failed dismally; out of 79 contested seats in the Assembly, the Congress won 70; the Leaguers, denied even official recognition, won in only 5 out of the 14 Muslim reserved constituencies.[11]

This surprised none, for till after the 1937 elections, the League in the CP and Berar—as elsewhere too—existed on paper only,[12] and this in spite of the provincial capital, Nagpur, having hosted the annual sessions of the party twice—in 1909 and 1920.[13] The party had established by then its full-fledged provincial set-up with branches in all the districts of the province and some of the party members had attended all the annual sessions of the League at different places, besides serving for long on its different committees.[14] But then, the League's provincial body had soon degenerated into a non-functional set up; it had failed to create a clout among even the small Muslim élite—let alone secure a mass base for itself. The élite had no reason to view the League as a representative organization of the Muslim community, far less as the only organization of this kind.

CP and Berar counted very little in the League's political calculations at the national level; and that because the local Muslim population was very small among whom the Congress, the League's main rival, could claim no large following worth the name. In fact, it was only in the period 1919-22 that the Congress message had made some impact on the Muslims but that too only because the message had then been delivered in the Khilafat package. No League leader of national standing, least of all M.A. Jinnah, had visited Nagpur after 1920, when Jinnah had left the city in a huff, not even caring to attend the annual session of the League there, which he was slated to preside over.

III

The elections of 1937 stung the Muslim League into activity in CP and Berar. Shaukat Ali, once a staunch Khilafatist and a Gandhian alike, visited Nagpur in 1936 as a League leader to reorganize the party for the elections; his first task was to compose the differences between the local Leaguers; he failed in his mission, despite his mother, Begum Mohamed Ali, exhorting the men to be united under the League banner, convincing them that they were 'Muslims first and last'.[15] Abdul Rauf Shah and S.W.A. Rizvi, both of whom had been MLAs earlier and both close to Raghavendra Rao, their common benefactor, had no love lost for Muhammad Yusuf Shariff, a veteran leader, who too had been an MLC earlier and had clambered up to a ministership,[16] again with Rao's help. The reconstituted provincial organization of the League got sharply divided immediately after it was set up, with the followers of the Rauf Shah-Rizvi combine and those of Yusuf Shariff trading charges against one another. Even Jinnah's appearance on the scene to mend matters served no purpose; he left Nagpur in despair, resolved to withhold official recognition to either section till the elections were over.[17] Thus, divided internally, the League went to the polls; Shariff's group bagged five seats while Rauf Shah and Rizvi's followers won eight seats.[18] Shariff soon walked over to the 'Congress parlour'[19] to become the Law Minister in the Congress cabinet, the Premier, N.B. Khare, having decided, on Maulana Azad's advice,[20] to include a Muslim in his team to give a lie to the League propaganda that the Congress was a Hindu party.

During the Congress rule for a little over two years (July 1937 to November 1939) Hindu-Muslim social relations at the mass level worsened as did the relations between the Hindu and Muslim élite at the political level.[21] This was due to four reasons: the frequent communal riots all over the province; the rapid spread of the Muslim League to every nook and cranny of the province; the Congress ministry's programme, which upset the Muslims; and the clear polarization of the

Hindu and Muslim public opinion on communal lines, caused by the activities of some communal organizations.

Communal spirit ran high during electioneering, the Hindu Mahasabha and the Congress having set up candidates with criminal records who engaged toughs to ensure their victory.[22] The Hindu Mahasabha accused the Congress of 'pro-Muslim sympathies' for garnering Muslim co-operation at the cost of Hindu interests. The Hindu press lambasted Jinnah's 14 points as an impediment to national unity; the Leaguers were accused of being 'conmmunalists first and nationalists afterwards'.[23] No wonder, serious riots at places made the situation tense before the elections.

Even small townships and villages in the remote recesses of the province with no earlier record of communal violence became disturbed places when Hindu and Muslim religious celebrations coincided and when elections to local bodies took place. The Congress, the Mahasabha and the League all determined to capture these bodies with the help of the RSS, the Muslim National Guard and other communal organizations.

The most serious riot took place at Chandur-Biswa in Buldhana district in March 1939 when a local Congress leader, Jagdeo Patil, was killed by a Muslim mob. The Congress government packed off almost all Muslim males—some of them 14 years old—to jail and clamped a heavy punitive fine on the Muslims alone. The sessions court sentenced six Muslims to death and 24 others to transportation for life. The sentence, however, was set aside by the High Court, Justice Vivian Bose being particularly critical of the way the local authorities had conducted the enquiry into the incident.[24] The case served as grist to the League's propaganda mill; it vindicated the charge that the Congress ministry was heavily biased against the Muslim community.

Muslim MLAs acted as a solid communal bloc, some asserting 'separate national identity' for their co-religionists who, they claimed, were 'Muslims first and Indians afterwards'.[25] This, no doubt, served the Hindu Mahasabha's propaganda interest.

After the Lucknow session of the Muslim League in October 1937, the CP and Berar provincial organization was reorganized and all the Muslim MLAs, with the exception of Yusuf Shariff and three others, joined the League. Their one-point programme was to condemn the policies of the Congress ministry as harmful to Muslim interests. The secretariat of the Berar Muslim League warned the local Muslims against the 'suicidal consequences of joining the Congress', which had reportedly made some headway in its mass contact movement among the Muslims.[26] Developments such as the Congress flag being declared the national flag, the *Vande*

Mataram the national song, the implementation of the Congress programme of rural education, called the Vidyamandir scheme, and the spinning of *charkha* in schools—all these were held out as 'evidence of a subtle attempt to impose a Hindu culture on the Muslim minority'.[27]

The Leaguers unfurled their party flag beside the Congress flag on the Jabalpur Municipality building causing local tension.[28] The Muslim MLAs refused to sing *Vande Mataram* at the start of the proceedings in the Assembly.[29]

The Vidyamandir scheme was a comprehensive programme to tackle the problem of rural illiteracy and promote rural development, local people's active involvement in the scheme being its special feature. The people would themselves donate land for schools, teachers being paid out of the proceeds of the model agricultural farms attached to the schools. All departments of the government engaged in rural reconstruction would be associated with the scheme which, so it was hoped, would 'in near future ... make village life interesting and happy and relieve the village people from the misery in which they lived'.[30]

The curriculum provided in the scheme was an eminently practical one, having a bearing on the problems of rural life in respect of hygiene and sanitation, agriculture and cottage industry. The scheme was to meet the needs of 24,000 villages with no schools at the time and no prospect of schools in near future either, due to the government's inability to fund them.[31]

The Muslims opposed the scheme tooth and nail; they would have nothing to do with any *mandir*, a place for idol worship; thus the name of the scheme itself went against the very grain of Islam.[32] This was the constant refrain of the Muslim League propaganda at the local and national level. The common Muslims were soon convinced: the Vidyamandir scheme was indeed a sinister design of the Congress ministry to Hinduize the Muslims.

A Muslim satyagraha was organized at Nagpur by local Leaguers; apprehending a serious situation, Jinnah dispatched Liaquat Ali Khan to the city where the latter managed to extract from Ravishankar Shukla, the premier,[33] an undertaking that the scheme, which was to be given a new Muslim name,[34] would provide for some special concessions for Muslim pupils. The local Muslim press gloated in what they hailed as a victory: the Hindu Congress ministry had been forced to concede an 'educational communal award' to the Muslims.[35]

Later, in 1942, Sir Azizul Haq, Vice-Chancellor of the University of Calcutta, Speaker of the Bengal Legislative Assembly and prominent

League leader, conducted an enquiry into the Wardha scheme of education, which Shukla too hoped to implement in the province. Haq condemned the author of the scheme, Zakir Husain, as a 'Congress Muslim', who was 'credited with a desire to merge the specially Muslim culture in a single Indian culture'.[36]

The communal problem in the CP and Berar received national attention when the Pirpur Committee's report came out in November 1938, saying that 'Muslims in no other province have suffered so much as in the Central Provinces and Berar'.[37] The Committee—and later another one, headed by Fazlul Haq, a prominent leader of Bengal and the Premier of the province—framed a litany of charges against the Congress ministry: discrimination against Muslims in respect of government service and educational opportunities; bias in criminal cases involving Muslims; economic disabilities clamped on the Muslims;[38] and a systematic process of deculturization of Muslims through education. The conclusion arrived at was that there indeed lay 'something like an identity of purpose between the Congress and the Hindu Mahasabha',[39] both having launched a political and cultural onslaught on the small, helpless, inoffensive Muslim minority in the province.

The Congress ministry's point by point refutation of all the accusations in a press statement[40] had no effect either on the continuing League propaganda or on the general Muslim mind. The League's recruitment drive clearly indicated this.[41]

That the charges were hollow and just a propaganda ploy was amply made clear by the governor, Sir Francis Wylie, in his private communication with the Viceroy, Lord Linlithgow. The Viceroy, having received a letter from Sir Ziauddin Ahmad, a member of the Central Legislative Assembly, alleging injustice suffered by the Muslims, asked the governor to enquire into the allegations.[42] Lord Zetland, the Secretary of State, also wished to know if the Congress government really discriminated against the Muslims in respect of public employment, preferring pro-Congress 'good Muslims'.[43]

Wylie, who held the Congress ministers in utter contempt and scorn[44] found the allegations baseless. Muslims had suffered no 'positive injustice' whatever except some 'pin pricks' like arbitrary transfers, which too the governor had often succeeded in preventing. As for government jobs, Muslims held about 22 per cent of them though they were only a little above 4 per cent of the population.[45] And this was notwithstanding the fact admitted by the governor himself: the CP Muslims in general were 'not exactly out of the top drawer', who could 'boast of no leader with either intelligence or influence'. Worse were the Berar Muslims, who only wallowed in the nostalgia of their ancestors' greatness.[46]

Wylie clearly saw that the Muslims were using the Vidyamandir scheme as only a 'pretext' and as 'the necessary peg for a considerable agitation' against the Congress ministry.[47] Personally, the governor had a 'sneaking liking' for the scheme as a means of dealing with rural illiteracy, but he knew it would 'almost certainly fail'.[48] The Muslim grievance regarding Urdu schools was also unjustified; there were already enough Urdu schools in the province; they numbered 10 per cent of all schools. One could really see no reason why Muslim children should not go to Hindi schools although all of them easily spoke that language. In fact, in UP Hindu and Muslim children went to common primary schools despite there being a large number of Urdu schools.[49]

The governor knew well that Muslim grievances against the Congress ministry were grounded on no base other than their morbid fear of 'permanent subjection to a Hindu majority'; he, of course, appreciated their sense of a great loss: 'a fair—perhaps a preferential—deal' they were accustomed to receiving under the old administration; but then, Wylie wondered how that could be helped in the changed circumstances.[50]

The Viceroy was assured that the governor would save the Muslims from 'anything resembling grave injustice', convinced as he was that his ministers were as careful to maintain the secular image of their party as they were fearful of a governor's rule following any act that might appear to him as being blatantly anti-Muslim.[51]

Jinnah did not accept the Congress offer that the charges against the Congress ministries be investigated by the Chief Justice of the Federal Court,[52] which only confirmed the truth repeated 30 years later by Wylie himself in London: the League accusations were mere 'moonshine'.[53] The Viceroy too had the same feeling.[54]

IV

Between 1939 and 1947, communalization of the provincial political life kept pace with its integration with national political currents as shaped by the Congress, the Muslim League and the Hindu Mahasabha and the communal organizations associated with the latter two parties. A Hindu-Muslim fracas in a remote village, the appointment and transfer of a minor government employee, the attitude of a petty policeman in a township, the maintenance of a denominational primary school—all these were drummed up into issues involving the very *izzat* (self-respect), of either the Muslim or the Hindu community itself. National leaders often made much of these small local incidents to reap political harvests for themselves and their parties. A furious war of words would rage in the press and public platforms where the leaders would spew fire and brimstone, adding to the problem of local peace keepers.

The Muslim League was worth nothing in provincial political life till 1937; ten years later it had become the sole guardian of local Muslim interests. The provincial committee of the party was thoroughly re-organized, Rauf Shah being made its chief and a member of the national executive of the party. A planned membership drive was launched and a propaganda machinery set up: local funds were created and a grassroot leadership assiduously built up. The League made its appearance in almost every *taluka* of the sprawling province. The party held regular meetings at many places, its proceedings at all organizational levels were widely publicized through the local and national press as were any national and international events and issues with any bearing whatever on the Muslim community as such. Jinnah himself visited the province several times to both deepen and widen the League's influence and to rally the Muslims against the Congress. He often made disturbingly communal speeches, as reported by the local authorities.[55]

As elsewhere in the country, Jinnah's was the last word in whatever concerned the local Muslims. As directed by him, Muslims in the CP and Berar cooperated with the government during the Second World War; they kept clear of the Congress individual satyagraha and the Quit India movement. The local Muslim press echoed Jinnah's reaction to the Cripps Mission, the Federation scheme, the Rajagopalachari formula, the Simla Conference, the Cabinet Mission Plan and, above all, the Pakistan scheme. Muslims in the province had, as directed by the League High Command, no truck with the agitation in the country over the INA trials in Delhi.

With the League forging forward, the Congress lost whatever little remained of its influence among the local Muslims. It could win no bye elections held during the war years for Muslim constituencies, all of them going to the League.[56] It had to bring in nationalist Muslims from elsewhere, the Khudai Khidmatgars, in particular, for propaganda purposes.[57] Shariff, the one prominent Muslim Congressman, failed to influence the local Muslims against the Pakistan scheme.[58] Spurned by the Muslim community as a political turncoat and a suspect in Congress eyes, Shariff ultimately left the Congress in 1943.[59]

With local units of some Muslim organizations—the Ahrar party, the

All India Momin Conference and the Khaksars, for example—the League had no love lost. In this and in their challenge to Jinnah's leadership,[60] Congressmen found some ammunition at least to use against the local Leaguers' claim that their party alone represented the provincial Muslim interests and that Jinnah was the undisputed leader of the entire Muslim community.

During the Congress rule, and more so in later years, the Hindu Mahasabha grew rapidly in membership and local influence. Its president, V.D. Savarkar's tours through the province were very successful,[61] *Akhand Bharat* being his rallying cry and opposition to communal electorates his consistent stand. The Muslim League and the Congress were his common targets of virulent attack; communal riots squared well with the Mahasabha's scheme of Muslim bashing and organizing the Hindus for the purpose. But then, the glowing personal image of Mahasabha leaders, including B.S. Munje and Savarkar, was no index to the political clout of the party as measured particularly by the results of the elections in 1937 and 1946.[62] In the elections to local bodies, however, the party scored some successes, but during the war years, the Congress was rendered ineffective by the government's repression, when many local Congressmen were serving long jail sentences. The Mahasabha, no doubt, roused the feeling of Hindutva, particularly during communal riots, but, due to the solid opposition of the Congress and the League, it failed to turn the feeling into political support strong enough to challenge the two parties.

The RSS also spread its wings, making the most of communal riots and the resultant anti-Muslim feelings among the Hindus. During the war years, as an organization it avoided any avowed political activity and open involvement in communal disturbances but allowed its members freedom of action in their individual capacity. The government kept track of its close association with the Hindu Mahasabha and knew of its involvement in the violent incidents at Chimur during the Quit India movement.[63] Although knowing it to be a Hindu communal organization and that its members were implicated in many communal riots, the government never banned it altogether; in 1933, the government had issued an order barring its employees from any association with the RSS. It was kept under constant watch by local authorities, and during the war its members were prevented from publicly parading in military uniforms. The RSS leadership never defied the ban; M.S. Golwakar, the chief, acquiescing in the policy of adjustment with the government.[64] By then the RSS-Mahasabha relations had developed some strain,[65] which was some relief for the local authorities which had dealt with communal troubles in which the two outfits had earlier made a common cause against the Muslims.

The government closely watched and compiled annual reports on the activities of the Muslim volunteer organizations as well, especially the Khaksars and the Muslim National Guard. The Khaksar movement, founded by Inayatullah Khan Mashriqui in 1930, was a bitterly anti-Muslim League organization and it blamed Jinnah for stoking Muslim communalism, which it viewed as a threat to Indian nationalism. It organized branches in several places of the province, particularly in the Berar districts; its members performed drills and military exercises while emphasizing the need for intercommunal unity. The government banned it in 1941; its activities were greatly hampered due to the strong Muslim reaction to the attempt made by one of its members on the life of Jinnah. Mosques were used by Khaksars as their hideouts until they were flushed out of them by the police. It had little influence on the local Muslims. Soon after the war, many Khaksars flocked to the Muslim League.[66]

The Muslim National Guard was a volunteer corps set up by the Muslim League, its members taking to military drills and assisting the League in propaganda work. In the war years its increased membership and its activity during communal riots led the government to take up the matter with the League national leadership. It also brought the organization under the rule banning military drills at public places. Intelligence reports had it that it received financial support from the Nizam's government.[67]

V

The League berated the Congress as a Hindu party, no different from the Hindu Mahasabha. No doubt the League needed to damage the Congress image for propaganda purposes. But Congressmen of the province themselves provided some substance to the League's accusation. Almost the entire Hindu élite, for long only high caste men, had connections with the Hindu *sangathana* movement, spearheaded by the Hindu Mahasabha, the Arya Samaj and the RSS. The connections survived the flux in their political fortunes, change in their party affiliation and variations in political situations. In the movement were involved, in varying degrees of openness, Tilakites and Swarajists, moderate Congressmen and their radical detractors, Independents and Liberals, pro and anti-establishment elements.

Sir Moropant Joshi, S.B. Tambe and S.M. Chitnavis,[68] for example, who for long had served the government and enjoyed its confidence, had strong links with the RSS all through their lives. They disliked the government's branding of it as a communal organization. M.B. Niyogi, a distinguished lawyer, who became a judge of the High Court, had life-long involvement with the Hindu unity movement. Khare found no contradiction whatever in his being a sincere Congressman and an ardent admirer of the RSS. His friendship with L.V. Paranjpe did not abate a bit even when the Hindu Mahasabha set him up against him (Khare) in the 1937 elections. Khare's colleague, Ramrao Deshmukh, presided over the civic reception of Savarkar in December 1937[69] and listened impassively to the fire-eating anti-Muslim speeches delivered by the Mahasabha president. With the communal situation worsening due to the Mahasabha activities, Khare had, of course, to take action against the Mahasabha, but later he became the president of the party while publicly declaring his admiration for the organization and discipline of RSS workers.[70] In fact, not until 1938 did the Congress ban its members' association with the Hindu Mahasabha. This must not have missed the notice of the government.

The Hindi speaking leaders of the CP and Berar,[71] though far less enamoured of the RSS than their Marathi speaking colleagues, were equally zealous in defending Hindu interests against what they feared as the growing Muslim challenges. Governor Wylie dismissed Shukla and his colleagues, D.P. Mishra and D.K. Mehta, all blue-blooded Brahmins, as rank communalists whose prejudices against Muslims needed to be checked for the sake of the morale of the administration. Muslim police officers were Shukla's particular targets; Wylie took them under his wing as protected wards. The governor's pressure alone saved them from 'penal transfers' as punishment for their supposed bias against the Hindus involved in communal riots.[72] Wylie wondered why Shukla, though unwell, rushed to Chandur-Biswa, not an easily accessible place, to attend the funeral of Jagdeo Patil, the slain local Congress leader. Shukla, despite the governor's plea immediately transferred the local police officer, a Muslim, without even an enquiry into his conduct.[73]

D.P. Mishra, the ablest hand in the Congress cabinet, demanded the peremptory transfer of Niaz Ahmad, the Deputy Superintendent of Police, Jabalpur,[74] who had been dealing with the case involving Mishra—the case that rocked the entire province.[75] Khare, the then premier, who alone showed 'no marked communalism in his official actions',[76] threatened to resign rather than oblige Mishra.[77] He also confirmed Imam-ur-Rahman, the only Muslim ICS officer in the province in his post (Deputy Commissioner, Yeotmal), in spite of his colleagues' strong opposition.[78]

Yusuf Shariff, the Provincial League president turned Congressman and Law Minister in the Khare cabinet, was not free from communalism either. He appointed 'a disproportionate number of Muslims as Assistant Public Prosecutors', after creating the posts 'without sufficient justification'. He was liberal in his clemency to Muslim offenders and even acted as their counsellors—a practice for which the governor, H.C. Gowan, had to pull him up.[79]

Shariff released from jail Zafar Hussain, the Muslim Inspector of Schools and a Khan Bahadur, who had been convicted to three year's rigorous imprisonment for a civil crime.[80] This misplaced clemency provoked an unprecedented public outcry; it cost Shariff his ministership and earned Khare, his protector, rather a bad name.[81] D.K. Mehta, the Law Minister in Shukla's cabinet, was equally communal in outlook; but for the governor's opposition, he would have freed from jail Sitaram Gaikwad who had been undergoing a sentence of rigorous imprisonment for attempting to kill Shariff for having released Zafar Hussain.[82] Wylie opposed as 'disingenuous' the Shukla ministry's plan of controlling the goings on in mosques where criminals had reportedly been harboured and arms stored for use during communal riots.[83] Wylie claimed that, but for his intercession, Shukla would have put all Muslim communal elements in prison, overlooking the deeds of Hindu communalists.[84]

Wylie was convinced of his ministers having 'almost certainly ... secret sympathy' with the Hyderabad satyagraha[85] launched by the Hindu Mahasabha and the Arya Samaj, in 1938-9, as a reaction to the Nizam's anti-Hindu policy. The satyagraha sharply polarized the Hindu and Muslim public opinion in the province, the one supporting and the other opposing it. Hundreds of satyagrahis from all over the province and many from far away places in the country went to Hyderabad through the bordering Berar districts, causing local tensions. Shukla and his colleagues could neither openly support the satyagraha nor strongly oppose it; either course would be playing into the hands of the Hindu Mahasabha. The Congress support would strengthen the movement, which would raise the political stock of the Mahasabha while smudging the secular image of the Congress; open opposition would only justify the Mahasabha's accusation that the Congress was indifferent to the suffering Hindus. Above all, the ministry had to heed to the governor's warning: effective measures be taken to prevent the passage of the satyagrahis through the Berar districts.[86]

In such circumstances the ministry decided to represent to the Crown Representative in Hyderabad against the anti-Hindu policy of the Nizam's government in regard particularly to the Hindu temples, Hindu schools and Hindu conversion to Islam. The ministry sympathized with the cultural object of the satyagraha as was made clear by the Arya Samaj; it had nothing to do with the political object, which the Mahasabha sought to promote.[87]

Wylie was hardly impressed by this stand taken by his ministry, much less so when he knew of its decision to send the Congress Speaker of the Assembly, Ghanashyam Gupta,[88] to the Viceroy to bring to his notice the 'just religious and cultural grievances of the Hindus' in the Nizam's state. Gupta would also negotiate with the Nizam's government about the matter. Wylie foiled this plan of his ministry. Linlithgow, on Wylie's suggestion, refused to see Gupta.[89] Convinced that his ministry would do little about the tense situation developing in Berar, the governor privately instructed the Commissioner at Amravati to exercise his executive powers to deal with the situation.[90]

The worsening communal situation in the province was in no small measure due to ministerial interference with routine administrative matters at lower levels where officers dealing with the law and order situation were under constant fear that their decisions would be set aside by the ministers, who gave more weight to local Congress workers' interpretation of the prevalent law and order problems than to reports of government officers on them.[91]

During the war years, governors of the province succeeded in building up a counterforce to the Congress for the sake of war operations. The Hindu Mahasabha, the Muslim League and all the others, who for various reasons, were hostile to the Congress, constituted the counterforce, the last led by Khare, the dismissed premier who had his own scores to settle with the Congress High Command.[92] All the Congress opponents fully cooperated with the government in its army recruitment drive, each, of course, for his own reason. The Hindus with military training would be better able to take on the Muslims after the war, so hoped the Mahasabha;[93] for local Leaguers, who blindly followed Jinnah's directive, it was implementing the party's policy of keeping well with the government; for Khare, cooperation with the government was essential to realize his ambition of becoming the premier once again with the support of the Muslims and the governor himself.

Both the Hindu Mahasabha and the League celebrated the Congress demission of office as deliverance from misrule. Khare rejoiced at the development. No punitive fines were imposed on the Muslims of Ashti and Chimur where violence had taken the toll of many policemen's lives in August 1942.[94] The governor suspended the realization of the punitive fines earlier imposed on the Muslims of Chandur-Biswa, and refunded the sums realized when the Congress ministry was in office.[95] Local authorities closely watched and carefully reported the activities of communal parties without being very harsh on them as long as they refrained from open indulgence in criminal activities.[96] Free from political pressure, local peace keepers, who enjoyed the trust and support of the governor, prevented the communal situation from getting out of hand; they encouraged the assumption of local responsibility for local crimes when forming peace committees to deal with communal troubles.

Khare's single-minded aim after the Congress ministry's resignation was to become the premier again by somehow cobbling up a minority ministry with non-Congress MLAs and prospective Congress defectors,[97] among whom he held the Marathi speaking men as the most important. For the purpose he consistently courted the 14 Muslim MLAs,[98] offering them as a bait even a disproportionately large share of ministerial berths—two out of six. He banked greatly on Rauf Shah, the President of the Provincial Muslim League, his long-standing friend, and S.W.A. Rizvi, whom he hoped to rope in with the help of Raghavendra Rao, who though out of active provincial politics then, still commanded considerable clout among the local Muslim population,[99] Rizvi having for long been his most favoured protégé.

H. Twynam, the governor, not only encouraged Khare in ministry-making but by pressure and persuasion sought to influence Muslim legislators in Khare's favour. Troubled by the Congress and worried over the worsening war situation, Twynam viewed the restoration of an Indian administration in the province as a political necessity. He had confidence in Khare's ability to win over not only non-Congress MLAs but even some discontented Congressmen, particularly the Marathi speaking ones. Twynam, who had served in Bengal earlier, knew the Muslims thoroughly; he, like Khare, was hopeful of winning over Rauf Shah, in particular, 'a mild mannered moderate little man', scarcely enthusiastic about Pakistan,[100] the League's main plank. As for Rizvi, Twynam would use the good offices of Raghavendra Rao, the Man Friday of successive governors of the province.[101] Twynam tried to prevail over the Leaguers, disabusing them of their suspicion of Khare and encouraging them to make the most of the 'solid bloc' position, which they would acquire in the ministry, a position which the governor would strongly support.[102]

For about three years Khare and Twynam persisted in their ministry-making efforts till ultimately they gave it up for one great reason: their failure to draw for the scheme the clinching factor for its success—'Jinnah's blessings'.[103] And that in spite of Khare's plea to Jinnah that the scheme be viewed as perfectly feasible and that his bonafides as a true friend of the Muslims be trusted.[104]

Jinnah was wary, though—for a time at least—not wholly averse to the idea of the League joining a coalition ministry. But he had also some strong reasons to withhold his consent—for the moment at least. He had a sneaking suspicion that Khare's object was just to use the Muslims for his own political ends, and that the Muslims might play into his hands. It was not a groundless fear: most Muslim MLAs had been only recent recruits to the League; some had long political association with Khare; and not a few were hankering after personal power and position, regardless of party interests. Besides, the provincial unit of the party had internal dissensions caused by ego clashes between the leaders.[105]

What made Khare's scheme all the more suspect was its support by M.S. Aney.[106] Aney's image among the Muslims was that of a rabid anti-Muslim, who, as a member of the Viceroy's Executive Council, was opposed to the general Muslim desire that Berar be restored to the Nizam as a reward for his services during the war.[107] Khare's efforts to win over the four non-Leaguer Muslim MLAs[108] appeared to Jinnah as a sinister move to divide the local Muslims, whose unity under his own leadership and his party was Jinnah's main political mission.

Above all, Jinnah knew for sure that, composed of small and separate groups, miscalled parties, Khare's projected ministry would fall like a house of cards the moment it confronted the solid Congress opposition in the Assembly. Finally, at that time Jinnah was having enough troubles with the Muslim ministries in Bengal, Sind and Assam to feel tempted to let his party strike its political fortune in the CP and Berar.[109]

Jinnah decided to wait and watch; he would neither reject the offer out of hand nor accept it with open arms; his partymen were only to keep talking to the governor and Khare, demanding further assurances from the one and wringing better terms from the other, all the while taking care that the flock stayed together. Jinnah did not even reply to Khare's letter.

Khare was sorely disappointed; he recalled the warning of his friend and former colleague, Ramrao Deshmukh: 'not to deliver himself hand and foot over to Jinnah as the latter would exact a heavy price'.[110] However, undaunted, Khare met the governor again, hoping that the Leaguers could be persuaded to at least observe neutrality whenever the minority ministry needed to seek the vote of confidence in the Assembly.[111] By now about three years had passed; Twynam's enthusiasm seemed flagging, he wondered if Khare was only day dreaming, for he had dismally failed to win over even Marathi speaking MLAs, his main hope, let alone effect any defection in the Congress party. He had got promises from many, firm commitment to his plan from none. Khare had indeed proved himself a poor judge of men while still trying to build 'on sand' the castle of his ministry.[112]

Khare was down but not yet out. He now requested Twynam to make him at least his non-official adviser. The governor would readily oblige provided Khare acquiesced in having Rauf Shah as his colleague in the same capacity. Twynam hoped that Khare and Rauf Shah, old friends and political co-workers, would make a good team,[113] both being equally anti-Congress and equally eager to piggyback to power with the governor's support.

But then, the Quit India movement which had just begun changed the situation. The emergency situation created by the Congress demanded that the governor strengthen his own personal rule instead of persisting in his fatuous experiments for a democratic administration with the help of either a minority ministry or Indian advisers. However, Twynam was not an ungrateful man nor one to ignore the fact that Khare did wield considerable political influence among the Marathi élite, which could be helpful to the government. On his strong recommendation, the Viceroy made Khare an Executive Councillor, 'a fitting reward for the valuable services he had rendered' to the governor by keeping him posted with the Congress game plan both at the provincial and national levels.[114]

The pot of a coalition ministry with Muslims in it was kept boiling by T.J. Kedar, Khare's trusted lieutenant.[115] Kedar kept seeing the governor and writing to Jinnah, besides confabulating with Muslim MLAs, to help him become the premier in a coalition cabinet of seven members of whom four would be Muslims,[116] all Leaguers, if possible, or no Leaguers, if it were considered necessary. Kedar failed more dismally than Khare, and much sooner too; the Viceroy was surprised at the 'inordinate demand' of the League in respect of ministerial berths, which Kedar had conceded.[117] Four Muslim ministers in a seven-member ministry was 'clearly ludicrously in excess' of the Muslim ratio in the population of the province;[118] it, however was a clear measure of the eagerness of Kedar to become the premier.

Unlike Khare, who was generally held in high esteem by the governor and the Muslim political élite, Kedar's image was that of a time-server, a chameleon, a 'volatile and unscrupulous' 'careerist', who was incapable of doing anything useful to further the government's war efforts, and this Twynam plainly told him.[119] Muslims distrusted Kedar far more than they did Khare; the former had changed his party labels oftener than even his clothes, as Abdur Rahman, the League leader, confided to the governor.[120]

Interestingly enough, Jinnah's stand on the ministry-making efforts was clear to all the League legislators, except Rauf Shah, their chief, who still harboured a flickering hope of ultimately making it to a ministry. He kept giving willing ears to Kedar until bluntly snubbed by Jinnah: '... you might as well enter into treaties and pacts with the lamp posts', Jinnah thundered, ridiculing Rauf Shah's continuing negotiation with Kedar and other leaders of small groups, which he fondly hoped could somehow be cobbled into a ministry.[121]

Jinnah, having been aware of Kedar trying to rope in non-Leaguers and seeking the governor's help for the purpose, pointedly reminded Rauf Shah of the firm stand of the party: the League alone represented Muslim interests in the country; it would never let a ministry be formed with any non-Leaguer in it nor allow any Leaguer to join such a ministry; and that non-Leaguers were not even true Muslims.[122] Jinnah warned Rauf Shah against agreeing to any terms offered for the League joining the projected ministry without getting them approved by the party High Command. Abdur Rahman had already warned Twynam that the certain League opposition to any ministry having non-Leaguers in it would plunge the whole country—not just the province—into chaos.[123]

The message went home. The government had better not annoy Jinnah any further when his cooperation was vital during the war years and in consideration of his having kept the Muslims away from the recent Quit India movement. Thus ended the fond idea of a 'make-shift ministry' 'dominated by careerists' and constituted by 'something like the King's party of George III'.[124] Twynam told Kedar that he wanted a stable ministry alone, if one could be formed by local leaders themselves, and that such a ministry must help the government in its war operations. The governor now left neither Kedar nor Muslim leaders with any hope whatever that he would either render 'active benevolence' to or exert 'gentle pressure through his officers on the many wavering personalities in local politics' to form a ministry to cooperate with the government.[125]

It was now past the middle of 1943; with the Congress leaders put behind the bars, the Quit India movement having petered out[126] and the tide of the war turning in favour of the Allied powers, the political crisis had ended; Governor Twynam had been able to manage the affairs by his own powers under the Government of India Act, 1935; the local political leadership lay divided, a section of it even solicitous of the governor's favours;[127] and the communal problem had been effectively dealt with by local executive authorities.

VI

The imminence of the end of the British rule and the inevitability of the Partition of the country on religious grounds influenced the course and character of communalism in the politics of the province. The Congress bounced back to power after winning the elections in 1946; the administration, now progressively Indianized, had no need to play off one section of the people against another for political purposes; local Leaguers acquiesced in the Congress rule in a spirit of resignation; and Hindu communal forces were kept in check by the Congress government and were unable to use Muslim bashing as a means of political mobilization. Communalism ceased to be a factor in local politics, though lingering for some years as a feeling, particularly among those, both Hindus and Muslims, who paid dearly for the country's independence in the form of life and much else held precious by them.

The Congress, the Hindu Mahasabha and the League plunged themselves headlong into the electioneering campaign. Opposition to the Pakistan scheme, the Wavell Plan and the Interim Government at the centre were the main election planks of the Mahasabha whose members fanned out to rural parts to enroll new recruits to the party—the targeted figure being 20,000 by October 1945. It set up a parliamentary board and launched a fund collection drive to raise money with which to pay its propagandists.[128] The League too set up an election fund, to which all its local committees were required to contribute so that it could raise Rs. 1,05,000. It set up a camp at Jabalpur for imparting training in election techniques.[129] The Congress too was successful in its enrolment drive, Berar alone accounting for 93,112 persons in a few months. The Congress received a shot in the arm: Aney returned to the party's fold, convinced that the Mahasabha's Hindu militarization policy was unsound and that the Congress alone could achieve independence for the country.[130]

Unlike in 1937, electioneering in 1946 was free from any grave communal disturbances, despite the withdrawal of restrictions on communal voluntary organizations after the war. Only in some villages local Hindus resorted to social boycott of their Muslim neighbours as a retaliation to the latter's objections to the playing of music before mosques.[131] The police in Berar having found no nexus whatever between the RSS and the Mahasabha or RSS involvement in any local communal dispute[132] indicated a welcome change in the situation.

The election results fully justified the League claim that it alone represented the Muslims. It won 13 out of the 14 Muslim reserved seats, its two candidates, Rauf Shah being one, having been elected unopposed; Khaksars and others who contested as independents were routed. Both the Congress Muslim candidates lost. However, another Congress Muslim won one of the two reserved Commerce constituencies and yet another won the Nagpur university constituency, who later became the Minister for Health in the Cabinet formed by Ravishankar Shukla. The Mahasabha won just one seat;[133] one of its candidates, in fact, discreetly left the field at the last moment fearing damage to his extensive interests in landed property and money-lending business when, as he was sure, Congress would come to power.[134]

The League legislators' generally low key posture was in sharp contrast to the aggressive stance they had adopted in the 1937-9 Assembly; it indicated their acquiescence in the Congress rule. Their only avowed concern was over what they viewed as the still inadequate educational and employment opportunities for their community. They pleaded that Urdu and Hindi be made the medium of instruction in the newly set up university at Sagar—and this as a gesture of consideration for the minority community.[135] The changed attitude of the Muslim legislators proved helpful for the conservation of communal peace. As for the Hindu Mahasabha, the RSS and Muslim voluntary organizations, the Shukla ministry continued with their earlier policy: non-interference with their propaganda work till it sparked off a communal fracas anywhere; and all these organizations were kept under close watch.[136]

Although disturbances in Calcutta in 1945 created great excitement among students, for which the convocation ceremony of Nagpur university had to be dropped,[137] the Muslim League's Direct Action Day in August 1946 passed off peacefully everywhere in the Central Provinces, except Berar. During the great Calcutta killings, the communal situation was 'peaceful but not cordial';[138] between September and November 1946, only three persons were reported killed and thirteen injured.[139] As directed by Jinnah, Muslims of the province observed 2 September 1946—the day on which the Interim Government under Nehru took office—as Black Day.[140]

Berar alone was the nagging problem, and so it remained for some time even after the country's independence. Bordering on Hyderabad, with which it had historical and cultural ties, Berar was a strong base of both Hindu and Muslim communal forces. Akola was the headquarter of the provincial branch of the League, which claimed a large membership among the local Muslims constituting about 8 per cent of the local population. The Hindu Mahasabha was very active in Berar when led by B.G. Khaparde, in particular.[141] Aney, Tambe and Moropant Joshi were all Beraris and involved in the Hindu unity movement.

Berar's retrocession to the Nizam was a live issue influencing both the political and communal aspects of the local life. Muslims were a solid bloc to support the retrocession while the Hindu opposition to it was weakened by the non-Brahmins and backward class men preferring the Nizam's rule to the continuance of Brahmin domination in the local political life.

This came to the fore particularly in 1945-7 when the prospect of the Nizam getting back Berar as a reward for his war services intensified the local Hindu-Muslim bitterness and the Brahmin/non-Brahmin clash of interests. The Prince of Berar and Sir Mirza Ismail, the Dewan of Berar, undertook a tour of the tract with a view to feeling the pulse of the people and, as the Commissioner suspected, 'to keep alive Hyderabad's claim to Berar'. The Hindu Mahasabha was divided on the issue of the Prince's visit, a section being determined to boycott it and even planning to bring in Savarkar for the purpose while another group opposed the boycott plan but rejected the idea that the Nizam's rule be restored in Berar. As for local Congressmen, non-Brahmins among them favoured the Prince's visit, Brahmins were opposed to it, while many others were just indifferent.[142]

Sir Mirza Ismail's visit was a great success, going by the reaction of the backward class men and non-Brahmins, who were led by Dr Punjabrao Deshmukh.[143] Deshmukh entertained Sir Mirza at his own home and received from him a handsome grant for the Shivaji Education Society.[144] The visit strengthened the local Muslim hope of their again being the subjects of the Nizam in the near future.

Berar was tense in 1946-7. A serious riot took place at Badnera in August/September 1946 as a reaction to the killings in Calcutta, in particular. Police firing killed several Muslims who had hung up black flags condemning the Interim Government in New Delhi. The League took up the issue to discredit the Congress government. A committee was sent to Badnera and in its report it asserted that the local police was determined 'to annihilate the Muslims and curb down their spirit and to establish the Hindu domination' at the place.[145] Congressmen colluded with the police, creating insecurity among the local Muslim population, it added.

In an open letter to Shukla, the League condemned his 'hymn of hate' against the Muslim community; Shukla responded by a stern warning to the local Leaguers that their unceasing vilification of the police and rumour-mongering would land them in trouble.[146]

The Shukla ministry rose equal to the difficult situation in July-August 1947. With stories of atrocities on Hindus in East Bengal, West Punjab and Assam freely circulating and with movement of refugees to and from several parts of the province taking place,[147] the situation would have been graver but for the attitude of the local Leaguers and Hindu Mahasabhaites. By now both had resigned themselves to the reality of the country's independence and of the country being divided on communal grounds. Abdur Rahman and Rauf Shah's demonstrative participation in the Independence Day celebration evoked considerable appreciation among local Hindus who reciprocated by agreeing to re-route their planned musical processions to avoid mosques[148]—a concession to Muslim susceptibility and for long a cause for prolonged Hindu–Muslim riots. The Mahasabhaites fully shared with their erstwhile Congress rivals the success of many Independence Day celebrations at many places.

The Shukla ministry followed a twofold policy: it would restore the Muslim sense of security and reassurance; and it would also weed out from the province those elements who were actually or potentially a security risk. The government checked the Muslim exodus from Berar, in particular, by public appeal and strict ban on unrestricted travel to Hyderabad by rail and road. Local peace committees were set up, all party conferences arranged and press statements issued for the purpose.[149]

The security risk was internal and external, both often interconnected as was proved particularly by the situation created by the uncertainty over Hyderabad's merger with the Indian Union and the police action which followed it. The police needed to keep a close watch on Muslim Leaguers in Berar and to stop some local Muslim schools, earlier centres of the League activity,[150] from functioning as pro-Pakistani or pro-Hyderabad bases. House to house searches led to seizure of arms stored by some local Muslims[151] at a time when reports came thick and fast about movements of the Hyderabad police and army units in border villages and their intrusion in tracts from where Hindus fled to safer areas.[152] As a precautionary measure Muslim officers in border areas were either promptly transferred or even retired, their anti-Hindu and pro-Nizam leanings confirmed by secret reports.[153]

All this created a situation in which anti-Pakistani sentiments often overlapped with anti-Muslim feelings, which caught on with the men even holding high offices. Shukla, the Premier himself, for example, decided to cleanse the administration of 'Muslim elements' though not declaring it. While publicly disclaiming any change in the existing policy regarding recruitment to public services,[154] he laid out a confidential scheme to end the long-standing overrepresentation of Muslims, in the services.[155] He would retire all Muslim employees—and those in the police department, in particular—who had completed 25 years of service; and not recruit Muslims till their strength in the government service fell to such a degree that it matched their proportion in the population of the province. However, Shukla could not immediately have his way because the general opinion of his staff was against the step, it being both morally improper and legally untenable.[156] So there the matter rested for the time at least, administrative discipline prevailing over political expediency.

VII

Communalism became an important factor in the CP and Berar politics after the 1937 elections when the Congress formed a ministry in the province. Before that its only manifestation was in the riots between Hindu and Muslim riff-raff, which were a law and order problem for the local peace keepers to tackle. A section of the Hindu élite was involved in the riots but not the Muslim élite, who were a disorganized group of men keen on piggybacking to power with the support of some Hindu leaders and the government, the latter two often acting in tandem.

The Government of India Act, 1935, in broadening the electoral system made the competition for power keener among the political élite who pandered to mass religious passions and sentiments as a means of political mobilization and support. This alone accounted for the steady growth of the Muslim League in the province after 1937 and the polarization of Muslim political opinion, so long a desideratum. Hindu communal groups, particularly the Hindu Mahasabha and the RSS, also adopted the same technique to gain political clout at the grassroots level.

The Congress, too, appeared to the Muslims as no different from a Hindu communal party, three factors deepening the impression: the party's failure to create any Muslim following worth the name, the desertion of some prominent Congress Muslims to the League and the close association of some important Congressmen with the Hindutva movement. Even the keen political rivalry between the Congress and the Hindu Mahasabha did not diminish the admiration of some Congressmen, mostly high caste Maharashtrians, for the RSS, for long the strong arm of the Mahasabha. This, no doubt, served as grist to the League's propaganda mill.

Finally, in the 1940s even local issues and events, however trifling in themselves, came to be viewed in the context of the intensifying power struggle between the Congress and the League. Although no large scale communal killings followed in the province, communal feelings ran high due to such killings elsewhere. Thus the people in this backward province ultimately joined the mainstream of the national life then buffeted by the communal maelstrom.

NOTES

1. Sir E. Raghavendra Rao, a leading politician of the province, was at first a follower of Tilak and Annie Besant. He formed the Independent Congress party and became a minister in 1927-8; later he organized the Democratic Party, which dominated the provincial legislature for some years before the 1937 elections when the Congress swept the polls. Rao, a blue-eyed boy of successive governors, became the Home Member in the Governor's Council from 1930 to 1936, and he was made the acting governor when the governor was on leave.
2. The CP and Berar legislature, constituted in 1914, was called the Legislative Council till, under the Government of India Act, 1935, it was renamed the Legislative Assembly.
3. *Central Provinces and Berar Legislative Council Proceedings* (hereafter *CPLC*), September 1922, Vol. II, pp. 268 and 254-8; and 1923, Vol. I, pp. 236-50.
4. Ibid., August 1921, Vol. II, pp. 374-8; August 1923, Vol. III, pp. 397-9.
5. S.W.A. Rizvi, a member of Rao's Democratic Party, was elected the president of the Legislative Council in 1931, Hindu MLCs hailing his election, ibid., 25 August 1931, Vol. II, pp. 133-4. Rizvi was praised as an 'upholder of Hindu-Muslim unity'.
6. Ibid., August 1921, Vol. II, pp. 780-4, 816, 822 and 823; and August 1925, Vol. I, p. 447. S.M. Chitnavis, the minister, was opposed to restrictions on trade in hides, for fear of economic loss to the government. Chitnavis, a liberal Hindu, was associated with the Hindu unity movement.
7. There were 33 riots between 1923 and 1930 in which 31 persons were killed and 721 injured, ibid., January-March 1936, Vol. I, p. 191. David Baker, 'The Muslim Concern for Security: the Central Provinces and Berar, 1919-1947', in Mushirul Hasan, ed., *Communal and Pan-Islamic Trends in Colonial India* (New Delhi, 1981), pp. 238-9.
8. The Hindu Mahasabha, the Arya Samaj and the RSS sought to organize the Hindu, socially and politically, following large-scale atrocities on the Hindus by the Muslims in the 1920s, beginning with the Moplah rebellion. B.S. Munje, the Hindu Mahasabha leader, set up rifle clubs and gymnasia for physically strengthening the Hindus and enabling them to take on the Muslims during the communal riots. Reconversion of Hindu converts to Islam was an important programme of the Hindu unity movement.
9. The Muslim population never exceeded 4.6 per cent till 1947.
10. Under the Act, the number of Muslim reserved constituencies was increased to 14.
11. Home Department (Political) (hereafter HD[P]), File No. 111/37 – Pol (1) of 1937 (Elections of 1937), National Archives of India, New Delhi (hereafter NAI).
12. Z.A. Zaidi, 'Aspects of the Development of Muslim League Politics, 1937-47', in

C.H. Philips and M.D. Wainwright, eds, *The Partition of India: Policies and Perspectives, 1935-1947* (London, 1970), pp. 245-6.

13. Syed Sharifuddin Pirzada, *Foundations of Pakistan: All India Muslim League Documents, 1906-1947, Vol. I, 1906-24* (Karachi, 1969), pp. 128 and 545.
14. Khan Bahadur H.M. Malak of Nagpur was one of the earliest members of the League. He was in the Aga Khan's delegation to Simla in 1906. He was one of the earliest vice presidents of the League, ibid., pp. 128, 320 and 391.
15. N.N. Mitra, *Indian Annual Register, 1936*, Vol. II (1st repr., Delhi, 1990), pp. 273-4.
16. He was a minister in 1933-4 for less than a year. At first he was a Rao loyalist and later his bitter baiter for Rao's partiality towards Rauf Shah, Shariff's bitter rival in Muslim politics.
17. HD (P) File No. 18-12/1936, Fortnightly Reports (hereafter FR) of first and second half of December 1936, NAI.
18. Home Department (Reforms) File No. 20/1936, NAI.
19. P.N. Chopra, ed., *Towards Freedom, Vol. I, 1937* (hereafter *TF*) (New Delhi, 1985), p. 722.
20. J.R. Joshi, *Dr Kedar Yanche Charitra* (in Marathi) (Nagpur, 1956), p. 191. Kedar, a follower of Khare, was a prominent political leader of the time.
21. For details, see K. Mojumdar, 'The Congress Ministry in the Central Provinces and Berar, 1937-39', in P.K. Mishra, ed., *Aspects of Indian History and Historiography* (New Delhi, 1996), pp. 22-47.
22. Sinha Papers (hereafter SP), File No. 280121, pp. 30 and 33. Notes from personal files of Deputy Commissioners, W. Grigson, Deputy Commissioner, Jabalpur, to Hyde Gowan, Governor, 1 November and 1 December 1936. SP are the typed copies of the many Political and Military Department files of the CP and Berar government which were used by the committee set up by the Madhya Pradesh government to compile the history of the freedom movement in the province. The chairman of the committee was D.P. Mishra, the Chief Minister. Professor R.M. Sinha was a member of the committee. Nagpur university procured the files from Professor Sinha.
23. Ibid., File No. 280060, extracts from newspapers, April 1936.
24. HD(P), FR, File No. 18/5-1940, second half of May 1940, NAI. Correspondence of Lord Linlithgow (hereafter LC), in Microfilm Reel No. 2195, Governor Twynam to Linlithgow, 23 March 1939, NAI ; ibid., Reel No. 2197, 22 August 1940.
25. *CPLC*, 7 November 1939, Vol. VII, p. 352.
26. LC, Gowan to Linlithgow, 6 July 1937, cited in *TF*, p. 722.
27. LC, Reel No. 2195, Governor Wylie to Linlithgow, 29 December 1938.
28. SP, File No. 280069, pp. 54-6, Chief Secretary's Note, 22 March 1939.
29. R. Coupland, *Indian Politics, 1936-42* (London, 1944), p. 102.
30. Government of CP and Berar, *Vidya Mandir Scheme: A Way to the Spread of Free and Compulsory Mass Education Within a Fixed Period* (Nagpur, 1938), pp. 12-13.
31. Mitra, *Indian Annual Register, 1937*, Vol. I (1st repr., Delhi, 1990), pp. 288 and 344.
32. *C.P. and Berar Legislative Assembly Debates* (hereafter *CPLA*), 14 August 1939, p. 783.
33. Shukla succeeded Khare as the premier, the latter having to step down after his differences with the Congress High Command. Khare was expelled from the Congress party. Continuing as a MLA, he opposed the Shukla ministry tooth and nail. He sought to rally the Marathi speaking politicians of the province under his leadership against Shukla and his colleague, D.P.Mishra, the two leaders of the Hindi speaking politicians

of the province, D.E.U. Baker, *Changing Political Leadership in an Indian Province: The Central Provinces and Berar, 1919-1939* (Delhi, 1979), pp. 177-99.
34. The name was Bait-ul-Ilm or Madina-ul-Ilm, *CPLA*, 1 November 1939, p. 3.
35. SP, File No. 280069, p. 68, *Jaddo Jehad* (Nagpur), 19 February 1939. *Jaddo Jehad* was a Muslim newspaper brought out in Urdu.
36. Khursheed Kamal, *A Documentary Record of the Congress Government, 1937-39, Related to Muslims under Congress Rule* (Islamabad, 1988), Vol. I, pp. 81-2.
37. *Pirpur Committee Report* (Lucknow, 15 November 1938), p. 53. The League appointed the Committee under the chairmanship of Raja Syed Muhammad Mehdi of Pirpur to report on the conditions of the Muslims in all Congress-ruled provinces.
38. A.K. Fazlul Haq, *Muslim Sufferings under Congress Rule* (Calcutta, 1939).
39. *Pirpur Committee Report*, op.cit., pp. 11-12.
40. *Hitavada* (Nagpur), 10 February 1939. It was a moderate newspaper run by the Servants of India Society.
41. In 1938, there were 23,000 members of the League; the number increased to 56,541 in 1943, Gowher Rizvi, *Linlithgow and India: A Study of British Policy and the Political Impasse in India, 1936-43* (London, 1978), p. 124.
42. LC, Reel No. 2196, Linlithgow to Wylie, 14 January 1939, NAI.
43. Ibid., 10 June 1939.
44. Ibid., Wylie to Linlithgow, 23 March 1939 and 18 November 1939. Shukla was described as strongly anti-Muslim and anti-Maharashtrian besides being 'a byword for dilatoriness', files lying with him 'for weeks and months'.
45. Ibid., Wylie to Linlithgow, 18 April 1939 and 23 July 1939.
46. Ibid., 23 June 1939; and ibid., Reel No. 2197, 22 January 1940.
47. Ibid., Reel No. 2195, 9 December 1938.
48. Ibid.
49. Ibid., Reel No. 2194, Hugh Bomford, Acting Governor, to Linlithgow, 23 March 1938.
50. Ibid., Reel No. 2195, Wylie to Linlithgow, 9 December 1938.
51. Ibid., Reel No. 2196, 18 April 1939.
52. Rizvi, op.cit., p. 101.
53. Francis Wylie, 'Federal Negotiations in India, 1935-39 and After', in Philips and Wainwright, eds, op.cit., p. 523.
54. Rajmohan Gandhi, *Patel: A Life* (Ahmedabad, 1992), p. 289. Rizvi, op.cit., p. 102.
55. SP, 280068, File No. 31/1939, Note on Communalism by C.M. Trivedi, 10 November 1938.
56. Coupland, op.cit., p. 333.
57. HD(P), File No. 18/5-1940, FR, second half of May 1940.
58. Ibid., File No. 18/6-1941, FR, first half of June 1941.
59. Ibid., File No. 19-7/1943, FR, for first half of July 1943.
60. Ibid., File No. 18-6/1938, FR, second half of June 1938; and ibid., File No. 18/4-1943, FR, second half of April 1943.
61. Ibid., File No. 18/12-1937, FR, first half of December 1937.
62. In both the 1937 and 1946 elections the Mahasabha won just one seat in the Assembly, B.B.Misra, *The Indian Political Parties* (Delhi, 1976), pp. 556-7; and HD (Reforms), File No. 20/1936, Election Returns, Provincial Legislatures, 1937, NAI.
63. The violent mob set a police outpost afire killing some policemen. The RSS and the Hindu Mahasabha were held 'entirely responsible' for the incident. Tukdoji Maharaj, 'originally a leader of the revivalist type' was implicated in the incident, LC, Reel

No. 2199, Twynam to Linlithgow, 5 October and 28 November 1942.

64. HD(P), File No. 18/10-1944, FR, first half of October 1944; SP, File No. 280076, Note by Chief Secretary on RSS, 19 September 1942 and Governor's Note, 15 October 1942.
65. V. Deshpande, 'Militant Nationalism in Maharashtra, 1925-51' (unpublished Ph.D. thesis, University of Jammu, 1989), pp. 103-4 and 110.
66. SP, File No. 280077, File No. 93/1944, Note on Volunteer Organizations in CP; and ibid., File No. 280070, Note on Khaksar movement in the province, 29 May 1939.
67. Ibid., File No. 93/1944
68. Joshi was Home Member in the Governor's Council and Chitnavis was a Minister handpicked by the governor, Sir Frank Sly, in the early 1920s. Tambe, a Swarajist, was a Home Member from 1925 to 1930 before he became the acting governor. M.S. Aney, a Member of the Viceroy's Council and earlier a Tilakite and a Congressman, was also closely connected with both the Hindu Mahasabha and the RSS.
69. HD(P), File No. 18-12/1937, FR, for first half of December 1937.
70. N.B. Khare, *My Political Memoirs or Autobiography* (Nagpur, 1971), pp. 213-15 and 246. He was the Mahasabha president 1949-51.
71. The politics of the CP and Berar was characterized by keen rivalry and jockeying for position and power between the Hindi speaking leaders belonging to the Mahakoshal region and the Marathi speaking leaders belonging to the Nagpur region. In the Berar region the local Marathi leaders had no love lost either for the Hindi leaders of Mahakoshal or Marathi leaders of the Nagpur region. For details see Baker, op.cit.
72. LC, Reel No. 2196, Wylie to Linlithgow, 18 May 1939; and ibid., 8 August 1939, enclosing R.N. Banerjee's letter to Laithwaite, 26 August 1939.
73. Ibid., Wylie to Linlithgow, 23 March 1939.
74. Ibid., Banerjee to Laithwaite, op.cit.
75. Before becoming a minister in the Khare Cabinet, Mishra was allegedly involved in a controversy. The matter was raised in the Assembly by Muslim MLAs, *CPLA*, December 1937, Vol. II, pp. 276-8. See also D.P. Mishra, *Living an Era*, Vol. I, *India's March to Freedom* (Delhi, 1975), pp. 260-2.
76. LC, Reel No. 2196, Banerjee to Laithwaite, 26 August 1939.
77. Ibid..
78. Khursheed Kamal, op.cit., pp. 134-5.
79. LC, Reel No. 2196, Banerjee to Laithwaite, 26 August 1939.
80. Ibid., Reel No. 2194, Hugh Bomford, Acting Governor, to Linlithgow, 7 April 1938.
81. Ibid., Reel No. 2194, Gowan to Linlithgow, 23 March 1938; HD(P), File No. 18/3-1938, FR for second half of March 1938; and N.B. Khare Papers, No. 108 (XII), Khare to Shariff, 5 April 1938, NAI.
82. LC, Reel No. 2196, Wylie to Linlithgow, 8 August 1939.
83. Ibid., 22 May 1939.
84. Ibid., 23 March 1939 and 18 April 1939.
85. Ibid., 4 June 1939
86. Ibid., 7, 10 and 23 June 1939.
87. SP, File No. 280070, pp. 71-121, Note by D.P. Mishra, 13 June 1939.
88. Gupta was president of the All India Aryan League.
89. LC, Reel No. 2196, Wylie's telegram to Linlithgow, 10 June 1939.
90. Ibid., Wylie's telegram to Linlithgow, 7 June 1939.
91. Ibid., Wylie to Linlithgow, 23 March 1939 and 18 April 1939.

92. Khare's ouster was condemned by the Hindu Mahasabha leaders, N.K. Kelkar and B.G. Khaparde and liberal Muslim leaders, Samiullah Khan and Maulana Abdul Natiq. Harijan leaders also supported Khare and criticized the Congress High Command's decision to sack him, HD(P), File No. 18 August 1938, FR, first half of August 1938.
93. LC, Reel No. 2198, Twynam to Linlithgow, 22 June 1941.
94. As in Chimur in Chandrapur district, in Ashti, a village in Wardha district, also a mob burnt a few local policemen during the August movement.
95. Maharashtra State (Vidarbha) Archives, Nagpur (hereafter MAVN), Police Department, File No. 6-2/1940.
96. The government needed to soft pedal both the Hindu Mahasabha and the Muslim League for their active cooperation with the local recruitment drive launched by the government. Local Mahasabha leaders sat with the Leaguers in the provincial war committees.
97. Khare hoped to rope in the non-Brahmin group, the backward classes group, the Berar group and the Muslims. He claimed to have 11 MLAs who formed his own group, LC, Reel No. 2199, Twynam to Linlithgow, 13 February 1942.
98. Of the 14 Muslim MLAs, 10 were Leaguers, one (Shariff) was a Congressman, close to Khare, and three were Independents.
99. Khare stayed in touch with Rao, the two men forgetting their old rivalry when Rao, close to successive governors, was often criticized by Khare, a devoted Congressman, till he was ousted from the party, LC, Reel No. 2196, Wylie to Linlithgow, 26 April 1939. It appears that even before the Shukla ministry resigned in November 1939, Khare and Governor Wylie had been trying to cause the fall of the ministry, the latter taking advantage of the former's grouse against the Hindu ministers who had caused his ouster.
100. LC, Reel No. 2198, Twynam to Linlithgow, 15 September 1941.
101. Rao was close to all governors, Montague Butler, Hyde Gowan, Francis Wylie and Henry Twynam, see Baker, op.cit., pp. 127-8, 143-4 and 163.
102. LC, Reel No. 2198, Twynam to Linlithgow, 26 August 1941.
103. Ibid., Reel No. 2197, 30 June 1942.
104. Ibid., Khare wrote to Jinnah that he could get the support of 49 MLAs, and if the Muslim League MLAs, numbering 10, joined him, his party, with a total membership of 59, would form the majority in the Assembly having a strength of 112 members. He added, 'I have been fair to Muslims all my life and my Congress friends have condemned me, among others, for this failing too', Khare to Jinnah, 7 February 1942, enclosed in Twynam's letter to Linlithgow, 13 February 1942, LC, Reel No. 2199.
105. Siddiqui Ali Khan, Member, Central Legislative Assembly, representing the League, and Rauf Shah, president of the Provincial Muslim League, were rivals in provincial League affairs.
106. Aney, a leader from Berar, was an early Tilakite and later an ardent Congressman who took a leading part in the Civil Disobedience movement. He, however, opposed the Congress stand on the Communal Award issue. He became a member of the Viceroy's Executive Council from which he resigned when Gandhi was imprisoned during the Quit India movement.
107. LC, Reel No. 2198, Twynam to Linlithgow, 26 August 1941.
108. One was a Congressman (Shariff) and the other three Independents.
109. LC, Reel No. 2199, Twynam to Linlithgow, 28 January 1942.
110. Ibid., Reel No. 2198, Twynam to Linlithgow, 15 September 1941.

111. Ibid., Reel No. 2199, 2 March 1942.
112. Ibid, 30 April 1942.
113. Ibid., 12 August 1942.
114. Ibid., 2 September 1942. Khare was the 'real active leader of the National War Front in the province and the Chief Warden of the ARP in Nagpur'. Twynam praised his 'rare honesty of character', ibid., 11 January 1943.
115. Kedar was a close follower of Khare and like him was expelled from the Congress, Joshi, op.cit.
116. LC, Reel No. 2200, Twynam to Linlithgow, 23 June 1943.
117. Ibid., Linlithgow to Twynam, 15 June 1943.
118. Ibid.
119. Ibid., Twynam to Linlithgow, 23 June 1943.
120. Ibid., Kedar was a member of the Nationalist Party, then a leader of the non-Brahmin group in the Assembly. He joined Rao's Democratic Party and became a minister for a short while and later he fell out with Rao. He formed a 'people's party' as well, Baker, op.cit., pp. 113, 162, 184 and 189-92. Also see Joshi, op.cit.
121. LC, Reel No. 2200, Twynam to Linlithgow, 12 and 14 July 1943, enclosing intercepted letter from Jinnah to Rauf Shah, 23 June 1943.
122. Ibid.
123. Ibid., Twynam to Linlithgow, 23 June 1943.
124. Ibid., Linlithgow to Twynam, 15 June 1943; and ibid., Twynam to Linlithgow, 28 July 1943.
125. Ibid.
126. The Congress movement was 'truly dead' in the province by October 1942, so claimed the government, HD(P), File No. 18/10/1942, FR for first half of October 1942.
127. Apart from all Muslim MLAs, the governor counted Aney, Khare, Kedar and Ramrao Deshmukh as pro-government at the time. The Mahasabhites also were cooperating with the government's war efforts.
128. MAVN, Political and Military Department, File No. 32/1947, FR for second half of July 1945 and first half of August 1945. The RSS urged students to move about villages for propaganda work, ibid., HD(P), File No. 18, September 1945.
129. Ibid., FR for second half of September 1945 and first half of December 1945; HD (P), File No. 18-9/1945, FR for first half of September 1945; also ibid., File No. 18-12/1945, FR for first and second half of December 1945.
130. MAVN, Political and Military Department, File No. 5/1945, FR for second half of October 1945.
131. Ibid., FR for first half of August 1945.
132. Ibid.
133. Reforms Department, File No. 94/4/1945, NAI, Statistics Relating to the election to the provincial Legislative Assembly, letter of the CP and Berar government to V.P. Menon, Secretary to the Governor-General (Reforms), 23 July 1946.
134. HD(P), File No. 18-10/1945, FR for second half of October 1945.
135. *CPLA*, 14 September 1946, pp. 318-19; 28 September 1946, pp. 738-40; 30 September 1946, pp. 765 and 766; and 16 November 1946, p. 974.
136. Ibid., 18 March 1947, p. 641; and 8 October 1947, p. 10.
137. HD(P), File No. 18-11/1945, FR for second half of November 1945.
138. Nicholas Mansergh, editor-in-chief, *The Transfer of Power*, Vol. IX (London, 1980), pp. 49 and 188.

139. Ibid.
140. MAVN, Political and Military Department, File No. 10/1946.
141. Khaparde was a minister in 1934 and again, for a very short while, in 1937, just prior to the formation of the Congress ministry, Baker, op.cit., pp. 108, 109, 164 and 177.
142. MAVN, Political and Military Department, File No. 3/1945, FR for first half of January 1945.
143. Ibid., File No. 16-53/1947; and File No. 63-B/1947.
144. Ibid.
145. Ibid., File No. 10/1946.
146. Ibid., SP, File No. 280079.
147. MAVN, Political and Military Department, File No. 32/1947; File No. 15-54/1947; and File No. 16-7/1948, *CPLA*, 6 November 1947, pp. 11-12.
148. MAVN, Police Department, File No. 24/1947, Rauf Shah, leader of the Muslim League party in the Assembly made a speech on the Independence Resolution moved by Shukla, saying that Muslims would be loyal to independent India, *CPLA*, 6 October 1947, Vol. IV, pp. 9-10.
149. Ibid., 6 November 1947, Vol. IV, p. 11; and MAVN, Political and Military Department, File No. 32/1947.
150. MAVN, General Administration Department, File No. 30/1947; File No. 39/1947; and Political and Military Department, File No. 42/1948.
151. *CPLA*, 6 November 1947, p. 12.
152. MAVN, General Administration Department, File No. 30/1947.
153. Ibid., Secret, File No. 29/1947; Political and Military Department, File No. 150/1947; Police Department, File No. 38/1947; File No. 6/1947; and File No. 8/1947. There were reports of some policemen having deserted their ranks and some opting for Pakistan and leaving their service, ibid.
154. In February 1947, Shukla said on the floor of the Assembly that the government, in matters of recruitment to public services, 'is not going to act on communal representation. It acts only on qualifications'. He gave an assurance that Muslim representation in the services would not be scaled down, although they were over-represented in them. He also gave an assurance that no retrenchment would take place either, *CPLA*, 25 February 1947, Vol. I, pp. 23-4.
155. Muslims had always constituted more than 20 per cent in public services, though they were never more than just 4.6 per cent of the local population.
156. MAVN, General Administration Department, File No. 17-58/1949, Note by Shukla, 11 June 1947. Officers advised him to wait till India became a Dominion after 15 August 1947, ibid., Department Notes.

Princes, Prajamandals and Partition: Congress Politics and the Rajas of Orissa, 1937-1949

JAYANTA SENGUPTA

The thesis of the singularity of '1947' has been criticized, most importantly, by historians working on the micro-history of the transfer of power in India and its immediate aftermath. This research has made clear that the political settlement of 1947-50 was a very restricted one both in the strictly constitutional sense and in the sense that it was thrashed out by a very small circle of élite and rather socially conservative politicians; and that, despite appearances, the transfer of power to Indians in 1947 had little immediate impact either on the way of governance or on the make-up of the governing class.[1] In spite of such strong features of continuity, however, 1947 continues to be commonly described as a revolutionary and watershed event in the context of integration of the erstwhile princely states in the Indian Union. Echoing the States Minister Vallabhbhai Patel's own verdict in a speech to the Constituent Assembly, William L. Richter has talked about a 'bloodless revolution from princely to republican rule'.[2] Not to be outdone, R.L. Handa has described the integration of the states as 'the world's biggest bloodless revolution'.[3] This paper examines the Congress' role in organizing people's movements in the princely states of Orissa. It tests the above argument with particular reference to the case of the integration of the Orissa states and examines how the states' question in general influenced Oriya regional politics in the run-up to the Partition in 1947.

THE *GARHJAT* POLITICAL SYSTEM AND THE NATURE OF PRINCELY RULE

A feature of nationalist politics in the subcontinent till the mid-1930s was that the Indian National Congress had geared its movements and political organization essentially to the political situation in British India, and was unwilling to commit significant resources to agitational political activity in the Indian princely states. But the forging of new 'mass contacts' by the Congress, in the mid-1930s, and the consequent broadening of its social base, took place concurrently with a geographical expansion of its influence. This was a direct outcome of the new Congress interest in the issues and problems affecting politics in princely India. The party's remarkable electoral success of 1937, followed by its initiation in the new experience of governance, raised popular expectations to unprecedented levels. In the feudatory states of Orissa, where princely rule had perpetuated an autocratic, semi-feudal system of administration, impoverished peasants were cajoled by a 'paternalistic' Congress policy into organizing a movement for political and agrarian reform during 1937-40. This presented the Congress with an opportunity to draft the states people's struggle in *Garhjat* or princely Orissa—launched by popular bodies called prajamandals—into the fold of agitational politics that the party organized in coastal Orissa against the British government and the big zamindars. This paper seeks to describe the various phases in the evolving Congress policy towards the prajamandal movement. It shows how the tendency of the Utkal Provincial Congress Committee (UPCC) leaders to veer between non-interference, compromise and withdrawal, at crucial stages of this movement reinforced the distrust that *Garhjat* people traditionally nurtured about coastal politics.

The 26 Oriya-speaking princely states, variously known as the *Garhjats*, the 'Tributary Mahals' and the 'Feudatory States', made up one of the largest and least accessible forest areas of central and eastern India. Originally ruled by tribal chiefs, these tracts were subsequently penetrated by upcountry adventurers from northern India who during the late ancient and early medieval period carved out petty principalities for themselves. Through the period of Mughal and Maratha rule over *Mughalbandi* or coastal Orissa, these hill chieftains had successfully retained their autonomy in return for making periodic payments of tribute or *peshkash* to the Mughal or Maratha overlords. The British conquest of Orissa during the Second Maratha War of 1803 brought the *Garhjats* into some administrative relation with the coastal tracts, which were under the direct control of the East India Company. Although British regulations were not introduced in the princely states and the avowed policy of the government was one of non-interference in their internal administration, the Governor-General Lord Moira proceeded in 1814 to establish the office of the Superintendent of the Tributary Mahals for the better administrative supervision of these territories. The superintendent held discretionary powers of interference in the states' affairs—a power that was invoked in 1840 and again in 1848 to confiscate the states of Angul and Banki, respectively, from their rulers on the charge of maladministration. In 1906, a new office of the Political Agent and Commissioner of the Orissa Feudatory States was created to take over the responsibilities previously vested in the superintendent.

It has been argued recently that the quality of government in a princely state in the twentieth century did not hinge solely on the ability and inclination of the ruler, because—contrary to popular opinion—the princes did not, and could not, rule autocratically in the literal sense.[4] However, although the standard of government in the feudatory states varied considerably, what distinguished them all was the personal nature of the administration. P.T. Mansfield, recollecting his days in the states as Additional Political Agent during 1919-21, commented that 'there was no democracy in the States, but personal government . . . some Rajas were enlightened and educated administrators; others were, well, not so good, but the standard generally was rising'.[5] Personal government had both its benefits and its disadvantages. The government was certainly closer to the people, less remote and impersonal than in the British districts. Similarly, the judicial system in princely Orissa, as an official observed in 1940, 'even if not as highly legalized as in British India, is very definitely more prompt'.[6] On the other hand, in the absence of bureaucratic procedures, people had no constitutional redress against a bad ruler. R.K. Ramadhyani, whose settlement work in the late 1930s and early 1940s gave him close access to most of the ruling chiefs, had some very pessimistic comments to offer on the nature of the rule in the states:

> I think it can safely be said that a Ruler who is a successful *ma bap* is indeed very exceptional. The 'hash' which many Rulers, who have received a satisfactory education and training, have made of their affairs shows that the circumstances and atmosphere surrounding them are such that it can only be a very exceptional person who can wield autocratic powers without abuse. Besides, in these states with far from princely revenues, efficiency of administration cannot well go hand in hand with a large privy purse, and generally the interests of the people become opposed to the interests of the Ruling Chiefs.[7]

These comments echoed the ones made half a century earlier in an annual administrative report, which stated that even colonial official supervision—exercised through short visits by superintendents during the winter months—had a very limited restraining influence on the Rajas. As a result, 'oppression and misgovernment' went unnoticed till popular discontent escalated into 'a general rising or disturbance', forcing the government to intervene to quell the rebellion. Yet, such a turn of events hardly succeeded in breaking the ongoing cycle of oppression and revolt and as the report stated: 'The Raja-oppressor makes the most fulsome promises of reform, and is reinstated, only to begin the process of provoking revolt all over again'.[8]

Indeed, tensions inherent within the *Garhjat* agrarian society resulted, in the second half of the nineteenth century, in intermittent outbreaks of rebellion against the chiefs. Uprisings in Athmallik in 1863, in Mayurbhanj in 1866, in Narsinghpur in 1878, in Nayagarh in 1849-52 and 1893-4 and in Keonjhar in 1867-8 and 1891-3 were all directed against an assortment of local, mostly agrarian, grievances—for which reason they have been dubbed, not entirely without justification, by some scholars as 'anti-feudal'.[9] About the political potency of these grievances, official and non-official opinion varied considerably. A committee appointed by the Congress in 1939 to enquire into the nature of the states subjects' grievances reported that 'land is heavily taxed [in the states] without regard to the capacity of the peasants to pay', and held that 'this heavy and iniquitous burden has broken the backs of the peasantry and created conditions ripe for an agrarian revolution'.[10] On the other hand, the Political Agent of the states in the 1920s, C.L. Philip, thought that 'on the whole the actual cultivators manage to exist fairly well' despite revision settlements in most of the states in the 1920s and the attendant increases in rent levels.[11] Likewise, an official report prepared in 1940 by the Additional Political Agent on the nature of administration prevailing in the states held that the overall level of rents in the states 'compare very favourably with rents in force in British India, even taking into account the cesses which are taken in addition to the rent'.[12]

The commonest of such 'additional' impositions—of which the official spoke—included cesses for the building and use of roads, for imports and exports, for the use of state-owned agricultural implements, as well as those exacted on a wide range of festive and social occasions.[13] These were often commuted into cash payments but sometimes levied in kind. The cesses, coupled with the forest tax or *nistar*—a commutation rate levied on subjects for the use of part-reserved forest produce—and the customary payments made to village *chowkidars*, hiked up the rental by sometimes more than 50 per cent.[14] The most unpopular among all exactions was the notorious custom of *beth begar* or *bethi*, defined as the 'liability to forced labour, or rendering of commodities free or at privileged rates, either to the Ruler, or their *thekadar* or headman, or to the zamindar or tenure-holder, or similar imposts'.[15] Usually such labour service was exacted from the states' subjects to maintain public roads and to cultivate the Rajas' own farms.

British official reaction to the custom of *bethi*, which had been the crux of agrarian discontent in princely Orissa for many decades, ranged from connivance to repulsion. A disapproving official had forewarned, as early as 1891, that 'the time is not far distant' when the Rajas would 'find it impossible to exact labour without payment', and that they would thus be 'well advised . . . [to] allow the custom to gradually die out'.[16] On the other hand, such levying of unpaid or nominally-paid labour, according to another official report of 1930, was 'not ordinarily excessive', seldom exceeded 15 days' work in a year, and was 'a natural system at the stage of development where rents and taxation are alike low and money does not circulate freely or rapidly'. The same report also noted that the concerned chiefs were taking steps to abolish the system and that the practice was thus gradually dying out.[17] Indeed, under mounting pressure from Political Agents, the ruling chiefs of the states were forced to accept the commutation of *bethi* into an additional cess on the land revenue. Yet, even well into the 1940s, abolition orders were far from fully effective and villagers in states like Patna, Baramba, Narsinghpur, Keonjhar, Bonai and Hindol remained liable to construct and maintain village roads, rest houses and temples and to clear forest boundary lines.[18] Where commutation came into force, the commutation fee worked out at nearly 33 per cent of the land revenue in states like Khandpara and Patna, and between 25-28 per cent in the rest of the states. In conjunction with the forest cess or *nistar*[19] and the customary payments made to village chowkidars, the cesses burdened the peasantry quite heavily, usually adding up to about half of the land revenue.[20]

Revenue in the *Garhjat* states was collected through village headmen variously known as *gaontias*, *ganjhus*, *sarbarahkars* and *pradhans*. Indeed, the agrarian social structure of the states centred around the institution of the *gaontia*, which must have arisen out of the process of reclamation of forests for cultivation. The pioneering or the oldest surviving clearer was usually considered the headman of the village. He became, in course of time, an important official of the ruling chief, undertaking the combined tasks of revenue collection and rural control. During the later days of Maratha rule in the late eighteenth century, the village headman as an official incumbent began to be replaced by the lessee or *thekadar* of the village. R.K. Ramadhyani, a settlement official who did pioneering compilation work on the system of land tenure in the states in the 1940s, wrote that 'at the present day it is this system of hereditary village headmen or lessees [*thekadars*] which exists throughout the States of the Agency with more or less modification'.[21] In most states the *gaontia* was allotted a fixed percentage of the total village rental, usually received in the form of a rent-free home-farm called *bhogra*. But he was not a tenure holder in any sense of the term, since, unlike his counterpart in Sambalpur, he did not have proprietary rights over such land.

No intermediate rights in the soil existed in the *Garhjat* agrarian society, except in the case of service tenures and other beneficiary grants, made most frequently to Brahmins and Paiks.[22] In some cases beneficiaries of service tenures held grants, or were assigned the revenues, of entire villages. Such grantees were known as *khorposhdars* or maintenance grantees and their rights in the soil bordered on zamindari rights. These grants—often exempting up to one-third of the total cultivable land in some states—caused an enormous alienation of land revenue for the states concerned.[23] The chiefs, originally slow to realize its implications, resorted to drastic measures to prevent this loss of revenue in the twentieth century when economic depression helped to reveal the unsoundness of the states' economies. Their endeavour in the 1930s to organize a large-scale resumption of these lands by evicting the original reclaimers of the soil caused much resentment in some states like Nilgiri and Hindol.[24]

In fact state encroachment on the customary privileges and rights of the upper categories of tenure holders and dominant peasant groups undermined the traditional patron-client linkages that had held *Garhjat* society together. A new revenue settlement concluded in Bonai in 1913 stipulated that Gond *jagirdars*—described as 'the most unreasonable, obstinate, and mulish people imaginable when any question of what they regard as an infringement of their rights or dignity comes up'—were to pay one half of the net land revenue assessed on their previously revenue-free *jagirs*.[25]

The chiefs of the states began to fish further in troubled waters when this belated drive for revenue maximization brought them into conflict with the *gaontias* or *sarbarahkars*, the traditional leaders of rural society in *Garhjat*. In areas where the office of the *gaontia* had developed a strong hereditary tradition, rulers usually continued to award the title deed or *patta* to the same family for over several generations. Therefore, it was possible for the *gaontia* to develop strong local ties over a long period of time and, in the process, to acquire quasi-tenurial rights.[26] But from the 1890s on they sought increasingly to undermine the hereditary principle by terminating the *patta* every few years. In 1892, village headmen 27 in number of Gangpur state complained to the Commissioner of the Orissa

Division of having been deprived of their *khuntkatti* villages by the Raja.[27] Relations thus soured continued to deteriorate further, as the Rajas went on behaving in the same way well into the twentieth century. In the mid-1920s several chiefs were reported to be by no means averse to selling *gaontia* offices on rather flimsy pretexts.[28] The agrarian discontent of the dominant peasantry was whipped up to a large extent by frequent cases of arbitrary removal of *sarbarahkars* by Rajas and the resettlement of villages with royal favourites or persons offering financial inducements. By the middle of the 1930s the powers of the *gaontias* were being considerably reduced in all the states, and in Baudh they ceased to be entrusted with even their basic task of revenue collection.[29] In some states like Nilgiri and Hindol considerable dissatisfaction of the *gaontias* resulted from a few cases of resumption of *bhogra* land and their assessment to rent, or their resettlement as *raiyati* tenure.[30] Even more objectionable were the instances where rulers sought to exact money as *salami* or *nazrana* in the disguise of a mutation fee.[31] Such attempts at limiting the powers of village headmen heralded the beginning of a long phase of struggle between the ruling chiefs and the peasants led by the *gaontias* and encouraged by Congress in the 1930s and 1940s. These prajamandal agitations gave Congress ample opportunity to project its new-found anti-feudal, pro-peasant image in the Orissa states.

The personal nature of the rule in the feudatory states fostered a semi-feudal administration characterized by a lack of personal liberties and representative institutions. In almost all the states laws were not codified, and even where they were put down on paper, actual practices could be markedly different. As R.K. Ramadhyani wrote in 1942, orders, proclamations and notifications modifying or cancelling previous ones 'which perhaps existed on paper, followed one another with bewildering rapidity'.[32] The widespread prevalence of favouritism meant the proliferation of unqualified persons in administrative jobs.[33] Excepting a very few, none of the states had an annual budget and this made it virtually impossible to administer or regulate the personal and domestic expenses of the ruler. 'There is no clear distinction,' the Orissa States' Enquiry Committee reported, 'between Public Treasury and the Raja's Privy Purse' and, consequently, 'the Rulers generally spend about half the public revenues on themselves and their families'.[34] Finally, basic civil liberties were virtually non-existent in the *Garhjat* political system. In the 1930s only a handful of states like Mayurbhanj and Nilgiri allowed their subjects to hold public meetings and form representative assemblies or prajamandals.[35]

On the whole, the Orissa feudatory states remained relatively poor arenas of élite politics. The growth of a professional middle class was a process aborted in the states by the twin operation of a semi-feudal administration and the lack of educational facilities. At the beginning of the twentieth century only 2.7 per cent of the states' population could read and write.[36] Little progress was subsequently made in education, and this all but put paid to the *bhadralok* as a political category in the states. Naturally, national political parties like the Congress, always found it difficult to build up an organizational base in this area, for they tended to depend upon organizers and leaders from the middle classes.[37] Moreover, the *Garhjat* people were always suspicious of the coastal Oriyas, whom they pejoratively called *katakis*.[38] The odium that the people of the coast incurred in the hills thus raised serious problems of political mobilization before 1947 and integration afterwards.

THE BEGINNINGS OF CONGRESS INVOLVEMENT

The general attitude of most British Indian political organizations, including the Congress, toward the Indian states had been one of non-interference in their internal affairs. It was not until 1921 that the Indian National Congress opened its membership to states' subjects. A major development during the 1920s that would drastically affect the future of the Indian princes was the rise of pressure groups and associations—consisting of British Indian activists and a small but militant number of states' subjects—advocating political and social reform in princely India. Since most princes proscribed all forms of political opposition to their administrations and policies, these newly-formed associations were usually forced to meet on British Indian territory, preferably near the state boundaries. They contained a sizeable number of British Indians and states' subjects living in British India.[39]

The first prajamandals, or public associations in the states, were founded in Mysore, Indore and Bhor between 1917 and 1921.[40] In 1927 an over-arching organization called the All-India States People's Conference (AISPC) was formed to coordinate the work of the local prajamandals and to put the states people's case for constitutional reform before the Indian Statutory Commission, which was rumoured to be tinkering with the idea of an all-India federation of provinces and states. Between 1930 and 1934 some hundreds of *khadi*-clad men and women from princely India, including about 60 from Orissa, responded enthusiastically to Gandhi's call for Civil Disobedience against the Raj.[41] However, the absence of an effectively coordinated Congress programme and prompt action on the part of the Political Agent and the state *durbars* concerned prevented the movement from taking off in the *Garhjat*.[42] The ruling chief of Kalahandi smugly declared in 1931 that 'in my state there is no sign nor symptom of this deplorable movement . . .'.[43] The Sonpur chief, likewise, congratulated himself on his ability 'to keep the people off from the baneful influence of the teachings of a particular class of political agitators of British India', who were described as engaging in 'highly pernicious and destructive work'.[44] In the midst of Civil Disobedience in British India, attempts were made to organize the states' subjects in favour of a civil and political rights campaign. In June 1931, the Orissa States People's Conference (OSPC) was convened at Cuttack at the initiative of a group of educated upper caste states' subjects that included Radhanath Rath from Athgarh, Madhusudan Patnaik from Tigiria and Balukeswar Acharya and Gangadhar Mishra from Ranpur. The Conference, presided over by the Swarajist legislator, Bhubanananda Das, called for the establishment of representative governments in the states.[45] However, during the years that immediately followed, the organization 'sank into a state of inactivity' and became virtually defunct.[46]

THE REJUVENATION OF THE ORISSA STATES PEOPLE'S CONFERENCE AND THE FORMATION OF PRAJAMANDALS

Notwithstanding the reservations of the Congress High Command about the party's possible entanglement in the politics of the Orissa feudatory states, the course of events in the coastal districts in the mid-1930s certainly worked in favour of the politicization of these territories. The formation of the Orissa branch of the Congress Socialist Party, the spreading organization of the Utkal Krushak Sangha and the formation of the ministry following the party's sweeping electoral victory in 1937 were all factors that militated in favour of an organizational expansion of Congress activities in the feudatory states. Although the core leadership within the AICC as well as the UPCC continued to show little interest in the states, the UPCC's Left wing drifted towards them during the 1936-7 election campaign. The question really was, therefore, how long could the UPCC and the Congressmen within the states continue as silent spectators.[47]

Political initiative in the states came mainly from the middle and substantial peasantry, led by the headmen (*sarbarahkars* or *gaontias*) who had a long history of defending their own receding agrarian social power against increasing princely encroachment in the late nineteenth century.

Belonging mostly to the Brahmin, Khandayat and Chasa castes, these groups traditionally exercised authority at the village level by virtue of their economic strength as well as their superior caste status compared to the mass of poor peasants, artisans and other labouring groups. Since they served as intermediaries between the administration and the ordinary villagers, it is on them that poorer peasants depended for employment and for rural credit facilities. When adversely affected by the states' agrarian policies, these dominant caste substantial cultivators tried to mobilize peasant movements. In the early decades of the twentieth century these rural local magnates started one such endeavour to organize a movement of the *Garhjat* tenant farmers against the feudal practices and abuses perpetuated by the Rajas, in favour of liberal agrarian legislation. Gandhi's no-tax movement in Bardoli in 1928 inspired the *Garhjat* peasantry to launch similar agitations.[48]

In 1936-7 fresh attempts were made to revitalize the organization of the OSPC by Sarangadhar Das, a subject of the Dhenkanal state. At his initiative the OSPC held its second session at Cuttack in June 1937 under the presidentship of Pattabhi Sitaramayya. The veteran Congress leader from Andhra, who was also the President of the AISPC expressed the desire of the Congress to 'harness the immense latent powers of the masses in the states'. He further said that the people of the states were entitled to form Congress committees in their respective territories and to appeal to the Congress Working Committee for the redressal of any constitutional maladies perpetuated by their chiefs.[49] The Conference adopted several resolutions, which were focused on issues like the attainment of responsible government, the rights of the states' people (that is, rights of occupancy on holdings and their fundamental rights of citizenship), the abolition of feudal practices like *bethi* and *rasad* and the setting up of an enquiry committee to look into the basic grievances of the states' subjects.[50] The committee that subsequently came into being consisted of Satish Chandra Bose, Balwantray Mehta, Brajasundar Das and Sarangadhar Das.[51]

The trend towards the politicization of the states' subjects was given a further boost by the installation of a popular Congress ministry in Orissa in July 1937. People from the Orissa states had attended some of the UPCC election meetings as well as those organized by the Krushak Sangha earlier. Their hopes and enthusiasm were raised to an even higher pitch by the massive Kisan Day rally that took place on 1 September 1937. As Sarangadhar Das reported, it was from this point onwards that they started looking upon the Congress government as their own government and towards Gandhi as their saviour.[52] It was the formation of the prajamandals and the development of political struggles under their leadership, which had, however, primarily ended the isolation of the states' people and linked them with the broader tide of Indian nationalism.

THE PRAJAMANDAL MOVEMENT IN THE ORISSA STATES, 1937-40

In the early 1930s, most senior Congressmen felt that the state-based organizations were simply too weak and unreliable to justify making common cause against imperialism. As one scholar has suggested, the Congress' suspicions would seem to have been well-founded, because in the mid-1930s prajamandals existed in only a handful of states and had few active members.[53] The States People's Conference in Orissa at this time probably had a membership of only around 200.[54] But what was the nature of the politics that the prajamandals brought into being? What measure of popular support did they have behind their organization? A confidential official report of 1938 had this to say on the subject:

> The prajamandal is an organization for promoting political agitation in the states. It consists of the discontented elements in the states. . . . Some members reside in the states but most of the leaders reside in British India [some of whom are not the states' subjects]. This organization has gained widespread sympathy in bringing to light those grievances of states' subjects which have been substantiated; and for bringing about reforms long overdue by means of 'concessions' and in some cases political reorganization as well. It leans for support on the Congress. The price of this support appears to be the furtherance of Congress influence throughout the states and the adoption of Congress methods and ideals. . . . The political object of this organization appears to be to bridge the gap which now exists between the political state of British India and in the same sense the backwardness of the states. The prajamandal is so overpowered by the influence and support of Congress that the difference between the political object of Congress in British India and that of the states' subjects within the states is ignored.[55]

The same report attributed the burgeoning movement in the Orissa states to 'administrative shortcomings sometimes amounting to tyranny'. It was also convinced that the leadership of the movement came from 'states subjects who are qualified for posts in the administrations, but are excluded on "Political" grounds and for reasons of personal differences with their rulers' who were said to be indulging in considerable 'favouritism, nepotism and intrigue'. The Congress exercised its influence over the movement, the report observed, 'through [communistic] "cells" formed among the . . . discontented elements'. It went on to offer a straightforward solution to the problem of political order brought into being by the prajamandal movement, 'provided that abuses are checked, long standing grievances redressed and the influence of "cells" removed, it would seem that the people would be content with any form of government, representative or otherwise'.[56]

The assumed 'backwardness' of the states' people made them, in the official perception, vulnerable to outside instigation and prone to outbreaks of violence. Thus in February 1939, by which time the movement had affected almost every single Orissa state, the Secretary of State for India reported that 'owing to the backward character of the population, agitation [in princely Orissa] has been accompanied by no little violence'.[57] Indeed, this perception was shared by some sections of the non-official British as well. Agatha Harrison, the Secretary of the India Conciliation Group, in London, and an informal intermediary for Gandhi with India Office officials, was appointed an observer to the Orissa states by the Mahatma in early 1939. She thought that the tribal population of the states were 'the kind of people among whom it often happens that a surface appearance of quiet acquiescence will conceal during long periods a mass of discontent and resentment which will at least be manifested in sudden and explosive violence'.[58] However, these observations made too much of the so-called 'violence' supposedly perpetuated by the prajamandal movement, which on the whole remained peaceful at least until 1939. Indeed, whatever violence characterized states' politics in the tumultuous last years of the 1930s came from the repressive state administrations, which were by no means hesitant to use force to quell agitations.

Following the pioneering and militant examples of Nilgiri, Dhenkanal and Talcher, prajamandals were formed during 1938-9 in most of the other feudatory states in Orissa, and people began their agitation in Athgarh, Ranpur, Pal-Lahara, Bonai, Tigiria, Nayagarh, Hindol, Keonjhar and several other *Garhjat* principalities. Interestingly, political propaganda by prajamandal organizers showed a firm faith in Gandhian leadership, in general, and in guidance from Congressmen of the coastal regions, in particular. A Raja in 1939 noted that 'Mr. Gandhi's name is a magic word to the agitators', who could be 'appeased by no concessions until dictated by the Congress high command to cease agitation'.[59] Indeed, frequent references were made to 'the fight taken up by the Congress' as a result of which 'the people in British India have to a little extent been able to heave a sigh of relief'.[60] It was also strongly stressed that in order to attain similar objectives the states' people 'shall have to act according to the advice of Mahatma Gandhi, the sponsor of Truth and Non-Violence'.[61]

The Rajas usually attributed the agitations to 'exotic influence', claiming that it was 'engineered and fomented by outside agitators'.[62] They also claimed that the movements had a narrow social base, that they grew out of the 'personal grievances' of 'refractory state subjects'.[63] It was a measure of the effectiveness of the Congress methods of mobilization that it could politicize local grievances and turn them against the Rajas. The colonial police observed the Congress tendency to time its satyagrahas to coincide with the time of tax collection by the states, thus appealing to potential revenue-defaulters.[64] Even without tangible economic or agrarian grievances to seize upon, the Congress success in working up a 'certain amount of discontent' in the Khond tribal tracts of Nayagarh state impressed colonial officials. One of them commented in 1939 that 'there is no real grievance here and there is certainly no oppression; but the lack of interest by state officials has led to lukewarmness on the part of the Konds and has rendered them a ready prey to the influence of outside agitators'.[65]

In all the states the prajamandals were declared unlawful and in some cases the Rajas approached the Political Agent for military assistance. In spite of such repression the states people's movement was characterized almost everywhere by peaceful civil resistance. However, mounting provocation at last led to a violent incident in the small state of Ranpur in January 1939, when the Political Agent, R.L. Bazalgette, was killed in an outburst of mob violence.[66] The incident was deeply deplored in the Indian press, including Congress newspapers, whose regret—as the Secretary of State acidly remarked—'was not uninspired by the realisation of the adverse effect of the incident on their own cause'.[67] The Congress Working Committee and Jawaharlal Nehru both regretted that the incident would greatly hinder the states people's movement.[68] Oriya leaders actively participating in the prajamandal movement also realized that it was time to put brakes on a movement that was starting to show dangerous signs of breaking out of the control of its leaders. Thus Sarangadhar Das, the Secretary of the OSPC, instructed the states' people 'not to launch upon any mass movement of direct action in the present circumstances'.[69] H.K. Mahtab, who had headed the Orissa States' Enquiry Committee, thought that the Congress 'must wash its hands clean of the whole thing'.[70] Thus the Bazalgette murder was taken by various levels of the Congress leadership as the signal for retreat. Along with this Congress retreat, the colonial administration also stationed 1,200 soldiers in Orissa in order to strengthen the coercive apparatus.[71] The presence of troops created an atmosphere of terror, which climaxed in the massacre of 32 unarmed Lutheran Munda tribals at Gangpur on 28 April 1939.[72] Indeed, after the

Bazalgette murder the movement lost sight of its non-violent intentions and became a form of guerilla warfare. The agitation continued sporadically until late 1939, when there ensued a period of compromise, with the agitations ceasing and some of the Rajas announcing moderate constitutional reforms.

In July 1939 the much-publicized report of the Orissa States' Enquiry Committee was published. It hardly offered anything new and clearly compromised with landlordism. It advocated that the treaties (*sanads*) with the *Garhjat* states should be cancelled and they should be treated as permanently settled estates 'without doing any violence to the rights of the chiefs'. It also suggested certain controls on their privy purses and the shifting of the states to the jurisdiction of the Orissa province. Finally it advocated the preservation of the states and reinforced Gandhi's position that activities such as freedom for outsiders to enter the states, and those connected with civil liberty and freedom of association, were to be tolerated 'so long as . . . [these] are not directed towards the destruction of the states'.[73]

THE WAR, THE SECOND CONGRESS MINISTRY AND THE ROAD TO MERGER, 1940-9

Lord Linlithgow, the Viceroy, visited Orissa in the first week of August 1939 and the affairs of the feudatory states drew his immediate attention. He discussed the problem with the Congress ministry in Orissa and a few feudatory chiefs also met him. Speaking at Cuttack, the Viceroy made special reference to relations between the people of Orissa and those of the neighbouring Eastern States. He admitted that there was as such no geographical boundary between the two parts and the people were closely interlinked in various ways. 'Provinces and states,' he said, 'are and must always be neighbours. They have each their own part to play in the progress of India, but the parts must be played in harmony, and not in dissonance.'[74] But before any concrete step could be taken for the solution of the problem on a permanent basis, the war broke out and the Congress ministry went out of office. Therefore, in spite of all efforts, the administration of the *Garhjat* states could not be properly streamlined in the interests of the people.

During the Second World War the colonial authorities strengthened their grip over the feudatory states and the ex-prajamandal leaders who were expected to create trouble were arrested under the Defence of India rules. However, the lull was broken during the Quit India movement in

1942 when there was a recrudescence of prajamandal activities in some of the states. These assumed serious proportions in Dhenkanal and Talcher. In the former, a Karan leader, named Baishnab Charan Patnaik, and 17 others brought an entire sub-division under their control and established popular administration for a fortnight before military troops reoccupied it.[75] In Talcher, the most prominent prajamandal leader of the late 1930s, Pabitra Mohan Pradhan, escaped from prison and in September led an attempt to capture the palace of the Raja. The situation became so serious that on 7 September the state authorities, with the help of the British military police, had to resort to aerial bombing in order to disperse an armed and increasingly violent crowd, which assembled in front of the palace.[76] In the face of a punitive and ruthless military force, the movement failed to make much headway in any of the states. However, notwithstanding the fact that some prominent leaders like Baishnab Charan Patnaik and Pabitra Mohan Pradhan had to abscond and others were kept in jail through the war period, underground activities still continued unabated. This situation remained unchanged till 1946 when the release of most political prisoners and the return of Congress to power gave a new fillip to the prajamandal movement.

By this time, both sides, the Rajas and the Congress, had reorganized and bigger armies, so to speak, on the field. In late 1946 the Rajas attempted to combine in a Union of the Eastern States, to include the Chotanagpur states, the Orissa states and some Chhattisgarh states. Their opponents worked at two levels. During 1945-7 an Orissa and Chhattisgarh States Regional Council, under the leadership of Sarangadhar Das, reorganized the prajamandals and directed their agitations. At the same time, the battle was also fought at the higher level of diplomacy, between the consortium of rulers and the Government of Orissa, backed by the Union Government. The scale of the struggle on the eve of independence and immediately afterwards, was larger than it had ever been before the Second World War. It took place between two relatively large and integrated forces and was no longer an affair of piecemeal harassment and counter-harassment.

By 1946, with the arrival of the Cabinet Mission, it was clear that the British were about to leave India and that this was the time to stake in claims for power soon to be left vacant. The rulers of the Eastern States Union attempted to form a unit big enough to exist as a separate state within the Indian Union. Such a state, although backward in every respect, had potential forest and mineral wealth. But, if this state came into existence, Orissa would consist only of the four coastal districts and some enclaves in the hills, and, crucially, it would be without the forest and mineral wealth of the hill areas. To the leaders of the Congress in 1946-7, therefore, it seemed that they were fighting for the very existence of Orissa as a viable state in the new Indian Union.

The necessity of the administrative integration of British and princely Orissa in the Indian Union was frequently acknowledged in official circles in the 1940s. In fact, even in 1930 the Orissa Sub-Committee of the Indian Statutory Commission had recommended that the Orissa feudatory states 'should be brought into relationship with any administration set up for Orissa'.[77] Sir Francis Wylie, Political Adviser to the Crown Representative, anticipated in a note of August 1940 that 'the day may quite clearly come when these small states will disappear altogether and be merged in the neighbouring province'.[78] While touring the Orissa states in early 1946, the Resident for Eastern States commented that the 'developmental' needs of these states tied their future with that of the Orissa province:

> The more I see of these Eastern States, with their vast forested uplands...the plenitude of minerals, the regularity of the monsoons, the more I feel that they ought to be playing a greater part in the economy of India. Left to themselves they can do little; development on any large scale will demand help from without in expert survey, in bold planning, in finance.[79]

Even the Viceroy, Lord Wavell, showed his commitment to this solution of the states' question when he commented that a merger of the states with the province was not 'outside the scope of practical politics' and that 'an effective Oriya province could be established only if Orissa and the Eastern States were amalgamated'.[80] The combination of these twin imperatives of the 'development' of the states and the 'viability' of the Orissa province was thus clearly apparent in the official position on the merger question by 1946.

Following the sweeping Congress victory in the elections of 1946, H.K. Mahtab, the new Chief Minister of Orissa, made serious attempts to bring about a complete change in the position of the states. On 6 April 1946, in course of meeting the Cabinet Mission and discussing the political settlement of India, Mahtab raised the problem of the feudatory states of Orissa and pleaded for the amalgamation of these states with the province. He argued that the Orissa states were originally zamindari estates, with no treaty rights with the paramount power, they were given feudatory status by the government 'by historical accident'. Therefore, the Cabinet Mission, Mahtab continued, should consider the Orissa states as a unique case and put an end to their anomalous existence by merging them with Orissa.[81] A UPCC memorandum, submitted to the Cabinet Mission at the same time, argued that British and *Garhjat* Orissa were 'part and parcel of one economic, political, geographical, historical, linguistic unit' and that they should be brought together in an integrated and comprehensive scheme of post-colonial economic planning.[82]

It was becoming clear to colonial officials that the states were crucial for the economic future of Orissa within the Indian Union. With an area of only 32,000 square miles and a revenue of less than Rs. 30 million, the Orissa province was unable to balance its budget without a large central subvention. The Orissa states had a total area of 29,000 square miles and a revenue of nearly Rs. 20 million, in addition to large potential economic assets in the form of unexplored forest and mineral resources. The prospects of a merger was, therefore, economically very attractive for the Orissa province. 'The Congress Party in Orissa,' wrote the Resident for the Eastern States, in May 1946, has 'been dreaming not only of swallowing the States but also of stealing districts from Madras in the south and Bengal and Bihar in the north.'[83]

Similar arguments were made by the Rajas, who strove to convince the government of the economic motives behind the Congress policy. R.N. Singh Deo, the Raja of Patna—who went on to pioneer sub-regional interests in electoral politics by becoming the leader of the Ganatantra Parishad—wrote to Lord Wavell about the danger of political and economic exploitation of the states' people and resources by the Orissa province.[84] The Raja of Seraikella claimed a separate 'cultural identity' for the feudatory states, in an elaborate note presented to the Resident for Eastern States. He cited ancient Puranic texts and epics to argue that the states near the northern and western borders of the Orissa province—like Seraikella, Kharswan, Mayurbhanj, Patna and Sonpur and the Sambalpur district—had never been conquered by the kings of Orissa. On the other hand, he contended, they belonged to the ancient Kosala kingdom of middle India. He concluded that the Orissa states, along with Sambalpur, differed fundamentally from the coastal tracts in 'habit and custom' and that they had always been exploited in the past by the British province.[85]

Thus, while the Oriya 'cultural identity' had appealed to the 'nation-building' imperatives of the Raj before 1936, a withdrawing colonial administration now found itself arbitrating between competing 'cultural identities'. The 'umpiring' ideology of the colonial reformist discourse, which had previously been called upon to unite the Oriya-speaking country, was now called upon to divide it. The concept of an overarching cultural identity for 'natural Orissa' thus came to be contested by many Oriyas themselves.

As negotiations over the second half of 1946 failed to arrive at a solution of the states' question, there were fresh outbreaks of prajamandal agitations in several states. Between May 1946 and December 1948, a number of states, most notably Dhenkanal, Talcher and Nilgiri, experienced sustained periods of popular upheaval involving flag marches, rallies, *hartals*, economic boycotts and even acts of civil disobedience. In December 1946 the Resident for the Eastern States reported that most of the 'subversive agitators are State subjects . . . but they proclaim their allegiance to the all-India Congress Party and they are undoubtedly being encouraged and probably financed from without'.[86] He also noted that the provincial press had taken up the cudgels for the Congress ministry's merger proposals and that UPCC leaders like Sarangadhar Das and Malati Choudhury were touring the states, 'preaching [the] virtual extinction of the Rulers'.[87] Such activities were now coordinated by the Orissa and Chhattisgarh States Regional Council, led by Sarangadhar Das, and consisted mostly of prajamandal leaders who had organized the agitations of 1937-9. With the AISPC trudging along warily, control tended to gravitate into the hands of inexperienced young men and fierce adivasis from the forests. In Dhenkanal, prajamandal activists and tribals terrorized officials, occupied government buildings and surrounded the palace. In the neighbouring state of Nilgiri, adivasis made off with grain from the fields of Hindu cultivators and looted village shops.[88]

In August 1947, the Rajas of the Orissa and Chhattisgarh states formed an Eastern States Union, which was financed by contributions from the constituent states.[89] The Union adopted an elaborate constitution, vesting executive power in a board of seven rulers, headed by a president who was to be assisted by ministerial advisers. The new Governor of Orissa, K.N. Katju, attacked the constitution as 'a complete eyewash', on the ground that the ministers were appointed by the board and were not responsible to the people.[90] Unperturbed by such attacks on its representative claims, a key text of this burgeoning Koshal movement claimed a separate cultural identity for the states, which subverted the idea of Oriya nationalism itself:

> . . . [the] natural division of Orissa into the highlands and coastal plains has favoured the formation of two Oriya blocks. The coastal plains corresponding to the old Kalinga Empire are one compact block with different traditions and outlook as well as some differences in culture and language. This makes it administratively convenient for grouping them into one Unit. The highlands with different traditions, outlook and cultural and linguistic differences as well are another compact block which should form another Unit. The two divisions have had different evolutionary

trends and when nature and history have made them separate, it will be in the interest of both to evolve as separate entities.[91]

Cashing in on Sambalpur's disenchantment with the coastal leadership over the Hirakud Dam issue, the Eastern States Union also included this marginal district in its territorial scheme. It was claimed that the influence of Hindi and Chhattisgarhi in the Sambalpuri dialect pointed to the district's cultural affinities not with Orissa but with Koshal.[92]

The movement's political aspirations, however, evaporated rapidly during the later months of 1947, as it became clear that in the absence of British mediation and patronage the Union could not hold out for long against the increasingly hard line policy of the States Ministry in the new Indian Union. In October 1947, local adivasis in the Nilgiri state—taking advantage of the disorder caused by the prajamandal agitation—began to seize the property of the non-tribals in the area and to redress long-standing economic grievances by direct action.[93] The Orissa government intervened and the Collector of Balasore was ordered to take over the administration of the state. This was achieved on 14 November. Four days later Nabakrushna Choudhury, the Revenue Minister in Mahtab's cabinet, warned the Rajas that 'the principle applied to Nilgiri may have to be pursued in case of all other States, if they went the same way'.[94] This was intimidating enough, and by and large the rulers had resigned themselves by this time to the impossibility of holding out against a government infinitely more powerful than themselves. But in some states where the rulers retained some popularity and respect, there was some ambivalence about the merger. More importantly, these sentiments were shared by influential leaders within the prajamandal movement, such as Harekrushna Mahtab himself.[95] After a visit to Orissa, the AISPC leader, Sarangadhar Das, too, remarked ruefully: 'I have always believed that feudalism has to be removed lock, stock and barrel. But unfortunately I found towards the end [of my visit] that many of my [prajamandal] colleagues do not agree with this … view point.'[96]

However, in December 1947 princes belonging to the erstwhile Eastern and Chhattisgarh political agencies were summoned to a meeting at Cuttack and were persuaded by V.P. Menon, the States Department Secretary, in the course of an all-night sitting, to sign covenants integrating their states with the province of Orissa. The princes capitulated and signed the Merger document. So, on 1 January 1948, the Congress government in Orissa assumed responsibility for the government of all the former feudatory states, with the exception of Mayurbhanj, Seraikella and Kharswan. In early December, the Raja of Mayurbhanj had handed over his administration to the local prajamandal. His 'Prime Minister'—a prajamandal leader named Sarat Chandra Das—was reported to be of the opinion that 'the state's best interests would be served by "good neighbourly relations" with Orissa rather than by direct merger . . .'.[97] Mayurbhanj eventually merged with Orissa on 1 January 1949, till which date the new Orissa province had no territorial border with the northern states of Seraikella and Kharswan. In May, amidst considerable murmurs of protest from the ex-Rajas, these two states were handed over to Bihar as a temporary administrative arrangement. This continued to embitter Bihari-Oriya relations and became the focal point of a widespread agitation in 1956.

The merger agreement sought to strike a compromise with the ex-Rajas. They were given privy purses which was exempted from all taxes, besides various other concessions. The basic idea was that 'the Government of India should not create as an aftermath of merger any social or economic problems for rulers or for their dependants',[98] which shows how a compromise was made with the ex-Rajas. Among the latter, many thronged the Congress, some of them became its leaders and sought advice from Congress leaders about their business prospects.[99] As can be expected, the merger movement had succeeded in uniting Orissa, but tensions did persist even in 1949 as some of the ex-Rajas continued to champion divisive politics.

Post-colonial Orissa thus became the single Indian state where states based parochialism remained strong enough into the 1950s to spawn a short-lived but quite successful political party, the Ganatantra Parishad. Thus, while the theory of 'one-party dominance' was applicable to most of the states, which had developed a 'Congress system',[100] politics in Orissa deviated from this pattern from the very beginning, and the states became a problem for the Congress. Regional political parties in Orissa became strong contenders in electoral politics, and they prevented the Congress from gaining an absolute majority in the state legislature for a long time.

REPRESENTING THE ORISSA HILLS: THE LEGACY OF PARTITION AND MERGER

In 1948, the Rajas of ex-princely Orissa were pensioned off—having been granted privy purses, based on their states' income, an allowance to meet religious obligations and certain tax concessions. At the higher levels of policy-making it was possible to discern a distinct effort to be conciliatory, or at least to avoid vindictiveness.[101] But within a few months of the merger, officials of the new Indian bureaucracy were already complaining that the Rajas were creating difficulties 'in the way of the [Orissa] Provincial Government . . . in arrangements to give effect to integration of administration'.[102] 'The Rulers', it was further warned, 'have thought of cutting themselves away again from the Province of Orissa and have made proposals for forming Unions on the pattern of the Saurashtra Union or even as a Centrally Administered Province like the Himachal Pradesh.'[103] Faced with this new secessionist challenge, the Orissa government felt compelled to adopt sterner measures. There were Adivasi risings in 1948 in the states of Bamra, Gangpur, Bonai and Pal-Lahara. The newly reconstituted state police put these down, some people were killed, others were detained and collective fines were imposed on villages.[104] In Kharswan there was a particularly unpleasant outbreak, resulting, according to the official enquiry, in 14 and, according to an unofficial estimate, in several hundred deaths.[105]

The tortuous process of administrative adjustment gave rise to considerable tension, as men found themselves in new administrative posts and the previously unfamiliar bureaucratic rules of the provincial administration became operative in the merged areas. A second, crucial factor was the long-established antipathy between the hill and the coastal areas and the deep-seated mistrust of the *katakis*—the blanket term of abuse commonly used throughout *Garhjat* to refer to 'outsiders' from the more advanced eastern districts. In an effort to speed up the process of administrative adjustment, the new Congress government acted with an impatience that, consequently, cost the party dearly in terms of political support. Instead of allowing the administration to continue for some time under the old *Garhjat* dewans for a smooth transition and psychological adjustment, the new ministry of Harekrushna Mahtab sent some of the senior Deputy Collectors (promoted to the newly-constituted Indian Administrative Service) down to the western districts. These new bureaucrats allegedly descended on the ex-princely areas like an army of occupation, consequently helping only to reinforce the traditional image of the *katakis* as 'conquerors' and 'exploiters'.[106] As a result, the administration ran into many difficulties and the *Garhjat* peasantry, used to the somewhat lax and intimate administration of a landed aristocracy, and suddenly exposed to the cumbersome processes of bureaucratic rule, came quite soon to regret the passing of the old order. The old élite, both in the plains and in the hills, was thus embittered and began to devise ways of fighting back.

It was subsequently held by the ex-Rajas that Orissa's coastal areas had benefited financially from the merger at the expense of the ex-princely areas. It was argued that in 1947, that is, immediately before the merger, the Orissa province had a total revenue of Rs. 62 million as against an expenditure of Rs. 72.4 million. The resulting deficit of Rs. 10.4 million was reduced during 1949-50 to Rs. 6.5 million, owing to the inclusion of the resources of the feudatory states in the revenues of the province.[107]

Even a sizeable number of Congressmen in the states, who had outlived the patriotic fervour of the 1930s and whose political ambition could not be realized in the changed circumstances, seceded from the Congress and joined in the murmurs of protest that were now starting to rise from many of the *Garhjat* districts. These men, alongwith prajamandal dissidents and anti-merger agitators, came forward with a plan to have a party of their own and, in October 1948, goaded the Rajas of Bolangir-Patna and Kalahandi into forming a new political organization, called the Koshal-Utkal Praja Parishad, with its headquarters at Sambalpur. Branches of the Parishad were opened in Kalahandi, Sonpur, Gangpur, Bonai, Keonjhar, Athmallik and Baudh. Paid workers were employed to propagate the party's ideals vilifying the Congress administration and government employees, and to canvass for the support of the states' people who were advised to vote for the Parishad candidates in the next general election.

During 1948-50 the Parishad's influence spread to other areas in western Orissa, and in the latter year the party changed its name to Ganatantra Parishad. The conflict between the coast and the hills, whose interests the Ganatantra Parishad came to champion, may in a sense be regarded as a political legacy of the Oriya provincial movement, which aimed at securing constitutional concessions from the Government of India as well as from neighbouring provincial governments. Just as the Oriya nationalists of the 1920s and 1930s complained of 'administrative apathy', 'hostile neighbours' and 'extreme poverty', and clamoured for a 'fair deal' in the form of provincial autonomy and central subsidies, similarly the Oriya politicians of the 1950s protested against 'central neglect' and demanded greater allocation of resources, greater share in centrally-funded development projects and an 'Orissa for the Oriyas'. The image of the wronged Oriyas, perpetually denied a 'fair deal', was, thus, an enduring one. If anything, it acquired great emotive power and electoral significance after 1947, by virtue of universal adult suffrage in a state which had the smallest electorate of all earlier British provinces.

Political integration of Orissa's ex-princely and ex-British areas, which closely approximated the state's fundamental geographical cleavage between hill and coast, introduced another dimension of complexity in this politics. Soon after the merger of the princely states in 1949, the hill districts began to smart under coastal political domination and to feel perpetually short-changed in the state level distribution of resources, just as state level leaders always thought themselves to be in short supply of central patronage. Thus, whereas inter-regional resource allocation and related issues of development were dramatized at the national level, the actual distributional and welfare implications for the most deprived segments of the population were brought out at the intra-regional level. In other words, the basic contours of centre-state relations in post-independence Orissa were replicated within the state itself in something of a core-periphery relationship between the coast and the hills. At the end of the day, therefore, while the integration of the princely states during 1947-9 refashioned the political map of Orissa and opened the door to further political change, the informal conventions of governance, political behaviour and the social composition of the ruling élite in the states remained for a long time pretty much the same.

NOTES

1. See, for instance, H.V. Hodson's classic, *The Great Divide: Britain, India and Pakistan* (London, 1969), which concludes with the reflection that the transfer of power was 'but a passing scene' in the 'huge panorama of the rise and decline of [Indian] empires', p. 542.
2. William L. Richter, 'Princes in Indian Politics', in *Economic and Political Weekly*, Vol. VI, No. 9 (27 February 1971), p. 538.
3. R.L. Handa, *History of the Freedom Struggle in Princely States* (Delhi, 1968), p. 6.
4. Ian Copland, *The Princes of India in the Endgame of Empire, 1917-1947* (Cambridge, 1997), p. 6.
5. P.T. Mansfield Papers, Centre of South Asian Studies, Cambridge, Vol. II (19 October 1919 to 19 July 1920), 'Foreword' (written in 1969).
6. J. Bowstead, Additional Political Agent of the Orissa States, 'Report on the Administration of the Orissa States and the Alleged Grievances of the State Subjects', para 48, Crown Representative Records (hereafter CRR), R/1/1/3585(1), File No. 22(4)-P (Confidential) of 1940 (Political Department), India Office Library and Records, London (hereafter IOR).
7. R.K. Ramadhyani, *Report on Land Tenures and the Revenue System of the Orissa and Chhattisgarh States*, 2 Vols (Berhampur, 1942), Vol. I, p. 5.
8. G. Toynbee, *Report on the General Administration of the Tributary Mehals of Orissa, 1890-91* (Calcutta, 1891), para 89.
9. See, for instance, P.K. Misra, *Political Unrest in Nineteenth-Century Orissa: Anti-British, Anti-Feudal, and Agrarian Uprisings* (Calcutta, 1983); and S. Pradhan, *Agrarian and Political Movements, States of Orissa: 1931 to 1949* (Delhi, 1985).
10. *Report of the Orissa States Enquiry Committee, 1939* (Cuttack, 1939), pp. 8 and 10. The Report provides a checklist of the highest levels of rent for the best classes of land in various states.
11. 'Confidential History of Dhenkanal State' (n.d.), p. 19, CRR, R/2/306/120, and

'Confidential History of Bonai State (up to 1927)', p. 51, CRR, R/2/305/18, IOR, where C.L. Philip commented that 'the rates of rent are on the whole low'.

12. Bowstead, op.cit., para 28.
13. Philip's 'Confidential History of Ranpur State (1926)' Appendix A, provides a 'Long list of extremely vexatious cesses' typically exacted in most of Orissa States, CRR, R/2/306/133, IOR. See also the *Report of the Orissa States Enquiry Committee, 1939*, p. 17, which dwells at length on the forced requisition of provisions (*rasad*) and money (*magan/mangan*).
14. Ramadhyani, op.cit., Vol. I, pp. 31 and 87.
15. Ibid., p. 30.
16. Toynbee, op.cit., para 37.
17. J.A. Shillidy, Secretary to Government of India to Under-Secretary of State for India, Economic and Overseas Department, India Office, London. Note entitled 'Forced Labour in Indian States', No. E and O 1914 (1930), Confidential, dated 20 February 1930, p. 4, Political and Secret Department File on 'Slavery in Indian States', L/P and S/10/1180, IOR.
18. Ramadhyani, Vol. I, op.cit., p. 30; Sir Francis Wylie, Political Adviser to the Crown Representative, 1941, 'Note on his Tour in the Eastern State Agency', pp. 16-17, CRR, R/1/3684, IOR.
19. A commutation rate levied on people for the use of part-reserved forest produce. It was not levied on tribals in some states like Keonjhar and Kalahandi, where shifting cultivation was permitted.
20. Ramadhyani, Vol. I, op.cit., p. 87.
21. Ibid., p. 12.
22. Wylie, op.cit., p. 9.
23. According to Ramadhyani's estimate for 1942, the amount of revenue lost ranged from Rs. 4,200 in Bamra to Rs. 43,000 in Khandpara. In Athgarh the revenue alienated through these grants amounted to one half of the actual land revenue collected by the state. See Ramadhyani, Vol. II, op.cit., pp. 2, 20 and 152.
24. Ibid., Vol. I, pp. 22-3.
25. Philip, 'Confidential History of Bonai State (up to 1927)', pp. 35-6, CRR, R/2/305/118, IOR.
26. Ramadhyani, Vol. I, op.cit., pp. 12-13.
27. Philip, 'Confidential History of Gangpur State', p. 19, CRR, R/2/306/121, IOR.
28. Idem., 'Confidential History of Rairakhol State', 1926, p. 27, CRR, R/2/306/130, and Philip and S.L. Marwood, 'Confidential History of Sonpur State', 1927, Appendix II, p. 14, CRR, R/2/306/133, IOR.
29. Ramadhyani, Vol. I, op.cit., p. 13.
30. Ibid., pp. 12-14. Ramadhyani also cited instances of entire villages being made into *khamar* (ruler's personal land) when the *gaontia's* office fell vacant through death or eviction. Their reconversion into ordinary villages, Ramadhyani reported, depended on the amount of *nazrana* available for the post of *gaontia*, ibid., p. 20.
31. Ibid., pp. 12-14 and 20-3.
32. Ibid., p. 6.
33. For instance, it was noted in 1939 that the business of administration in some of the states had become virtually a family affair. In Talcher, for example, the heir apparent was the sessions judge, the Raja's second son combined the offices of the Revenue Officer, Magistrate and Controller of the State Accounts; one brother of the Raja was the Assistant Revenue Officer and another the Forest Officer, two of his cousins were

tahsildars, and two others were the Chief Police Officer and the Excise Officer, respectively. See *The Report of the Orissa States Enquiry Committee, 1939*, op.cit., p. 13. The *Report* also claimed to 'have evidence of even Dewans and Rulers accepting bribes in consideration of services to be rendered', ibid.

34. Ibid., pp. 10 and 55. Bowstead in 1940, too, noted that in quite a number of states' budgets the head 'unforeseen expenditure' was used for the personal expenses of the Raja, which he did not wish to show under the head 'domestic', see J. Bowstead, op.cit., para 45.
35. The Political Agent of the Orissa States, letter No. R-2-1/46, dated Sambalpur, 16 November 1946, to the Resident, Eastern States Agency, files from the Divisional Revenue Commissioner's Office, Sambalpur, Orissa State Archives, Bhubaneswar (hereafter OSA).
36. L.F. Cobden-Ramsay, *The Feudatory States of Orissa*, p. 106.
37. F.G. Bailey, *Politics and Social Change, Orissa in 1959* (Berkeley, 1963), p. 176.
38. Ibid., p. 137.
39. For an account of the evolution of Congress involvement in the Indian states and the growth of political organizations therein, see B.N. Ramusack, 'Congress and the People's Movement in Princely India: Ambivalence in Strategy and Organization', in R. Sisson and S. Wolpert, eds, *Congress and Indian Nationalism: The Pre-Independence Phase* (Berkeley, 1988), pp. 377-403; B.N. Ramusack, *The Princes of India in the Twilight of Empire: Dissolution of a Patron Client System, 1914-39* (Columbus, OH, 1978); I. Copland, 'Congress Paternalism: The "High Command" and the Struggle for Freedom in Princely India, *c*. 1920-1940' (hereafter 'Congress Paternalism'), in J. Masselos, ed., *Struggling and Ruling: the Indian National Congress 1885-1985* (New Delhi, 1987), pp. 121-40; and for the most recent account, idem., *The Princes of India in the Endgame of Empire, 1917-1947* (Cambridge, 1997). For detailed studies of the regional variations of the Congress involvement, see the collection of articles edited by R. Jeffrey, *People, Princes and Paramount Power: Society and Politics in the Indian Princely States* (Delhi, 1978).
40. Copland, 'Congress Paternalism', p. 122.
41. Sarangadhar Das, Secretary, Orissa States People's Conference, letter dated 12 July 1938, to Pattabhi Sitaramayya, File No. 127, Part I, of 1937-40, All India States People's Conference Papers (hereafter AISPC Papers), Nehru Memorial Museum & Library, New Delhi (hereafter NMML). For details of civil disobedience in selected states, see India Office note dated 11 March 1931, Political (Internal) Collections (Pol Ind) 13/1, CRR, R/1/29/629, IOR.
42. See J. Bowstead, *General Review of the Administration of the Feudatory States of Orissa, 1931-32* (Calcutta, 1932), para 71, for a brief account.
43. Address presented by the ruling chief of Kalahandi at Bhawanipatna, Kalahandi, 10 January 1931, p. 147, H.L. Stephenson Papers, Box II, Vol. II, Centre of South Asian Studies, Cambridge.
44. Ibid. Address presented by Sir Bir Mitrodaya Singh Deo, Sonpur chief, at Sonpur, 12 January 1931, p. 155.
45. *Prajatantra*, 29 June 1931, cited in Pradhan, op.cit., p. 90.
46. L.M. Patnaik, *Resurrected Orissa* (Cuttack, 1941), p. 329; see also M.N. Das, ed., *Sidelights on the History and Culture of Orissa* (Cuttack, 1977), p. 285.
47. S.N. Dwivedy, *Quest for Socialism: Fifty Years of Struggle in India* (Delhi, 1984), p. 61.
48. In the State of Bamra in princely Orissa, a no-rent campaign along the lines of Bardoli

was organized in 1928 by the local *sarbarahkars* and *gaontias*, to protest against an increase in land rents brought about by the year's settlement, see Pradhan, op.cit., p. 91.

49. N.N. Mitra, ed., *The Indian Annual Register, 1937*, Vol. I (repr., Delhi, 1990), p. 256.
50. 'Orissa States: Correspondence of Sarangadhar Das', AISPC Papers, File No. 127/1937-40, NMML; see also Pradhan, op. cit., p. 93-6.
51. Mitra, ed., op.cit., p. 358.
52. Statement of Sarangadhar Das, dated 27 November 1938, AICC Papers, File No. G-35 (Part I) 1938, NMML.
53. Copland, 'Congress Paternalism', op.cit., p. 125.
54. Sarangadhar Das, 'A Statement of the Popular Movement in Dhenkanal State (Orissa)', dated 27 November 1938, appended to Das's letter to J.B. Kripalani, AICC General Secretary, dated Cuttack, 29 November 1938, All India Congress Committee Papers, File No. G-35 (Part 2) 1938: 'Indian States: Kathiawar, Kalsia, Dhenkanal', NMML. The estimate is based on attendance figures at the OSPC's second annual session at Cuttack in June 1937.
55. 'A Note on Praja Mandal', CRR, R/2/28/14, 'Special Disturbance File [Confidential]', IOR.
56. 'Comments on Military Aid to Civil Power in the Orissa States with some Observations on Removing the Cause which Requires this Aid', ibid. (All citations are taken from this section.)
57. 'Congress and the Indian States—Possibilities of Resignation of Congress Ministries in British Indian Provinces' (prepared for the Cabinet in February 1939), Memorandum by the Secretary of State for India, 'Development of Congress Inspired Agitation in the States', Private Office Papers, L/PO/5/20 ('Congress and the Indian States'), Secret CP 44 (39), IOR.
58. 'The Indian States: Reform and Federation', prepared by a Committee of the India Conciliation Group (hereafter ICG), with a foreword by Miss Agatha Harrison (London, 1939), p. 15 (Temporary Mss. 42), Box 42, Folder No. 42/1/1939, ICG Papers, Library of the Religious Society of Friends, London.
59. Raja of Hindol, Confidential letter dated 2 January 1939 to R.L. Bazalgette, Political Agent of the Orissa States, CRR, R/293/37, IOR.
60. 'Congress Activities in the Khandpara State', English translation of the Oriya *Yuddha Niyan* (War Conflagration), Bulletin No. 2 of the Khandpara Prajamandal, CRR, R/2/293/39, IOR.
61. 'Congress Activities in Athmallik State', English translation of the Oriya leaflet *Nibedan* (Submission), signed by Bhagaban Behera, President of the Athmallik Prajamandal, CRR, R/2/291/28, IOR.
62. 'Congress Activities in the Dhenkanal State', Raja of Dhenkanal, Confidential letter dated 10 September 1938 to the Rajas of Mayurbhanj, Patna, Keonjhar, Baramba, Bamra, Athmallik and Gangpur, CRR, R/2/287/13, IOR. See also the similar complaints of the Raja of Keonjhar in 'Congress Activities in the Keonjhar State', Balabhadra Narayan Bhanj Deo, Raja of Keonjhar, Confidential letter dated 16 September 1938 to R.L Bazalgette, Political Agent of the Orissa States, CRR, R/2/293/38, IOR.
63. 'Congress Activities and trial of Bazalgette murder case in Ranpur State', Raja of Ranpur, letter dated 9 December 1938 to Daubeny, Assistant Political Agent of the Orissa States, CRR, R/2/290/26, IOR.

64. 'Congress Activities in the Khandpara State', Central Intelligence Officer, Bihar and Orissa, Patna, Secret Note dated 25 September 1939 on 'Satyagraha in Khandpara State', CRR, R/2/293/39, IOR.
65. 'Congress Activities in the Nayagarh State', Forest Officer, Eastern States, Confidential letter dated 15 March 1939, to C.S. Searle, Political Agent of the Orissa States, CRR, R/2/294/42, IOR.
66. 'Congress Activities and Trial of Bazalgette murder case in Ranpur State', CRR, R/2/290/26, IOR.
67. 'Congress Activities in the States', Memorandum by the Secretary of State for India, Secret, C.P. 44(39), 'Development of Congress Inspired Agitation in the States', dated February 1939, para 3, Political and Secret Files, No. L/P and S/13/888, IOR.
68. For the CWC's statement deploring the incident, see Mitra, op.cit., *1939,* pp. 308-9; for Nehru's, 'Congress Agitation in Indian States', extract from J.L. Nehru, 'Lessons from Ranpur Tragedy', published in the *National Call,* 14 January 1939 (PY 204/1939), Political and Secret Files, Nos L/P and S/13/887, IOR.
69. 'Orissa States: Correspondence of Sarangadhar Das', AISPC Papers, File No. 127/1937-40, NMML.
70. 'Congress and the Indian States', H.K. Mahtab, Member, All India Congress Working Committee, letter dated 7 January 1939, to Girija Bhusan Dutta, MLA, Angul (produced to the authorities by a 'source'), Private Office Papers, L/PO/5/20, IOR.
71. *National Front,* 15 and 29 January 1939. Cited in B. Pati, 'Peasants, Tribals and the National Movement in Orissa, 1920-1950' (Ph.D. dissertation, Delhi University, 1989), p. 208.
72. 'Agitation in the Gangpur State', CRR, R/2/292/35, IOR; and Home (Political) Proceedings, 18/3/1939, National Archives of India, New Delhi.
73. H.K. Mahtab, et al., eds, *Report of the Orissa States Enquiry Committee* (Cuttack, 1939), pp. 57-60.
74. *Samaj,* 2 August 1939.
75. 'Dhenkanal State Affairs', CRR, R/1/3960, IOR.
76. *Talcher Prajamandalara Itihas* (in Oriya) (Calcutta, 1950), pp. 51-8.
77. *The Report of the Indian Statutory Commission,* Vol. II (London, 1930), Appendix IV, para 3.
78. Cited in Ramadhyani, Vol. I, op.cit., Appendix I, p. 102.
79. 'Reports Containing General Impressions on States Visited by the Resident for the Eastern States', H.J. Todd, Resident for the Eastern States, 'Tour Impressions: Kalahandi State', dated 21 February 1946, CRR, R/1/1/4536, IOR.
80. Record of meeting between the Cabinet Delegation, Viceroy Wavell, B.G. Kher, G.B. Pant, S.K. Sinha, R.S. Shukla and H.K. Mahtab on 6 April 1946, p. 89, Public and Judicial Proceedings, L/P and J/5/337, IOR.
81. Summary of H.K. Mahtab's statement before the Cabinet Delegation, in Nicholas Mansergh, editor-in-chief, *The Transfer of Power, 1942-7,* Vol. VII (London, 1977), Item 62, p. 157.
82. 'A Plea for Amalgamation of Orissa Feudatory States with the Province of Orissa', in H.K. Mahtab, *Beginning of the End* (rev. edn, Cuttack, 1974), Appendix II, pp. 67-70.
83. H.J. Todd, Resident for the Eastern States, D.O. No. C 30-13/46-P (Secret), dated Calcutta, 6 May 1946, to Conrad Corfield, Political Adviser to the Crown Representative, ibid., Appendix III.

84. R.N. Singh Deo, letter dated Camp Srinagar, 30 June 1946, to Lord Wavell, ibid., Appendix IV.
85. Note presented to the Resident for Eastern States, H.J. Todd, on 30 July 1946, by the Ruler of Seraikella, ibid., Appendix V, pp. 91-100, *passim*.
86. 'Prajamandal Propaganda Against Rulers in Orissa States', H.J. Todd, Resident for Eastern States, D.O. No. 753T/46, dated 4 December 1946, to C.M. Trivedi, Governor of Orissa, CRR, R/1/1/4510, IOR.
87. Ibid.
88. V.P. Menon, *The Story of the Integration of the Indian States* (Madras, 1961), p. 146.
89. Ibid., pp. 145-6.
90. K.N. Katju to Jawaharlal Nehru, in Durga Das, ed., *Sardar Patel's Correspondence, 1945-50*, 10 vols (Ahmedabad, 1971-4), Vol. III, Item No. 543, p. 494.
91. Koshali (pseud.), *Whither Koshal*? (Calcutta, 1946), pp. 3-4.
92. Ibid., p. 11.
93. Fortnightly Report for the province of Orissa for the first half of November 1947, L/P and J/5/237, IOR.
94. *Amrita Bazar Patrika*, 20 November 1947.
95. Ian Copland, 'The Integration of the Princely States: A "Bloodless Revolution"?', in D.A. Low and Howard Brasted, eds, *Freedom, Trauma, Continuities: Northern India and Independence* (New Delhi, 1998), p. 161.
96. Note by Sarangadhar Das, 27 November 1947, and report by Das on the merger of the Orissa and CP States, 2 February 1948, AISPC Papers, File No. 129/1947-48, Part I, NMML.
97. 'Mayurbhanj Affairs', extract from the Fortnightly Report No. 5 on the Eastern States, for the period ending 30 December 1947, Political and Secret L/P and S/13/1040, IOR.
98. Menon, op.cit., p. 154.
99. Mahtab's Correspondence (No. 141/44) with the Raja of Dhenkanal. The Raja wanted his advice for joining the Bengal Breweries (letter dated 20 August 1950) and Mahtab's Private Secretary replied to the Raja (letter dated 22 August 1950) expressing Mahtab's inability to give such advice. Cited in Pati, op.cit., p. 402.
100. For discussions of the 'Congress System', see R. Kothari, 'The Congress System in India', in idem, ed., *Party System and Election Studies* (Delhi, 1967), pp. 1-18, and idem, *Politics in India* (Delhi, 1970); W.H. Morris-Jones, 'Parliament and Dominant Party: The Indian Experience', in *Parliamentary Affairs*, Vol. XVII, No. 3 (1964), pp. 296-307; R. Kothari, 'Dominance and Dissent', in *Government and Opposition*, Vol. I, No. 4 (July-September 1966), pp. 451-66.
101. This is indicated by the strong emphasis placed by senior leaders like Mahtab on the need for restraint in the *Garhjat* areas during the administrative takeover. See Mahtab, letter dated Cuttack, 31 May 1948, to Nabakrushna Choudhury, H.K. Mahtab Collection (List No. 105), Instalment I (1937-54), subject file 13, NMML.
102. Copy of D.O. Letter No. F. 191-P(S) 48 (Ministry of States, New Delhi), dated 26 May 1948, from M.K. Kripalani to Sir B.N. Rau, Constitutional Adviser to the Government of India. Cited in Mahtab, *Beginning of the End*, op.cit., p. 294.
103. Ibid.
104. Political and Secret Files, Nos L/P and S/13/1040A, IOR, and Pradhan, op.cit., Chapter 4 *passim*.

105. R. Ghosh, 'The 1948 Blood Bath in Kharswan', in *Mankind*, Vol. III, No. 1 (Hyderabad, 1958).
106. K.V. Rao, 'The Pattern of Orissa Politics', in Iqbal Narain, ed., *State Politics in India* (Meerut, 1968), p. 212; and F.G. Bailey, 'Politics in Orissa', Part VIII, 'The Ganatantra Parishad', in *The Economic Weekly*, Vol. XI (24 October 1959), p. 1471. See also R.P. Taub, *Bureaucrats under Stress* (Berkeley, 1960), Chapter 2.
107. Speech by R.N. Singh Deo, former Raja of Patna. Deo spoke especially of the forest resources of the Orissa States, which increased the provincial forest revenue from Rs. 4 million to Rs. 7.2 million after the merger, *Orissa Legislative Assembly Proceedings, 1951*, Vol. I, Part II, No. 27 (Cuttack, 29 April 1951), pp. 18-19.

Road to Nowhere: The Akalis, Cripps and the Azad Punjab Scheme

BIR GOOD GILL

In Punjab during the fateful decade of the 1940s events were getting precipitated by the day at a pace faster than anywhere else in India. The presence of the Sikhs, as the third claimant to a political share had deepened the shade of the communal problem and further charged the political atmosphere. Although a minority in the state, they had been the past rulers of Punjab and had played the largest role in Punjab affairs before the annexation by the British. They, therefore, demanded a share larger than warranted by their numbers, in proportion to their historical, religious, martial and economic importance. The Shiromani Akali Dal was the leading political organization of the Sikhs since the 1920s. After the Sikh Gurudwara Act of 1925 it had consolidated its position among the Sikh masses. The Shiromani Akali Dal had supported the Indian National Congress in the Bardoli satyagraha and the boycott of the Simon Commission. It had also fought the first elections under the Government of India Act of 1935 in collaboration with the Congress and won 10 out of the 14 seats that it contested. It joined hands with the Congress to form the opposition to the Unionist Party.

The main leaders of the Shiromani Akali Dal included Master Tara Singh, Giani Kartar Singh, Giani Dhanwant Singh, Ganga Singh, Harnam Singh Advocate, Giani Gurmukh Singh Musafir, Ishar Singh Majhail, Gopal Singh Quami, Darshan Singh Pheruman and Sohan Singh Jalalusman. Baba Kharak Singh was the president of the Shiromani Akali Dal. In 1930, however, he broke away from it and in March 1934, formed a new party, the Sikh National League, which was later named the Central Akali Dal. Among its main leaders were Amar Singh (editor of *Sher-e-Punjab*), Mehtab Singh, Jathedar Kartar Singh Jhabbar and Harbans Singh Sistani. The Central Akali Dal, however, could never replace the Shiromani Akali Dal (popularly known as the Akalis) as a party of the Sikh masses. By the 1940s the Akalis found themselves faced with some difficult issues.

The outbreak of the Second World War and the launching of the Pakistan scheme by the Muslim League had changed the political scenario. The Congress which was at the helm of affairs at the centre had moved to the background in Punjab. It had lost contact with the masses and people were getting weaned away to other Sikh and Hindu organizations.[1] The political power in the Punjab at the time rested with the Unionist Party, which had formed the government with Sikander Hayat Khan as premier. The scheme for the division of India had induced a sense of insecurity among the Sikhs. Any scheme, based on counting of heads, they felt, would not do justice to the Sikhs. The various parleys by the British and Indian leaders to settle the communal issue without their consent induced them to act and react. This paper is an attempt to understand the Akali leadership, their fears and aspirations in the politically charged period of the early 1940s.

The British necessity of gaining allies for its war efforts had given a fresh spurt of energy to political activity in India. The Sikh support in the army was vital to these efforts. Although, the feudal section of the Sikhs headed by the Maharaja of Patiala had already created the Khalsa Defence of India League in the beginning of 1941, to the British that was not enough. They knew that as far as the Sikh masses were concerned the real recruiting base was the rural belt. And here, it was the Akalis who held the key. The government, keeping in mind the need for the Akali cooperation in the war efforts, was contemplating the inclusion of a Sikh member in the Defence Council. The Hindus of Punjab had also demanded the inclusion of a Hindu member in the Council to check the communal dominance of the Muslims. But the Viceroy, Lord Linlithgow brushed it aside. He wrote to Sir Bertrand Glancy, the Governor of Punjab, 'The Punjabi Hindus need have no fear that their position will not be well looked after by their co-religionists.'[2] The Sikh claim, however, he justified on the basis that Akalis had a separate entity which needed to be represented in the Defence Council: 'We cannot overlook the importance of the Akali issue.'[3] The Akalis at this point of time were perched on the horns of a dilemma between their martial interests and political interests that pulled them in opposite directions.

The Akalis making a virtue out of necessity decided to side with the British in the war efforts and even conveyed that they no longer regarded Khalistan as a practical solution to their political problems.[4] It had been a difficult decision to take.[5] The recruitment in the army was essential for the preservation of the Sikh identity. Besides the economic angle, it was the valorous Sikh character that found a befitting expression in a military career. In such a situation where the majority community were trying to squeeze maximum perks for their brethren, the Akalis were compelled to toe an independent line of action. The Akalis, especially Giani Kartar Singh, successfully promoted Sikh recruitment, and with Master Tara Singh advocated a token arrest policy in line with Gandhi's Civil Disobedience. The Sikh dilemma was summed up by Glancy in a letter to Linlithgow, dated 22 November 1941. He wrote 'the Sikh community is growing more and more uneasy and there is a feeling that it must move in . . . some direction or the other to ensure its survival'. In such a situation the Akali decision to encourage Sikh enlistment in the Army on the one hand and their support to the Congress on the other had been dubbed as 'sailing in two boats'. But with the relations between the Muslims and the Sikhs becoming more and more strained the policy does not seem out of place. This, when even the Hindu response to Gandhi's campaign was cold in Punjab. The Hindi press, *Vir Bharat* and *Milap* wished the campaign to be terminated,[6] as it was not effective enough.

The British War Cabinet in a bid to woo Indians during the crucial phase of Axis-Allied confrontation had decided to send Sir Stafford Cripps on a twofold mission—(a) the immediate problem of securing full Indian cooperation in the war effort; and (b) to ascertain a long term policy, which was necessary to attain the first goal. As regards the former he had to consult the Viceroy and as to the latter, he had a draft declaration to hold discussions with the leaders of various political parties.[7] Glancy expressed his grave fears over the forthcoming draft declaration in connection with Punjab, which was circulated to the War Cabinet. He wrote about the unprecedented intensification of bitterness between the Muslims and Sikhs and that recruitment would be seriously affected as all communities would wish to keep their young men at home to defend their own interests.

Glancy had a hunch that in such a situation the Muslim League would gain strength in Punjab and create a large scale disruption. The chances were that the premier, along with his ministers would resign.[8] In such a situation cooperation from Punjab in the war effort would not be forthcoming. Linlithgow considered that the idea of the local option clause would be of little help in easing the mounting tension. He wrote to Lord Amery, Secretary of State, that it would arouse 'gravest apprehensions and bitterest feelings among Sikhs in the Punjab unless accompanied by specific renewal of our pledge',[9] as prospects of a predominantly Muslim and separate Punjab would frighten the Sikhs who would then cause trouble. Once the Sikhs became troublesome, the Muslims, too, would look to their own defences resulting in the intervention of the Muslim League to promote the Pakistan scheme. There were, also, the Viceroy warned, a 'good many clandestine arms in the Punjab'.[10] He suggested that only something similar to the 'August Offer' could help the situation.[11] Glancy, however, felt that the Sikhs could derive no solace from such an incorporation unless assurance was given to them that the 'minority clause' could be implemented to their advantage.[12]

Having been checkmated, the British War Cabinet planned their next move and announced the Cripps Mission, accordingly. The arrival of Cripps on 23 March 1942 filled the atmosphere with hope and ecstasy. Every political party was holding its breath in anticipation as to what Sir Stafford Cripps could be carrying for them. Linlithgow, on the contrary, was doubtful about the success of the mission and worried more about the war effort. Keeping his fingers crossed, the best he could have hoped for was that 'Cripps may be able to get the scheme over in such a way that, even if it is not accepted its presentation may not cause serious mischief to our war effort.'[13] The local option clause not only could adversely affect the heavy Sikh recruitment, but even give an impetus to communalism appearing in the army.[14] This the British could ill afford at this juncture.

Cripps did not understand the complexity of Indian politics and hence did not see the gravity of the situationm. He concentrated mostly on the Congress. As he hurriedly met delegation after delegation, things became more tangled. Tej Bahadur Sapru found Cripp's attitude very non-serious.[15] There was panic among the Sikhs that the Constitution would place power in the hands of the majority. This could result in 'unprecedented intensification of bitterness'[16] between the Muslims and the Sikhs. The Sikh delegation comprising Baldev Singh, Ujjal Singh, Master Tara Singh and Sir Jogendra Singh met Cripps on 27 March 1942. After going through the documents they raised the vital question of protection of the Sikh minority. Cripps pointed out to them that they could protect themselves under the local option clause. Cripps wrote in his Note:

> I pointed out to them the successive stages at which they might hope to be able to exert pressure which would enable them either to remain part of the single Indian Union or to get some provincial autonomy within the second union, if such was formed.[17]

He extended his argument that the Congress would not have a majority in the Constituent Assembly and would desire to get the support of the smaller minorities such as the Sikhs. The Sikhs, in return, could ask for protection under the new Constitution. 'This would set up a standard minority protection which might well be satisfactory to the Sikh community and might even entail the subdivision of the Punjab into two provinces or the setting up within the province of Punjab of a semi-autonomous district for the Sikhs.' And in case the Muslims decided not to remain within the Indian Union then it would be necessary for them to obtain a vote of non-accession by plebiscite in Punjab and in this they would try to get the Sikh support offering minority protection clauses going further than those already offered by the Indian Union. Sikh leaders who had expected some concrete offer rather than vague assurances felt that they were shabbily treated and were thoroughly disillusioned. Master Tara Singh found the whole question of the treatment of minorities was much too vague. Angry over the outcome and knowing the pressure point, Master Tara Singh went straight to the Secretary, Defence Department, and declared that so far as the Sikhs were concerned 'it was more likely to cause a complete cessation of the war effort than to encourage them to do more'.[18] He elaborated that the only thing that would satisfy the Sikhs, if this scheme were to be implemented was that Punjab should be divided and that the whole area south of the Sutlej plus the districts of Lahore (except Lahore city), Amritsar, Gurdaspur, Jullandur, Hoshiarpur and Kangra should be made into a separate province.[19] The Sikh All Parties Committee also conveyed their disappointment in a joint note summing up that they had lost all hope of receiving any consideration from the Cripps Mission and would not, therefore, like to labour the point anymore.[20]

Rejection of the Cripps Proposals by one and all relieved the Akalis of immediate danger but it did not help them overcome their apprehensions. The type of constitution that the Congress favoured could provide little room to the Sikhs in the government of independent India and joining Pakistan would be suicidal. They knew that the Hindus of Punjab could look elsewhere in India to counter the communal dominance of the Muslims but the Sikh problem and the solution to it lay in Punjab only. They were in a real tight position. As a way out of their problem the readjustment of provincial boundaries was taken up seriously by the Akalis. They advocated redistribution of provincial power between the eastern and western Punjab in order to carve out a province in which Sikhs would have a decisive voice and be a large balancing force between the Hindus and the Muslims. Having this in mind, the Akalis under the leadership of Master Tara Singh took the matter to better judges—the press and the public platform.

The *Akali* (Lahore), a leading Punjabi daily, was the first to bring out an editorial on the failure of the Cripps Proposals.[21] It argued that if a separate state could be carved out from the existing Punjab to give lease to the minorities, then why had the British annoyed the Sikhs? If Sind could be separated from Bombay only for the sake of 38 lakh Muslims then why not a separate province for Sikhs and Hindus from a population of 384 lakhs in the Punjab?[22] The Cripps plan had given the right to Muslims and the princely states to secede but no right to Sikhs to stay with the Centre. The paper exhorted the Sikh masses to send resolutions to Cripps that the Sikhs would not see themselves as scapegoats and thereby accept their political death.[23] On 7 April, the Sikh congregation at Sialkot unanimously passed a resolution to condemn the Cripps Proposals.[24] A Jhelum delegation did the same.[25] The main argument was that if the Muslim League wanted partition on the basis of the right of self-determination of the Muslim community then the Sikhs, should be permitted to be a part of India on the basis of that very principle. Cripps who proved to be 'a poor statesman and a poorer negotiator',[26] saw the sparks of the fireworks created by him even before his departure. His glaring mistake was that he assumed that the only party that mattered in India was the Congress and the one person in the Congress who mattered was Jawaharlal Nehru.[27] Within the Congress circles as well, there was a realization that Cripps had alienated large section of people, such as the Hindu Mahasabha and the Sikhs.[28]

The Sikh retaliation worried the British and resulted in the process of appeasement. David Taylor Monteath, the permanent Under Secretary of State for India and Burma suggested in the Minutes, dated 24 April 1942, that while there was 'no way of putting back the clock in the Punjab', means could be found to ease the tension. He suggested that something could be said about the 'eventual adjustment of provincial boundaries and the provision be made in Section 290 (of Government of India Act of 1935)'.[29] In line with this policy Cripps put forward the Sikh case in the House of Commons on 28 April. Amery too complimented the martial Sikhs. Added to all this were the assurances given to Master Tara Singh, through Major Short, the Civil Liaison Officer of Lahore, that the government would appease the Sikhs.[30] These assurances were not lost on the Akalis. From then onwards, there was a definite move to promote the British war effort. In return, Master Tara Singh was hopeful of the inclusion of a Sikh member in the Viceroy's Executive Council and of an Akali representative in the Punjab Cabinet.[31] After the war they hoped for a readjustment of provincial boundaries that would enable the Sikhs to exercise provincial autonomy and cultural self-determination. Master Tara Singh in his letter of thanks to Cripps brought up the case of readjustment of territories. He wrote:

If the British Government be prepared to accept this proposal of the Sikhs, there is likelihood of the final solution of the communal problem. In that case, I may be able to persuade the Congress and the Hindu Mahasabha to agree to the communal solution outlined in your proposals and as amended by the Sikhs proposal.[32]

Cripp's reply that anything the Sikhs could do to bring about an agreement on the Indian situation would be much appreciated by the British,[33] encouraged the Akalis to pursue their line of communal settlement.

The next task was to convince the Congress and the Mahasabha of the intrinsic value of the scheme, which Master Tara Singh thought would not be a difficult task, as the Azad Punjab scheme, as he called it, was both for the Hindus and Sikhs of Punjab. Unlike the Pakistan scheme, it was not separatist but was rather a move to resist the delinking of Punjab from the centre and the mainstream. The Akalis also joined the Hindu Mahasabha in celebrating 10 May 1942 as Anti-Pakistan Day and in passing resolutions all over India opposing the Pakistan scheme.[34] In the meantime, the Muslim League seeing the wind blowing in the adverse direction passed a resolution on 20 August demanding an immediate declaration of the right of self-determination for the Muslims, if the Muslim masses were to be roused to intensify the war effort.[35] This was in contrast to Sikander Hayat's unconditional support to the British war effort, and shows that the Muslim League was gaining ground in the Punjab and was demanding much more than mere lip sympathy from the Unionists. Jinnah who had protested against overemphasizing the territorial limits of the provinces in his Muslim League address in April 1942, wrote to Mahatma Gandhi on 21 September 1942 that the Muslims be considered as a nation and not as a territorial unit. Yet he insisted that Bengal and Punjab as they existed be regarded as the homeland of the Muslim nation![36]

The battlelines were now drawn. The Akalis took up the case of Punjab. They decided on a two point programme: (1) to demolish the Pakistan scheme, and (2) to establish Azad Punjab. This was pursued through the platforms of the press and at conferences. The All India Akali Conference declared that whereas they were against the Muslim League's Pakistan demand, they favoured the reorganization of Punjab boundaries in such a way as to create a province where no one community had a majority.[37] At the Montgomery Conference on 10 October they demanded that the Sikh shrines in West Punjab should be spared from majority vote while considering the new boundaries.[38] Later Giani Kartar Singh suggested a special status for Nankana Sahib and other shrines in that part of Punjab but did not stress his point. Had it been pursued in earnest there could perhaps have been room for a Vatican status for Nankana Sahib, the birthplace of Guru Nanak Dev.[39]

The Sikander formula was also not acceptable to the Sikhs and caused much resentment. The *Akali* in its special issue tried to convince the Sikh masses that it was a farce. According to the formula, Punjab had the right to stay with or disassociate from the Centre on the basis of a 75 per cent vote. The Sikhs were only 19 per cent in the Punjab Assembly. The other 81 per cent could easily fulfill the condition even if all the Sikhs voted against it.

The Sikhs would never be a party to such a decision. They said that even if the condition of a 50 per cent community vote was added, it would not be practical. The only solution to them was the appropriate division of the province. Their fear was further accentuated because there were by then many Hindus, with strong positions at the Centre (C. Rajagopalachari, for example) who thought that there was no harm in accepting the Pakistan demand. The Akalis stressed the rights of the Sikhs on the basis of their special entity, their sacrifices for Punjab, their religious shrines and their land revenue. The only solution, it was felt, was the readjustment of the boundaries to carve a province in which no community was in a majority.[40] The Akali conference at Nankana Sahib held on 25 November 1942, asserted the same demand, to gain an effective platform in Punjab politics.[41]

Giani Kartar Singh, MLA (Lyallpur), explained in the *Akali* that those who clubbed new boundaries of the Punjab and the Pakistan scheme together, did not understand either. He elaborated that there were 11 provinces in all, out of which seven had a Hindu majority and four a Muslim majority. The Hindus were safe at the centre, the Muslims wanted a separate state. The Sikh predicament was that they could neither stop Pakistan at the central level nor break it at the provincial level. Kartar Singh was bold enough to say that the Sikhs should work for the unity of India as a whole but aim at an appropriate partition of the Punjab. He supported his argument on the basis of what the British had done earlier with NWFP in 1901, Delhi in 1911 and Sind in 1935 where states were created on a linguistic basis. The Sikhs could, however, not ask for a separate state on the basis of language, because under the influence of their respective leaders the Hindus and Muslims assumed Hindi and Urdu, as their mother tongue. In the Census of 1941, Punjabi was shown to be the mother tongue of a small number, and that too, scattered all over the province. Also Punjabi was of two types—Lahori and Multani,[42] which weakened the case, dividing the issue into East and West Punjab. Master Tara Singh argued that ethically only the Sikhs were the real claimants to the Punjab as the others who had disowned their very mother tongue had no right to be there.[43]

On 13 December, Kartar Singh finally declared that an impartial commission for Punjab should be set up by the government to draw a line of division on the basis of population, property, land revenue, etc. Two provinces should be carved out—on one side the Muslim majority areas and on the other those areas where no community was in a majority. A provision should be made for the transfer of population and property at government expense and religious places should be controlled through the central government.[44]

Master Tara Singh further clarified the stand of the Akali Dal at the famous Azad Punjab Akali Conference held at Ferozepur on 18 December 1942. In his presidential address he declared that:

> The last five years of the dominance of one community by majority rule has convinced me that the Sikhs cannot live under any such dominance. . . . It is alleged that I demand Khalistan on the pattern of Pakistan. This is not true. My scheme is opposed to Pakistan. Pakistan means communal dominance and an attempt to break away from the Centre. My scheme attempts to break the communal dominance and opposes the idea of severing relations with the Centre.[45]

In the new Punjab it was argued that there would be 40 per cent Muslims, 40 per cent Hindus and 20 per cent Sikhs. Sikhs were nowhere in a majority and Master Tara Singh countered this by arguing that he only hoped to push their position to the status of a balancing power between the two communities in Azad Punjab.

The only man happy with the Cripps Proposals was Jinnah.[46] He could now see things falling in line for the first time in Punjab. This was the right time to canvas for and strengthen the hands of the Muslim League.[47] Sikander Hayat Khan could not withstand the mounting pressure of the League and had to attend its Lyallpur meeting. This open shift exposed the inherent weaknesses of the Sikander-Baldev Pact. Master Tara Singh openly criticized both Jinnah and Sikander at this juncture. He alleged that even the Census of 1941 was manipulated. The Muslim officer-in-charge of the Census had conducted its operations at that time of the year (winter) when lakhs of Pathans, besides a large number of Kashmiri Muslims come down to Punjab from the North-Western Frontier. This had helped to swell Muslim figures.[48] Against this calculated move of the Muslim community, the Akalis gave a cry both to the Hindus and the Sikhs to preserve as large a portion of Punjab as possible from Muslim rule. He categorically said that 'the portions so preserved is [to be] called Azad Punjab'.[49]

The scheme of Azad Punjab, however, did not have as smooth sailing as expected.[50] Criticisms came both from expected and unexpected quarters. Some sections, of the Hindi press, like *Vir Bharat* and *Milap*, attacked the scheme. The *Tribune* too, Master Tara Singh regretted, had misrepresented the Sikh interests and misreported news. This had caused tension in the Hindu-Sikh relations and damaged their combined front against Pakistan.[51] Within the Sikh leadership Baba Kharak Singh, president of the Central Akali Dal, took the lead to undo the scheme and left no opportunity of condemning it. The *Fateh*, a socio-political weekly, voiced the opinions of leaders of the Central Akali Dal. The Sikhs of western Punjab, whose fate had hung in the balance, were the most easy to convince. The *Fateh* argued that the Akalis had never come to the rescue of the Sikhs of this region in the past.[52] It criticized the scheme as a 'stunt' of Giani Kartar Singh and Master Tara Singh. It pointed out that the vast areas, which the scheme was planning to hand over to the Muslims had nine lakh Sikhs and property worth lakhs of rupees besides large fertile holdings in Sialkot, Gujranwala, Lyallpur and Sheikhupura. It mooted the idea that Lahore, Amritsar, Jullundur and Hoshiarpur, where Akalis were concentrated, had little land to give in compensation. The crisis of identity had no solution in the scheme of Azad Punjab.[53]

The Central Akali Dal came out with its own slogan of 'Akhand Punjab' (United Punjab) in tune with the Akhand Hindustan movement.[54] It labelled the Azad Punjab scheme as a scheme envisaging the future slavery of the Sikhs. At the Gujranwala conference, the Central Akali Dal chalked out a programme to hold conferences throughout the country to condemn the scheme.[55] Baba Kharak Singh had taken up the case of the people living beyond the Ravi, that is, of the areas comprising Lyallpur, Sialkot, Gujranwala, Sheikhupura and Rawalpindi as supporting the Akhand Punjab demand.[56] Master Tara Singh was accused of having secret meetings with Jinnah and the Muslim League president, Aurangzeb Khan, and of trying to divide Punjab in collaboration with Jinnah.[57] Resolutions were passed by the Central Akali Dal at various conferences during August, September and October 1943 to counter the Azad Punjab scheme. Baba Kharak Singh, Labh Singh, Baba Madan Singh Gaga and Durlabh Singh all from the Central Akali Dal labelled the Azad Punjab scheme as 'anti-national', 'another face of Pakistan' and 'nothing but castles in the air'.[58] The Akali leaders were even accused of embezzlement of the Gurudwara funds for purposes of party propaganda.[59]

The Central Akali Dal and the Hindus bitterly criticized the permission granted to Ajit Singh Sarhadi to join the Muslim League ministry in NWFP. The Akali decision was in tune with the policy of the Hindu Mahasabha. Veer Savarkar had declared that coalition ministries were desirable wherever a Muslim ministry was unavoidable. It had happened also in the Sind and Bengal. Veer Savarkar's statement received a mixed response, while the Akalis were reproached for negotiating with the enemy camp. [60] This 'Realism in Politics',[61] was, felt to be the need of the hour and the Sikhs could not afford to lose whatever little chance they had of self-assertion.

On 5 June 1943 the Working Committee of the Shiromani Akali Dal stated that it had received enquiries from various places about its notion of the Azad Punjab and its boundaries. It issued a clarification:

> The Shiromani Akali Dal hereby declares that in the Azad Punjab the boundaries shall be fixed after taking into consideration the population, property, land revenue and historical traditions of each of the communities. An independent and impartial commission alone can finally decide the demarcation of boundaries. Further the Shiromani Akali Dal is of the opinion that if the new demarcations are effected on the above mentioned principles then the Azad Punjab shall comprise of Ambala, Jullandur, Lahore Divisions and out of the Multan Division, Lyallpur District, some portion of Montgomery and Multan Districts. The Shiromani Akali Dal shall make its demand of these demarcations and shall fight for the same.[62]

In the wake of the controversy, the *Akali* traced the background of the scheme to 1931 when, at the time of the Gandhi-Irwin Pact, Sikhs of all ideologies sent a deputation to present their demands. In that delegation Sir Sunder Singh Majithia, Shivdev Singh Sialkot, Sant Singh, MLA (Lyallpur), Giani Sher Singh, Giani Kartar Singh and Master Tara Singh were all present. The 17-point programme of the Sikhs had carried a demand for new boundaries of Punjab. This demand was presented by Sampuran Singh and Ujjal Singh before the Round Table Conference. The same demand was put in front of Cripps and made to the Congress Working Committee, where it was considered under the 'Self-determination Clause'.[63] It was, therefore, not a bolt from the blue as alleged nor was it in retaliation to the Pakistan demand. Master Tara Singh added that the Azad Punjab demand would stand even if the Muslims gave up the Pakistan demand because its aim was to free Hindus and Sikhs from the yoke of the factional rule of the Muslims. He also said that when Cripps in his proposals agreed to give Pakistan to the Muslims, the Sikhs were unhappy as they were, so to say, being thrown to the wolves. Cripps had professed sympathy for the Sikhs and agreed to it being a genuine demand but expressed his helplessness to commit himself to anything without consultation with his colleagues. Amery too had said that whenever India's new constitution would be formed the proposal to re-carve the province would be considered. This is why it is sometimes referred to as Amery's scheme. Amery added 'the Scheme, has connection with the separation of Sind. If a province could be created to give dominance to one community why not a separate province to grant safety to another?'[64]

At a series of counter conferences in the West Punjab the Akalis continued their propaganda. The first one was organized at Panja Sahib on 14 and 15 August 1943 to propagate the scheme. Thousands of Sikhs came from Jhelum, Peshawar and Rawalpindi to display their support.[65] Processions were taken out and resolutions were passed for Azad Punjab. At Goindwal, in Amritsar, it was even suggested that the Sikhs would be ready for sacrifices if need be.[66] At Dera Baba Nanak and Dhudial, in East Punjab, Giani Kartar Singh, Principal Ganga Singh, Giani Dhanwant Singh, Secretary Shiromani Akali Dal, delivered fiery speeches in favour of the scheme.[67] At the Akali Conference, Peshawar, Master Tara Singh stressed the need for safeguarding the rights of minorities in that part of Punjab.[68] Harnam Singh Advocate, president, Central Sikh League, Lahore, gave a reply to the allegations of Baba Kharak Singh and his supporters. To the allegation that Gurudwara Nankana Sahib and Panja Sahib would be left out if the Azad Punjab scheme was accepted, he asserted that Harmandir Sahib, Dera Sahib and other Lahore Sikh shrines, Gurudwara Taran Taran, Takht Keshgarh Sahib and the gurudwaras in the Multan division would be in Azad Punjab. But, he said, it would be wrong to say that Nankana Sahib and Sacha Sauda would go to Pakistan.[69] To the criticism that this demand was anti-national, Harnam Singh retorted that even the Congress had supported the readjustment of boundaries both in Punjab and in Bengal in their resolution to Cripps. To the attack that it was an offshoot of Pakistan, he replied that Jinnah in his famous 14-point programme, had agreed that whenever it became necessary to alter the boundaries of the provinces it would have no effect on the Muslim majority in Punjab, Bengal and the NWFP. From this point of view the Azad Punjab scheme was just the opposite of the Pakistan scheme. Jinnah himself confessed that Azad Punjab, was a serious threat to the Pakistan scheme. [70]

The Akalis by now were weary of criticism and were disturbed by the Pakistan bogey. The fear of the Congress-League settlement in which the Sikhs might be ignored was creeping into their minds. Even the Hindu

Mahasabha was nervous.[71] The atmosphere was heavy with resentment. This was when Rajagopalachari forward his formula. The Hindus called it a tool for the 'vivisection of India'. The Sikhs, one and all, vehemently, condemned it.[72]

The Akali leadership, caught in the crossfire of the resultant controversies, had to spend most of its time in clarifications and in defending its stand. The name Azad Punjab did them more harm than good. The name instantly brought to mind the idea of secession contrary to the intentions of its promoters. It was a misnomer. The Azad Punjab scheme spread like a forest fire, but much before its arguments were put to test, it was abandoned and the well-meaning scheme was lost in the maze of endless controversy. Its chances of survival were bright, in the beginning. The Muslim League was intially silent about it. The British circles were of the view that the scheme sprang from the heart of India[73] and was not engineered by separatist forces like that of Pakistan. Even some Congress leaders were contemplating that territorial readjustment was necessary, whether the question was approached from the angle of the two-nation theory or from that of the residuary powers being vested in the provinces.[74]

The Azad Punjab scheme was a reflection of the way in which the contemporary Akali mind functioned. To the Akalis the Pakistan fear was far more real than it was to the leaders of the national mainstream, elsewhere in India. Their whole concentration was to free the Sikhs and the Hindus of Punjab from the Muslim yoke, lest 'plunges into the outer darkness of Pakistan'. The epicentre of the problem was Punjab, so the remedy was how to solve it and yet let Punjab remain in India. If the scheme was accepted, the Akalis felt, it would make Pakistan unviable because by doing so, it would snatch from the Muslim majority areas of the west, the valuable resource material of the central and eastern Punjab and reduce the former to a state of financial impotence. The scheme, no doubt, had some lacunae and needed refinement. It did not, for example, have a satisfactory solution for the Sikhs in the western Punjab. But had it been discussed and debated by the various political parties and leaders with an open mind, it had the potential to act as a counter to the Pakistan scheme, especially for Punjab. Also had the scheme been accepted, it might not have made much of a difference to the Radcliffe line, but one of the most heinous bloodbaths in recent history could, perhaps, have been avoided.

The most positive feature of the scheme was that it reiterated that the

Sikhs wanted to remain within India. The Akali leaders stressed the point again and again, that the scheme was both for the Hindus and the Sikhs of Punjab. But criticized vehemently by opponents and ignored by the major political parties, the scheme died a premature death. While the ill-starred Azad Punjab scheme was drowned in the hue and cry raised against the Rajagopalachari formula, little did one foresee that contemporary events in the Punjab were moving towards a more tragic finale.

NOTES

1. This was admitted by the Secretary, Punjab Congress Assembly Party, in a letter to Rajendra Prasad, 20 December 1941, Valmiki Choudhary, ed., *Dr. Rajendra Prasad Correspondence and Select Documents*, Vol. V (New Delhi, 1986), p. 116.
2. Lord Linlithgow to Sir Bertrand Glancy, Simla, 3 July 1941, in Linlithgow Papers, Microfilm Roll 90, Nehru Memorial Museum & Library, New Delhi (hereafter NMML).
3. Ibid.
4. Glancy to Linlithgow, Lahore, 22 November 1941, in ibid.
5. Even the British War Cabinet acknowledged that 'The Sikhs present a somewhat separate problem from other classes. They are [a] separate, warlike and politically minded community.' The Sikh recruitment in the army was as high as 12 per cent of the whole in 1941. Note by Major General Lockhart, India Office, 25 February 1942, Nicholas Mansergh, editor-in-chief, *The Transfer of Power 1942-7* (hereafter *TOP*) Vol. I (London, 1970), Document (hereafter Doc.) 180.
6. Home Pol., 18/7/1941, Appendix 1, National Archives of India, New Delhi, (hereafter NAI).
7. Amery to Linlithgow *TOP*, Doc. 315.
8. Glancy to Linlithgow, Lahore, 4 March 1942, ibid., Doc. 236.
9. Linlithgow to Amery, 6 March 1942, ibid., Doc. 248.
10. Linlithgow to Amery, 6 March 1942, ibid., Doc. 253.
11. On 8 August 1940, the Governor-General, had issued a statement that weight would be given to the views of the minorities in any revision of the constitution.
12. Glancy to Linlithgow, 10 March 1942, *TOP*, Doc. 298.
13. Linlithgow to Amery, 24 March 1942, ibid., Doc. 372.
14. Glancy to Linlithgow, 10 March 1942, in ibid., Doc. 298. Also see R.J. Moore, *Churchill, Cripps and India, 1939-1945* (Oxford, 1979), pp. 70-1.
15. Sapru commented that Cripps was like an actor in a comedy 'playing to the gallery and trying to earn cheap popularity with the press', Tej Bahadur Sapru to Jagdish Prasad, 19 August 1942, Roll 4, P. 254, Sapru Papers, NMML.
16. Glancy to Linlithgow, 4 March 1942, *TOP*, Doc. 236. See also Glancy to Linlithgow, 5 March 1942, Linlithgow Papers, Roll 9, NMML.
17. Note by Cripps, 27 March 1942, *TOP*, Doc. 396.
18. G. Ogilvie to Leonard Pinell, Acting Private Secretary to Viceroy, 30 March 1942, ibid., Doc. 455.
19. Ibid.
20. Joint Note to Cripps by Baldev Singh, Tara Singh, Jogendra Singh, Ujjal Singh and Mohan Singh, 31 March 1942, ibid., Doc. 467.

21. *Akali* (Punjabi daily, Lahore), 1 April 1942.
22. Muslims enjoyed only a narrow majority over the Hindus and Sikhs combined. The latter had the advantage over Muslims in educational and economic fields, Satya M. Rai, *Partition of the Punjab* (New Delhi, 1965), pp. 33-4.
23. *Akali*, 2 April 1942.
24. Ibid., 11 April 1942.
25. Ibid.
26. Sapru to Jagdish Prasad, 14 April 1942, Roll 4, P. 252,. Sapru Papers, NMML.
27. Sapru to B. Shiva Rao, 12 April 1942, Roll 5, P. 216, in ibid.
28. Sapru to Jagdish Prasad, 19 August 1942, Roll 4, P. 254, in ibid.
29. Minutes by Patrick and D. Monteath, 24 April 1942, *TOP*, Doc. 675.
30. Central Intelligence Officer, Lahore, 12 May 1942, Home Poll (1), 219/1942, NAI.
31. Ibid.
32. Master Tara Singh to Cripps, Amritsar, 4 May 1942, *TOP*, Vol. II (London, 1971), Doc. 17.
33. Cripps to Master Tara Singh, 10 July 1942, ibid., Doc. 244.
34. Home Poll (1)222/1942, NAI; also *Tribune* (Lahore), 2 and 19 April 1942.
35. Resolution of Muslim League Working Committee, Bombay, 20 August 1942, *TOP*, Vol. II, op. cit., Doc. 598.
36. P.R. Das to Sapru, Patna, 18 December 1944, Roll 1, D. 53, Sapru Papers, NMML.
37. *Akali* (editorial), 30 September 1942.
38. Ibid., 12 October 1942.
39. Kartar Singh later put forward this point to Jenkins, Governor of Punjab, for declaring Nankana Sahib and its neighbouring villages as a 'free city', but somehow he was not forceful enough, Latif Ahmed Sherwani, *The Partition of India and Mountbatten* (Karachi, n.d.), p. 106.
40. The Nirankari Number of *Akali*, 22 November 1942.
41. *Akali*, 27 November 1942.
42. Ibid., 11 December 1942.
43. Master Tara Singh to Sapru, Amritsar, 10 January 1945, Roll 5, S. 280, Sapru Papers, NMML.
44. *Akali*, 13 December 1942.
45. Ibid, 20 December 1942.
46. Cripps noted that the only suggestion Jinnah made was some change in phraseology in the proposals to promote a Second Dominion, 25 March 1942, *TOP*, Vol. I, Doc. 380.
47. Ian Talbot, *Khizr Tiwana, the Punjab Unionist Party and the Partition of India* (Surrey, UK, 1996), p. 85.
48. Master Tara Singh to Sapru, Roll. 5, S. 280, Sapru Papers, NMML.
49. Home Poll, 18/11/1942, NAI.
50. Master Tara Singh had the hunch that the only party that would object to the division of Punjab as proposed by the Sikhs could be the Muslim League, in *TOP*, Vol. II, Doc. 17.
51. *Akali*, 17 October 1944; also see Home Poll, 18/10/44, NAI.
52. *Fateh* (Punjabi weekly, Lahore), 21 January 1943.
53. The editorial adds that the *Milap* always referred to Sikhs as 'Hindu community' and if the Sikhs of the west did not wish to migrate, the community would be divided into two camps, *Fateh*, 28 January 1943.

54. Ibid., 4 February 1943.
55. Ibid., 18 February, 11 and 25 March 1943.
56. Ibid., 6 and 13 May 1943.
57. Ibid., 23 July 1943.
58. Ibid., 27 August, 23 September, 7 October and 2 December 1943.
59. Home Poll (1), 18/12/1943, NAI.
60. Home Poll (1), 18/5/1943, Appendix 1, NAI.
61. K.C. Gulati, *The Akalis Past and Present* (New Delhi, 1974), p. 104.
62. N.N. Mitra, *Indian Annual Register, 1943, Vol. I* (repr., Delhi, 1990), p. 298.
63. *Akali*, 11 July 1943.
64. To Master Tara Singh, ibid., 25 July 1943.
65. Ibid., 19 and 20 August 1943.
66. Ibid., 5 and 17 September 1943.
67. Ibid., 6 and 7 October 1943.
68. The resolution stated that one Sikh should be in the NWFP Ministry and 12 per cent Sikhs in all state jobs. In the District Boards the claim to equal representation given in other provinces to other minorities, should be applicable to the Sikhs, too. Gurumukhi should be taught in schools if there were more than seven Sikhs. The Sikh seat should be fought on the Sikh ticket, ibid., 24 November 1943.
69. The Akalis had fixed the boundaries of Azad Punjab in June 1943. This made it geographically impossible to include the shrines in the proposed Azad Punjab. Perhaps the Akali minds were working to etch out a special status for these shrines.
70. *Akali*, 19 September 1943.
71. Home Poll, 18/6/1944, NAI.
72. Ibid., 18/8/1944.
73. Lt. Col. Birdwood, wrote in 1945, 'in one respect it [the Azad Punjab] has better logic than that [the Pakistan] demand in that the Sikh ambitions at least spring from the heart of the country affected and are unaffected by influences imposed from outside', quoted in Gulati, op. cit.
74. P.R. Das to Sapru, 18 December 1944, Roll 1, D.53, Sapru Papers, NMML.

Tribes, Partition and Independence

K.S. SINGH

Mainstream writings on Partition have centred on the roles and relationships of the major communities such as the Hindus, Muslims and Sikhs. The Christians and Anglo-Indians also figure in the discourse on Partition. But the tribals are generally left out or treated casually and briefly as communities living on the periphery, which they were, considering their situation in the *Transfer of Power* papers brought out by the former colonial authority[1] or in the *Towards Freedom* project material published so far.[2]

The objective of this paper is to explore the relatively uncharted area of tribal politics on the eve of Partition and through independence. It deals with tribal autonomy, tribal movements, the colonial plans for separation and integration, impact of the events leading to Partition and independence in the two major regions of tribal India, middle India and the north-east. The problems of the two regions were varied. The tribals were in control of their resources and enjoyed a larger measure of autonomy in the north-east, which was also relatively isolated. The territorial isolation of the area was enforced by such measures as the Inner Line Regulation, 1873. The tribals of middle India had a lesser degree of isolation. However, there were also similarities between the two regions, for example, the rise of a tribal middle class, shaped by education, received at mission schools and employed by the colonial administration, loosening of the hold of the traditional élites, opening up of the tracts, particularly during the Second World War, commercialization of crops and a greater role of the market forces. The rise of a tribal segment of entrepreneurship in some parts of the north-east was a special feature of the tribal situation there. The new middle class demanded a role for itself in constitutional politics and even beyond it.

One aspect of tribal politics had been the growing demand for a special dispensation for the tribal people articulated in some form or the other in the decade since the 1920s and for tribal autonomy or for the creation of a tribal state in the 1940s. The demand for a tribal state among the Bhils was reported around 1945; however it was in Chotanagpur that a well-organized tribal movement for the creation of a Jharkhand province out of the Bihar and adjoining provinces crystallized. There were several reasons that explain why Chotanagpur became the centre of such a movement. Chotanagpur was the most advanced of the tribal regions from the point of literacy, political consciousness and industrial development. Christianity had come in a big way to Chotanagpur and the major tribes were effectively evangelized. As Christianity spread it performed many roles: it gave them history and myths; it accentuated the notion of private rights in land; it promoted education and medical care; and it also emphasized a sense of separateness. The Chotanagpur tribes had a tradition of militant and organized struggles going back to over a hundred years, around land and forests. Lastly, there was a rich corpus of anthropological literature to draw upon in order to create a new sense of tribal identity.[3]

The period from 1938-47 saw the rise of the Adivasi Mahasabha. The immediate cause of the formation of the Mahasabha was the experience of the first elections held in 1937, under the Government of India Act of 1935. The Congress had swept the polls and had persuaded the Christians to form a joint body. The existing Chotanagpur Improvement Society led by members of different Christian denominations and non-tribals merged to form the Adivasi Mahasabha. This new body represented an advance on the earlier movement, in the sense that it had a wider political base, and a pan-tribal composition and objective. Two other sources of influence on the Mahasabha, were the Bengali-Bihari controversy and the Muslim League politics. The Bengalis felt that their interests in Bihar were not safe and, therefore, they could combine with the tribals to form a separate state. The Muslim League during the mid-1940s toyed with the ideas of forming a separate Muslim dominated region and a corridor passing through the tribal areas to link East and West Pakistan. They sympathized with the tribals and gave financial support to the Adivasi Mahasabha.

The Mahasabha was 'loyalist' but remained outside the mainstream of nationalist politics and the freedom movement. Professional political workers, some of them highly educated and articulate, led the Mahasabha. It became a Chotanagpur movement extending over both urban and rural areas and it involved tribals other than the Ranchi tribals. It demanded not the formation of a sub-state but complete separation from Bihar. A series of violent incidents occurred during this period, which underlined the militant nature of the movement. The Sabha was, however, routed in the elections held in 1946, by the Congress.[4]

The Adivasi Mahasabha threw up a charismatic tribal leader, Jaipal

Singh (1903-68). He was brought up by the missionaries of the Anglican Church and educated at St Paul's School, Ranchi, St Augustines' College, Canterbury, England, and St John's College, Oxford, England. He was an Oxford Blue at hockey and captain of the Indian Olympic hockey team at the Amsterdam Olympics in 1928, which won the world championship. He acted as Civilian Adviser, Eastern Command Selection Board; Minister for Colonization, Bikaner State; Headmaster-designate and Officiating Vice-Principal, Rajkumar College, Raipur; Member, Board of Secondary Education, Bihar; and Member, Standing Committee, Ministry of Works, Production and Supply. He became President of the All India Adivasi Mahasabha, in 1939, and President of the Jharkhand Party in 1949. [5] Jaipal Singh in an autobiographical note called himself a 'primitive nationalist'.[6]

This rising star of the tribal world of Chotanagpur, chose to stay at Jamshedpur. He was a personal friend of Narendra Nath Rakshit, Managing Director of the Tatanagar Foundry. Rakshit moved the first resolution on the formation of an Adivasi state at the Haripura Congress, presided over by Subhas Chandra Bose.[7] Bose entered the world of Chotanagpur through the labour politics of Jamshedpur, the course of which he steered, albeit briefly, as President of the Jamshedpur Labour Association. Both, Jaipal Singh and Subhas Chandra Bose, interacted with each other at least on one occasion. Bose tried to persuade Jaipal Singh to join the freedom movement and the nationalist mainstream. This, it was argued, would secure for the tribals the support of the nationalist forces and would be mutually beneficial. According to an informant, Jaipal Singh agreed to consider the proposal. But, at that time, he was too much of a loyalist to the tribal cause to join the mainstream.[8]

It was around this period that the idea of an industrial state to be formed out of the mineral rich regions of Bihar was mooted, a concept which was the forerunner of the notion of the Jharkhand state. Jaipal Singh also emphasized the separateness of the Adivasi workers of the foundry to break the strike called by the Congress-led union in 1939, which they did. We do not know to what extent the Adivasis were weaned away from the militant Left or Congress-led unions, though we do know that the tribal workers did sometimes join hands with the non-tribal workers to secure the acceptance of their demands, for example, in the TISCO strike of 1928. The tribals took the initiative in such situations. The Adivasi women workers, called *rezas*, were particularly active. Of special interest was the rise of tribal ethnicity, which was part of the tribal workers' movement during this period. It is a matter of record that the tribal workers of

Jamshedpur played a major role in the Adivasi movement and in the emergence of the Jharkhand party. The demands articulated by tribal workers became a part of the agenda of the tribal movement.

In a number of articles, Jaipal Singh explained the objectives of the Adivasi Mahasabha, its philosophy and linkages:

> Separation of Chota Nagpur and the Santhal Parganas is inevitable and the demand for the creation of a Governor's province out of the Aboriginal Tracts is nothing new. . . .
>
> The Adivasi Sabha is inspired by the principles of the Indian National Congress. It is working for the political and economic emancipation of the Adivasis and non-Adivasis of Chota Nagpur and the Santhal Parganas. The present position of our being enslaved to Bihar is not only intolerable but also grossly unjust. Partial exclusion has thrown the backward tribes at the mercy of the Biharis.
>
> The Adivasi movement is a national movement. The Aboriginal Tracts are and have always been distinct as an administrative unit, whether they were under Bengal or under Bihar and Orissa. Much of the present friction between Bihar and the Partially Excluded Areas would have been obviated had the Bihar Ministry treated Chota Nagpur and the Santhal Parganas which are very inadequately represented in the Legislatures, as an area calling for special attention and added consideration because of the fact of statutory differentiation.[9]

Jaipal Singh was obsessed with the status of the tribals and wrote extensively on the subject. This is, an example, of what he said:

> Hitherto we have been taught to think of aboriginals as being those people who inhabited this land before the Aryans came. For centuries the Adivasis have remained aboriginal. It made no difference what faiths the Adivasis embraced. Their racial identity was never tested by religious data. The Census operations of recent years have taken the line of least resistance in regard to racial origin. The demand for the separation of the Aboriginal Tracts into a separate province can be appreciated only when we understand who the Adivasis are. Our eyes tell us that about three-fourths of the present population is aboriginal.[10]

Linking up Adivasistan with India and Pakistan, Jaipal Singh conjured up a grand vision of the Adivasi cultural world:

> Its history too is wonderful. These parts are inhabited largely by those who are regarded as the original inhabitants of India. Their civilization differs in many respects from the civilization of other people. The discovery of old articles shows that this civilization is very old. The Adivasis belong to a different stock (Austric) from the Aryas (Aryans) and people of the same stock are spread towards the south-east of India in the many islands to a great distance. Their ancient culture is preserved in these parts to a considerable extent, perhaps more than elsewhere. It is not however, as if the Aryas and the Adivasis never mingled with one another.

As a matter of fact there have been considerable intermixture and exchange. Aryas have taken many things from them and they have taken many things from the Aryas. With all this, however, they have kept themselves apart. . . .

From Burma right down to the eastern shores of Indo-China civilization has been influenced by our mututal cooperation. Some 1800 years ago our people from Champa (Bhagalpur) migrated and established the Champa colony in Indo-China. That is an incident in the history of the past, which Bihar played among the Austrics of the south-east.

Historically, about 3500 years or more ago, the forefathers of the . . . light skinned nomads, began a series of invasions of Adivasistan and came through the Afghan passes and settled in the Gangetic plains. These interloping Aryas were contemptuous of the Adivasis; one theory of the origin of caste, varna, is that it was invented by the Aryas to prevent inter-marriage with the dark Adivasis.[11]

But Adivasistan was to be no more than a 'reunion of Bihar and Orissa to Bengal'. In 1940, Jaipal Singh was not enamoured by the Muslim League. He wrote:

What shall we say of Pakistan? The Moslems are a distinctly dissimilar people. Being the minority they consider themselves the injured party. Their list of grievances is long but when one analyses them in detail they become hard to grasp. The Moslems make what is beyond doubt the most difficult minority problem in the world. Pakistan will make for Hindu regeneration and this will come from the consequent emancipation of Hindu women. Mohammedanism is largely responsible for the low position that the woman occupies at the present time in India.[12]

Jaipal Singh further elaborated the objectives of the Adivasi movement, heritage and support for the Bengalis. He wrote:

The Jharkhand Province Movement stands for the moral and material advancement, for the political and economic emancipation of greater Chota Nagpur and the Santhal Parganas, and, in sum, for the creation of a separate province so that we may have an enlightened administration appropriate to the needs and traditions of the people. That there is nothing much in common between Bihar proper and Jharkhand is readily admitted. . . .

I mention the pathetic situation of Bengali Hindus to indicate that the Jharkhand Province Movement has every sympathy with the plight of the Hindu minority in Bengal but at the same time I must make it abundantly explicit that our demand is not made on a religious basis at all. We are fighting for a cultural autonomy, an arrangement wherein every culture will get its full scope to develop its own character. We do not want uniformity in any shape. We want a unity of purpose and . . . the preservation of the life and soul of the most ancient aristocracy of Hindustan, the Adivasis. In Jharkhand we number nine million out of a total population of ten million. With ninety per cent of the population of Adivasis, there can be no two opinons about the justice of the demand for separation. . . .

Separation is vital for the salvation of the people of Jharkhand, be they Bengalis, be they Adivasis. Separation is the only means we have to redeem our culture. . . .

It is universally admitted that a great civilization existed and flourished thousands of years before the influx of the Aryan hordes. The discoveries of Harappa and Mohenjodaro have yet to be deciphered before any adequate collation of facts can be made in regard to the Adivasi share in that ancient civilization. In any case we have abundant wealth left in the present Adivasi society to justify our having a place of honour in the national life of India. Our language is rich, our religion is the true founder of Hinduism, our social customs are the envy of democracy, the simplicity of our life is the desire of India, our race is famed for truthfulness and honest work, we are accommodating to all people and, in short, we Adivasis possess all the qualities which entitle us to play an important role in the struggle for Indian Independence.[13]

Jaipal Singh also supported the war efforts. The Adivasi Mahasabha however moved closer to the Muslim League on the eve of Partition and independence. The Muslim League in return proposed to champion not only the cause for self-determination for the Muslims, but also to speak for other minorities. The tribals were not explicitly mentioned but the Muslim League tried to forge links with tribals in Chotanagpur in the same way as they had recruited some members of the scheduled castes to their ranks. As M.A. Jinnah in his presidential address at the annual session of the All India Muslim League, held at Lucknow in October 1937, said:

The All-India Muslim League certainly and definitely stands to safeguard the rights and interest of the Mussalmans and other minorities effectively. That is its basic cardinal principle. This is the *cause belle*. . . . The Congress with its entire boast has done nothing in the past for the Mussalmans. It has failed to create confidence and to create a sense of security among the Mussalman and other minorities.[14]

Three years later in March 1940 the Muslim League's Lahore Resolution spoke of the need to provide effective and mandatory safeguards for the protection of the religious, cultural, economic, political, administrative and other rights and interests of the tribals in consultation with them.[15]

The Adivasis emerged as a political force in the general election of 1946 capturing three seats in the provincial assembly of Bihar; there were four Adivasi independents in Orissa; in Assam the Tribal League captured six seats. The Muslim League continued to speak of the rights of Muslims, Christians and other minorities, who they considered had been reduced to the status of irredeemable helots, socially and economically, by the Hindu caste system, which was a direct negation of nationalism, equality, democracy and all the noble ideals Islam stood for.[16]

The Muslim League in Bihar was reportedly preparing plans to divide Bihar and create a separate homeland for 47 million Bihari Muslims in 1947. The League pamphlet 'Divide Bihar' declared:

The Musalmans of Bihar fully support the demand of the people of Chotanagpur and Santhal Parganas for separation from Bihar. The Adivasis (aboriginals) and Muslims of Chotanagpur and Santhal Parganas together form a majority in that area and they have been demanding separation of Chotanagpur and Santhal Parganas for a long time. . . . Geographically, economically and culturally Chotanagpur with Santhal Parganas is a separate land and has nothing in common with Bihar. The districts demanded as the homeland for the Muslims of Bihar, Purnea, South Bhagalpur, South Monghyr, Patna, subdivisions of Jehanabad and Nawadah and some parts of Sadar division of Gaya form a contiguous area and may form some sort of union with Chotanagpur and Santhal Parganas and make a strong independent sovereign state.[17]

To the Muslim League the union of the beef eating Adivasis, who bury their dead, belonging to Chotanagpur, with Hindu Bihar was illogical and inconsistent:

There is no justification for making Chotanagpur attached to the Province of Bihar for exploitation by the caste Hindus of the province. . . .

Adivasi tribesmen of Bihar province will want to federate with Muslim Bengal and not Hindu Bihar. If a plebiscite of Adivasis were held, their verdict would be clear. If they had separate electorates today they and the Muslims would form a majority in the Bihar Legislature.[18]

There was also the enormous material resource base including mineral wealth of the Adivasi land that had to be considered:

Jamshedpur with Tata (iron) works is in the Adivasi country and all the mineral resources of the tract are today being exploited for the benefit of Akhand Hindustan. Adivasis, who eat beef and bury their dead, are as far apart from caste Hinduism as Islam or Christianity.[19]

Support for the tribal state was only part of a bigger plan drawn up by the Muslim League to form a larger tribal state, consisting of the Chotanagpur region and Central Provinces, which would eventually be joined by Hyderabad, the 'biggest Muslim state'. A secret document revealed:

That the Muslim League had plans to foment a movement for independent Jharkhand by the aboriginals of Chotanagpur and Santhal Parganas. Jharkhand would seek union with the aboriginals of the Central Provinces and a final link up with Hyderabad which was seeking an outlet to the sea at Goa on the western sea coast of India.[20]

There were to be three phases in the fulfilment of this 'Grand Design'. First, the exodus of the Muslims from communally tense areas within Bihar to its districts bordering on Bengal would be encouraged so that these border districts would be turned into Muslim majority areas. Secondly, the formation of Jharkhand out of Chotanagpur and Central Provinces would provide a link with Hyderabad and form the 1,200 mile long corridor running across India, Thirdly, this new acquisition would eventually join Pakistan. As Pyarelal analysed it:

> The demand for pockets [Muslim majority areas in Bihar] became a vital link in its [Muslim League] strategy. It was natural, while the feeling of insecurity prevailed for the Muslims to want to congregate in villages where they were in large numbers. The League sought to make this into a permanent feature of Bihar's polity. From the idea of selected, they proceeded to the idea of contiguous pockets to the division of Bihar itself, to provide an independent homeland for the Muslims which along with Jharkhand would join Pakistan. The bastion of Pakistan would thus protrude right up to Chotanagpur. If that happened, what could be more natural than that the aboriginal tribes of Central Provinces should desire to join their brothers of Chotanagpur. The big state of Hyderabad abutted on these areas and being the hereditary Muslim state had the 'right' to belong to this joint federation of Muslims and aboriginals. Goa was later declared to be the 'natural' outlet to the sea for Hyderabad. Secret negotiations were said to be proceeding for its sale to the Nizam. Here in the making was the 1200 mile long corridor running across India.[21]

This idea of a corridor needs to be discussed further. On 21 May 1947, Mohammad Ali Jinnah demanded the creation of a 1,200 mile long corridor to link up the eastern and western wings of Pakistan,[22] which would pass through the northern provinces of India. The prominent members of the Muslim League, including one Yunus from Bihar, [23] who suggested that the best corridor should be along the Grand Trunk Road, supported this demand. However the proposal was rejected by the Congress leaders: Sardar Patel, characterized it as 'such fantastic nonsense not to be taken seriously';[24] C. Rajagopalachari dismissed it as a matter of 'stark absurdity';[25] and Rajendra Prasad found the demand 'untenable'.[26] The *Times of India* in an editorial recalled that corridors had an 'evil reputation' of breeding trouble. It pointed out that while the Polish corridor was Polish, Jinnah's corridor would not have the justification of being predominantly Muslim.[27] The Muslim League paper, *Dawn*, however, recalled that there was nothing new in the demand for a corridor, which had been raised in the past as it was considered vital for the creation of Pakistan. The editorial went on to warn that if the Muslims could win Pakistan, they could just as well build a corridor 'somewhere' for the linking of the two segments of Pakistan.[28]

The idea of a corridor, therefore, did not die down, but continued to resonate for some time. It was to start from Goa and pass through Hyderabad, the tribal territories of Central Provinces, Jharkhand, contiguous tribal areas of West Bengal and Orissa and East Pakistan. The Muslim League continued to cultivate the tribal leaders assiduously. From Calcutta it provided funds and other material support for the tribal movement in Chotanagpur. As late as 1959, copies of letters purported to have been written by Muslim leaders to Jaipal Singh offering help and calling for rendering accounts, were in circulation to discredit the tribal leader and his movement.

The Muslim League particularly focused on Jaipal Singh. [29] The Feroz Khan Noon–Jaipal Singh correspondence referred to by Pyarelal show how close they had got to each other.[30] Jaipal Singh began to speak the language of the Muslim League. He said: 'Let them [Hindus] think the Muslims and Adivasis are not going to tolerate Hindu Raj for one second. We will fight for our religion and integrity and our racial *izzat*.'[31] Some of the tribal élite had also been roped in. Another tribal leader, who was the secretary of the Santhal Parganas Adivasi Sabha, spoke thus on the occasion of the Division of the Bihar Conference in 1947:

> It is the highest travesty of constitutionalism that the Adivasi who form the 70 per cent of the total population (?) have been reduced to very ordinary majority. Let the Mongols, Aryan or any race for that matter, quit and hand over the country to its genuine inhabitants, the Adivasis. . . . Racially and culturally we are distinct entities from the Hindus. Geographically, Jharkhand stands out from Bihar. What we want is simply that: 'Hands off Jharkhand'.[32]

The Muslim League ideologues, who envisaged the confederacy of Bengaman (East Pakistan and Adivasistan), looked upon Jharkhand as the potential area for the spread of Islam. Through the large scale conversion of tribals and intermarriages between Muslims and the tribals, they thought that they could one day tilt the demographic balance in favour of the former.[33]

The Adivasis of the regions adjoining Chotanagpur, the Santhals, Oraons and Mundas, who were culturally and linguistically akin to the Adivasis of Jharkhand, were getting restive on the eve of independence.

Those belonging to the princely states of Orissa and the Central Provinces wanted to join Chotanagpur, rather than be integrated with the provinces of Orissa and Madhya Pradesh. Led by the Adivasi Mahasabha and their own regional organizations, they agitated against the merger of Kharaswan with Orissa and Sarguja and Jashpur with Madhya Pradesh. Their agitation resulted in much bloodshed.[34] The All India Adivasi Mahasabha in its meeting at Ranchi on 28 February 1948 called for the immediate creation of the state of Jharkhand, comprising the Adivasi tracts, together with the adjacent areas such as Saraikela, Kharswan, Gangpur, Jashpur, Keonjhar, Bonai, Bamra, Sarguja and Changbhakar. These areas, they claimed, were historically part and parcel of the Chotanagpur plateau.

Nationalist opinion was rightly alarmed at the attempts made by the Muslim League in collaboration with a few of the tribal leaders to weaken the nascent Indian nation state. The Muslim League and the Jharkhand link-up were not a mere pressure ploy; it was a real threat. There were elements in the Chotanagpur Separation League, which talked of a sovereign tribal state. The intended corridor would, it was feared:

> Effectually cut off South from the North of India and enable the Dravidians to break off from the North, Pakistan would woo them as their 'deliverer'. Dismembered and weakened, the Indian Union, with the tentacles to Pakistan running deep through its flesh would not be able to control the various Indian Provinces, specially the Muslim rulers who would always have at their beck and call the powerful state of the Nizam.
>
> The utterances of Jinnah and the way in the which the Muslims League's political demand has been mounting up had created in the minds of the nationalists a lively fear that after partition, the next step would be for the League to make Pakistan a springboard for the subjugation and conquest of India. This was later embodied in the Muslim slogan, *Has ke liya hai Pakistan, Lar ke lenge Hindustan* (We got Pakistan by joke, we shall take India by force).[35]

While the fear and anxiety of the nationalist leadership over matters concerning the security of the nation state could well be appreciated, the idea of a corridor in 1946 did not look like a distinct possibility. The tirade against the Hindu society and the attempt to divide Hindus and minorities also did not actually cut ice in the long run. As Jinnah admitted:

> All other minorities such as Scheduled Castes, Sikhs and Christians have the same goal as the Congress. . . . Their goal and ideology is . . . of a united India. Ethnically and culturally they are very closely linked to the Hindu society.[36]

Although the Adivasis were not mentioned in this statement, it represented a belated appreciation of the sociological reality that underlay political processes. As Jinnah elaborated 'all the minorities in actual practice, invariably . . . vote . . . against us in Government'.[37]

The gory incidents leading to Partition, particularly the Calcutta massacres, deeply disturbed Jaipal Singh who was present in the city on that fateful night. Although the Muslim League and the tribal leaders continued to interact and collaborate on such platforms as provided by the Chotanagpur Separation League, which was dominated by the Muslim Leaguers, retired bureaucrats and friends of missionaries, rethinking on the part of tribal leaders had started. The Christians had played a positive role in constitution making and in contemporary Indian politics. With the attainment of Indian independence Jaipal Singh tried to live down his collaboration with the Muslim League in the immediate past and to make his peace with Indian nationalism and Indian unity. He quoted Rajendra Prasad to say that: 'for the last six thousand years Adivasis had been struggling stubbornly for their *izzat'*. He assuringly added that 'for eternity hereafter they would see to it that the honour of India does not in any way get impaired'. Jaipal Singh also said that he was committed to fully support the Fifth Schedule, relating to the provisions of the administration and control of the Scheduled Areas and Scheduled Tribes in India.[38] A subtle change had now come about in the Jharkhand movement as the call for Adivasistan was replaced by the call for Jharkhand. In fact the term Jharkhand had been in use since 1940. Swami Sahajanand Saraswati wrote his tract on 'Jharkhand ke Kisan' in 1941, which has now been published.[39]

II

A section of the British bureaucracy, which had worked in the north-eastern hills, envisaged a common agency of administration for the territories comprising most of the hill areas of Assam and Burma and also a part of the Chittagong Hill Tracts, inhabited by tribes of the 'Mongol stock', which bordered the ethnic territory of China. The roots of this idea went back to the Chin-Lushai Conference of 1892, which discussed for the first time the possibility of a unified administration for the tribes inhabiting the British territory in Bengal, Assam and Burma. The proposal fell through on account of the absence of infrastructural facilities, the fact that the Chins had nothing in common with the Lushais and the resistance offered by the Burmese authorities to any scheme to include the tribals living in Burma.

However J.H. Hutton revived the proposal into a full-blown form in the 1930s. He noted the commonalities of customs and languages and also considered the 'Chinese menace', which was likely to materialize in the future. Hutton's scheme was further elaborated by another civil servant, Sir Robert N. Reid, the Governor of Assam (1939-42). These hill regions formed the first 'southward projection of the main bulk of Asia, the Indo-Chinese Peninsula'. With other British civil servants, Reid shared his distrust of the political domination of the Indians over this region, the yawning gulf in the relationship between the tribesmen and plainsmen and the need for giving suitable protection to the hill people. The Assam administrator J.P. Mills even suggested the restoration of the old Ahom kingdom under a constitutional monarch but with democratic accountability. But there were many difficulties in the implementation of such a scheme: the financial cost being prohibitive and also the opposition of Burma to any loss of its territory.

Finally in 1945, Whitehall turned down the proposal to set up a north-east province of the Agency. The idea of a Crown colony was finally buried with the transfer of power in 1947, but as the eminent historian H.K. Barpujari says, 'the kaleidoscopic changes in North-Eastern India in the wake of India's independence bear enough testimony to the fact that erstwhile tribal experts clearly visualized the complexities of the problem of the tribesman and some of their comments and observations were indeed prophetic'.[40] Barpujari was probably referring to the notion of tribal autonomy, the large cultural and ethnic space shared by the tribal groups across the hilly areas of East Pakistan, Burma and India and the growing realization of the imperative need to maintain linkages, both commercial and cultural, among these people. Burma 'flirted' with Reid's plan for sometime and then closed the matter, declining to introduce even the Indian version of the scheme of excluded areas, which was designed to safeguard the identity and interest of its hill people.[41]

The tribal response to the idea of the Crown colony protectorate for the north-east India was varied.[42] The moderate Khasi leader, Reverend J.J.M. Nichols-Roy (1903-58) rejected the proposal because it was neither economically viable nor was it favoured by the educated people of the hills, who had some experience of democracy. He advocated that the hill people of Assam get a share of independence while maintaining their connection with the province of Assam. His colleague, Reverend L. Gadphol who represented the Jaintia Hills supported the scheme of a colony protectorate. The Garo leaders opposed the plan and voiced the desire of the Garos to be with Assam and India. Later, a lone Mikat Sangma, educated in Calcutta, protested against the partition of his land and proclaimed himself the chief of the Southern Garo Hills, but he was charged with sedition and imprisoned. The protest failed. The Naga leader

A. Zephu Phizo expressed his support for the British scheme as part of Naga 'spontaneous loyalty', but other Nagas opposed it vehemently as they had no affection for any kind of British imperialism and colonialism in their land. The Mizo Union also turned down the proposal and favoured an autonomous status for their hills within the province of Assam, because the upcoming Mizo middle class wanted to abolish the traditional chieftainship, which the British rule had propped up. Some Mizo individuals favoured union with Burma but the vast majority was against it.

This range of responses from different tribes shows how the British administrators who originated the scheme were cut off from ground realities. There were some exceptions, however. Reid's successor, Andrew Clow, was critical of the anthropologists' approach, which was isolationist, and saw no future in the hill tribes segregating themselves from the plains. The Deputy Commissioner of the Naga Hills district pleaded with the Nagas to get the 'tribal people thinking within the limits of the practical', 'his own profound conviction' being that the Nagas should 'plump for cooperation and get the best bargain they can'. But a section of the Nagas was not prepared to listen to him. The plainsmen, too, traumatized by Partition, failed to reciprocate and build up a relationship of trust with the hill people. A golden opportunity was thus lost for the time being.

The north-east also had three princely states and a cluster of 25 Khasi states under their chiefs (Syiems, Lyngdohs, Sirdars or Wahabadars). Some of them were also ritual heads of their communities and acted as priests. Manipur and Tripura never had tribal policies inspite of tribal or semi-Hinduized maharajas. There were also, the 'unadministered' tract of Tuensang and the region lying south of the Indo-Tibetan frontier, which 'theoretically' were and became a part of the province of Assam. Manipur and Tripura acceded to the Indian Union and became Union Territories in 1950, as part of the scheme of 'territorial' integration.

A section of the Khasis led by the redoubtable Reverend J.J.M. Nichols-Roy,[43] vociferously favoured participation in constitution making, creation of a separate, distinct Khasi-Jaintia-Garo district out of the British and the Syiem territories, merger with Assam and continuance in India. Nichols-Roy was born in a non-Syiem Khasi territory into a family which had the tradition of a liberal education. He was educated in Calcutta. He grew up to be an evangelist and an entrepreneur and went on to become a political activist, a minister in the Assam cabinet and a member of the Constituent Assembly. In the last capacity he stood out as an outstanding advocate of tribal autonomy against the assimilationist views expressed by some members. Along with Gopinath Bardoloi, now a Bharat Ratna,

Nichols-Roy could be credited with crafting the Sixth Schedule, which guaranteed a measure of autonomy to the tribes in terms of control over resources in land and forest or self-management. Nichols-Roy was one of those moderate leaders who lived on to see their dreams realized.

However there was another section of the Khasis who were 'ambivalent'. They were clearly confused by Partition and felt unsettled by its economic impact. Pakistan had declared an economic blockade of the hills, in a bid to pressurize the tribals to join Pakistan. The territories of some of the Khasi states extended into Sylhet along the foothills, which was going to be part of East Pakistan. Therefore, while they did not want to join Pakistan, they needed time to sort out their problems. But events were moving fast. Twenty out of 25 Khasi states joined the Indian Union after signing the Instrument of Accession on their own or as and when the policy of 'carrot and stick' was applied. The remaining followed suit, including the Syiem of Nongkhlaw, who had hesitated for a while. The Syiem of Jirang demanded that the two hills, Khasi-Jaintia-Garo should form one administrative unit outside Assam, which could be possible only if both the Instrument of Accession and the draft constitution of India had provision for it. The Darbar voted 46-40 in favour of this resolution against that of Nichols-Roy who favoured merger with Assam.[44] Ultimately the integration of the remaining Khasi states was effected but not without some problems.

The developments in the Naga territory took a different course. The Nagas had established their political identity by organizing the Naga National Council (NNC) in 1946. Many among the Nagas, under the leadership of Phizo, demanded independence, but there were some Naga leaders, who favoured a settlement with India.[45] While the story of the developments as they unfolded is well-known, it is perhaps necessary to recall a few matters regarding the relationship with the emerging nation state of India. The secretary of the NNC of Kohima, on 6 December 1946, declared:

> The NNC stands for the unification of all Naga tribes and their freedom. . . . Our country is connected with India, connected in many ways. We should continue that connection. I do not mind whether future India is a Congress government or a League government. But as a distinctive community, as I stated before, we must also develop according to our genius and taste. We shall enjoy home rule in our country, but on broader issues be connected with India. We must fight for it, we must get it; keep on watching.[46]

The NNC leader was voicing the Naga people's concerns and aspirations.

In a letter to the NNC leader, T. Sekhrie, Nehru wrote in August 1946:

> It is obvious that the Naga territory in Eastern Assam is much too small to stand by itself politically or economically. It lies between the two countries India and China, and part of it consists of rather backward people who require considerable help. When India is independent, as it is bound to be soon, it will not be possible for the British Government to hold on to Naga territory or any part of it. They would be isolated between India and China. Inevitably therefore, this Naga territory must be part of India and of Assam with which it has developed such close associations.[47]

Some members of the NNC led by Phizo met Mahatma Gandhi, in July 1947, and reportedly told him of the Naga's determination to stay out of the Indian Union. Gandhi is said to have assured the delegation that under no circumstances would force be used against the Nagas who, according to Phizo, were free to stay out of the Indian Union if they so desired.[48] According to another version, Gandhi is also said to have told Phizo that the hill people should feel that the plains were as much theirs as their hills. National unity was and is a matter of feeling.

It is not necessary here to go into the tortuous course the Naga story took, but the issues are still unresolved.

III

The course of events leading to Partition and independence produced a dramatic impact here on the tribal situation as elsewhere in India. There was a whole range of responses, a diversity of perceptions, a mix of romantic dreams of independence and autonomy and a sobering understanding of the harsher ground realities. The upcoming tribal middle class tried to formulate their responses as best as they could. In Chotanagpur the notion of Adivasistan emerged, alongside Pakistan and Hindustan, and a short period of honeymoon with the Muslim League followed. The League had its own plans to form a Muslim Adivasi dominated state and the tribal corridor to link-up the two wings of East and West Pakistan. This may look like a pipedream today, exaggerated and unrealistic, the work of the over-heated imagination of a people who had lost their nerve, the result of an overworked intelligence agency. But every word of the story was believed, when it unfolded in those days and the nationalist forces worked overtime to assuage hurt feelings and promote harmony. The tribal leaders gradually returned to their demand for Jharkhand and adopted constitutional means for achieving it.

Similarly, the developments in the north-east, as recorded by historians under the shadow of Partition and independence are extremely instructive. There was no major link-up between the tribal leaders and the Muslim League. The antagonisms between the plainsmen and the hill people, the resistance by the former to any notion of autonomy for the latter and the concept of assimilation versus autonomy and integration are all there in the Constituent Assembly's debates on the north-east. It is to the abiding credit of the moderates on all sides, among such tribes as Garos, Mizos, Khasis, etc., and of leaders of such integrity and vision as Gopinath Bardoloi and Nichols-Roy that the matter could be resolved for the time being within the constitutional ambit.

But other issues remain to be resolved. The vision of the north-east as the cultural and commercial bridge to South-East Asia, recently re-constructed by B.G. Verghese,[49] has a lot to commend itself. In its fulfilment lie the hopes of long term progress, peace and stability for the region as a whole. Secondly, many questions are now being raised about the processes at work in the 1940s. It is said that not all hill tribal leaders, with the exception of Nichols-Roy, were involved in the deliberations about the future set-up or were not represented in the Constituent Assembly.[50] It is also being argued by some people now, playing up isolated incidents involving the Khasis, Garos, Nagas and Mizos that the 'states' of the north-east were 'annexed' rather than integrated and that the idea of the right of self determination, which became the buzz word in the 1970s, is still to be exercized. Nation building is a continuous process. The many issues of identity and autonomy of tribal groups, involving understanding with non tribal groups and relationship with the nation state, and those of economic and cultural development should continue to be addressed sympathetically and democratically.

NOTES

1. Nicholas Mansergh, editor-in-chief, *The Transfer of Power, 1942-7*, Vols I to X (London, 1970-80).
2. Indian Council of Historical Research, New Delhi, 'Towards Freedom, 1937-47'. Of these three volumes have been published so far.These are for the year 1937, edited by P.N. Chopra (New Delhi, 1985); for 1943-4, edited by Partha Sarthi Gupta (New Delhi, 1996); and for 1938, edited by Basudev Chatterjee (New Delhi, 1999).
3. K.S. Singh, *From Ethnicity to Regionalism, Tribal Society in India* (New Delhi, 1984).
4. Ibid. Also see *People of India: An Introduction* (Anthropological Survey of India, Calcutta, 1992).
5. *Parliament of India, Who's Who* (Publication Division, Government of India, New Delhi, 1950), p. 46.

6. 'A Primitive Nationalist', in *Bihar Herald* (Patna), 4 December 1945.
7. K.S. Singh, 'Foreword', in Dilip Simeon, *The Politics of Labour under Late Colonialism: Workers, Unions and the State in Chotanagpur, 1928-39* (New Delhi, 1995).
8. 'Netaji Subhash Aur Chotanagpur, Ek Smriti' (in Hindi), in *Smarika* (Ranchi), 23 January 1978.
9. Jaipal Singh, 'The Adivasi Sabha', in *Bihar Herald*, 27 June 1939.
10. Idem, 'Adivasi Strength', in ibid., 4 July 1939.
11. Idem, 'Adivasistan, Hindustan, Pakistan', in ibid., 28 May 1940.
12. Ibid.
13. Idem, 'The Adivasi Movement', in ibid., 10 December 1940; idem,'Transitional Alignments', in ibid., 9 October 1945; idem,'Jharkhand Issues', in ibid., 13 November 1945; and idem,'The Adivasi Movement', in ibid., 4 December 1945.
14. G. Allana, compiled and ed., *Pakistan Movement: Historical Documents* (Karachi, 1967), p. 158.
15. Ibid., pp. 26-7.
16. Ibid., p. 408. Resolution dated April 1946.
17. Pyarelal, 'The Bitter Days', in *Mahatma Gandhi: The Last Phase*, Vol. I (Ahmedabad, February 1958), pp. 316-18.
18. Ibid.
19. Ibid., Syed Zafar Imam, President of the Bihar Provincial Muslim League, foreword to 'Divide Bihar'. A pamphlet issued by the Muslim Students Federation at the time of the second session of the Division of Bihar Conference, held at Gaya, in April 1947, quoted in Pyarelal, op.cit.
20. Ibid., p. 286.
21. Ibid., p. 316.
22. *Times of India*, 22 May 1947.
23. Ibid., 1 June 1947
24. Pyarelal, 'A Losing Battle', in *Mahatama Gandhi: The Last Phase*, op.cit., p. 205.
25. *Times of India*, 28 May, 1947.
26. Ibid., 24 May 1947.
27. Ibid., (editorial), 26 May 1947.
28. *Dawn* (founded by Quaid-i-Azam Mohammad Ali Jinnah) (Karachi), May 1947.
29. S.P. Sinha, *Conflict and Tension in Tribal Society* (New Delhi, 1994), pp. 281-97.
30. Pyarelal, 'The Bitter Days', op.cit.
31. Sinha, op.cit., p. 289.
32. Pyarelal, 'The Bitter Days', op.cit., p. 318.
33. Sinha, op.cit.
34. Commissioner's Records Room, Ranchi.
35. Pyarelal, 'The Bitter Days', op.cit., p. 316
36. Idem, 'The Changing Scene', in *Mahatma Gandhi: The Last Phase*, op.cit., p. 131.
37. Ibid.
38. *Constituent Assembly Debates*, Vol. X, 30-7-49 to 18-9-49, Book No. 5.
39. Walter Hauser, ed., *Swami Sahajanand and the Peasants of Jharkhand: A View from 1941* (New Delhi, 1995).
40. H.K. Barpujari, 'New Light on the Proposed Crown Colony: North-East India', in *Proceedings of the Indian Historical Records Commission* (1990).

41. D.R. Syiemlieh, 'Burma Flirting with Reid's Plan', in Milton S. Sangma, ed., *Essays on North-East India* (New Delhi, 1994).
42. Idem, 'The Crown Colony—Protectorate for North-East India: A Tribal Response', in *Proceedings of the North-East India History Association*, 11th Session (Imphal, 1990).
43. P.K. Kyndiah, *Reverend J.J.M. Nichols-Roy: Architect of District Council Autonomy* (New Delhi, 1993); also see O.L. Sanitang, *Memoirs of the Life and Political Writings by Shri Hon'ble Rev. J.J.M. Nichols-Roy*, Vol. I (published by Shri Shrolenson Marbaniang on the occasion of 50th anniversary of independence, Shillong, 1999).
44. D.R. Syiemlieh, 'Integration of the Khasi States into the Indian Union', in *Proceedings of the North-East India History Association*, First Session (Shillong 1980); idem, 'Response of the North East Hill Tribes of India Towards Partition and Independence', in *Indo-British Review*, Vol. XVII, Nos 1-2 (September-December 1989); and idem, 'The Political Integration of the Khasi State with the Indian Union', in B. Paken, ed., *Regionalism in India with Special Reference to North-East India* (New Delhi, 1993).
45. Udayon Misra, *North-East India: Quest for Identity* (Guwahati/New Delhi, 1988). Also Tirlottoma Misra and Udayon Misra 'Movements for Autonomy in India—North-East', in T.V. Satyamurthy, ed., *Social Change and Political Discourse in India, Vol. III, Region, Religion, Caste, Gender and Culture in Contemporary India* (Delhi, 1996).
46. Quoted in Udayon Misra, op.cit.
47. Ibid.
48. Ibid.
49. B.G. Verghese, *India's North-East Resurgent: Ethnicity, Insurgency, Governance and Development* (New Delhi, 1996).
50. V.S. Jafa, 'North-East and the Constitution of India', in *Grassroots Options* (August-October 1997).

Partition and Indian Business

DWIJENDRA TRIPATHI

The leadership of the Indian National Congress is often held responsible for the division of the Indian subcontinent. No doubt, history would have taken a different course—what course can be anybody's guess—had the Congress rejected the formula under which were carved two sovereign countries out of what until then was a single entity. However, the rejoicings and celebrations that greeted the advent of independence everywhere in India clearly proved that the nation as a whole regarded Partition as a small price to pay for ending the colonial rule. Perhaps it tells something about the enormous faith the Indian people had developed in the sagacity of the Congress leadership. But for a more definitive understanding, we require a series of micro studies probing the attitudes of different segments of the Indian population. This present paper seeks to deal with one of these segments.

I

By the time the move for Partition began to gain momentum following the adoption of the Pakistan Resolution by the Muslim League at its Lahore session in March 1940, Indian business had already emerged as a pressure group of some significance. It was no more an appendage to the British business interests, as it had been well up to the end of the First World War, and it had become quite conscious of its distinct identity. The emergence of the Federation of Indian Chambers of Commerce and Industry (FICCI) and the Indian Merchants' Chambers, along with a host of local or regional bodies, representing exclusively Indian interests, was an eloquent testimony to this development. Their representatives used every conceivable forum, including the floors of legislatures, to press for various kinds of concessions, and there were occasions when Indian business demonstrated remarkable solidarity against British interests.[1] There is, no doubt, that an Indian capitalist class had come into its own much before the separatist demand became a serious issue in Indian politics.

This class essentially comprised Hindus belonging to a variety of social backgrounds—Marwaris, Jains, Vaishnava Banias, Chettiars, Brahmins, etc.—and Parsis. Muslims were few in number and had little influence. Although Muslim traders, particularly in western India, had been active in maritime trade before the advent of the British, for a variety of reasons, they failed to take advantage of the new business opportunities that emerged in the wake of the British occupation of the subcontinent. For one thing, only a few Muslim traders attempted to enter modern industries and still fewer of those who did were successful. Ebrahim Currimbhoy, a Bombay-based merchant prince of Khoja Ismaili descent, for instance, built a huge textile empire during the closing years of the nineteenth century, but could not stand the rigours of the Great Depression. In Ahmedabad, next only to Bombay as a cotton manufacturing centre, only one Muslim trader entered the industry in 1912 but soon sold out his company to a Hindu Patel. In Kanpur, another textile centre, no Muslim ever attempted to take to manufacturing. Some of the wealthiest business families, such as the Ispahanis in Calcutta, the Haroons in Karachi and the Sherwanis in the United Provinces (now Uttar Pradesh), too, remained confined to trade. In fact, the Adamjees of Calcutta were perhaps the only Muslim family who achieved a measure of industrial success. They were among the first Indians to enter the Calcutta jute industry, till then controlled tightly by the Europeans, and their company was noted for the efficiency of its management.[2]

As a group, the Muslims lagged behind in trade as well. Even though trade remained the principal occupation for a large number of them, particularly in western India, they operated on a rather modest scale, barring the few distinguished exceptions mentioned earlier. They were totally absent from banking. The Bohras' Bombay Mercantile Cooperative Bank was the only banking institution that the community controlled in 1940,[3] and this, too, was very small. The Muslim business community, thus, consisted primarily of small traders and merchants most of whom dealt in leather, glass and silk.

This is not the occasion to discuss why the Muslims, from whose ranks had emerged some of the most dominant business leaders in pre-British India, were reduced to a secondary position in more recent times. But the failure of the Muslim community to exploit the emerging industrial opportunities had serious consequences for its influence in the Indian business world. For, business leadership was gradually gravitating to industrialists ever since modern manufacturing gained a certain level of maturity, and passed almost entirely to this new class during the inter-war period. Purely commercial interests, no matter to what community they belonged to, were relegated to the background.

It is significant that it was Ghanshyam Das Birla, a trader turned industrialist, who dominated FICCI from its very inception. True, the names of a handful of trade leaders, including a few Muslims, appear among the original organizers of this apex body of Indian capitalism, and some were even elected its president.[4] But it was the industrialists like Birla, Lala Shri Ram and Kasturbhai Lalbhai who called the shots. Purshotamdas Thakurdas was perhaps the only representative of trading interests who wielded considerable influence among the native businessmen, but this was perhaps due to his having a very close link with industrial houses, including that of the Tatas. The industrialists had a dominant voice in the affairs of the Indian Merchants' Chamber too, another powerful organization of native business.[5] Operating at a modest scale as traders and industrialists alike—even those Muslims who set up industrial enterprises either failed miserably or achieved only moderate success, as the careers of the Currimbhoys and Adamjees illustrate—the Muslims in the Indian business world remained by and large on its fringes. Although a number of Muslims served on the boards of several industrial enterprises, board membership in the contemporary Indian situation carried with it far less power and substance than even today.

The industrialists had been sympathetic to the Congress from the very inception of this organization. In fact, the industrialists in Bombay, the centre of the burgeoning native capitalism, had actively encouraged and even provided financial assistance for the formation of the Congress. Later when the Indian Industrial Conference, representing this new class, came into being in 1905, it always acted as an appendage of the Congress, and the two bodies always held their annual sessions together until the dissolution of the Conference in 1926.[6] It was a matter of pride for industrialists in those days to serve as chairmen of reception committees for the annual sessions of the Congress.

The industry-Congress nexus posed no problem as long as the Congress remained a mere pressure group, clamouring for modest political economic privileges within the imperial scheme of things. But as the Congress became increasingly more militant, particularly after Gandhi appeared on the scene, it became necessary for the industrialists to adopt a new strategy. They could not abandon the Congress for, even the most moderate and pro-British sections among them had no doubt that 'Indian commerce and industry are only an integral phase [*sic*] of Indian nationalism, and that deprived of its inspiration in Indian nationalism

Indian commerce and industry stand reduced to mere exploitation.'[7] With the growing conflict of interest between Indian industry and British expatriate firms, witnessed after the First World War, losing the support of the nationalist forces would have been suicidal. For the same reason, however, the industrialists could not afford to alienate the government of the day as well.

The strategy adopted to accommodate these rather conflicting objectives can be described as one of equidistance between the Congress and the government, a sort of middle path. It did not emerge from a pre-planned design; instead it unfolded itself gradually in response to the exigencies of the situation. The new strategy, nevertheless, was reflected on several fronts. First, the visible association of Indian industrialists with the Congress, a characteristic feature of national politics before the First World War, became a thing of the past. Not a single prominent leader of Indian business had an active link with the Congress after 1919. Secondly, even though some industrialists, notably G.D. Birla, generously supported various constructive programmes launched by Gandhi, they refrained from advancing any financial support *directly* to the Congress. Also, while working in unison with the Congress with regard to issues affecting Indian business in peace time, they kept aloof from the confrontational-agitational aspects of the freedom struggle. It is significant that no industrialist of any standing gave any vocal support either to the Non-Cooperation movement of 1921 or the Civil Disobedience programme of 1932.[8]

While the majority of the industrialists seemed to subscribe to the strategy of maintaining equidistance during the inter-war period, a very strong section of the Bombay industrialists, led by the Tatas, differed from this approach. To them it seemed to be heavily weighted in favour of the Congress. Socially closer to the ruling race, these elements remained suspicious of the Congress leadership and leaned towards the government.[9] They were more vocal in denouncing the agitational programmes of the Congress and went to the extent of organizing an anti-non-cooperation society in Bombay. A few years later they even attempted to promote an anti-Congress formation within the Central Legislative Assembly to foster cooperation with European interests. But they were dissuaded by the saner elements amongst themselves on the ground that this would be 'the surest method of alienating the sympathies of the various political parties'[10] that were supporting the cause of Indian commerce and industry.

The attitude of the mercantile interests—Gordon's category of 'marketeers'[11] including traders, speculators, brokers, etc.—to the Congress was an essay in contrast to that of the industrialists. Unlike the industrialists, they were rather lukewarm and, on occasions, even hostile to the Congress during the formative phases of the organization.[12] With the rise of Gandhi, however, they as a group emerged as the most solid and dependable allies of the Congress. They were much less inhibited and more open in their support, financial and otherwise, to the Congress during the periods both of political tranquillity and turbulence alike. They suspected the bonafides of the mill owning class and big industrialists who, they believed, were hand in glove with the government in pushing them to the brink. The inter-war period, it may be recalled, was one of extreme commercial difficulties.

What has been said above should not, of course, be construed to mean that the Indian business community was neatly divided between the industrialists and traders. Most industrialists were still engaged in trading operations, and some traders were closely linked with industrialists—Purshotamdas Thakurdas serving on the boards of many Tata companies, was an excellent example. Further, there were groups within groups. For instance, those who sympathized with the Congress were divided between the moderates and militants, and in the loyalist group some were more vocal in their support to the government than others. The divisions within the Indian business community, thus, were complex and the dividing lines were often blurred.

II

One thing is, however, undisputable. The communal division was yet to make an appearance or, at least, become clearly visible, when Mohammad Ali Jinnah took over the leadership of the Muslim League in 1936. A weak and demoralized organization the Muslim League was yet to make a meaningful impact on the imagination of those for whom it claimed to speak. The elections of 1937 for provincial legislatures held under the Government of India Act of 1935 must have brought home to the League leadership that much more needed to be done to win the support of the Muslim population, including businessmen, to establish the claim that the League was the sole representative of the Indian Muslims. The League won less than one-fourth of the seats reserved for the Muslims—only 104 out of a total of 489. The electorate even in the Muslim-majority provinces of the Punjab and Bengal preferred regional parties to the League. That the Congress performance in these provinces was also relatively poor would have been only a cold comfort to the League leadership.[13]

Stung by the results, Jinnah and his team threw themselves wholeheartedly into the task of organizing various interest groups among the

Muslims. The efforts directed to this end became still more vigorous after the adoption of the Pakistan Resolution in March 1940. Encouraging Muslim businessmen to organize their own trade associations—exclusively for the members of their community—was among the important steps taken to win over their support. Some feeble attempts to set up separate organizations for Muslim business had been made earlier, but with little success. The Madras Muslim Chamber set up in 1928 was perhaps the earliest experiment in the field, but it remained virtually defunct. Likewise, a Bombay based organization bearing the grandiose title of All India Chamber of Commerce and Industry did not achieve even a semblance of a representative character. Promoted in 1939 by two prominent businessmen of the city, Sir Sultan Chinoy and S.M. Jamail, it was suspect in the eyes of a large number of traders and industrialists, and its influence, whatever it was, remained confined to the Presidency. Most of the important trade associations in Bombay remained non sectarian, befitting the cosmopolitan character of the metropolis.[14]

The only trade association of the Muslims, founded before the emergence of Jinnah, that attained a modicum of respectability was the Muslim Chamber of Commerce in Calcutta (1932). Two of the most influential business families of the city, the Ispahanis and the Adamjees, were behind its formation. Caste-based organizations of Memmons, Khojas and Bohras, the three most important trading groups among Gujarati Muslims, did exist but concerned as they were with social and business matters alike, they were more like the *mahajans* and *panchayats* that existed in commercial centres in western India rather than modern trade associations.

Moreover, none of the business organization of Muslims set up before 1940 had anything to do with communal politics. Instead, they were in line with a host of formations that various communities constituting Indian business had been promoting since the closing years of the nineteenth century. It is also noteworthy that none among the organizers of the so-called All India Chamber of Commerce and Industry in Bombay had close association with the Muslim League, and the Ispahani and Adamjee families were yet to come under the spell of Jinnah at the time of the birth of the Muslim Chamber in Calcutta. Efforts to organize the Muslim business community into a discrete pressure group, thus, had made very little headway before the emergence of Jinnah as the supreme leader of the Muslim League.

Jinnah's leadership of the League provided a new impetus to the efforts to organize Muslim businessmen. An influential section of big traders and industrialists flocked under his banner. Not only Mirza Ahmad Ispahani and Sir Adamjee Dawood, undoubtedly the most important Muslim business figures in Calcutta, but also Sir Sultan Chinoy, S.M. Jamail and Habib Rahimtoola in Bombay drew much closer to the League than ever before. Other prominent Muslim business leaders who gravitated to the League after Jinnah came to the helm included men like Yusuf Haroon, G. Allama (both based in Karachi) and Nasir A. Shaikh and Martib Ali Shah of the famous Wazirali family (both from Lahore). Some of them like Mirza Ahmad Ispahani and Sir Adamjee Dawood not only became major financiers for the League but also rose to great heights in its organizational hierarchy. At Jinnah's urging, they helped promote an airline and a shipping company and to reorganize an existing insurance company. A Bombay based merchant Mohammad Ali Habib was persuaded to set up a bank, the first Muslim enterprise of this kind in the country.[15] These initiatives aimed at making the Muslim presence felt on the industrial horizon and inspiring the community to make a transition to modern business.

In the meantime Jinnah, soon after the adoption of the Pakistan resolution, had undertaken an extensive tour of the business centres of the country, exhorting Muslim businessmen to organize themselves. Even though he made a great impression on his audiences, it took some time before the Muslim businessmen in the major commercial centres could be persuaded to set up their own trade associations. By 1943, however, Muslim chambers had already sprung up in Madras, Karachi, Dacca, Chittagong and Lahore. Even so, the birth of the All India Federation of Muslim Chambers of Commerce and Industry had to wait for another two years largely because of the mutual jealousies of the leaders of the pre-existing Muslim Chambers in Calcutta and Bombay. It finally held its first convention in April 1945 where all provinces, with the exception of the Central Province, were represented. Sir Adamjee Dawood was elected the first president of this body whose organizational linkages with the Muslim League were all but formal.[16]

Jinnah, once the 'brightest jewel in Hindu Muslim unity', to quote the words of Sarojini Naidu, had finally brought home his separatist message to the Muslim businessmen in India, industrialists and traders alike. He was equally or even more successful with other segments of the Muslim population in the country. For in the elections for the central legislatures, held in 1946 under the Government of India Act of 1935, the Muslim League registered a resounding victory—winning 460 out of 533 seats reserved for Muslims. Significantly, no reserved constituency returned an anti-League candidate. In the absence of a desegregated account of the voting pattern, it is difficult to assess the contribution of the Muslim businessmen to the League performance, but it can be safely assumed that it must have been substantial. In view of the fact that voting rights were contingent on certain conditions, including property qualifications, limiting the franchise to less than 20 per cent of the total adult population, it is obvious that the business segments of the Muslim electorate must have tilted the balance significantly in favour of the separatist candidates.

How did this spectacular change in the political preference of the Indian Muslims, particularly those engaged in trade and commerce, occur within a space of less than a decade, in fact within five or six years, if we date the beginning of the process to the Lahore Resolution? What had happened in the ten years since 1937, when the Muslim League had been rejected by the Muslim electorate, that by 1946 the party could legitimately assert its claim to be the most representative political formation of the Indian Muslims? Was it due to Jinnah's charisma? Was it due to his and his lieutenants' organizing capabilities? Or was it simply the deep appeal of a separate homeland for themselves that brought about this transformation among the Indian Muslims.

No definite answer to these questions is possible. Perhaps an explanation lies in a combination of all these factors plus a host of many others. An analysis of the situation must start with the fact, often ignored, that the Muslims as a group had never been very actively associated with a broad national front that the Congress was ever since its birth. Special exigencies on occasions, such as the Khilafat agitation of 1920, undoubtedly bridged the distance, but by and large the community's feelings towards the Congress had always been lukewarm. The attitude of the Muslim business class is no exception. Few of this class had close links with the Congress even during the organization's early phases when its anti-government posture was yet to become pronounced. Nor were Muslim business leaders actively associated with the efforts to promote non-sectarian trade associations, representing Indian interests as a counterpoise to European dominated fora in the 1920s. By the beginning of the 1930s, however, their indifference to a broad-based political and commercial formation seems to have yielded place to a growing desire to demonstrate their separate identity. The emergence of commercial bodies representing exclusive Muslim interests around this time was a significant, though feeble, pointer to this trend. It is also noteworthy that the Muslim trader in Bombay extended only limited or no support to the Civil Disobedience movement, unlike the non-Muslim elements in this class because of whose enthusiasm for the Congress an English governor of the province scornfully termed the city as 'the keep of Gandhism'.[17]

At the same time, there seems to be no evidence to suggest that the Muslim masses or the businessmen among them were fired by a great deal of enthusiasm for the Muslim League well until the end of the decade. The result of the 1937 elections irrefutably proved this. It seems that the Muslim middle classes had hoped that a Jinnah-led League would be an alternative to a choice between political aloofness and proximity to the Congress. But Jinnah and his colleagues were still functioning at the time of the 1937 elections within the broad framework of a pan-Indian nationalism. His position around this time in his own words, was:

> There has been no change in me, not the slightest since the day I joined the Indian National Congress. It may be I have been wrong on some occasions. But it has never been done in a partisan spirit. My sole and only object has been the welfare of my country. . . . India's interest is and will be sacred to me and nothing will make me budge an inch from that position.[18]

Though he asked the Muslims to strengthen *their* organization, he also enjoined upon them to 'prove that their patriotism is unsullied and their love of India and her progress is no less than that of any other community in the country'.[19] It is also necessary to remember that the League did not enter the election on a pronounced communal platform, its main pro-Muslim planks being the protection of the Urdu language and its script and measures to improve the general conditions of the Muslim masses. The choice that Jinnah and his League offered to their electorate in 1937 was only that of tweedledee over Congress tweedledum, when it was looking for a clearer alternative.

Obviously, a tottering political formation as the League was at the time of the 1937 election, could not have been transformed into a fighting machine within a brief span of nine years, of which the results of the 1946 elections were an eloquent testimony, only because of Jinnah and his associates' organizing capability, considerable though it was. There must have been some objective conditions that they exploited to advantage. This line of reasoning gives credence to the suggestion that the Muslim middle classes had been nursing some deep-seated grievances, real or perceived, against the majority community. Whether their relative backwardness was their own doing or their progress was thwarted by the Hindu bourgeoisie is beside the point. The perception seems to have developed among them that the latter was the case.[20] If this was so, the dream of a promised homeland seemed to offer a lasting remedy. Both the feelings of grievance and the suggested cure must have had such a tight hold on the imagination of the Muslim electorate that they were ready to repose their faith even in a man whose Islamic credentials were at best tenuous.

Significantly, Jinnah seldom went deeply into the economic and administrative implications of his plan to divide India,[21] and yet he carried conviction with his audience. It is not very often remembered that the open session of the League at Lahore where the Pakistan demand was endorsed, was addressed by Jinnah in English—a language which only a few in the audience could have followed. But they did not have to, for it was the feelings and not arguments that prepared the public opinion for Pakistan. The feeling among the Muslim masses of having been wronged must have been deeply entrenched indeed. Be that as it may, there is no question that by the mid-1940s, the Muslim business community of India almost as a block, industrialists and traders alike, had come to identify themselves totally with the Muslim League. Only a few of their ranks, such as the Sherwanis of the United Provinces, remained sceptical. Whether for Jinnah the demand for Pakistan was simply pressure tactics and whether he was perfectly open until the end for an arrangement within the framework of a united India, as has been suggested in certain quarters,[22] would always remain a subject of speculation. But to his followers he had held out a promise that they would not have been easily ready to compromise with.

III

The attitude of the non-Muslim elements in Indian business in the meantime underwent little change. The trading interests' support for the Congress remained as steadfast as ever before; if anything it became even more intensified with the intensification in the Congress-League competition after Jinnah assumed the latter's leadership. The pro-Congress among the industrialists, subdued during the years of civil disobedience, resumed their role as counsellors and intermediaries after the end of the political turbulence, while the group that had been less appreciative of the Congress tactics and programmes, during the 1920s and early 1930s, seemed to have become less hostile. One reason for this change of heart was the performance of the Congress ministries formed after the elections of 1937 in several provinces. During the two years that these governments held office, they gave little evidence of the rabid socialism that many had feared.

In fact, in many cases, the Congress ministries seemed to provide the kind of facilities and support only governments can provide for enterprise creation and growth. Yet another factor that could have diluted the scepticism, even hostility, of a section of industrialists towards the Congress was the way the National Planning Committee (NPC), appointed by the Congress in 1938, functioned. Keen to avoid the impression that the committee might become an instrument of a doctrinaire approach to economic reconstruction, its chairman, Jawaharlal Nehru, right from the beginning made it a broad-based platform, involving persons of all shades of opinion in its deliberations. On one hand, Nehru drafted persons like Ambalal Sarabhai of Ahmedabad in the task; on the other hand, he invited middle-roaders such as Purshotamdas Thakurdas, and even those who had been seen as distant from, or even critical of, the Congress so far. The motives of the Congress and its economic ideology were much less suspect in the eyes of even those who had been distrustful of it so far.[23]

All this seems to have reduced the gulf between those among the industrialists who had been relatively more sympathetic to the Congress and the others more ambivalent or even hostile. Both the groups had no difficulty in professing their loyalty to the government while remaining in full accord with the essentials of the Congress demand for freedom and transfer of power. The equidistance strategy that only one section had pursued so far now seems to have been adopted by the other group as well. Nothing illustrates this better than the way the industrialists responded to the impending crisis of 1942. Just before the adoption of the Quit India Resolution by the Congress, a group of industrialists, including G.D. Birla and J.R.D. Tata—the leaders of the two opposite camps—assured the Viceroy of their opposition to a policy of conflict. 'We are all businessmen', they wrote in their memorandum, 'and therefore we need hardly point out that our interest lies in peace, harmony, goodwill, and order throughout the country'.[24] And during the holocaust that engulfed the country following the arrest of the Congress leaders, they lived up to this assurance. We know of no case of open support extended to the agitators by any section of the industrial bourgeoisie. Some are reported to have extended clandestine help and a few others acquiesced in the strikes of the workers in their factories. But no industrial leader expressed open sympathy for the Congress, unlike the mercantile elements, which downed their shutters upon the arrest of the Congress leaders and kept business suspended for several months.[25]

As peace returned and the end of the colonial rule seemed to be in sight, the industrialists resumed their dual policy—of demonstrating their loyalty to the government through support to the war efforts, on one hand, and re-establishing a claim on the gratitude of the Congress, on the other. Some of them resumed their financial contribution to the Congress, as well. G.D. Birla went to the extent of objecting to the colonial government's proposal to appoint a committee to plan for post-war reconstruction. 'Who is going to plan for India, this Government or a national Government?'[26] He also remained expressly critical of the committees the government had appointed around this time to deliberate on post-war planning and reconstruction.

To demonstrate, however, that the industrial community was not against the idea of planning *per se*, a group of industrial leaders, representing all sections of their community produced, in 1944, what has since then come to be known as the Bombay Plan. Although then branded as the Tata-Birla Plan by many, particularly the Leftists in the Congress and outside,[27] the document anticipated the fundamentals that guided the formulation of free India's industrial policy and many features of the First Five Year Plan. The authors recognized the need for planned development, justified state control over key industries and concurred with the idea of a central directing authority to ensure successful implementation. While they did assign a legitimate role to the private sector, they emphasized that the private sector must be ready to accept tight state control. 'Practically every aspect of economic life [in independent India] will have to be so rigorously controlled by the government'; and they conceded unhesitatingly, 'that individual liberty and freedom of enterprise will suffer a temporary eclipse'.[28]

Barely 13 years earlier, the FICCI leadership had cried wolf when the 'fundamental rights and economic programme' resolution, adopted at the Karachi session of the Congress, mildly hinted at the need for state regulation of key industries. If the idea of planning by now had caught up with the entire capitalist class, of which the Bombay Plan was an eloquent testimony, it could have been partly due to the capitalist association with the NPC since 1938, or possibly the capitalist class was simply anxious to demonstrate to the prospective leaders of post-colonial India that Indian business was ready to move with the times. Nobody in 1944 would have been in doubt that Nehru, with whom planning was an obsession, would occupy *a*, if not *the*, critical position in the post-British dispensation. Be that as it may, the Bombay Plan was an important indicator of the fact that the ranks of the industrialists were much less divided in their appreciation of the Congress programme, even as they did not feel as close to Congress as the non-Muslim 'marketeer' groups in Indian business.

IV

All said and done, however, the non-Muslim Indian business never developed an organic relationship with any political formation. Individuals, of course, interacted, in some cases rather closely, but as organizations, the non-sectarian trade bodies functioned independently of the Congress or any other political group. Unlike the associations of Muslim businessmen, these bodies had an autonomous origin and development; they came into being and grew up because of the exertions of businessmen themselves. Again, unlike the Muslim League, no business figure had any formal association with the decision making apparatus of the Congress. The non-sectarian associations normally took no explicit position on such issues, as the prospects of Partition, that did not have a direct bearing on their operations. Individuals, however, did react, and a random assortment of such reactions may help us get a feel of how the articulate section of the non-Muslim business community responded to this momentous possibility.

G.D. Birla was first and foremost among such individuals—first in articulating his views and foremost among those who did so. As early as 11 January 1938, almost around the same time as Jinnah began to voice the Partition demand but more than two years before the Muslim League formally adopted it, Birla wrote to Gandhi's secretary:

> The chief difficulty [impeding a settlement with the British government] still seems to be the Hindu-Muslim question. . . . I wonder why it should not be possible to have two federations, one of the Muslims and another of Hindus. The Muslim Federation may be composed of all the provinces or the portions of the provinces which contain two-thirds Muslim population and the Indian states like Kashmir which is composed of Muslims. Another Federation may be of Hindus and such states as are composed of Hindus. I fear if anything is going to check our progress, it is the Hindu-Muslim question—not the Englishman, but our own internal problems.[29]

By this time, perhaps, C. Rajagopalachari had already started toying with the idea of Partition as a price for independence. Birla met Rajaji, sometime after the above letter to Gandhi's secretary was drafted. Rajaji perhaps, gave Birla some idea of his thinking, for, Birla wrote to him, on 12 October 1938, commending the idea. Asserting that Kashmir would go to 'Muslim India' under a scheme of division, he added: '. . . if we want to have a peaceful India, we must encourage the division and after that we will have no reservation of seats [for Muslims in the legislature], no minority problem and no communal problem'.[30] We have no idea of Birla's reaction to the Muslim League's Lahore resolution. It seems that even if Birla gave further thought to the matter, he kept his counsel to himself. Perhaps the lull in the political atmosphere during the initial phases of the war (individual satyagraha, notwithstanding) had a dampening effect on his counselling propensity. His views on Partition at this time were expressed only in privileged communications. There is no evidence that he made his ideas public at this stage.

The credit or discredit of being the first non-Muslim business personality to publicly voice his support for the Pakistan idea belongs to Birla's fellow Marwari, Ramkrishna Dalmia. In 1940, perhaps, soon after the Lahore session of the League, he advised the country, as he put it, 'to accept Pakistan, as being the only solution under the circumstances'. Many 'denounced [him] as anti-Hindu and called [him] all sorts of names'. Dalmia claimed that he was the 'first Hindu' to back Jinnah's demand. He had known the League leader for some time and Jinnah had even been his house guest 'for a couple of days'.[31]

Nothing came out of this early support to the League's demand at that time, but Birla again returned to his mediating role with the rise in the political temperature, in 1942. Soon after the Congress had rejected Rajaji's proposal to grant to the Muslim majority provinces the option of seceding from a future all-India federation, as Cripps' Mission proposals envisaged, Birla wrote to the Mahatma's secretary on 14 July 1942:

> You know my view about Pakistan. I am in favour of separation and I do not think it is impractical, or against the interest of the Hindus or of India. As long as we will quarrel, there is no salvation for India. Besides, we should not forget that the Muslims—every one of them—now want it. Even the Congress Muslims are no longer an exception.

The Mahatma's reply was, characteristically, a delightful blend of clarity and vagueness. 'The question as such is not of Pakistan or separation as such', his secretary wrote to Birla communicating Gandhi's reply, 'but of the real content of these conception [*sic*].'[32] To Jawaharlal Nehru, Birla offered the following advice, flaunting his business credentials:

> If in a partnership business, one partner is discontented, he would be given the right to separate himself from the erstwhile common concern. Partition should be reasoned and reasonable, but why oppose partition? . . . . Had I been a Muslim, I would never have demanded Pakistan nor accepted it since, after partition, Islamic Bharat will be a very poor state, bereft of iron and coal. This is for the Muslims to determine. I am confident that if you agree to Pakistan, the Muslims will reject it. Whether they accept it or not belongs to the future. But our opposition to partition will intensify their desire for it.[33]

It is not known whether Nehru reacted to this reasoning. But he certainly did not act on it.

Birla seems to have confided only with political figures. There is no record of his writing or speaking to his business colleagues about his ideas—not even to Purshotamdas Thakurdas with whom he communicated very frequently. Why he behaved in this fashion can be anybody's guess, but one thing is clear that there were many others in the non-Muslim business circles who thought differently. For instance, Lala Shri Ram, probably the most respected business figure in the Delhi-Punjab region, was clearly against the division of the country. In a letter to Purshotamdas Thakurdas on 29 September 1942, when the agitation had not yet quite subsided, he declared in unambiguous terms: 'We should not pay any price for Independence to the Muslims, either in the way of Pakistan or increase in the percentage of seats in the Centre or residual power in the provinces.'[34] Ever since the days of the Lala's presidentship of FICCI, his relations with the Marwari tycoon had been rather cool, but their disagreement on the Partition issue cannot be attributed to their personal differences. Birla and Shri Ram, at any rate, would not have known the contents of their private communications to their respective correspondents.

At least two major figures in other parts of the country and unrelated to FICCI's internal politics echoed the Lala's views. One of them was V.N. Chandavarkar, the President of the Indian Merchants' Chamber. Addressing the annual meeting of the Chamber in March 1942 he warned that 'any scheme that was likely to result in the disintegration and disunity of the country was not likely to be welcomed'.[35] The most cogent and powerful arguments, however, came from one of the most influential business figures in Bombay, Sir Ardeshir Dalal. Closely associated with the House of Tatas, Dalal would later serve for a short period on the Viceroy's Council as a member-in-charge of the Department of Planning and Reconstruction. In a pamphlet entitled *An Alternative to Pakistan*, Dalal pointed out to the 'innumerable problems' Pakistan, if created, would face and then added:

> It [Pakistan] will cut itself from the great economic and industrial future which a self-governing India may look forward to. There will be a great urge to impose heavy custom duties on goods from 'Hindustan' to fill its depleted coffers and that in itself will not only hinder industrial progress but might be a futile source of trouble between the two states.[36]

Dalal, incidentally, was the only prominent business figure who argued against Partition, in economic terms—unless Birla is counted as one by virtue of his vague allusion to the poverty of the future breakaway state, in his above mentioned letter to Nehru. Both, however, viewed the matter from Pakistan's point of view, while no Muslim proponent of division ever placed great accent on economic benefits to justify the demand. Jinnah and his associates harped on the danger to Islam more often than anything else, and even the business supporters of the League seldom campaigned for a separate Muslim state in the name of possible economic gain. Nor did the non-Muslim businessmen ever cite harm to their own interests as a ground for their support, or opposition, to the Pakistan demand. Most of them kept their counsel to themselves, and major trade organizations like FICCI expressed no opinion. Also their contemporaries too did not relate the businessmen's views of the politics of division to narrow and selfish business interests.

V

And yet some scholars have suggested exactly this.[37] According to this view, the big business, largely in the hands of non-Muslim interests, opposed the scheme of Partition simply because it would have hurt their operations spread throughout the land. The areas that were proposed to be included in a future breakaway state were either a source of raw material or market for finished goods produced in major centres such as Bombay, Calcutta, Ahmedabad, Kanpur and Coimbatore. Most of the business houses—Tata, Birla, Shri Ram, Mafatlal, etc.—also had factories in areas in Bengal and the Punjab that were sure to go to Pakistan. They would have preferred a united India in the normal course of things. However, when they sensed that the alternative to Pakistan was a loose federation, with a weak central authority, incapable of protecting their all-India operations or providing a strong support to their industrial schemes, the economic explanation would have us believe, they veered round to the idea of division. Apart from being speculative, the proposition ignores the fact that G.D. Birla and Dalmia, not ordinary figures in the non-Muslim ranks, came out in support of Pakistan quite early in the game, much before there was any proposal to dilute the role of the central authority in India's governance, and their position remained unchanged throughout.[38] Likewise, Lala Shri Ram and persons like him never came round to supporting the idea of division—not even after the Cabinet Mission Plan, envisaged seriously for the first time a rather weak centre. The suggestion also ignores the position of the numerous class of merchants whose preference for a united India had little room for concession until the end.

An economic explanation of the attitude of Indian business, thus, appears to be a post facto rationalization of a complex historical reality.

Even the Muslim business communities, which gave solid support to the Muslim League were swayed not so much by the calculations of economic gain, but by spontaneous emotivity inherent in the lure for a separate homeland, natural for a community left behind in the race for progress. It is significant that some of the wealthiest Muslim business families, who openly supported the League, did not move to Pakistan until riots in their home towns forced their hands. Many of these families, as they later confided to an American author in personal interviews, had planned to conduct their operations in both countries, while remaining in India.[39] Likewise, it was only after large scale rioting in their region that the Khoja, Bohra and Memon traders, concentrated in the Bombay Presidency but active elsewhere too, moved to Pakistan in hordes. It is also important to remember that the All India Muslim Chambers of Commerce and Industry[40]—an 'instrument of unity and commercial and industrial strength . . . *so necessary for achieving independence*', to quote one of its principal promoters—was allowed to wither away once the Muslim League's demand for Pakistan had been conceded.

The reactions of the non-Muslim segments in Indian business to the Pakistan agitation were much more varied and confused—perhaps as varied and confused as of the rest of the Indian populace. Such elements can be divided, albeit at the cost of over-simplification, into three groups. One would comprise persons like Birla and Dalmia, who were essentially suspicious of the Muslims as a community and believed rather simplistically that the Partition would provide a good riddance, or bring home to the Muslims the value of a united India. Such persons seem to have been influenced, directly or indirectly, by the ideas of Lala Lajpat Rai and V.D. Savarkar, whose stress on the Hindu-Muslim chasm sometimes sounded identical to the two-nation theory.[41] Though not fanatic, businessmen in this category looked upon the Muslim community as an encumbrance rather than a partner in the nation-building tasks. G.D. Birla, for instance (though more magnanimous towards the Muslims than his brother B.M. Birla, who hated them from the core of his heart), could not always hide his distrust of them. Once in the mid-1920s, reacting to communal riots in northern India, he went to the extent of advocating proselytization of Muslims by force.[42] There must have been many more like Birla in the non-Muslim business circles who thought that Partition would provide a lasting solution to the Hindu-Muslim problem.

For the second group of persons, Partition appeared to be an emotional tragedy. Undivided India was too sacred a concept for them to accommodate the idea of bisection, whatever the reasons. Most non-Muslims, particularly Hindus including businessmen, belonged to this category. In the case of some people, such as Lala Shri Ram, this feeling might have been reinforced by their business interests, but the primary reason for their opposing Partition remained emotional. The group consisted of both die-hard communalists and persons of more liberal persuasion. A vast majority of the opponents of Partition may be said to have belonged to it. They probably never seriously believed that the country would actually be divided, but acquiesced in the decision once it ultimately materialized.

The third category of the opponents of Partition may be said to consist of a rather small section of the business community, who wanted to convince the supporters of Pakistan that the demand was detrimental to the interests of the Muslims themselves. Instinctively committed to the idea of an undivided India, they avoided advancing cultural or historical arguments, because such arguments would have had little impact on those who were clamouring for the creation of the new state on the basis of the two-nation theory. Instead they tried to reason out that the new state would be an economic cripple. Influential businessmen belonging to communities other than Hindus or Muslims, people like Sir Ardeshir Dalal, who did not want to get entangled in Hindu-Muslim controversy, comprised this category.

Regardless of how one classifies the non-Muslim business elements, one thing is certain. They had very little influence on the developments that determined the political fate of the subcontinent. Functioning at the periphery of the national movement, they had very little power to mould the events to suit their preferences or interests. Thus the suggestion that Birla's proximity to Sardar Vallabhbhai Patel might have been a factor in the Congress High Command veering round to the Partition proposition[43] appears to be rather far-fetched. It is also unjust to the Sardar. He was too shrewd to be trapped by any machination and too independent to succumb to either pressure or persuasion.

NOTES

1. For a more detailed account, see D. Tripathi, 'Congress and the Industrialists, 1885-1947', in idem, ed., *Business and Politics in India: A Historical Perspective* (New Delhi, 1991), pp. 86-123.
2. The industrial transition among Indian Muslims has not been adequately explored. Thomas T. Timberg, 'Industrial Entrepreneurship among the Trading Communities of India: How the Pattern Differs', in *Economic Development Report No. 136* (Centre

for International Affairs, Harvard University, Cambridge, Massachusettes, 1969) is among the few works (see pp. 74-8) that have made some attempt in this direction. Three volumes compiled by S. Playne, *Southern India, Bengal and Assam, Bihar and Orissa and the Bombay Presidency, United Provinces, Punjab, etc.* (all published by Foreign and Colonial Compiling and Publishing Co., London, between 1915 and 1920), contain useful primary data.

3. Timberg, op.cit., p. 75.
4. A list of FICCI presidents can be found in H. Venkatasubbiah, *Enterprise and Economic Change: 50 years of FICCI* (New Delhi, 1977), pp. 172-3.
5. Stanley Kochanek, *Business and Politics in India* (Berkeley, 1974), p. 142.
6. Ibid., pp. 157-8.
7. Purshotamdas Thakurdas to N.M. Mazumdar, 7 June 1929, File No. 42/II, Purshotamdas Thakurdas Collection (hereafter PT Collection), Nehru Memorial Museum & Library, New Delhi.
8. For a more detailed discussion, see Tripathi, op.cit., pp. 92-7. Edward C. Benthall, senior partner in the Calcutta based Bird and Co. (who later served on the Viceroy's Council) and leader of the British business interests in India had information that Birla had paid two full days' pay to the workers of his Kesoram Mills on the condition that they went out on *hartal* on the day of Gandhi's arrest. See Benthall's Diary entry of 22 May 1930 in Benthall Papers, Box VIII, file containing papers of 1929-33 (Centre of South Asian Studies, Cambridge University). A few days later on 2 June 1930, he entered in his diary the following: 'I am informed by Baladeodas Bajoria [a Birla rival in Calcutta business] that the next move in the Civil Disobedience campaign is for a month's *hartal* in Bombay, the mill-owners having agreed to pay their workers half wages, the shop owners having agreed not to charge rent for their shops', see ibid. On 8 June 1931 Benthall's diary entry alludes to business donations to Congress and adds: 'Rs. 7 lacs weekly came from Ahmedabad alone via Ambalal Sarabhai', see ibid. Even after the end of the Civil Disobedience, the Law Member of the Viceroy's Council maintained that Birla was the 'most generous donor of funds' to the Congress during the movement. For his letter to Benthall, 7 November 1935, see ibid., Box IX. Birla, however, always maintained that he never gave funds to the Congress but financed Gandhi's constructive programmes. Even if these suspicions in official circle or among European businessmen might contain some truth, there is no evidence of industrialists' *open* support to the agitation, either financially or morally.
9. Referring to the differences between the two camps Benthall wrote to a friend: 'There is a feeling amounting to bitterness among people like Modi [Sir Homi Mody] and Cowsji [Sir Cowasjee Jehangir] to the Ahmedabad Congress millowners.' See Benthall to Sir Herbert Carr, 6 May 1931, Benthall Papers, Box VII, file covering 1929-34.
10. Thakurdas to Mazumdar, 7 June 1929, PT Collection, op.cit.
11. A.D.D. Gordon, *Businessmen and Politics: Rising Nationalism and a Modernising Economy in Bombay, 1918-1933* (Delhi, 1968), pp. 1-4.
12. The Marwari traders, for instance, opposed the swadeshi agitation of 1905 in Bengal, because the boycott of foreign cloth affected a major source of their profit. See J.H. Broomfield, *Elite Conflict in a Plural Society: Twentieth Century Bengal* (Berkeley, 1968), p. 31.
13. In Bengal a Muslim dominated coalition led by Fazlul-Haq's Krishak Praja Party and in the Punjab a Hindu-Muslim agrarian outfit, the Unionist Party, won the majority of seats.

14. Stanley Kochanek, *Interest Groups and Development: Business and Politics in Pakistan* (Delhi, 1983), pp. 105-6.
15. Hanna Papanek, 'Pakistan's Big Businessmen: Muslim Separatism, Entrepreneurship, and Partial Modernisation', *Economic Development and Cultural Change*, Vol. XXI, No. 1 (October, 1972), pp. 8-16.
16. Kochanek, *Interest Groups*, op.cit., pp.106-9.
17. Quoted in Gordon, op.cit., p. 238.
18. Quoted in S. Gopal *Jawaharlal Nehru: A Biography*, Vol. I (New Delhi, 1976), p. 223.
19. Quoted in Z.H. Zaidi, 'Aspects of the Development of the League Policy, 1937-47', in C.H. Philips and M.D. Wainright, eds, *Partition of India, Policies and Perspectives 1935-47* (London, 1970), p. 250.
20. Sir Mohammad Iqbal's Presidential Address at the Allahabad session of the Muslim League in May 1930, among other things, provide some insight into these conditions. He lamented that the Hindus and Muslims had failed to discover the 'principles of internal harmony' because 'we suspect each other's intentions and inwardly aim at dominating each other'. Quoted in M.H. Saiyid, *The Political Study of Muhammad Ali Jinnah* (New Delhi, 1986), Vol. II, pp. 478-9. The poet-philosopher, it may be recalled, had been a votary of Hindu-Muslim unity until not long before that. His famous poem *Shikwa* (Lament) is also regarded by some as an oblique expression of Muslims' grudges against the Hindus. In this poem written in 1909, the poet complains to Allah for being unfair to the Muslim community and laments the decline of Muslim power and the taunts flung at them by infidels. A translation of the first 16 of his 31 stanza long poem can be found in Khushwant Singh, *Not a Nice Man to Know* (New Delhi, 1993), pp. 179-83. W.C. Smith, *Modern Islam in India* (Lahore, 1943) also relates Muslim communalism to the feeling on the part of the community that its progress was thwarted by the Hindus. See the chapter on 'Communalism', pp. 185-224.
21. Sir Percival Griffiths, who had met Jinnah on several occasions, gives the following account of discussions with Jinnah about Pakistan shortly before the Lahore session of the League: Jinnah 'went on to develop cogently and impressively, his two-nation theory and to expound the full Pakistan demand, which was to be adopted by the Muslim League in March 1940. The writer [Sir Percival] and others present raised all the obvious objections—economic changes, frontier problems, military and administrative difficulties. Mr Jinnah brushed them all aside and completely refused to discuss details. This capacity for adhering to a clear-cut idea and ignoring all difficulties of details and procedure was perhaps Mr Jinnah's greatest source of strength.' See Sir Percival Griffiths, *Modern India* (New York, 1965), p. 29.
22. A. Jalal, *The Sole Spokesman: Jinnah, the Muslim League and the Demand for Pakistan* (Cambridge, 1985), p. 175.
23. On 1 February 1940 Benthall entered in his diary: 'The business community is anti-Congress as a whole and wants to make money in peace.' Diaries of Edward Benthall, Benthall Papers, Box VII, Item 3, Diary of 1940. The basis of Benthall's assertion is not quite clear; it seems to be an expression of desire rather than fact.
24. Frank Moraes, *Sir Purshotamdas Thakurdas* (Bombay, 1957), pp. 2, 13 and 219.
25. For details see Tripathi, op.cit., pp. 114-17; also S.K. Ghosh, *The Indian Big Bourgeoisie* (Calcutta, 1985), pp. 226-9.
26. Venkatasubbiah, op.cit., p. 49, also see p. 42.
27. Ibid., p. 71.
28. Purshotam Thakurdas, et al., *A Brief Memorandum Outlining a Plan of Economic*

Development for India (Bombay, 1944), p. 48; also see H.V.R. Iyengar, 'A Look at the Bombay Plan in the Light of Today', *Forum of Free Enterprise, The Bombay Plan and Other Essays* (Bombay, 1968), pp. 1-17.

29. Birla to Mahadeo Desai, 11 January 1938, G.D. Birla, *Bapu: A Unique Association* (Bombay, 1977), Vol. III, p. 144.
30. Birla to C. Rajagopalachari, 11 October 1938, Birla Papers, Series II, File No. R.8, in possession of the Birla family.
31. Ramkrishna Dalmia, *Some Notes and Reminiscences* (Bombay, 1948), p. 24.
32. Birla to Mahadeo Desai, 14 July 1942, Birla, op.cit.,Vol. IV, pp. 315-17; Mahadeo Desai to Birla, 16 July 1942, ibid., p. 319.
33. Quoted in Ram Niwas Jaju, *G.D. Birla: A Biography* (New Delhi, 1986), p. 136. Jaju has not given the date of this letter, but the context indicates that it was written sometime in 1943.
34. Lala Shri Ram to Purshotamdas Thakurdas, 29 September 1942, PT Collection, File No. 239.
35. Quoted in *Times of India*, 25 March 1942.
36. A.R. Dalal, *An Alternative to Pakistan* (Bombay, 1943), p. 45.
37. Claude Markovits, 'Businessmen and the Partition of India', in D. Tripathi, ed., op.cit., pp. 284-307.
38. As late as 1948, Dalmia explained his position thus: 'Had Pakistan in some form been conceded at the earliest stage, the Muslims would never have thought of severing their ties with the rest of India and they would have soon realised the futility of their demands and would have been compelled to come back to the Indian union', Dalmia, op.cit., p. 25.
39. Papanek, 'Pakistan's Big Businessmen', op.cit., p. 13.
40. M.A.H. Ispahani, quoted in Kochanek, op.cit., p. 109.
41. M.H. Saiyid, op.cit., Vol. II, p. 479, asserts that Mohammad Iqbal's ideas about Hindu and Muslim being separate cultures, enunciated in his Presidential Address at the Allahabad session of the Muslim League were in line with the thinking initiated by Lala Lajpat Rai. In his Presidential speech at the Hindu Mahasabha session in 1939 Savarkar unreservedly declared: '. . . we Hindus are marked out as an abiding Nation by ourselves', N.N. Mitra, *Indian Annual Register, 1939*, Vol. II (July-December), (repr., Delhi, 1990), p. 317. A few years later he was even more explicit about his faith in the two-nation theory. Presiding over the Hindu Mahasabha session, he said: 'I have no quarrel with Mr Jinnah's two-nation theory. We Hindus are a nation by ourselves, and it is a historical fact that Hindus and Muslims are two nations,' ibid., *1943*, Vol. II (July-December), op.cit., p. 10.
42. Birla to Gandhi, 11 June 1928, Birla, op.cit., Vol. 1, p. 9. Birla writes in this letter: 'There is no doubt whatever in my mind that once we convert a number of Muslims to Hinduism (through *shuddhi* or purification as advocated by the Arya Samajists like Lajpat Rai), they would begin to love the rest of the Hindus in the same way that a Hindu does another.'
43. Markovits, op.cit., p. 300.

Economic Irrationality of the Partition of India

SHRI PRAKASH

The movement for political independence of India was unique. It had a major socio-economic programme as its essential part. The social emancipation of the masses and the rapid balanced development of the economy formed an integral part of it. The movement for the boycott of imported goods and the promotion of *khadi* and other cottage and small scale industries, appointment of the Planning Committee in the 1930s and the formulation of the Bombay Plan, Peoples' Plan and Wardha Plan, during the 1940s—all these highlighted the importance attached to the economic aspects of political freedom.

The economic objectives of political freedom were primarily threefold: (i) the freeing of the Indian economy from colonial exploitation, the greatest proponent of which was Dadabhai Naoroji,[1] who highlighted that the British were draining Indian resources through trade, home charges and remittances on various counts and other indirect underhand means; (ii) the eradiction of poverty of the masses through the reduction of inequalities of income and wealth and the equalization of opportunities; and (iii) political empowerment and social upliftment of the masses.[2]

Pre-British India was highly developed and industrialized. Britain in those days was struggling to move out of its underdevelopment trap.[3] India was the major exporter of cotton and silk textiles, spices, artifacts and handicrafts. Upto the end of the eighteenth century, India led Europe, including Britain, in technology, product designs and the production cost of cotton and silk textiles and numerous handicrafts.[4] The British government protected its industry against imports of the cheaper, though superior, Indian goods, both through legal measures (1701 and 1720) and heavy duties. Use of printed Indian calicoes was banned.[5] There is evidence that up to the end of the eighteenth century, India was 'a great manufacturing country'.[6] The East India Company had initially nothing to offer in exchange for its imports from India. The Company was allowed by the British government to export gold, silver and coins worth £30,000 per year to India to settle India's favourable balance of trade and balance of payments with Britain.[7]

The British needed the colonial markets for selling the rising output of their industrial goods. To eliminate competition to British goods in the colonies from indigenous goods, numerous policy instruments were used for the radical alteration of the pattern, structure, composition and direction of India's foreign trade.[8] The East India Company encouraged the production of raw silk and discouraged the production of silk fabrics in Bengal (1769), by forcing silk winders to work in the Company's factories. They were not allowed to work on their own account even at home after factory hours.[9]

The Indian agriculture was fairly developed and self-reliant. Only about 5 per cent of the total cultivated area was under non-cereal crops, though horticulture and floriculture were adequately developed. Cultivation was carried out on scientific lines in the context of the then 'state of the knowledge' and 'agricultural technology'. Economic structure and cropping patterns in India were changed to suit the requirements of British economy. They promoted the exports of such agro raw materials as cotton, jute, tea, coffee, indigo, rubber and minerals at extremely low prices from India to promote their nascent industries. The British encouraged the diversion of area from cereal to non-cereal crops for this purpose.

For the elimination of competition to British goods, the British also followed a policy of de-industrialization of India, which resulted in its de-urbanization also. As artisans and craftsmen left big cities, such as Murshidabad, Dacca, Lucknow, Agra and Delhi, urban decline set in.[10] The de-industrialization and de-urbanization trends of early nineteenth century operated upto the early decades of the twentieth century. Agriculture had to absorb the excess urban population of skilled artisans and craftsmen as unskilled agricultural labourers. Consequently, India emerged from colonial rule not only primarily as an agricultural country but also as a producer of raw materials for foreign industries.

This is supported by the fact that, according to the Census of 1881, about 61 per cent of the total Indian population depended on agriculture; in the 1921 census, the share of population dependent on agriculture increased to 73 per cent.[11] Population pressure on agriculture increased roughly by 1.2 per cent per annum and only a fraction of this additional burden was the result of the natural population growth. A substantial proportion of the increased population pressure was accounted for by the reverse urban to rural migration. The possibility of rural to urban migration was arrested also due to the want of urban jobs. This inflicted a heavy loss of human capital on India, while the economic structure was transformed from a balanced economy to one that was primarily dependent upon agriculture. Besides, this also generated both open and disguised unemployment and it accentuated poverty.[12] Indian exports at extremely low prices in the altered pattern of trade consisted largely of primary goods, including food grains and agro raw materials. India imported manufactured goods from Britain at high prices. Thus the composition, direction and terms of Indian foreign trade during the colonial era were manipulated and distorted to subserve the British national interests.

The changes in the economy and the decline of Indian industries destroyed the self-reliant and self-sufficient character of both rural and urban India.[13] Diversion of as much as 18 to 20 per cent of cultivable area from food grains to cash crops transformed India from a self-sufficient into a food deficit country. Paddy production, especially, fell extremely short of requirements. The change in the cropping/production pattern accentuated the food shortages in India. These shortages were mitigated to some extent by the incorporation of Burma and Sri Lanka into the Indian dominion. But this leverage was lost subsequently.

In 1951, 83.3 per cent of the total cultivated area was under food grains, while non-food crops accounted for 16.7 per cent of the gross cropped area. The proportion of area between food and non-food crops in India had hovered around the ratio of 4:1 for long,[14] though the area under non-food crops had increased continuously, partly through the monetary incentives provided by the British and partly by coercion. The changes in the cropping pattern were neither preceded nor were they accompanied by a rise in the crop yields. Consequently, India became a food deficit country in the colonial era.

The impact of food shortages was further heightened by the frequent occurrence of floods and famines and the consequent crop failures. Inequalities of income distribution and hence low purchasing power of the masses made them quite vulnerable in times of distress. Neglect of investment in agriculture, in general, and irrigation, in particular, accounted for the frequent occurrence of floods and famines. This neglect is in sharp contrast to the high priority accorded by the British to the development of railways to connect the ports with the sources of supply of raw materials and food grains and of the markets for the sale of their manufactures.[15]

During the first half of the nineteenth century alone, seven famines occurred, resulting in 15,00,000 starvation deaths. During its second half, there were four major famines. From 1854 to 1901, 22,82,500 persons are estimated to have died due to starvation.[16] Thus on an average, 46,000 people died every year due to starvation caused by food shortages, low purchasing power and unaffordable high prices. During the Second World

War period also, supply of food grains fell extremely short of demand, while the prices rose steeply. Consequently, the available food supplies became inaccessible to the poor. A serious famine occurred in Bengal in 1943, resulting in 35,00,000 starvation deaths. Shortage of food grains accounted only partially for starvation deaths. These were caused largely by the mismanagement of the available supplies.[17]

Besides the want of investment in such yield-raising inputs as high yeilding seeds and fertilizers and also in dams, canals and barrages for the expansion of irrigation and the generation of power, made Indian agriculture vulnerable to the adverse weather conditions, which occurred periodically. Hence there was no change in the farm technology and irrigational facilities, which improved only marginally in nearly 190 years of the British rule from 1757 to 1947. In 1951, only 17.1 per cent of the gross cropped area had irrigational facilities, making cultivation a gamble in the monsoons.[18] A substantial proportion of this area was irrigated only because of the private investment in traditional wells and community investment in tanks, etc.

The deliberately designed British policy of keeping the agricultural prices low also inflicted serious damage on the agriculture of undivided India. Both national and international agriculture-industry terms of trade, had been kept against agriculture, condemning the farmers to live perpetually in penury and misery and keeping agriculture permanently underdeveloped. Frequent occurrence of floods and famines not only compounded the problems of de-industrialization, resulting in industrial backwardness and agricultural underdevelopment but also inflicted a heavy loss on life and property. Such disasters reduced the agriculturists periodically to penury and misery. Adverse international terms of trade, low agricultural prices and cyclical fluctuations in output and trade made the Indian farm economy highly unstable around the low equilibrium trap. Severe food deficiency before the attainment of Indian independence forced the British to launch the 'Grow More Food' campaign during the 1940s.[19] The country also inherited a low, narrow and lop-sided industrial base, which was surrounded by the backwaters of a backward agriculture.

Under these circumstances, economic rationality warranted that the geographical division of the country into two independent countries, India and Pakistan, should have been based on such parameters as the population to be supported, gross cropped area relative to the size of population to be supported, the crop yield rates and the irrigational facilities available in different regions and parts of the country, socio-economic infrastructure capacity for industrial production and its raw material needs.

The human and physical capital endowments and the actual and potential capacity for trade might have been used as an additional criterion for the geographical and demographic partition of undivided India. But political considerations, based on communalism, swamped economic rationality.

The problem was further compounded by the voluntary and involuntary population transfers between the newly independent countries. It resulted in a situation where the man-land ratio favoured Pakistan, while it was not favourable to India, not only in quantitative but in qualitative terms also. This is supported by the fact that in 1948, independent India had a little over 77 per cent of the total geographical area of undivided India, but it had to support 82 per cent of its population. As against this, Pakistan received 23 per cent of the total land area to support only 18 per cent of the total population of pre-1947 undivided India. This inequitable distribution of land and population resulted in the decline of the land-man ratio in independent India, both in relation to Pakistan and in relation to undivided India. According to the land utilization statistics, 92.5 per cent of the total geographical area, excluding 7.5 per cent of the unsurveyed and inaccessible land mass, was equal to 30.42 crore hectares.[20] This implies that only 0.59 hectare of land was available per person in India. The population transfers on communal lines made the already bad situation worse, since more Hindus and Sikhs migrated from Pakistan to India than did Muslims from India to Pakistan.

The inequity inflicted was not in quantitative terms alone, the situation was even worse qualitatively. Independent India could produce at best only 68 and 63 per cent of the total output of paddy and wheat, respectively, produced earlier in undivided India. Consequently, per capita availability of wheat and rice improved by 2.2 and 1.9 percentage points, respectively, after Partition in Pakistan, while it declined by 8.4 and 7.01 percentage points in independent India. Partition, therefore, reduced not only the actual supply but also the potential per capita supply of food grains in independent India.[21] Supplies of other cereals, pulses, fruits, vegetables and oil seeds were similarly affected adversely. This further deepened the import dependence of India for food grains and other agricultural goods.

The food deficiency of independent India became worse than that of undivided India, resulting in the continuation of war-time rationing and imports to cover the gaps between the national output and demand. Consequently, the First Five Year Plan of India focused mainly on agricultural development, on the one hand, and on the continuation of the earlier schemes in various stages of implementation, on the other.[22] This warranted the according of a very high priority to land reforms, investment in irrigation, acreage-augmenting and yield-enhancing inputs and the restructuring of the cropping pattern to face the consequences of Partition and to meet the challenges of development. This delayed the launching of the programmes of industrialization of independent India at least by eight to ten years.

Besides, India got a disproportionately larger share of the urban population and a relatively larger share of such manufacturing industries as jute and cotton textiles, sugar and tea. As against this, Pakistan emerged mainly as an agro-based rural country. Urban areas accounted for approximately 17.62 per cent of the total Indian population in 1951.[23] The share of the urban areas in Pakistan's total population was substantially lower. The reason was that, whereas four out of seven metropolitan areas came to India, only Lahore, Karachi and Dacca became part of Pakistan. Besides, the number of such medium sized cities as Lucknow, Allahabad, Varanasi, Meerut, Agra, Aligarh, Bhopal, Indore, Jabalpur, Jaipur, Jodhpur, Ajmer, Udaipur, Patiala, Amritsar, Ludhiana, Hissar, Rohtak, Bangalore, Hyderabad, Mysore, Guwahati, Shillong, Gwalior, Trivandrum, Cochin, Coimbatore, Madurai and many other such cities in India, was many times more than similar cities in Pakistan. Urbanization and the development of infrastructure is a slow, time consuming and costly process. This naturally adversely affected economic development in general, and industrialization, in particular. Pakistan suffered more on account of this than India.

Several major industries had developed in colonial India. The pace of industrialization was accelerated a great deal in the 1940s by the urgency of war time needs. Pakistan's share in the industries of undivided India was meagre. The following industries were reasonably developed on the eve of independence:

Tea, coffee, rubber, leather and leather products, iron and steel, cotton textiles, jute textiles, match boxes;

Paper and paper products with an output of 1,06,000 tons and employment for 18,800 persons;

Sugar with an output of 12 lakh tons;

Ferro-alloys, non-ferrous metals and fabricating industries, mechanical industries, diesel engines and pumps, sewing machines, machines and cutting tools, chemical goods industries;

Woolen textiles; and

Cement with an output of two million tons and employment for 21,800 persons emerged as the major industry of independent India.

It is obvious from this list that the industrial economy of both colonial and independent India was dominated by such consumer goods as cotton and jute textiles, sugar, salt, soap, leather goods and paper and paper products. The lopsided nature of the industrial structure of India is well reflected in the following table showing value added by different groups of industries in 1950-1:

	Consumer Goods	Intermediate Goods	Capital Goods	Others	Total
Value Added (Rs. in Crores)	261	90	31	3	385
Percentage Share in Total Value Added	68	23	8	1	100

Source: Vadilal Dagle, ed., *A Profile of Indian Industry, 1975-76.*[24]

Slightly more than two-thirds of value addition was the contribution of the consumer goods industries. Capital or producer goods industries accounted for only 8 per cent of the net industrial income. Intermediate goods contributed slightly less than one-fourth of the net industrial income. Import dependence of the Indian economy for intermediate goods has not been mitigated even now. Thus, heavy and intermediate goods industries, taken together, accounted for hardly one-third of the industrial income. In the first instance, industrial sectors accounted for hardly 12 to 14 per cent of the total GDP. Secondly, the range, number and technological base of the industrial production were extremely narrow and limited. The accentuated nature of the lopsidedness of the industrial structure of independent India should be seen in this perspective. The economic structure reflected the underdevelopment and the industrial and agricultural backwardness of the Indian economy.

As has already been pointed out land suitable for the production of raw materials for several of these industries was located in Pakistan. Agro-climatic conditions of the land mass of India was not suitable to several of these crops. Producer and intermediate goods industries were very few and such as those that existed were inadequately developed and operated on a small scale with obsolete technology, making competitive imports of all such goods inevitable. Export earnings were required to grow commensurately with the import requirements of the changed structure of the economy on the one hand, and needs of development, on the other. Both machinery and intermediate goods, agro-raw materials and food grains were required to be imported.

Indian economy, in fact, faced the shortages of food grains, foreign exchange, capital, industrial enterprise and exportable surpluses. These constraints, accentuated by Partition, limited the development of the Indian economy. Indian industries had experienced a steep slump in the post-Second World War period, owing largely to (a) the demand recession in the international markets; (b) the difficulties in getting supplies of raw material and intermediate goods; (c) the transport bottlenecks; (d) the backlog in replacing worn and torn machinery and equipment; and (e) the necessity of upgrading the technological base of production.[25]

Partition disrupted the internal sources of supplies of several raw materials and numerous intermediate goods. It also snatched away the demand for finished and semi-finished goods that used to emanate from the markets of the Pakistani parts of undivided India. Transport and communication links were almost totally disrupted. Alternative road and rail routes had to be constructed. Water and airways had been dislocated. The north-east, Rajasthan, Gujarat, Punjab and Kashmir faced this problem in varying degrees of severity. Even such communications and transportation facilities as remained within India had to be used for the transportation of millions of refugees on a priority basis, causing a heavy drain on the scarce resources, which could have been used alternatively for development.

As against India, Pakistan received a relatively larger share of rural population and the lion's share of the irrigated and highly fertile land, which was much more suitable for the cultivation of wheat, fine varieties of paddy and some agro raw materials. This created the new problem for India of arranging adequate supplies of raw materials against hard currency of such major foreign exchange earning export industries as cotton and jute textiles. It resulted not only in aggravating the existing food shortages but in inflicting multi-faceted blows to the Indian economy. These were firstly, India was now deprived of the foreign exchange earned from the exports of such agro raw materials as cotton, jute, dry fruits, etc.; secondly, the earlier indigenously available supplies against rupee payment had to be imported against hard currency at much higher prices; and thirdly, these supplies had to be hauled over long distances from far flung third countries, raising tax, transport and trade margins and hence a loss to the Indian economy.

The human tragedy involved in the population transfers between India and Pakistan, mostly as involuntary refugees, also inflicted a heavy loss of human capital on both countries. It deprived thousands of people of their means of livelihood and innumerable men had to change their occupations in which process their earnings were reduced. There was also the related problem of rehabilitating these refugees and making them self-reliant. Hindus and Sikhs, by and large, were endowed not only with industrial and commercial enterprise but also possessed physical capital required for such enterprises. In fact, commercial and industrial, physical and financial capital and entrepreneurship were almost exclusively owned by the Hindus and Sikhs, while the lower and lower middle class artisans, craftsmen, semi-skilled and skilled workers were largely Muslims. The latter were either directly employed by non-Muslim producers and traders or non-Muslim traders provided the financial and material needs and the marketing channels for the output. In most cases, such traders purchased the goods produced by the Muslim craftsmen. Thus, the marketing of the produce of the Muslim artisans and craftsmen was done mainly by non-Muslim financiers and/or traders.

Large-scale transfers of population on communal lines from both the countries almost totally destroyed the human capital base of production, trade and commerce of an extremely large number of production activities. Both countries were forced to start many of these activities almost from scratch, wherever such economic irrationalities had totally snapped the complementarities that existed between the economies of these two newly independent countries.[26]

Development efforts, aided by favourable weather conditions, enabled independent India to achieve high levels of output during the last two years of the First Five Year Plan, which facilitated the lifting of controls and the rationing of food grains. It also instilled the confidence that India had achieved self-sufficiency in the production of food grains. This led to the shifting of focus from agriculture to industrial development during the Second Five Year Plan, though this belief of self-sufficiency was belied by subsequent developments. However, the objective of self-sufficiency in food grains was attained after the fructification of the Green Revolution in the mid-1960s. For nearly a decade, the country had to live from 'ship to mouth' as the output-demand gap was covered by imports from the USA under its PL-480 food grants. Rice was imported from such countries as Burma and Thailand, while the USA, Canada and Australia emerged as the major suppliers of wheat.

Independent India inherited a predominantly agriculture based backward rural economy with an extremely weak industrial base, a lopsided industrial structure, grossly underdeveloped infrastructure and a stagnant economy with its development arrested for decades by colonial exploitation. These problems were further compounded by the calamitous dislocating events of the division of colonial India into two independent countries. The political partition of India on a communal basis was in total disregard of agro-climatic conditions, population to be supported by each country and the agricultural and industrial economy to be inherited. This made the already vulnerable economy still more vulnerable.

The partition of the two provinces of Punjab and Bengal resulted in their bifurcation into West and East Punjab and West and East Bengal whereas all other provinces were transferred to one or the other country in their totality. East Punjab and West Bengal became part of the Indian Union, while West Punjab and East Bengal formed part of the newly-born country, Pakistan. The importance and economic irrationality of this unnatural geographical partition arose from the fact that West Punjab and Sindh were not only the most irrigated and most fertile areas of undivided India, specializing in the production of wheat, finer varieties of both paddy and cotton, in accordance with their agro-climatic conditions and irrigational endowments, but these also accounted for a very high proportion of the output of these three goods. And again, East Bengal accounted for almost the entire jute growing area and a substantially high proportion of the course paddy growing area of undivided India. Naturally East Bengal was the main source of supply of coarse paddy and raw jute. On the other hand, West Bengal had the privilege of being the location of nearly 98 per cent of the total jute mills of undivided India. Similarly, Ahmedabad, Bombay and Kanpur were the major locations of cotton textile mills of undivided India. Though East Punjab was much better endowed with the agro-climatic conditions and irrigational facilities than the rest of independent India, yet it compared very poorly with West Punjab and Sindh. The latter were, in fact, known as the granary of undivided India. They were also agro-climatically more suited to the production of the finer varieties of paddy and long staple cotton. Other parts of West Pakistan, Multan, Baluchistan and the NWFP were major centres of production of dry fruits and other agro raw materials.

On the whole, independent India inherited most of the industrial economy of undivided India, alongwith its physical and human capital, including 90 to 98 per cent of the cotton and jute textile mills. Pakistan got most of the areas producing agro raw materials and food grains. The consequence of this irrational division was that a large number of industrial goods as well as such agro manufactures as cotton and woolen textiles, sugar, betel leaves and betel-nut, steel, chemicals, etc., which the Pakistani part used to get as domestic supplies from the Indian part of undivided India, had now to be imported against foreign exchange from other countries, while India had to find new export markets for its surpluses. Trade with Iran and Afghanistan through land routes became dependent upon the cooperation of Pakistan and it was not easy to get this from Pakistan. Thus, besides the accentuated shortfalls in domestic output of food grains caused by Partition, it also affected other segments of the agricultural and industrial economies of independent India due mainly to the structural mismatch between the production of agro raw materials and the natural raw materials needed for the agro-based and other industries of India.

Independent India emerged as the net importer of long staple cotton, raw jute and mesta, necessitating allocation of foreign exchange. Political factors impeded direct imports from Pakistan. Jute and long staple cotton were imported from such far flung countries as Egypt, Sudan and Nigeria. Imports of Pakistani raw materials substantially raised the costs since trade, transport and tax margins got added to the export price of raw materials, like Pakistani jute, supplied through third countries. Enhanced production costs due to enhanced procurement costs and, hence, high prices of these Indian exports made it difficult for India to retain its foothold in its traditional markets and thwarted its efforts to penetrate new markets in the face of the intensifying competition offered by other countries. Dilution in the quality of raw materials made these twin tasks still more difficult. Uncertainties and long lead times involved in the procurement of supplies of raw materials and intermediate goods of requisite quality affected production and supply schedules. These factors directly affected the modernization and development programmes of these industries, which impinged upon export earnings. Propagation of the cultivation of cotton, jute and mesta in areas less suitable to their cultivation and investment in yield augmenting inputs facilitated the achievement of self-sufficiency over a period of time, though it involved a heavy cost to the economy, in general, and to industry, in particular.

As a result exports of jute and cotton textiles from India were at a distinct disadvantage in the face of stiff competition from developing textile industries of such new entrants into the market, as Pakistan, Japan, Ceylon, South Korea and Taiwan. Concerted efforts under different development plans enabled India only over a period of time to overcome these handicaps and maintain its foothold in international markets.

Geography does not recognize political boundaries. But the political division of India into two independent countries resulted in its geographical partition. All assets, including natural wealth, had to be shared between two independent countries. In most cases, ingenious means and ways to divide natural phenomena like land, can be devised but the division of such geographical assets as climate, rivers, oceans, mountains and hills pose almost insurmountable difficulties. Consequently, the sharing of the waters of common rivers between India and Pakistan became a disputed subject. Infinite quantity of water from the rivers common to East and West Punjab and East and West Bengal flowed into the seas/oceans without being used for meeting the drinking water needs of the growing population, for irrigating the fields or for generating the much needed hydroelectric power both in India and Pakistan. The development of the river system for navigational purposes could also not be undertaken. Waterways had constituted an important means of conveying both men and materials in undivided India. But these have now almost disappeared as a means of transportation in independent India. Settlement between the two countries on the sharing of river waters was reached after many long discussions but sharing of the Ganga water between India and Bangladesh is still awaiting a final settlement—a temporary settlement, notwithstanding.

It is not easy to estimate the total losses of the potential output of a variety of goods and services due to the economically illogical partition of the subcontinent. For example, north-east India had to be connected by 'circuitous' road and rail routes, since the shortest routes could be developed only through Bangladesh. Besides the capital cost of the development of these longer road and rail routes, the additional cost of transportation of men and materials borne by the Indian economy due to these longer routes can well be surmised. Bangladesh would also have derived economic benefits if such road and rail routes had been developed. Of course, some irrationality where this is concerned was eliminated by mutual exchange of some islands between India and Bangladesh at a much later date through mutual consent.

Economic irrationality of the political division would have been contained if both the newly independent countries had decided to cooperate economically with each other. Let us hope, history will not repeat itself and that the Indo-Pakistan and Indo-Bangladesh economic cooperation will proceed smoothly under SAARC (South Asia Association for Regional Cooperation). If all three countries move towards SAPTA (South Asian

Preferential Trade Arrangement), economies of the region will derive immense benefits and its development would be greatly accelerated.

NOTES

1. Dadabhai Naoroji, *Poverty and Un-British Rule in India* (Delhi, 1969, 1st edn, London, 1901).
2. *First Five Year Plan* (Planning Commission, Government of India, New Delhi, 1951).
3. 'At a time when Western Europe, the birthplace of the modern industrial system, was inhabited by uncivilized tribes, India was famous for the wealth of her rulers and for the high artistic skill of her craftsmen. Even at a much later period than when the merchant adventurers from the West made their first appearance in India, the industrial development of this country was, at any rate not inferior to that of the more advanced European nations.' Report of Industrial Commission (1918), cited in P.G. Gadgil and P.L. Gadgil, *Industrial Economy of India* (New Delhi, 1985), p. 281. Also see Paul Baran, *Political Economy* (London, 1953).
4. The cotton and silk goods of India could be sold for a profit in the British market at a price from 50 to 60 per cent lower than the fabricated ones in England. See H.H. Wilson, *History of British India*, Vol. I, p. 538, cited in Gadgil and Gadgil, op.cit., p. 5. When tariffs from 70 to 80 per cent failed to check the imports of Indian textiles, England passed prohibitory laws in 1701 and 1720 to ban the use of Indian calicoes. The government levied an excise duty of 5 per cent on Indian products. Excise duty was totally unknown upto that time. Besides, the Court of Directors opposed the use of Indian ships in Indo-British trade. Tata was not allowed to set up a steel plant in the Central Provinces in the 1880s.
5. 'Had this not been the case, had not such prohibitory duties and decrees existed, the Mills of Paisley and Manchester would have been stopped at their outset, and could scarcely have been again set in motion, even by the power of steam. They were created by the sacrifice of the Indian manufacture', H.H. Wilson, op cit., p. 385, cited in R. Palme Dutt, *India Today* (Calcutta, 1970), p. 101.
6. T. Raychaudhri, 'A Re-Interpretation of Nineteenth Century Indian Economic History', in *Indian Economic and Social History Review*, Vol. I (March 1968).
7. Palme Dutt, op.cit., p. 101.
8. 'Custom duty of 78 per cent on Indian imports into Britain was imposed. But British exports to India continued duty free.' The purpose of such policies was to create a market for British goods in India and to transform India into a producer of primary goods. For details, see S.K. Mishra and V.K. Puri, *Indian Economy* (Bombay, 1983).
9. *Select Committee on Administration of Justice in India, House of Commons, Ninth Report (1783)*, Appendix XXXVII, expected the then industrialized India to change its economic structure in order to make it 'produce crude materials for the manufactures of Great Britain', cited in Mishra and Puri, op.cit., p. 93.
10. For example, the population of Dacca during this period declined from 150 thousand to 30 to 40 thousand only. See ibid., p. 85.
11. See ibid., p. 92.
12. Naoroji, Atkinson, Baring, Horne, Curzon and Giffen estimated per capita income of India to be in the range of Rs. 23.5 in 1867-8 and Rs. 31.5 in 1895. See Moni Mukerji,

'National Income', in V.B. Singh, ed., *Economic History of India, 1857-1956* (New Delhi, 1975), p. 672.

13. Daniel H. Buchanan observed that 'the armour of the isolated self-sufficient village was pierced by the steel rail and its life blood ebbed away'. See his *Development of Capitalist Enterprise in India* (London, 1966), p. 189.
14. Government of India, Ministry of Finance, *Economic Survey* (Publication Division, New Delhi, 1995), Statistical Tables.
15. For details, see Vera Anstey, *The Economic Development of India* (London, 1952).
16. William Digby, *Prosperous British India* (London, 1901), cited in Palme Dutt, op.cit., p. 124.
17. Sir W.W. Hunter, Director General of Statistics, Government of India, wrote that 'forty million of the people of India habitually go through life with insufficient food', cited in P.C. Ray, *The Poverty Problem in India* (Calcutta, 1895), p. 149. Similarly, Charles Elliot, Member of the Governor-General's Council, stated 'I do not hesitate to say that half the agricultural population never knows from one year's end to another what it is to have a full meal', cited in G.V. Joshi, *Writings and Speeches* (Poona, 1912), p. 763.
18. *Economic Survey*, op.cit.
19. G.P. Khare, *Planning in India* (Bombay, 1963).
20. Acreage data for later years have been taken from Mishra and Puri, op.cit., p. 121.
21. Calculations are based on data taken for 1961, from *Economic Survey*, op.cit.,
22. Ibid.
23. Kingsley Davis, *The Population of India and Pakistan* (Princeton, 1951); and Government of India, Registrar General's Office, *Pocket Book of Population Statistics* (New Delhi, 1972).
24. Adapted from Gadgil and Gadgil, op.cit., p. 295.
25. See Pramit Chaudhri, *The Indian Economy* (New Delhi, 1978).
26. For the role of human capital in development, its forms and the evolution of the concept, see Shri Prakash, *Cost of Education* (New Delhi, 1997), Chapter II.

Paradoxes of Partition

PARTHA SARATHI GUPTA

On the fiftieth anniversary of independence historians have been looking back into the processes that led to it. Since independence came with the Partition of the subcontinent, there has been as much interest in the causes of Partition, as there has been over the character of the Indian struggle for freedom, or the imperial calculations that led Britain to withdraw the apparatus of colonial rule from the subcontinent. Supplementing the Mansergh-Moon volumes on the *Transfer of Power* and the published and forthcoming volumes of the *Towards Freedom* series of the ICHR, we now have another project of documentation, specifically on Partition.

It is a truism that archival material, when carefully selected and published, are a great aid to the historian. Most of us who write monographs (also called secondary authorities) exercise our own judgement in the selection of evidence and make interpretative generalization about the historical process thereafter. There is thus a considerable degree of abridgement of the narrative of the past in the works of every historian. Apart from the historian's own predilections, constraints imposed by publishers (concerned about printing costs) force the historian to distil in one sentence or paragraph the essence of an argument, which can really be susbtantiated by pages of original sources laid out *in extenso*. For a phenomenon like the Partition the importance of a collection of documents as a corrective to stereotyped accounts of the process cannot be exaggerated. As explained below, these documents are illuminating.

The Jamia Hamdard (Hamdard university) of New Delhi, encouraged its Centre for Federal Studies to undertake this task in 1990. The Centre has, in a relatively short period of five years, built up a unique collection of more than 4,000 documents. Under the editorship of S.A.I. Tirmizi, three volumes have been planned, covering the years 1937 to 1947. The first volume, which is under review, deals with the calendar years 1937 to

* This article is based on S.A.I. Tirmizi, ed., *Paradoxes of Partition (1937-47), Vol. I (1937-39)* (New Delhi, 1998).

1939 and contains 579 documents. Many are from private archives in Pakistan and India, but a fair proportion have been selected from volumes of documents already published, like the works of Jawaharlal Nehru, the correspondence of Rajendra Prasad and other printed collections of documents, which are listed in its bibliography.

The volume is user-friendly. All the documents are arranged in a chronological sequence, preceded by a 45-page summary, giving the author, content and date of the document and the page of the volume, where it is to be found. Readers interested in pursuing specific themes can turn to the index; there are two of them, a subject index and a name index. An 81-page introduction, well annotated with citations to standard authorities, gives the editor's understanding of the communal question during British rule, from its very beginning. This makes it rather long. The portion of this introduction relevant for the period after 1935, starts only at page 31, after which the text of the introduction is further peppered with the serial number of the documents in this volume, wherever appropriate. There are biographical data about the important personages mentioned in the documents, in the form of footnotes. There is also a glossary of Indian words. Surprisingly, there is no list of abbreviations. Readers will presumably know what the AICC stands for, but they may have to think a little to realize that *SWJN* means the *Selected Works of Jawaharlal Nehru*.

The editor has nowhere explained why he has chosen to divide the project in terms of calendar years. After all, the historical process is a continuous flow of events; bends and turning points in the stream of time are not necessarily to be found on 1 January of each year. One very good reason, to my mind, for making 1937 the beginning is that 'provincial autonomy', under the Government of India Act, 1935, became operational after the elections of 1937; the contrasting performance of the Congress party as between the Muslim-majority provinces and the Muslim-minority provinces, was a pointer to the future. The terminal year, 1947, was the year of independence and Partition.

Strictly speaking, the election results came out in February, and office acceptance by the Congress took place in the second quarter of 1937, not on 1 January. In 1939 the Congress ministries resigned, sometime in November, not on 31 December. The editor can justify his choice of starting the volume on 1 January 1937, by pleading that he had to give documents on the election campaign and on the uncertain political climate, between the declaration of the results and the assumption of office by the Congress, and to illuminate the state of tension among the contending political parties.

He can similarly justify ending at the end of 1939, to give documents on the immediate fallout of the resignation of the ministries and the celebration of the event by the League as a day of deliverance.

It will be interesting to see what yardstick the editor uses to split the remaining six and a half years, till 15 August 1947, into two volumes which have been promised. There are well-known landmarks for the editor to choose from—the session of the League in March 1940, which adopted the resolution on Pakistan, the British government's announcement in August 1940 that the minority groups will have a 'veto' on India's constitutional progress, the clause in favour of provincial option in the Cripps offer of 1942 and the failure of the talks at Simla, in June 1945. It is to be hoped that, in the introduction to the next volume, the editor gives the rationale for his periodization.

In the preface the editor has posed the following questions about the possible causes of the Partition of the subcontinent:

> The story of partition is, in fact, the story of opportunities missed and dreams shattered. The debate on partition raises a number of questions. Should partition be analysed only in terms of Congress-League strategies as is often done, or should the debate not be deepened by investigating the causes of the uneven socio-economic development of the bourgeois of the two sister communities? Did the Hindu bourgeois, having close links with the Congress Right and the Hindu Mahasabha, support a strong unitary centre while the Muslim bourgeois favour a weak federal Centre with autonomous provinces? How far the interests of the Hindu and the Muslim bourgeois converge on the question of partition? It is true that the Congress, as an umbrella party aspired to be a national organisation but was it not at every cross-road of constitutional dealings with the Muslims and other minorities not influenced by clever manoeuvring of communal elements inside and outside? The result was that the Muslim and other minorities lost faith in its national character. How did the Muslim League, which was in wilderness since the Khilafat days, rise from the ashes during the last decade preceding partition under the leadership of Jinnah, who, though tutored in the liberal and secular traditions of Dadabhai Naoroji and G.K. Gokhale, now totally transformed, propounded the untenable two-nation theory in total opposition to the composite cultural nationalism of the Congress? Jinnah's task was facilitated by the Hindu Mahasabha's strident advocacy of the *Hindu Rashtra*. (pp. vii-viii)

These are good questions, but not all of them can be answered within the time span of this project; one needs a larger time scale. However, some of these questions do get partial illumination from the documents assembled here. For example, the uneven development of the educated middle classes of the two communities in Bengal and the consequent competition for jobs and clamour for quotas and reservations is revealed, among others, in Doc. No. 409, where the Bengal governor concludes a letter to the Viceroy, saying, 'it is quite the biggest problem that has confronted the Bengal Government and involves every aspect of the communal question at some point or other' (p. 697). Equally relevant is the correspondence, between the Chief Accountant of the Reserve Bank of India and the Muslim Chamber of Commerce on the question of less than proportionate recruitment of Muslims in the staff of the Bank (Doc. Nos 79, 93, 127 and 284). The liberal nationalist face of the earlier Jinnah can still be seen in some of his speeches during the election campaign (Doc. Nos 1, 5 and 13), and even in his first press interview after the election results (Doc. No. 26). Nehru's electioneering speeches against Jinnah offended some Muslim sympathizers of the nationalist cause. One of them, Maulana Habib-ur-Rahman Ludhianvi, an old Khilafatist and founder of the Ahrar party, wrote critically to Nehru:

> The late Dr. Ansari had rightly remarked that there was no strife in India rather the pitch had been queered by the personal bickering of the leaders. . . . After so many years the environment is becoming amiable once again. We would do well if you do not let the harsh words spoil it. Your speech about Mr. Jinnah has been commented upon by the entire Muslim Press. Ideologically Mr. Jinnah is near to you. He is a moderate. None is better than him. Please try to bring him closer to you. (Doc. No. 18, p. 115)

What the documents do bring out, in disastrous detail, is how the wheeling and dealing of party politics and ministry making, plus a fair amount of egocentricity on both sides, prevented the creation of a united stand against the undemocratic constitution imposed on the people of this subcontinent by the Raj. This was further aggravated by the ideological stance of a communal nature of influential personalities like Sir Mohammad Iqbal and Vinayak D. Savarkar, who was, in 1937, released from the restrictions confining him to reside within the confines of the Ratnagiri district in Bombay Presidency. Certain letters of Iqbal obtained from a private collection in Karachi (the Shamsul Hasan Foundation), are a revelation. Doc. No. 37, shows a pan-Islamic thrust, Doc. No. 55, a strong anti-Congress bias and Doc. No. 81, shows Iqbal's belief that for the Muslims the ideals of Islam would be a far better guarantee of equality than Nehru's Bolshevik-inspired socialist ideas. Extracts from all three are included below:

Doc. No. 37, Iqbal to Jinnah, 20 March 1937:

> I suppose you have read Pandit Jawaharlal Nehru's address to the All India National Convention and that you fully realise the policy underlying it in so far as Indian

Muslims are concerned. . . . While we are ready to cooperate with other progressive parties in the country, we must not ignore the fact that the whole future of Islam as a moral and political force in Asia rests very largely on a complete organization of Indian Muslims. I, therefore, suggest that an effective reply should be given to the All India National Convention. You should immediately hold an All India Muslim Convention in Delhi to which you should invite members of the new Provincial Assemblies as well as other prominent Muslim leaders. To this convention you must re-state as clearly and as strongly as possible the political objective of the Indian Muslims as a distinct political unit in the country. It is absolutely necessary to tell the only problem in the country. From the Muslim point of view the cultural problem is of much greater consequence to most Indian Muslims. At any rate it is not less important than the economic problem. (p. 137)

(The speech of Nehru referred to in this letter is printed in this volume just before this, as Doc. No. 36. It was his speech to a Convention of Congress legislators in Delhi on 19 March 1937. It emphasized the need to work among the Muslim masses, 'provided we approach them rightly and on the basis of economic questions', p. 136.)

Doc. No. 55, Iqbal to Jinnah, 22 April 1937:

As the situation is becoming grave and the Muslim feeling in the Punjab is rapidly becoming pro-Congress for reasons which it is unnecessary to detail, I would request you to consider and decide the matter as early as possible. The Sessions of the All India Muslim League is postponed till August, and the situation demands an early re-statement of the Muslim policy. If the Convention is preceded by a tour of prominent Muslim leaders, the meeting of the Convention is sure to be a great success.

Doc. No. 81, Iqbal to Jinnah, 28 May 1937:

The League will have to finally decide whether it will remain a body representing the upper classes of Indian Muslims or Muslim masses who have so far, with good reason, taken no interest in it. . . . The Muslim has begun to feel that he has been going down and down during the last 200 years. Ordinarily he believes that his poverty is due to Hindu moneylending or capitalism. The perception that it is equally due to foreign rule has not fully come to him. But it is bound to come. The atheistic socialism of Jawaharlal is not likely to receive much response from the Muslims. The question, therefore, is: how is it possible to solve the problem of Muslim poverty? . . . Happily there is a solution in the enforcement of the law of Islam and its further development in the light of modern ideas. After a long and careful study of Islamic Law, I have come to the conclusion that if this system of Law is properly understood and applied, at least the right to subsistence is secured to everybody. But the enforcement and development of the Shariat of Islam is impossible in this country without a free Muslim State or States. . . . But, as I have said above, in order to make it possible for Muslim India to solve these problems, it is necessary to redistribute the country and provide one or more Muslim States with absolute majorities. . . . Perhaps this is the best reply you can give to the atheistic socialism of Jawaharlal Nehru. (pp. 183-4)

While Iqbal thus egged on Jinnah towards getting the Muslim community organized in favour of a separate political existence, the speeches of Savarkar and the activities of the Hindu Mahasabha generally (including crypto-Mahasabhaites within the Congress) were not conducive to communal harmony either. Doc. No. 166, gives an extract from the fortnightly report for the Central Province and Berar, for the first half of December 1937, with reference to a speech by Savarkar:

The burden of his speeches was that there must be Hindu rule as India is the land of the Hindus, and that Hindus should tolerate all minority communities except the Mohammadans because the latter would be certain to join Muslim invaders from the North when India obtains Swaraj. (p. 297)

By December 1939, Savarkar said the following at the twenty-first session of the Hindu Mahasabha in Calcutta:

We Hindus, in spite of thousand and one differences within our fold, are bound by such religious, cultural, historical, racial, linguistic and other affinities in common as to stand out as a definitely homogenous people as soon as we are placed in contrast with any other non-Hindu people—say the English or Japanese or even the Indian Muslims. That is the reason why today we the Hindus from Kashmir to Madras and Sindh to Assam will be a nation by ourselves—while the Indian Muslims are on the whole more inclined to identify themselves and their interests with Muslims outside India than Hindus who live next door, like the Jews in Germany. (Doc. No. 573, p. 947)

One of the special merits of this volume is that while amply documenting the political contest between the Congress and the Muslim League, and giving the points of view of other Muslim groups and associations like the Jamiyat al-ulama-i Hind (Doc. Nos 40, 135, 370 and 371) and the Ahrar party (Doc. No. 66, 72, 254 and 421), it also has many useful documents on the recrudescence of Hindu communalism, culled from the papers of B.S. Munje, M.R. Jayakar and newspapers and periodicals. One other set of papers that the editor should have examined in this connection, but has not, are those of K.M. Munshi, who was the Home Minister in the Congress government of the Bombay Presidency. Savarkar and a number of Maharashtrian Hindu Sabhaites lived in that province, and so did Jinnah himself. Munshi, like Malaviya, was of a

Hindu communal frame of mind, and it would have been illuminating to have something from his papers or his notings as Home Minister.

One oft-repeated topic in connection with the Partition story is the refusal of the Congress to form coalition governments with other parties, especially the Muslim League. The Congress thus lost the prospect of developing a cross-communal alliance, like the Unionist Party of the Punjab, and pushed Fazlul Haq, the popular Krishak Praja leader of Bengal, towards an alliance with the Muslim League. In his memoirs Khaliquzzaman had made a big issue of the failure to create a Congress-League coalition in UP. The documents in this volume, which deal with this are Doc. Nos 39, 41, 43, 45 and 48. What Nehru wrote, on 30 March 1937, about this is worth quoting. It is not a new discovery, it has already been published in the *Selected Works of Jawaharlal Nehru,* Vol. VIII, from where it has been printed here at Doc. No. 41. It reveals his mind set:

> I am entirely opposed to this as I am opposed to all pacts and coalitions with small groups at the top. So far as I know my colleagues of the Working Committee are also opposed to it. (p. 141)

Well said, about small groups; but what about a situation where the Congress was in a minority, a small group, and the biggest single group in the Bengal Legislative Assembly was a non-League Muslim party, like the Krishak Praja Party? Historians from West Bengal and Bangladesh have passed adverse judgement on the Congress High Command's attitude to this question. We would have expected—but do not get—some documents on the abortive coalition efforts between Congress and the Praja party just after the elections in this volume. Eyewitness accounts by Abul Mansur Ahmad and Humayun Kabir are well-known sources. If these are dismissed as having been written long after the events they narrate, contemporary evidence does exist in the AICC papers and, more fully, in a file among the India Office Records (in the L/P and J sequence) entitled 'Formation of the Government in Bengal'. It is a pity that the editor has overlooked this.

While on Bengal, it is also necessary to point out that there is one glaring omission among the many archives and repositories explored by the editor to select documents—the Netaji Research Bureau in Calcutta. After all, Subhas Chandra Bose was the president of the Congress in 1938. While some letters from Bose (found in other collections) have been quoted, resources of that important institute have not been tapped. Similarly no effort has been made to explore archives in Bangladesh or Assam.

Nehru's fond belief was that since the election results showed that the Muslim League represented only the upper strata of Indian Muslims, the Congress which, had a socio-economic programme would be able to widen its support base among the Muslim masses by a mass contact programme (Doc. Nos 57, 61, 64 and 65). He was encouraged to do so by suggestions from young Muslim activists, from Meerut (Doc. No. 121). But by early July 1939, Nehru had to admit that the programme had been a failure. He wrote to Rajendra Prasad:

> It is true that in spite of our efforts, the situation has deteriorated and it may be said that there is more general ill-will among the Muslim masses towards the Congress than there has been at any time in the past. (Doc. No. 417, p. 707)

Jinnah and the Muslim League made it clear that they regarded the mass contact campaign, as a hostile act towards them, aimed at undermining the potential vote bank of the League. The observations of the president of the Jamiyat al-ulama of Bihar, Phulwari Sharif in November 1939, are worth quoting:

> But in launching this scheme the Congress committed two blunders. Firstly it was wrongly called Muslim Mass Contact, which led the Muslim leaders to believe that the Congress is attempting to alienate the Muslim mass[es] from their true leaders simply to capture their votes. This move of the Congress also provoked the Muslim leaders to oppose the Congress. Congress should not have started Muslim Mass Contact as there is nothing like Sikh Mass Contact, Christian Mass Contact. It simply developed a deep-rooted aversion for the Congress. (Doc. No. 511, p. 855)

This observation occurs in a 12-page statement; although some of its remarks are specific to the province of Bihar, one other general criticism it made of the Congress leadership was very valid:

> While the Nationalist and the Congressite Muslims openly condemn the reactionary and communalist movements of the Muslims, the Hindu leaders of the Congress do not condemn their co-religionists. The Hindu papers which claim to speak for the Congress, do not criticise them at all. Neither Gandhiji nor Panditji ever decry the misleading and inflammatory statements of Mr. Savarkar and Dr. Moonje. Panditji used to criticise them a few years ago; but there seems to be a distinct change in his attitude. (p. 863)

This long statement, from a nationalist Muslim leader of Bihar, was sent to the All India Congress Committee in November 1939. The editor has found it among the AICC papers.

There are similar documents revealing the misgivings felt by Muslim sympathizers of the Congress at the acts of omission and commission by the provincial governments and by the Congress party rank and file, for example, there is a letter from a moderate Muslim politician Khan Bahadur Mohammad Ismail of Bihar to Rajendra Prasad (Doc. Nos 133 and 143) and from K.M. Ashraf to Mahabir Tyagi (Doc. No. 208).

As the Muslim political classes increasingly began to consider the Congress provincial governments to be 'Hindu Raj', there emerged paper schemes for amending the Government of India Act; these in different ways anticipated the formation of Pakistan. Some visualized a confederation of the various provinces and the princely states, some others planned the grouping of provinces in terms of cultural zones, and a few thought of two separate sovereign states. By using the index under 'Pakistan' and 'Pakistan scheme', the reader will be able to get an idea of them. One of them was designed by no less a person than the Punjab premier, Sir Sikander Hayat Khan, which visualized an All India Federation on a regional basis, where there would be seven zones (Doc. No. 424). A remark of the editor indicates that he agrees with K.K. Aziz that Jinnah at that time did not want a total separation and was uneasy about the use of the word Pakistan (p. 704, fn. 3). That the young dreamers of Pakistan were not simply thinking on religious and cultural lines, but had a hard-headed awareness of economic realities and wanted the future Pakistan to be viable, is revealed in the letter of Ahmad Bashir, Secretary, Pakistan Majlis, Lahore, to Jinnah, on 22 March 1939:

> The Cultural Zone Scheme casts aside the half of the Eastern tracts of Kashmir and the Punjab and includes Bundelkhand instead. This Eastern portion of the Punjab and Kashmir possesses the richest mineral and economic resources of Pakistan. I may bring it to your kind notice that the Mandi Hydro-Electric Power Station in the Kangra valley, not only supplies electric power to about three-fourths of the Punjab but is also a potential source of revenue to the Province. If Kangra valley is seceded from the Punjab it will be a severe blow to its economic order, and a substantial gain of Hindu India. (Doc. No. 373, pp. 630-1)

By early August 1939, most of these schemes were in Jinnah's hands, and at his instruction they were sent to Liaquat Ali Khan for circulation to members of the Working Committee of the League (Doc. No. 430). This must have come as a disappointment to Liaquat, because only two months earlier he had written to Jinnah, hoping for a Congress-League settlement, being encouraged by a conversation with young Muslim members of the Congress:

> Mian Iftikharuddin of Punjab, and Dr. Zaheer and Sajjad Zaheer, all young Congressmen have had talks with me up here. They are most anxious that there should be a settlement between the League and the Congress as they feel that the country cannot progress any further without such a settlement. They gave me to understand that the left wing of the Congress is most anxious for a settlement.

They say that they will force the hands of the Congress High Command to acknowledge the League as the only representative organisation of the Musalmans but desire that some face-saving device be found. I told them that the League was always willing for an honourable settlement and the responsibility for the present situation rested entirely on the Congress. . . . I was given to understand that the Hindus of the left wing of the Congress also were most anxious for a settlement. (Doc. No. 406, p. 688)

Those who have followed the small print of the detailed constitutional arguments about the reforms, from the publication of the Report of the Simon Commission, in 1930, to the passage of the Government of India Act, in 1935, are aware that the questions of provincial autonomy and the distribution of powers between the centre and the provinces were at every stage overshadowed by the interests of religious minorities in each province. The British Raj expected to use the special powers of the provincial governors and the powers of supervision, direction and control of the Governor-General to look after British imperial interests as well as the claims of the minorities in each province. The working of the constitution in the Congress ruled provinces altered these expectations. To push the claims of pan-Indian nationalism as understood by the Congress High Command the latter exercized its own parallel supervision, direction and control in the Congress-ruled provinces. This caused irritation in gubernatorial and Viceregal circles. In April and May 1939, this irritation is reflected in a number of letters exchanged amongst them, namely, Craik, Punjab governor, to Linlithgow (Doc. No. 408, especially paras 2 and 4), Haig, UP governor, to Linlithgow (Doc. No. 380) and Hallett, Bihar governor, to Linlithgow (Doc. No. 404, especially paras 4 and 13). None of these worthies, however, thought of implementing the Pakistan idea. Craik, on the contrary, wrote:

Though all these schemes are visionary and ill-defined, it would, I think be a mistake to assume that the Pakistan idea is dead in the sense that we shall hear no more about it. I feel that it will continue to figure prominently in the columns of the more irresponsible Muslim newspapers and to be ventilated on the platform, but as a possible solution of our present difficulties I do not think it merits serious consideration. (Doc. No. 408, p. 692)

The excellence of the contents of the volume should make it a much sought after reference medium. It is all the more important, therefore, to remove the many regrettable instances of mistakes at the editing or the copy-editing stage, and the many printing mistakes, before a second impression is released in the market.

One Past Two Histories

LAL BAHADUR VARMA

It should be obvious that *two* here does not stand for *one* plus *one*; it signifies the two opposite sides, antagonistic in nature. The past of the people who were arbitrarily divided on 14/15 August 1947 remains one, but it was differently projected even before the division and it was instrumental in causing that division. Once Partition materialized it was natural that all efforts should be made in Pakistan to justify it and at the least to flaunt the confidence of achievement. History alone could cultivate that confidence and sustain it. Since it was not a natural outcome but an artificial creation, the history to sustain it too had to be concocted. The result is that even after more than half a century of existence the rulers of Pakistan dare not provide the people their full history. The history available to the ordinary citizens of Pakistan is not only distorted, it is incomplete.

In India things are better but not totally satisfactory. The textbook history in India is biased often in a subtle way but sometimes quite blatantly also. The strides made in the academic world in the quality of historiography—in concept, commitment and methodology—do not percolate to the people and the general perception of history remains dangerously superficial and sectarian. History is an instrument for making history. With blunted or twisted instruments the endeavours do not yield the desired result. Generations fed on wrong histories seldom take right decisions.

It is with this perspective that it is proposed to outline the different approaches to the Partition of India in the two countries. For reasons of space, however it cannot be a thorough review of the historiography of the two countries. It is just a small survey of the interpretations of the division of India done immediately after the event. Many profound researches and the changing political climate have resulted in some objective and convincing interpretations. Historians, particularly in India, have presented a more objective view of the past but the common citizen in both countries continues to view the same facts differently believing in the interpretation of the establishment that is.

While studying the prejudices of historians at Sorbonne, Paris, under the caring but critical guidance of Raymond Aron, taking up the Partition of India was an obvious choice in order for me to understand the communal and nationalist bias of Man who is the subject as well as the object of history, as Aron puts it.[1] It is natural that the same facts and figures of history are looked at differently, but this is not always rational and not always acceptable to an impartial historian. A historian is supposed to outgrow his natural reaction and abide by the norms of his vocation. Thus political interests are outlined to show how a colouring of facts is brought about to suit communal and nationalist interests. This paper mostly covers the historical writing during the first 25 years of the existence of the two countries.

The Partition of India is as significant an event in the history of modern India as its independence from the British rule and it continues to overshadow almost every aspect of the life of the two countries and the relations between them. One of the *raison d'être* of Partition was that diagonally opposed interpretation of the events of history were seen with subjectivity playing a greater role than objectivity. The same subjectivity continues to colour the vision of historians of the two countries, even after 1947, strengthening the communal and nationalist biases in the historiography on both sides of the frontier. A historian is not supposed to follow but to shape public opinion, playing to the galleries is in the nature of a politician. If a historian is fascinated by this game he remains neither fish nor fowl—perhaps not even a red herring.

India as a cultural entity had never fully corresponded with India as a political entity. The political frontiers of kingdoms and empires kept on changing, expanding and diminishing, but never was politics comprehended in terms of unification and division. It was only in colonial India that India was 'unified' and then 'partitioned'.

Was Partition a design, a natural culmination or an error of judgement? What was the real problem? Was this problem solved by Partition? Was Partition inevitable? If not, how did it come about? Politicians can never give satisfactory answers to these questions but historians can. Unfortunately they too have not succeeded fully.

Generally Indian historians play the simplification game and blame both the imperialist design of *divide et impera* and the megalomaniac ambitions of Jinnah, who played into the hands of the colonial rulers. But there are others who take into account the divisive distinctions between Hindus and Muslims. Failures on the part of the Congress are also considered by some to be an important factor. But the general perception and textbook history continues to uphold the simpler explanation. On the other hand most of the Pakistanis historians blame the Hindus and the Congress. They try to deny British complicity because it hurts one's self-esteem when you admit to playing someone else's game.

The general opinions about Partition appear to be almost uniform in each country but different from that in the other country. People, politicians and historians seem to have similar points of view—more so in Pakistan. It becomes difficult for the common man to comprehend history, when the historian becomes slave of the point of view, which is coloured by communal or nationalist interests.

Coming to a closer examination of the historiography of the two countries we could begin with the present. The burning questions raised by the now well-known journalist Najam Sethi of Pakistan, which led to his incarceration, are very pertinent. He said in Delhi recently:

> After 50 years Pakistan is unable to agree upon who we are as a nation, where we belong, what we believe in, where we want to go. Are we Pakistanis first and Punjabis, Sindhis, Baluchis, Pathans or Muhajirs afterwards? Or vice versa? Do we belong to South Asia or to Middle East? Are we Muslims in a modern Muslim state? Or Muslims in an orthodox Islamic state? Are we supposed to be like Saudi Arabia and Iran which are orthodox Islamic states or like Jordan, Egypt, Syria and Algeria which are liberal Muslim states? If none of these fits the bill, what then? Whose version or vision of Islam or plan do we follow? The *Quran* and Sunnah say some. Well, if the Qaid-e-Azam and Allama Iqbal had their own interpretations of how the *Quran* and Sunnah were to be applied in the real life of a modern state like Pakistan, the problem has been compounded by the myriad interpretations of their interpretations. And the problem doesn't end there.[2]

It is the question of 'visions' and 'versions', which is crucial to this whole issue and remains pertinent and relevant today even more, than it did through the decades. This is because these have created problems regarding the past and are creating even more problems in the present. The 'visions' and 'versions' are not limited to Islam, they shape and deshape history too. If Sethi's questions could be scientifically answered and not only in Pakistan but in India too, it would be easier to understand the phenomenal event of Partition and much more that has followed in the two countries.

Similar questions could be framed in the Indian context too, though differently but with the same motive. Such questions demand explanation in terms of *raison d'être*, nature and social dynamics and the orientation of the state. They disturb not only the rulers, who have the power to deal with them in a way that suits them, but also sensitive and sensible historians who have to frame questions and then try to find out answers to them.

We could now peep into the textbook histories served to the youth of the two countries. The history of Pakistan is said to begin with the invasion of Mohammed bin Qasim. Some even talk of 5,000 years of Pakistan or present Mohenjodaro as the ancient model of Pakistan.[3] But these historians have not succeeded in letting people know about the continuous past of the area on which Pakistan was carved in 1947. There is no mention of the instable conditions in India due to which 'the Muslims did not have to face much opposition and conquered *the whole of India without any difficulty*' (emphasis mine).[4] Coming to modern times it is said that 'the British with the assistance of the Hindus adopted a cruel policy of exodus against Muslims after the War of Independence of 1857'.[5] And again 'the creation of Pakistan was in fact the fulfilment of the earnest desire of the Muslims of India to mould their lives according to the principles of Islam, which they found was not possible in the united India under the hegemony of the British.'[6] It is this distorted and even truncated history which poisons all those for whom it is meant.

Another textbook of Pakistan Studies meant for all graduate students, BA, BCom, BSc, MBBS and Engineering, could be taken as more representative because of its wider reach. It feeds its history to all the would be intelligentsia of Pakistan.[7] This book compares Jinnah with Washington, Bismark, Cavour, Garibaldi, Lenin and Ataturk but finds Jinnah more remarkable because while others assumed the leadership of traditionally well-defined nations and espoused their cause or led them to freedom, 'he created a nation out of an inchoate and downtrodden minority and established a cultural and national home for it. And all that within a decade.'[8]

What a glorious achievement but what a monumental contradiction in its concept! On the one hand Pakistan is projected as a well defined nation, which is incompatible with another nation and on the other a genius or a magician like Jinnah creates Pakistan out of almost nothing. Mostly based on the writings of I.H. Qureshi, who always talked of two imperialisms, the Hindu and the British, this book is a good example of 'Machiavellian history', that is, it presents only those facts that suit one's cause. This cause is generally that of the rulers not the people in whose name all political crimes are committed.

In India too well-known facts are interpreted differently and betray prejudices. A popular textbook prepared, according to the latest syllabi, by the National Council of Educational Research and Training, is relatively more balanced and concludes by underlining six causes of the Partition: (i) divide and rule policy of the British; (ii) two-nation theory of the Muslim

League; (iii) appeasement policy of the British; (iv) bungling by the British missions sent to India; (v) lack of cooperation between the Congress and League; and (vi) communal riots.[9] But obviously even this tempered interpretation does not point a finger towards the lapses and mistakes by the Congress and some of its leaders. Similarly there is a chapter on 'The Great Leaders of the National Movement'. It takes note of Dadabhai Naoroji, Surendranath Banerjee, Gopal Krishna Gokhale, B.G. Tilak, Lala Lajpat Rai, Subhas Chandra Bose, Jawaharlal Nehru, Sardar Vallabhbhai Patel, Maulana Azad, Rajendra Prasad and, of course, Mahatma Gandhi.[10] They are all Congress leaders making the national movement synonymous with the Congress, a distortion that continued full scale through the first 25 years of independence and continues even now. There is no mention of Bhagat Singh, B.R. Ambedkar and, of course, M.A. Jinnah. Inclusion of Jinnah as one of the 'greats' of the freedom struggle against the British should be a litmus test for the objectivity of the historical account of it.

Focusing on the historiography of the two countries, there are the following interpretations of the Hindu-Muslim relations in Indian history:

1. Hindus and Muslims formed two distinct nations, which were incompatible. It was the British presence that kept them together.
2. Hindus and Muslims, in spite of their differences had lived together for centuries. If there were points of discord and diversity, there were even more tides of unity. It was the colonial presence of Britain that emphasized and promoted differences rather than unity and obstructed the coming together of the two. Once their divisive presence was gone, these communities would learn to solve their problems among themselves.
3. During the colonial rule, the Muslim community had lagged behind due to several historical as well as psychological factors. So they needed reservation of some kind.
4. During the national movement and in the course of the growing, though limited, democratization of the government the struggle for power and pelf took a communal turn. The forces that analysed Indian society in terms of class not communities or castes could not play a decisive role and sectarian interests, which were tacitly encouraged and promoted by the ruling classes, succeeded in giving a communal twist to nationalist politics.

The first premise leads to the inevitability of Partition, while the others hold persons, parties and policies responsible for the Partition of the country and consequently question the indispensability of it. Pakistani historians, generally, go by the first argument and insist upon the inevitability of Partition, while Indian historians, with many differences of detail, generally, support one or the other of the latter remaining interpretations, of course with reservations and modifications.

Let us look at the opposite views in Pakistan and India regarding the inevitability of Partition. In Pakistan, Mumtaz Hasan is of the opinion that the creation of Pakistan was 'a logical conclusion' to the relations between the two communities of India.[11] Chaudhri Mohammad Ali, a financial expert, who rose to become the Prime Minister of Pakistan, thought that the 'social organization and *weltanschauung* of the two communities were fundamentally different and any idea of common nationalism would be nothing but an illusion and a snare for the Muslims of India.'[12] According to him, Hindus were the natural allies of the English and this had aggravated the situation. Only the creation of a Muslim state could have resolved the problem. According to K.K. Aziz, religion is an essential element of nationalism, particularly in the Orient. But religion was not the only bone of contention between the two communities of India, psychological factors, myths, symbols, fears and heroes also separate them. History itself divided them. 'There was a conflict between two civilizations,' he further added, 'and nothing but the creation of two different states could resolve the issue.'[13]

Ali Tayyeb takes a different line of argument. According to him, Partition was only the most recent example among a succession of rivalries, discords and separatist tendencies, which have always characterized Indian history. He argues that areas on the periphery had always revolted whenever the central authority was weak. This happened after the decline of the Mauryas, the Tughlaqs and the Mughals and took place without religion being a factor.[14] He explains the separation of Pakistan in terms of political geography as the inevitable evolution of Indian history. Some historians like Z.H. Zaidi say that the 'the phenomenon can be explained neither in terms of charismatic leadership, nor a feat of propaganda and organization, nor even as a response to the appeal to religious emotions . . . the idea of Pakistan appeals to the sense of the deepest yearnings in the heart of the ordinary Indian Muslim.'[15] Eminent Pakistani historian I.H. Qureshi, presents Mohenjodaro as the 'prehistoric model' of Pakistan.

On the other hand in India, many historians, particularly those who belong to what could be called the Allahabad School of History, Sir Shafat Ahmad, Tara Chand, Mohammad Habib, R.P. Tripathi, Beni Prasad, Nurul Hasan and others, never gave much importance to the difference between the two communities. According to them, both the Indian communities have influenced each other to the core. The present composite culture popularly known as 'Ganga-Jamuni' does not allow any separatist design.[16] Others who talk of predominance of the Hindus, also refuse to accept separation. According to K.M. Panikkar, the history of India is essentially the 'history of Hindu people' to which the contribution of 'Islamic culture' brought a larger perspective.[17] R.C. Majumdar is of the opinion that Islam was never assimilated into Indian culture and, therefore, a permanent gulf existed between the two. Militant Islam had little influence on Hindu social order and differences between them have remained what they had been for centuries.[18] With all his insistence on the difference and pre-eminence of Hindus, Panikkar, too, did not propose separation as a solution. He is very critical of 'religious fanaticism' of the Muslims but is equally opposed to the 'social fanaticism' of the Hindus.[19]

Insistence only on differences or similarities is an over-simplification of the historical process. The argument that religious based nationalism leading to the two-nation theory, was the basis of the inevitability of Pakistan fell flat on its face when Bangladesh was created. Similarly, overemphasis on unity amid diversity, and not allowing cultural diversity an opportunity to flourish, not promoting the march towards egalitarian-ism and, finally, flaunting but not nurturing democracy, secularism and socialism have exposed the fissures in the arguments of composite culture and the pluralistic Indian society.

Anil Seal has a point when he says that India was not a nation but 'a graveyard of nationalities of ancient conception and a cradle of modern nationalities struggling to be born'.[20] Any objective observation of the Indian subcontinent putting country, nation and state in their proper per-spective will find that India has been neither one nor two nations. It is a country of nations and nationalities in different stages of evolution and maturity. The process has undergone catalysis several times with a negative as well as a positive impact accelerating or obstructing the natural process. The inevitability of Pakistan cannot be explained and understood in isolation. The myths, symbols, icons, heroes and villains, trends and tendencies of Indian history have to be again explained and understood in terms of the motive forces of society in the light of the latest researches in human history and with the help of the objective, yet committed, creativ-ity of the historian. For example, the plurality, adaptability and tolerance of Indian culture have to be put in their proper perspective. These attributes cannot be taken for granted. A society that breeds, tolerates and even justifies untouchability cannot be hailed only for having underlined *atmavat sarva bhuteshu* (all living beings as self) and a society that calls foreigners *mlechchha* should not be *glamourized* for having said *vasudhaiva kutumbakam* (the world is a family).

Indian society was like a traditional Japanese house with only four outer walls, the internal space was divided according to need. If a guest arrived an additional room could always be created. But nobody was allowed to build a house next door. Muslims were certainly not the first to come to India as aggressors. But those who had come earlier—the Aryans (now controverted), Greeks, Kushans, et al., merged into, even converted, the indigenous Indian society. Muslims not only refused to merge and get converted, they started converting the indigenous population. Thus arose a challenge before the toleration, plurality and catholicity of traditional Indian society which it failed to meet. The failure continues. Coexistence on egalitarian terms and democratic values were never cherished and promoted in traditional Indian society. Patriarchal, patronizing and parochial tendencies have shaped the Indian psyche in such a way that it is difficult to outgrow them. No wonder even the Muslims of India are less democratic and more hierarchy-ridden than elsewhere.

It was in such a society that the British experimented with all that was necessary to run a colonial and yet indispensably modern state. The outcome of this was a stillborn middle class, which remained crippled, dependent and blunted. Capitalism, nationalism, liberalism—nothing emerged and developed naturally here. The old was sick and dying but never died. The new was born and budded, but never blossomed. Generally there was an element of sham, show and superficiality in the individuals and communities that emerged in modern India. All the unresolved problems of Indian society mushroomed with the first shower of modernization. And there was a plethora of contradictions when the principal contradiction was posed as one between British colonialism and Indian nationalism. Any attempt to resolve the principal contradiction in a given society ignoring or sidetracking others, which are as effective, create more problems than it solves. One has not to go far to find a testimony of this. The India of today is a glaring example of unconsummated nationalism, weakened, though yet surviving, feudalism and rehegemonizing neo colonialism in a new form even after the glorious endeavour of the freedom struggle.

With this kind of perspective the creation of Pakistan can be better understood. The heroes and villains will appear less heroic or villainous and more as instruments of history. While making history they will appear also as products of history. Such a history may not promote antagonism and belligerence but comprehension and compatibility.

Even the most catholic view of history will not be able to absolve the British government and put the total sin of Partition on the head of the two warring communities of India, on their parties or on their leaders. While one pole of over-simplification lays the burden on the head of the involved communities, the second pole makes the colonial rulers out to be the sole culprits. But this explanation is too simplistic to be correct. We shall now see how the role of the British is viewed from the two sides of the frontier.

One protagonist of the Hindu-Muslim common cause, Ram Gopal, puts total blame on the calculating politics of the British. He points out how the British manipulated the Aligarh establishment to widen the gulf between the two.[21] Pattabhi Sitaramayya, the Congress leader and historian, emphasizes that the British played the same game everywhere they ruled. In the USA they encouraged the northern states against the southern states, in Ireland, Ulster against the rest of the country and, in India, they showed partiality to one community and to the native princes.[22] This view is corroborated by B.K. Gupta who says that as the Congress grew stronger, the British pitted Hindus against Muslims, princes against the bourgeoisie and moderate constitutionalists against the extremist followers of Tilak.[23] K.M. Panikkar underlines the same divisive policy in the organizing of the army into communal regiments, like the Dogra, Sikh, Rajput, etc. Tara Chand blamed the British on an idealist and philosophical plane when he wrote that they had failed to nurture confidence and harmony which should be the primary duty of any regime among the people. This appears to be a naive argument, but in the final analysis it implies the British attempt to keep India divided.

However, amidst this kind of credulous *naïveté*, there are mature assessments too. Two senior leaders of the Socialist Party, Ashok Mehta and Achyut Patwardhan, wrote a very perceptive pamphlet, *The Communal Triangle*, succinctly propounding the view that the British formed the base of the communal triangle, the other two arms being the Hindus and Muslims.[24] But others who blame the British for the divide, attribute to Indians such innocence as they did not have and such subtlety to the British as they were not capable of.

On the other hand, in Pakistan many writers absolve the British of even the natural divisive attributes of a foreign ruler. G.W. Chowdhury is of the opinion that the British neither provoked nor encouraged the differences between the two communities. Instead, their sincere goal was to leave India unified at the glorious end of their rule.[25] Aziz Ahmad also absolved the British and argues that Partition was the direct consequence and a logical culmination of a policy started by Syed Ahmad.[26] This logic is extended to say that the British were forced to accept Partition. I.H. Qureshi, the premier historian of Pakistan, strongly affirms that British imperialism was never an ally of the Muslims. On the contrary, he argues, it remained fundamentally opposed to them.[27]

It would have been a sad commentary on the historiography of the subcontinent if it had remained at that. Happily there are several historians on both sides of the frontier whose interpretation can be summarized in the words of K.K. Aziz: 'Indians divided themselves and left it to the British to use it.'[28]

It should not be difficult to understand why most historians accepted a simplistic interpretation of the Partition during the first few decades of freedom. Those were the days of the Congress supremacy in India and of the Muslim League in Pakistan. The general tendency was, therefore, to give credit to the Congress for the independence of India and to the League for the creation of Pakistan. Historians more or less toed this 'nationalistic' line and were not able to cultivate the courage of conviction to swim against the tide.

The Congress had all along the freedom struggle insisted on the one nation theory and had castigated anyone who pointed to any kind of fragmentation in Indian society. But subsequently, the leaders with fatigue and frustration accepted Partition. They did not quite develop a democratic temper and cherished their self-righteousness. Accepting one's own mistakes and shortcomings is part of the democratic process, which was never genuinely nurtured in India, and is not evident even today. Under such circumstances the blame was thrown on somebody else's shoulders. It did not require any great ingenuity to brand the British as bandits—they were, of course, the cruel colonial rulers. The thesis would be undisputable and incontrovertible for the common folk. Indian historians had generally tried to prove worthy fighters on the front of nationalism. They worked hard to substantiate this political line.

In Pakistan, of course, in the immediate post-independence period, things had to be different. If it were a British game how could Jinnah be the father and the Muslim League the mother of Pakistan? The more the British were proved to be anti-Muslim and pro-Hindu the more Herculean the task for the creators of Pakistan would appear. This alone would be the *raison d'être* of overlooking the obvious. Recent trends, moreover, of finding layers of historical reality have not yet reached textbooks and the general perception of history. Providing history not in terms of the handiwork of heroes and villians but as the product of social dynamics has not yet been fully realized in Pakistan—and, to a lesser extent, in India too.

Muslims, like Hindus, are not a homogenous monolith and yet at different junctures of history they have been portrayed as such. They had developed a peculiar psyche. Though a minority and mostly a product of religious conversion in India and that too from the downtrodden 'have not' castes, they had some psychological relief in Pakistan of belonging to a dominant and ruling religion. The Muslims of undivided India did not grasp the political reality after 1857 and felt dethroned. They never considered Hindus as their equals. But after 1857 they were condemned by the British as the main culprits of the 'mutiny', segregated by the Hindus and lost all their psychological and economic advantages. According to Aziz 'they got more and more alienated and lost', what he calls, 'their confidence in themselves and hope'.[29]

In the twentieth century, with the national awakening spreading and the process of self-government broadening, the Muslims faced a peculiar problem. The only ideology acceptable to all and sundry could be nationalism, which went along with liberalism. In a liberal democracy Muslims thought that they would remain a permanent minority to be oppressed, suppressed and exploited by the 'revengeful' Hindus—the permanent majority. Therefore, if they got integrated into the national movement they would remain a minority and if they wanted a Muslim fraternity they would have to be pan-Islamic. When the Muslim League was founded in 1906 it was not any more popular than the early Congress launched two decades earlier.

The Congress and its leaders, particularly Azad and Nehru, branded the League as 'negative'. Maulana Azad went on to call the League the 'creator of Pakistan'. Humayun Kabir has rightly pointed out that Jinnah is usually painted in a rather 'cavalier fashion'. Sinha sweepingly asserts that 'from Syed Ahmad to Jinnah, they all played in the hands of the British'.[30] He goes to the extent of comparing Jinnah with Hitler. For some others the importance of Jinnah lay in his becoming a symbol of separation and power. B.R. Nanda, the famous historian-biographer stresses this point differently: 'If Nehru was rather hot-tempered, even Gandhi with all his humility, Rajagopalachari with his *sang froid*, Subhas Bose with his radicalism and Rajendra Prasad with his sense of fair play, did not succeed in negotiating with Jinnah.'

In Pakistan, obviously, the argument is built around the fact that the British actually conspired with the Hindus against the Muslims. It is true that after the revolt of 1857, the British became very suspicious of the Muslims and discriminated against them but due to several factors, by the end of the century things had taken another turn. W.W. Hunter played no small role in this reconciliation, his book proved to be a turning point.[31]

Subsequently Aziz endorses the fact that the Muslims were the natural allies of the English for the following reasons: they were not agitators and did not believe in the agitational politics of the Congress; they were nearer to Christians than the Hindus; they respected the literature and philosophy of the English; the English were powerful and, therefore, the Muslims knew that the English alone could help them; there is an Islamic injunction that the Muslims must respect the established power and the English were the established rulers; and, finally, there was an immediate gain for the Muslims in being on the side of the rulers.[32]

The general tendency is, therefore, to insist on Muslims, Muslim League and Jinnah being responsible for creating Pakistan. The essence of this argument is seen in the vehemence of Qureshi when he argues that the Muslims had snatched their country away from two imperialisms—Hindu and British.[33] There seems to be a general uniformity among Pakistani historians on the role of Jinnah in the the creation of Pakistan. Jinnah once boasted that he created Pakistan with just his secretary and the typewriter. And for obvious reasons this view is endorsed in both countries. V.P. Menon, who played a crucial role during the transfer of power agreed that Jinnah created Pakistan almost alone. But the basic difference lies in the moral connotation of the two evaluations. While Jinnah is a supreme hero in Pakistan, he is a villain of the first order for the same deed in India.

Let the creation of Pakistan be a tragedy as perceived in India, or a triumph as in Pakistan, but calling it the creation of an individual and his party is not only history that is not genuine but it also displays a lack of a sense of social responsibility on the part of the propagandists—be they politicians, historians, teachers or just ordinary citizens. But this has been the general practice in spite of the fact that the historiography of the freedom struggle and Partition has undergone several modifications, particularly in India.

While during the first few decades of independence in India people never cared to probe into the Congress hand even if it were indirect in the Partition, in Pakistan the onus has been on the Congress. But here lies an irony. If the Congress was responsible for the miseries and deprivation of Muslims they were also indirectly responsible for giving the Muslims their homeland. This is why, without determining the role of the Congress in the creation of Pakistan, the writers simply put the full blame on the party. Abdul Aziz dedicates his trenchant pamphlet 'Discovery of Pakistan' to the victims of Brahminism and stresses upon the complicity between the Brahmins and the British.[34] Qureshi underlines the fact that the Congress refused to recognize the Muslim League as the third party and enumerates the wrongs done by it to the Muslims, more particularly after the elections of 1937. According to him, it was the misrule of the Congress that led the Muslims to observe the 'Deliverence Day' when the Congress ministries resigned and that even when the Congress accepted Partition it was sheer opportunism and deception.[35] According to C.M. Ali, the Congress wanted to inherit power all alone.

The Congress is criticized in India, too, but in a more nuanced manner. Even Nehru had accepted that the Congress had a 'Hinduized look'. Some historians have noted that behind the secular facade of the Congress there was, what is called by D.G. Dalton, the 'trans-political politics' of Gandhi. Some have noted that the Congress attracted Muslims of religious inclination, like members of Jamiyat al-ulama. The Congress is also blamed for not laying due emphasis on the diversity of India and being overemphatic about the unity aspect. According to B.N. Pandey, the Congress had only two alternatives *vis-à-vis* the League, that is, either to treat it as an enemy or as a concerned party. In the first case the Congress should have left no stone unturned to uproot it and in the latter case it should have come to some understanding with the League. He adds that in both the cases the unity of India could have been preserved. But the Congress was in a dilemma and continued to hesitate. It was British politics that rendered the creation of Pakistan possible and the Congress only concretized this possibility.[36] Campbell-Johnson, the Secretary of Mountbatten, the last Viceroy, officially responsible for actually making Pakistan a reality affirms that as the British aided the Congress in keeping its place, so did the Congress in making the Muslim League live and survive.[37]

C.H. Philips, in his introduction to the book he edited on the Partition of India makes a valid point. In India, the Partition is considered a tragedy, a dismemberment for which naturally one tends to find causes, fix responsibility and to show the nefarious consequences of it. In Pakistan one insists on the indispensibility of a Muslim state and finding the roots of such a state in history.[41] In India, Partition is a historic evil and in Pakistan, it was only the solution to a historic evil.[38]

In India the two-nation theory of Jinnah and the Muslim League is criticized. But Savarkar and Lala Lajpat Rai spoke almost the same language. Savarkar, who led the Hindu Mahasabha talked of two nations even before the Lahore resolution was passed. Lajpat Rai was prepared to give autonomy to areas with Muslim majority. Both of them were politicians, with a rightest orientation, but even historians, like R.C. Majumdar and K.M. Panikkar agreed that there were two distinct elements in Indian society.

We may conclude by emphasizing that the cliche-ridden and biased history being propagated in the two countries, due to indulgence of historians or in spite of them, caters to only sectarian beliefs and works like slow poisoning on a community. Historians on both sides of the frontier have a well defined two pronged task. Firstly, to probe deeper and explore wider to unravel the factors that led to Partition. It, however, must be made clear that arguments against Partition should not be aimed against the existence of Pakistan, which is a reality and cannot be wished away. Vehement opposition to the creation and even the existence of Israel and then accepting it as a historic reality by the Arabs need to be kept as an example to be followed. Secondly, historical researches need to be taken to the people by the experts through popular writing and textbooks of all levels. They should incorporate latest researches and should be regularly revised under authoritative guidance and supervision. Ivory tower academics are not only irrelevant, they are becoming an unnecessary burden on society.

NOTES

1. See Raymond Aron, *Dimension de la Consience Historique* (in French) (Paris, 1961).
2. Najam Sethi, quoted by Dinesh Kumar, in *Times of India*, 6 June 1999.
3. See I.H. Qureshi, *A Short History of Pakistan* (Karachi, 1967).
4. M.I. Rabbani and M.A. Sayyid, *An Introduction to Pakistan Studies* (Lahore, 1989), p. 3.
5. Ibid., p. 7.
6. Ibid., p. 8.
7. See M.D. Zafar, *Pakistan Studies* (Lahore, 1990).
8. Ibid., p. 26.
9. D.N. Kundra, *History and Civics* (New Delhi, 1997), p. 151.
10. Ibid., p. 156.
11. Mumtaz Hasan, 'The Background of Paksitan', in C.H. Philips and M.D. Wainwright, eds, *Partition of India—Policies and Perspectives, 1935-47* (London, 1970), p. 329.
12. Chaudhri Mohammad Ali, *Emergence of Pakistan* (New York, 1967), p. 37.
13. K.K. Aziz, *The Making of Pakistan: A Study in Nationalism* (London, 1967), p. 145.

14. Ali Tayyeb, *Pakistan, A Political Geography* (London, 1966), p. 96.
15. See Z.H. Zaidi, 'Aspects of the Development of Muslim League Policy, 1937-47', in Philips and Wainwright, eds, op.cit., p. 274.
16. What is called the Allahabad School of History is no school at all in the strict sense of the term. It is known for its emphasis on composite culture.
17. K.M. Panikkar, *Survey of Indian History* (London, 1947), p. 25.
18. R.C. Majumdar, *History and Culture of the Indian People*, Vol. IX (Bombay, 1967), pp. 615-31.
19. Pannikar, op.cit., p. 26.
20. A. Seal, *The Emergence of Indian Nationalism* (London, 1968), p. 339.
21. See Ram Gopal, *Indian Muslims A Political History (1858-1947)* (London, 1959).
22. See Pattabhi Sitaramayya, *History of the Indian National Congress*, Vols I and II (Bombay, 1947).
23. *Journal of Indian History* (August 1963), p. 29.
24. See A. Patwardhan and A. Mehta, *The Communal Triangle* (Ahmedabad, 1942).
25. See G.W. Chowdhury, *Pakistan's Relations with India 1947-67* (London, 1968), p. 747.
26. See Aziz Ahmad, *Islamic Modernism in India and Pakistan 1857-1864* (London, 1967).
27. I.H. Qureshi, *Struggle for Pakistan* (Karachi, 1965), p. 309.
28. Aziz, op.cit., p. 95.
29. Ibid.
30. See Sasadhar Sinha, *Indian Independence in Perspective* (Bombay, 1964).
31. See W.W. Hunter, *The Indian Musulmans* (London, 1872, repr. 1971).
32. Aziz, op.cit., p. 30.
33. Qureshi, *A Short History of Pakistan*, op.cit., p. 310.
34. See Abdul Aziz, *Discovery of Pakistan* (Lahore, 1964).
35. Qureshi, *A Short History of Pakistan*, op.cit.
36. B.N. Pandey, *The Breakup of British India* (London, 1981), p. 216.
37. Alan Campbell-Johnson, *Mission with Lord Mountbatten* (London, 1951).
38. See 'Introduction' to Philips, and Wainwright, eds, op.cit.

The Imperialist Distortion of the Partition of India: A Historiographical Critique of the Writings of Percival Spear and H.V. Hodson

BISHWA MOHAN PANDEY

The Partition of the Indian subcontinent into two sovereign states has been an issue of lively debate right from the day it was thrust upon the people, in 1947. What is noteworthy is that the discussions still remain as inconclusive as they were 50 years ago. The factors and circumstances which shaped the course of action, leading to the vivisection of India have generated differing responses and reactions and have been interpreted variously. Opinions are sharply divided over the role and responsibility of different parties, organizations and personalities involved in the tragic event that preceded India's independence. Broadly speaking, these interpretations could be categorized into three groups, representing the three sides, which were actively involved in the real drama of Partition—British, Pakistani and Indian.

The Partition of India found its earliest echoes in the colonial writings. Although its historians, including both amateurs and professionals, claim impartiality and objectivity, a close scrutiny and careful analysis of their writings reveal that nearly all of them share common biases, which differed only in relation to their personal background and group affiliations. It is, therefore, all the more pertinent to assess the extent of the gap between their professed claims of impartiality as historians and the histories they actually wrote. The historians of the imperialist school have been engaged in the presentation of India's Partition in a way that could justify the blunders of the colonial regime. India's socio-cultural history has been exploited to emphasize the theory of 'communal divide' and assert that its manifestation led to the emergence of communalism and ultimately to the Partition.

The historians of this group have produced a huge corpus of literature on the Partition. Some prominent scholars of this school are E.W.R.

Lumby,[1] David Page,[2] H.V. Hodson,[3] R. Coupland,[4] Percival Spear,[5] Alan Campbell-Johnson,[6] Penderel Moon,[7] Hugh Tinker,[8] C.R. Attlee,[9] H. Bolitho,[10] Peter Hardy,[11] C. Jeffries,[12] L. Mosley,[13] R.A. Smith,[14] P.N.S. Mansergh,[15] C.H. Philips,[16] R.J. Moore,[17] etc. These scholars have constructed highly biased and prejudiced versions in the name of objective history. It is against this background that the present paper seeks to analyse the world of colonial historiography in order to lay bare both the intricacies of the colonial period and the exploitation of the past by the alien rulers. The present exercise is limited to an analysis of the writing of Hodson and Spear, as these two historians, by and large, represent the entire group consisting of those who actually served the colonial regime and wrote on the subject, the former as an administrator turned historian and the latter as a professional historian.

Hodson remained associated with the British India government from 1930 in different capacities and was the Reform Commissioner, Government of India, during 1941-2. Spear, on the other hand, was Professor of History at St. Stephen's College, Delhi, with only a very brief participation in the colonial government during the Second World War. Both of them had first-hand knowledge of Indian realities and personally watched the last days of the British Raj in India. Though, they were better placed to explain events, they utilized history to defend the end of the empire as the completion of the English mission, to explain Partition as the natural result of Indian realities and to project independence not as the fulfilment of the national movement but as a generous gift of British liberalism. Moreover, the writings of these two historians reflect the impact of the classical imperialist ideology, whereas the writings of later historians of this genre reflect the reaction against nationalist assertions.

A number of factors went into the shaping of Spear and Hodson's approach to modern Indian history in general and to Partition in particular. Firstly, they were actively associated with the colonial regime in India when the Indian national movement under the leadership of Gandhiji and the Left was fatally eroding colonial hegemony. The colonial set-up, therefore, needed immediate ideological restrengthening. Secondly, communalism, which was a result of the 'divide and rule' policy of the British, was entering a violent phase, thereby affecting the freedom movement. Hence, it needed theorization by the imperial authority and a denial of the catalytic role of the British in its emergence, growth and fulfilment. Thirdly, the successful Socialist Revolution in Russia, its expansion and its unambiguous opposition to imperialism sounded an alarm. Fourthly, in the post-Second World War period the colonial policy needed defence so that the interest of this regime could remain safe even in the post-colonial period. That is why they needed fresh justification for their rule. Here it is pertinent to state that 'the classical imperialist historiography is mainly concerned with the rise, expansion and fulfilment of the British rule'.[18]

In tune with the colonial academic thinking, the Partition has been accepted as inevitable by both scholars. Spear traces the rise of the separatist tendency from the time of the Arab invasion of Sind, in the eighth century, while Hodson traces it back to the eleventh century, when Punjab was annexed by Mahmud Gazni. The former calls the medieval period of Indian history the Muslim period, and traces a separate identity for the Muslims right from the time of the Arab invasion. 'Muslims in India required separate treatment'[19] because 'unlike earlier invaders, Muslims could not be assimilated in the mainstream of Hinduism through the process of cultural adjustment and assimilation'.[20] This assimilation was not possible in the case of the Turks because they brought with them their own religion and culture.[21] Indian culture is regarded as heterogenetic, where there has been conflict between different traditions. This cultural conflict resulted in compromise, adjustment and impact. India has rightly been regarded as a melting pot of cultures by Spear, who asserted that, in spite of several cultural invasions, India has been able to maintain its uniqueness. However, he says that this cultural interaction produced strains and stresses, which inevitably led to the territorial division of 1947.

With a similar motive, but in a different tone, Hodson asserts the inevitability of Partition:

> What happened in 1947 was merely a by play, that the die was cast much further back, when the Cabinet Mission persisted in seeking consent to compromise rather than imposing compromise by arbitration or when Lord Wavell failed to secure National Government at Simla Conference or when Congress rejected Cripps offer in 1942 or when the Muslim League adopted Pakistan as its goal or when they failed to admit the Muslim League ministers in 1937 or at other dates perhaps earlier.[22]

Unlike Spear, he traces its roots from the eleventh century:

> The tale that ended in 1947 can be said to have had its beginning eight or nine centuries earlier. The transfer of power to two successor states was the end of the story, the preface of which was the annexation of the Punjab by Mahmood Gazni in 1018 AD and which began in earnest with the defeat of Prithviraj by Muhammad Ghori in 1192 AD.[23]

Thus, both scholars view Partition as inevitable and, to strengthen their assumption, they approach the medieval period with an imperial mindset. Spear calls it the Muslim period, because most of the rulers were Muslims. But he refrains from calling the modern period Christian though the rulers were all Christians. Hodson has nothing to say about the medieval period. He takes a long jump from the eleventh-twelfth century and comes to 1935, with the assumption that the Hindus and Muslims could not come together and this strengthened the emergence of a bipolar society. He asserts:

> What happened in 1947 was bound to happen. Linlithgow and Wavell, Mountbatten and Cripps, Gandhi and Jinnah, Sikandar Hyat Khan and Jawaharlal Nehru and all others were mere puppets moved by the historical forces which they had no power to deflect.[24]

The imperial school in general stresses the nature of Hindu-Muslim cultural contacts during the medieval and modern times. Spear, unlike Hodson, tries to buttress his hypothesis, by analyzing the socio-cultural aspects of medieval India. He relates the separatist tendency among Muslims to the nature of the proselytizing role of Islam in India. Amongst the various processes abetting the expansion of Islam, he lays emphasis on marriages between Central Asian Muslims and Indian women. He says that these Muslims never dissociated themselves from their original homeland and it is probably from among these groups that most of the later Muslim leadership emerged. They were responsible for generating 'a sense of separateness and a sense of mission which tended to bind together people of the most diverse racial and social origins into a cultural religious unity'.[25] This is apparently a rationalization of the hypothesis that the Muslims in India had a separate identity right from the period when Islam came to India and they consciously maintained it, thereby leading to the emergence of communalism.

The decline of the Mughals, the general antipathy of the Muslims towards Hinduism, the lack of a modern middle class amongst Muslims, etc., according to Spear, were also responsible for the emergence of communal-ism: 'The Mughal period was the classical phase of Islam in India and its decline had made Muslim community impoverished, divided and discredited.'[26] The Muslims had no middle class which could unify them. Hence, in order to arouse them they had to be made to feel that 'Islam was in danger'.[27] Islam and Hinduism have been depicted by Spear as antithetical to each other. He also said: 'Hindu feelings about the cows are as untranslatable into Western terms, as are Muslim feelings about idolatry and they are no less strong.'[28] In this way, his arguments were constructed around the nature of Islam and Hinduism which, he said, were responsible for the emergence of Muslim communalism and separatism culminating into Partition. The aim of these explanations were to construct a paradigm in order to absolve the colonial regime from any responsibility for the Partition.

The nineteenth century Indian renaissance finds a place in imperial writings but it has been interpreted as a divisive force. It was argued that Islam in India was politically depressed and culturally isolated in the eighteenth century.[29] In these circumstances an internal movement was started in Islam to purify it. The progress towards an Anglo-Islamic synthesis lagged a good generation behind that of the Anglo-Hindu synthesis.[30] Thus, Hindus and Muslims were further differentiated. Spear compares the reform movement among Muslims as a renewal or purification of the body of the people and says that then there was a movement of leaders which united in the Pakistan movement.[31] He further asserts that the impact of 'Westernization'[32] on Indian tradition through the introduction of English as the medium of instruction,[33] differed on religious lines. These movements underlined the distinct legitimacy and values of Hindu and Muslim civilizations, respectively. The political manifestation of these movements, he argues, were the Indian National Congress and the Muslim League, which spoke for the two nations.

Spear's explanation of the nineteenth century Indian renaissance and its effect and also of the foundation of the Congress and the Muslim League are distortions and attempts at a concealment of known facts. It is by now generally undisputed that the Indian renaissance was not a gift of the West. Similarly accusing the Indian National Congress of representing Hindu vision is ahistorical because it undermines the role of the nationalist Muslims, who were active in the Congress right from its inception. Further, to project the Muslim League only as a result of the Muslim reform movement is a concealment of the official encouragement given to it. Spear says that Sir Syed Ahmad's movement was inspired by the fact that the Muslims in India were a separate people or nation, that could not be absorbed into Hinduism and that the essence of Islam was consistent with the best that the West had to offer.[34] Thus, he suggests that Muslims came closer to the British due to elements of mutual commonality. 'Muslims preferred the British because they possessed more of a western outlook in their tradition',[35] and the Congress became 'both the cultural and political voice of the new Hindu India'.[36]

The initial stage of the national movement is called a mass movement by Spear, which he said got a Hindu character under the guidance of the

Indian National Congress. Contrary to known facts, he argues that Muslims allowed the Indian National Congress to become a dominantly Hindu body through their abstention.[37] He thus ignores the fact that Badruddin Tyabji presided over the third session of the Congress. He opines that Muslims formed the Muslim League in 1906, when they were alarmed at the Congress getting concessions. They demanded a separate electorate, which they got in 1909. The formation of the Muslim League by the élite to safeguard its interests is passed off as an act of the Muslim masses. Hodson says that with the formation of the Muslim League the conflict between the British government and the Congress became triangular and it was resolved only by the Partition of India.[38] On the issue of a separate electorate he says:

> Aware of the risk that one class or community might by virtue of its superior numbers, wealth and education come to dominate India's nascent political life and the counsels of the government, successive Viceroys supported the policy of separate communal or class representation.[39]

The impression is thus given that the British government was granting a major constitutional concession by providing a separate electorate. This imperial defence of the policy of divide and rule, was manifest in the form of the separate electorate provision of the Indian Council Act, 1909.

The aim of the Muslims in India, says Spear, became focused in the 1920s, especially in the phase of the post-non-cooperation movement: 'The end of Non-Cooperation left the Muslims as a whole disillusioned and fearful of their future.'[40] He further said that in the post-Khilafat period, the Hindu majority, personified in the enigmatic figure of Gandhi, seemed to be the main threat to a separate Muslim existence.[41] Also Indian Islam needed a more dynamic creed and a larger vision and they found this in the writings of Mohammad Iqbal: 'Sayyid Ahmad gave Indian Islam a sense of separate existence and Iqbal a sense of separate destiny.'[42] Spear has tried to malign the Gandhian leadership, which stood for communal harmony. Thus, he blames the Indian leaders of both communities for creating a separatist tendency.

The separatist movement got a further fillip towards the end of the 1920s. Spear asserts that the Muslim search for unity led to the reorganization of the Muslim League under the leadership of Mohammad Ali Jinnah and that the search for a positive programme became two dimensional, the first to safeguard the Muslim interest and the second, autonomy to Muslim majority areas. In 1930, Iqbal suggested the union of the Frontier Provinces, Baluchistan, Sind and Kashmir, as a Muslim state within a federation, while Rahmat Ali coined the term 'Pakistan',[43] in 1933. Spear summed this up when he wrote:

> The ideology of Iqbal, the visions of Rahmat Ali and fears of Muslims were thus united by the practical genius of Jinnah to bind Muslims together as never before during the British period and lead to effect an act of political creation.[44]

The constitutional reforms and growth of the national movement from the mid-1930s onwards further widened the divide between the two communities, argue both Hodson and Spear. To be more precise, the Government of India Act, 1935, was a turning point in the history of the Indian National Congress and the Muslim League *vis-à-vis* Hindu-Muslim relations. Spear believes that the Act of 1935 gave to the majority the power of cultural as well as political dominance over the minority thereby increasing their fear. The fear of dominance by one community over the other created an atmosphere, which made the Partition inevitable. According to Spear, in the late 1930s, the Congress was thinking not merely of getting rid of the British but of controlling India. Here they came up against the Muslims and henceforward the Congress was fighting on two fronts.[45]

The elections in the provinces to implement provincial autonomy, proposed in 1935, left the League in the wilderness in the six provinces and this made them regard the Congress as their mortal foe. The failure of the League in capturing power made the Partition inevitable. 'Muslims desired freedom from British as well as from Hindus', from here on, says Spear.[46] The result of the elections made the Muslims realize their twin weaknesses—disunity and lack of a mass base. They tried to overcome these under the leadership of Mohammad Ali Jinnah. Spear emphasized that the political foundation of Pakistan was laid down in 1937, when the Congress failed to accept the League as a coalition partner in the United Provinces.[47] He further argues that this failure on the part of the Congress was a bitter affront to the policy of cooperation and coalition of the Muslim League.[48] This 'converted a middle class Muslim nationalist movement into a popular Muslim resurgence'.[49]

Hodson assigns undue importance to the Act of 1935 for the growth of Muslim separatism. Jinnah blamed the Congress ministries of pursuing a Hindu policy. Hodson says that the religious or quasi-religious provocations were now combined with political and administrative accusations and that this resulted in Muslim apathy towards the Congress, which in turn resulted in Jinnah beginning to speak of two nations. The cry of 'Islam is in danger' was raised and the Congress Raj to the Muslims became a worse bogey than the British Raj had ever been. Hodson wrote that even the proposed federation could not have averted the Partition. R.J. Moore, who represents the latest trend in imperial writing, however, disagrees and says that a federation could have stopped the Partition.[50] Thus, imperial scholars accept the official stance of the Muslim League of putting the blame on the Congress. The intensification of the national movement because of the Congress rule is portrayed as giving a boost to the communal divide by these historians.

The imperialist historians criticize the Indian National Congress vehemently because by the late 1930s the anti-imperialist movement led by it showed signs of entering a decisive phase. They argue that the attitude of the Congress High Command and the Congress ministries, crystallized the Pakistan movement, sponsored by the Muslim League. Hodson says that the dictatorship of the Congress High Command heightened Muslim fears. Above all, the majority rule was seen to be Congress rule at the centre, dominated by the Hindu majority, through an organization, which brooked no opposition and refused to share its power. 'The conduct of provincial self-government from 1937-9 was a major cause of the spread of the two-nation theory and the Pakistan Movement.'[51] Hodson deliberately seems to forget that the Congress was leading a movement where unified command and strict discipline were needed.

The freedom movement and the Pakistan movement both entered the final stage during the Second World War. The colonial ideologues blame the Congress for the separatist tendency that became increasingly visible during this period. When the war broke out, and India also declared war, it was welcomed by the colonial regime and utilized by the League for the advancement of their goal. The Muslim League declared a 'Day of Deliverance' and 'Thanksgiving'. The Congress demanded the formation of a national government as a prerequisite for support in the war efforts, which was rejected by the colonial regime. The imperial authority then turned towards the Muslim League. Jinnah promised support on two conditions: justice and fair play for Muslims in the Congress-ruled provinces. He also wanted an assurance that no constitutional advance for India should be made nor any constitution framed or adopted without the consent and approval of the Muslim League. The government, for very obvious reasons, accepted the demands of the League and even encouraged it. The League passed the 'Pakistan Resolution' in March 1940, at its Lahore session, and the colonial government in turn promised full weightage to the minorities through the August Offer of 1940. This is a clear evidence of colonial and communal collaboration, which is refuted by the imperial ideologues.

Spear suggests that differences between the demands of the Congress and the League led to a deadlock, which steadily deepened the suspicions between the two.[52] He defends Churchillian imperialism, which denied India's right to self-determination as declared by the Atlantic Charter. The British government under Churchill did not want any reform in India. But Spear says that the constitutional deadlock was reached because the League insisted that any national government should be on a Hindu-Muslim 50-50 basis.[53]

Both Hodson and Spear, had served under the colonial regime during the Second World War, which is why they regarded the early years of the 1940s as crucial in the history of India. The best opportunity for reform came, says Hodson, in the form of the Cripps Proposals.[54] These were rejected by all parties though on varied grounds. The League rejected it because of a vagueness on the Pakistan issue. Gandhiji regarded it as a 'post-dated cheque on a crashing bank'. 'So the golden moment passed and with it the last real chance of establishing a united independent India. The rejection was a prelude to Partition.'[55] The failure of the Cripps Mission, Hodson says, was due to the differences among the Viceroy, Cripps and the War Cabinet, as well as among Indian leaders.[56] He too, like Spear, suggests that its failure widened the gulf between the Congress and the government and created frustration in the Congressmen.[57]

The Cripps Mission, which had been sent to India by the uncompromising Churchill under international pressure, was bound to fail. It was outdated, and both the colonial regime and the Home government allowed it to fail because of Cripps' association with Indian leaders. This proposal did not contain any major concessions but only future promises, yet it has been fulsomely praised by British historians. It was only an attempt to obtain India's cooperation in the war, but it succeeded in giving a fillip to the Pakistan movement, a fact denied by the imperialist historians.

The Quit India movement, which was the culmination of the freedom movement[58] has been interpreted as an 'insurrection'[59] or as a 'blunder committed by the Congress', which failed.[60] But it did not fail, rather it brought independence onto the Indian agenda. Spear says that the Congress had backed the wrong horse, which discredited it.[61] He further argues that during this period Muslim separatism had gained unprecedented strength and the League would not accept anything short of Partition. Where did this strength of the Muslim League come from? The imperial historians are silent because they know that the League's prestige was enhanced by the British regime itself. When the Congress sponsored movement entered its last phase, the colonial regime turned towards the League to counterbalance it.

The post-Second World War period was a difficult one for the British government so far as India was concerned. Due to recurrent economic losses, the Indian empire became a liability for the colonial regime. Economic pressures and the intensification of the national movement, leading to the erosion of the colonial hegemony, compelled the ideologues to devise new reasonings. Spear suggests that due to the Muslim suspicion of the Congress and Congress' underestimation of the League's strength, the British policy makers were put in a difficult position *vis-à-vis* the granting of self-government to a united India.

The new Viceroy, Lord Wavell, made efforts to reconstitute his Executive Council by inducting more Indians. Spear says that Wavell's task was to ensure cooperation between the two highly suspicious bodies, namely the Congress and the League, and the failure of cooperation would mean Partition. This became more apparent after the failure of the Simla Plan in 1945. Actually, the Simla Plan gave veto powers to Jinnah and both Jinnah and the British are equally responsible for its failure. But Spear does not say even a single word about this. Hodson writes that Lord Wavell convened the Simla Conference to discuss the formation of a 'politically representative' council.[62] Thus, he tries to conceal the real colonial motive by calling the communally planned body a representative body.

The Simla Conference failed due to the colonial and communal collaboration. Hodson says that the new Viceroy tried to solve the constitutional problem of India while the Secretary of State for India had his own formula to solve it.[63] He blames the Viceroy for its failure: 'If the Viceroy had been as adamant as Mr. Jinnah, the latter would have been obliged to give in.'[64] But Hodson again reiterates the inevitability of the Partition: 'All this may have been inevitable because the Muslim League's demand of Pakistan and the Congress demand of United India were incompatible.'[65] Both scholars fail to see the divisive forces let loose by the Simla Plan. It became certain at this time that Jinnah's consent was a necessary prerequisite for any future constitutional developments. But this has been consciously ignored and a blind eye turned to the catalytic role of the colonial regime in putting one community against the other.

The developments of 1945-6 have been highlighted by the imperialist historians to justify their preconceived conclusions, regarding the Cabinet Mission sent by the newly elected Labour government led by Attlee. It aimed at the preservation of a united India while giving reasonable satisfaction to the Muslims' claim to autonomy. Hodson asserts that the end of the war and the formation of the government by the Labour Party hastened the pace of events and heightened the hopes as well as reduced the patience of Indian politicians.[66] Hodson and Spear say that this attempt at reconciliation failed but both assign different reasons for it. Spear blames the Indian political parties: 'It failed because the commission was not enjoined to impose any solution,'[67] while Hodson blames the Labour government.

The Cabinet Mission, with its recommendations and its aftermath, is said to have further widened the gulf between the Muslim League and the Congress. The Mission rejected the Pakistan demand but by providing for the grouping arrangement there was implicit acceptance of it. When the Congress and the League interpreted it differently, the government sided with the latter. The Muslim League, refused to participate in the Interim Government and declared 16 August as 'Direct Action Day'. Spear writes:

> The terror that was unleashed could not be restrained within peaceful bounds. The hope of a united independent India was extinguished in the blood and monsoon passion of 1946.[68]

The colonial regime remained a silent spectator, a point not mentioned by either of the imperial historians.

Hodson says that both the Congress and the Muslim League took different stands. The former formed the National Government while the latter declared a 'Direct Action Day'. Spear suggests that the Partition became a necessity after the Cabinet Mission. He argues that henceforth there was a two-pronged strategy of the Muslim League, it continued violent riots and joined the National Government to wreck it from within. The League also boycotted the newly constituted Constituent Assembly, in December 1946. Thus, Spear concludes that after the Cabinet Mission the Partition of the Indian subcontinent was only a matter of time. But Hodson highlights the events of 1947 to justify his predetermined conclusion. In the beginning of 1947, Mountbatten replaced Lord Wavell as Viceroy. Hodson had a very soft corner for Mountbatten and tried to defend his actions.[69] He wrote that Lord Mountbatten wanted to have a united India, but it was impossible because division was opted for by the Indians themselves.[70] Hodson, working within a typical imperial framework, defends Mountbatten and goes to the extent of criticizing the Labour government. He starts with Atlee's Declaration, which he regards as an open license to Pakistan,[71] and argues that the mission of Mountbatten from the start aimed at the transfer of power to Indians even without any agreement being reached.

Mountbatten prepared the June Plan and proposed the Partition. Hodson reiterates that the Indians themselves had accepted the Partition and that it was merely announced by Mountbatten. Jinnah declared that once Partition was decided upon, all trouble would cease and people would live happily. He called upon the Viceroy to hand over power 'as soon as possible'.[72] Hodson writes that the Viceroy's discussion with the Congress leaders, other than Gandhi, also tended to go in the 'same direction'.[73] After protracted discussions, Mountbatten concluded that the only solution to the problem was the Partition of India into two sovereign states, in a situation where the Congress and the Muslim League were looking in different directions. The Congress concluded that Partition was a better alternative than any dilution of the Cabinet Mission Plan, while the League said 'no Cabinet Mission Plan at any price'.[74]

Thus Hodson explains that in the post-Cabinet Mission period, the Congress and the League parted ways. It is true that at this stage Partition became inevitable, but the events of 1946-7 should not be interpreted, in isolation. Actually the long term colonial policy of divide and rule was reaching its climax and communal violence decided the fate of the subcontinent. The British government promoted the League's action by its own inaction. But this reality hardly finds any reflection in Hodson's writings. In fact, Hodson like other scholars of his school, gives undue prominence to the happenings of 1946-7 obviously to show the inevitability of the Partition.

The imperialist historians were at crossroads. Their skill and profession demanded objectivity while their ideological commitments and affiliations made their writings biased and prejudiced. Hodson accepts that the mission of Mountbatten was to effect a transfer of power to Indians, with or without any agreement among Indians.[75] But in this process the fate of India was to be decided not by Indians but by the British. This assertion also goes against the declared aim of the imperialist historiography, because it shows that the British too were responsible for the Partition of India and they were not acting merely in accordance with Indian opinions but according to their own convenience. In order to give Mountbatten a clean chit, Hodson writes:

> Whatever other criticism may be made of Lord Mountbatten's plan for transfer of power it certainly can't be said that it was imposed without the fullest consultation with India's political leaders or that it was contrary to the ultimate consensus of their views. It may certainly be said that it was not he but the Indians who divided India.[76]

The Mountbatten Plan was made public on 3 June 1947 and, on its basis, the British Parliament passed the Indian Independence Act, which was implemented on 14 and 15 August 1947. This Plan had initially been rejected by the League and the Congress but subsequently it was accepted. Hodson states that India was divided because of the will of Indians. But why and how was Partition accepted? Hodson says that India was divided because Partition was accepted as a panacea for all ills. The imperial ideologues have ignored questions like—What were the other options? Why was Partition accepted without giving a chance to other schemes? And why and how was this particular date selected? These questions remain unanswered. And to answer the question as to why the Partition was affected at a lightning speed, Hodson says:

> Since the Partition was regarded as panacea of all evils, it was administered at the earliest possible date. The difficulties in governing India between the date of announcement and effective establishment of the successor authorities rendered it advisable.[77]

The final date, Hodson opines, was declared by accident. He thus accepts the role of chance in history, so that the real motive could be concealed.

The imperialist scholars invariably emphasized the imaginary and hypothetical theories of 'white man's burden' and 'civilizing mission',[78] when they talk about the nature of the British rule. In the process they try to cover the real intentions of the colonial power. Hodson writes: 'The British policy aimed at leading the people of India to a condition in which they would be able to govern themselves and grow out of imperial tutelage.'[79] To highlight their point these historians try to negate the role of the Indian national movement. What India achieved on the night of 14 and 15 August, Hodson asserts, was not the fulfilment of its cherished goal rather it was the culmination of the British long term policy of granting India self-rule, promised by Montague in 1917. Thus, independence has been interpreted as a gift of the British, but Partition which coincided, rather than preceded, and reduced the charms of freedom, has been interpreted as a natural corollary of India's pluralistic society.

To conclude, the imperialist historians of different generations approach the sensitive, epoch making and tragic developments leading to Partition, with a pre-determined mindset. Their aim is to justify the colonial policies and to absolve the colonial authorities of any responsibility. The Partition of India, which was in reality a manifestation of a series of short and long term colonial policies, has been viewed from the same stereotyped angle. The British Empire in India had been created on the basis of divide and rule and they felt compelled to elaborate upon this policy for the maintenance of this most important jewel of Pax Britannica. The imperial ideologues have naturally tried to emphasize that Indians were divided into watertight compartments on religious lines and that the British simply worked on it, they did not create the great divide. They wilfully ignore the intracommunity dissimilarities and intercommunity similarities :

> Hindus and Muslims lived in a village separated not only by religious creed and rituals but by whole modes of life and attitude of mind, each a permanent hereditary group without inter-marriage or mutual absorption.[80]

This is a deliberate negation of the composite nature of Indian society and culture. For Spear, in India communal affiliation was stronger than class affiliation.

It is true that a sense of social division on religious lines existed in Indian society. But it is equally true that the Hindus and the Muslims belonging to the same class or locality often had more areas of commonality with each other than with their co-religionists in other segments of society. The imperial historians are so obsessed with religion that they have interpreted class contradictions as contradictions based on religion. The class conflicts between the ruler and the ruled, between the imperial power and the nationalists, among the élites themselves, etc., have been viewed ahistorically. They kept on emphasizing that incompatibility of religious, economic, political and cultural interest, encouraged separatism, that culminated in the creation of Pakistan. In order to buttress their hypothesis they have distorted India's past and produced a constricted picture of reality. These explanations, of course, served their purpose and are still found useful in the domain of international power politics.

Colonial historiography projects the Pakistan movement as a national movement and considers it deep rooted in the Indian tradition. Spear asserts, that Muslims 'in their own eyes were not a minority at all, but a separate "nation" '.[81] Hence, this tantamounts to an extension of the ideological support to the Pakistan movement in a conservative imperial model. This stance is further elaborated:

> Before 1930 the word Pakistan had not been heard of, in 1940 it was adopted by the Muslim League as its official aim; in 1947 it appeared as a new state containing more than 70 million people. Clearly such a rapid growth leading to such spectacular success must have sprung from roots deeper than purely political motives and stretching far beyond the twenties of the twentieth century.[82]

Thus the issues related to the Partition of the Indian subcontinent have been distorted and manipulated to suit the interests of the colonial rulers.

In a way the imperial historiography of Partition is perfectly in tune with élite historiography, where the past is manipulated to justify the mistakes of the élite in the present and, in this pursuit, the aspirations and activities of the masses are left totally neglected. Since most of the British historians of the first generation writing on Partition were a part and parcel of the colonial regime, their writings are overburdened with intense and inalienable ideological pressures, symptomatic of an unsympathetic imperial mindset. History writing has a purpose. The imperial writings have now become obsolete. It is high time to deconstruct the myths, which have been deliberately and consciously woven, around the event of Partition by the imperial ideologues, if the past is to be understood more meaningfully and the neo-colonial interpolations are to be exposed.

NOTES

1. E.W.R. Lumby, *The Transfer of Power in India* (London, 1954); and idem, 'British Policy Towards Indian States, 1940-47', in C.H. Philips and M.D. Wainwright, eds, *The Partition of India-Policies and Perspectives 1935-47* (London, 1970).
2. David Page, *Prelude to Partition* (Oxford, 1982).
3. H.V. Hodson, *The Great Divide: Britain, India and Pakistan* (London, 1969); and idem, 'The Role of Lord Mountbatten' in C.H. Philips and M.D. Wainwright, eds, op.cit.
4. R. Coupland, *The Cripps Mission* (London, 1942); and idem, *The Future of India* (London, 1942).
5. Percival Spear, *India, Pakistan and West* (London, 1952); idem, *History of Modern India* (Delhi, 1961); and idem, 'A Third Force in India 1920-47: A Study in Political Analysis', in C.H. Philips and M.D. Wainwright, eds, op.cit.
6. Alan Campbell-Johnson, *Mission With Mountbatten* (London, 1951).
7. Penderel Moon, *Divide and Quit* (London, 1961).
8. Hugh Tinker, *Experiment With Freedom—India and Pakistan, 1947* (London, 1967); and idem, *India and Pakistan—A Political Analysis* (London, 1962).
9. C.R. Attlee, *As it Happened* (London, 1954).
10. H. Bolitho, *Jinnah: Creator of Pakistan* (London, 1954).
11. Peter Hardy, *The Muslims of British India* (Cambridge, 1972).
12. C. Jeffries, *The Transfer of Power* (London, 1960).
13. Leonard Mosley, *The Last Days of the British Raj* (London, 1961).
14. R.A. Smith, *Divided India* (New York, 1947).
15. P.N.S. Mansergh, *Survey of British Commonwealth Affairs, 1939-52* (London, 1958); and idem, 'Some Reflections on the Transfer of Power in Plural Societies', in C.H. Philips and M.D. Wainwright, eds, op.cit.
16. C.H. Philips, *The Partition of India, 1947* (Leeds, 1967).
17. R.J. Moore, *The Crisis of Indian Unity, 1917-40* (Oxford, 1974); idem, *Churchill, Cripps and India, 1939-45* (Oxford, 1979); idem, *Escape from Empire—The Attlee Government and the Indian Problem* (Oxford, 1983); idem, *Endgames of Empire—*

Studies of Britain's Indian Problem (New Delhi, 1988); idem, 'The Making of India's Paper Federation, 1927-35', in C.H. Philips and M.D. Wainwright, eds, op.cit.; and idem, 'British Policy and Indian Problem, 1936-40', in ibid.

18. A.T. Embree, *Imagining India—Essays on Indian History* (Delhi, 1989), p. 54.
19. Spear, 'A Third Force in India 1920-47', op.cit., p. 496.
20. Idem, *History of Modern India*, op.cit., p. 87.
21. The imperialist school argues that the Muslims remained separate as a distinct community. The effort to maintain this identity gave birth to communalism. Therefore, communalism was the natural corrolary of the social milieu of India. Opposing this view, the nationalists blame the colonial authority for the emergence and growth of communalism. A section of the historians views it as a game of élites.
22. Hodson, *The Great Divide*, op.cit., p. 181.
23. Ibid., p. 9.
24. Ibid., p. 12.
25. Spear, *History of Modern India*, op.cit., p. 357.
26. Ibid., p. 354.
27. Idem, 'A Third Force in India 1920-47', op.cit., p. 497.
28. Idem, *India, Pakistan and West*, op.cit., p. 90.
29. Idem, *History of Modern India*, op.cit., p. 358.
30. Idem, *India, Pakistan and West*, op.cit., p. 206.
31. Idem, *History of Modern India*, op.cit., p. 358.
32. It refers to a process of change brought about in Indian society and culture as a result of over 150 years of British rule and the term subsumes changes occurring at different levels—technology, institution, ideology and values. This concept was propounded by M.N. Srinivas, *Social Change in Modern India* (New Delhi, 1972).
33. Spear, *India, Pakistan and West*, p. 103.
34. Idem, *History of Modern India*, p. 360.
35. Idem, *India, Pakistan and West*, p. 206.
36. Ibid., p. 200.
37. Idem, *History of Modern India*, p. 362.
38. Hodson, *The Great Divide—Britain, India and Pakistan*, op.cit., p. 12.
39. Ibid., p. 13.
40. Spear, *History of Modern India*, op.cit., p. 362.
41. Ibid., p. 361.
42. Ibid., p. 362.
43. The term 'PAKISTAN' was coined by Rahmat Ali—a visionary from Cambridge. That he was under the influence of British Home authority is a possibility. 'P' stands for Punjab, 'A' for Afghan areas, 'K' for Kashmir, 'S' for Sind and 'STAN' is the Persian suffix for Baluchistan. The literal meaning of the term Pakistan is 'a pure country or place'.
44. Spear, *History of Modern India*, op.cit., p. 363.
45. Idem, *India, Pakistan and West*, op.cit., p. 203.
46. Idem, *History of Modern India*, op.cit., p. 374.
47. Ibid., p. 375.
48. Ibid., p. 374.
49. Ibid., p. 375.
50. Moore, 'The Making of India's Paper Federation', op.cit., pp. 54-94.
51. Hodson, *The Great Divide*, op.cit., p. 75.

52. Spear, *History of Modern India*, op.cit., p. 381.
53. Ibid., p. 382.
54. The Cripps Mission was sent to India by the Conservative British government, headed by Churchill. Its aim was to obtain India's active cooperation in the war efforts. It gave fillip to the Pakistan movement.
55. Spear would like to convey the impression that the Cripps Mission did not fail, but faced Indian rejection. Actually, it failed due to Churchill-Cripps-Linlithgow Axis, as discussed by Moore, *Churchill, Cripps and India*, op.cit., p. 103.
56. Hodson, *The Great Divide*, op.cit., p. 103.
57. Ibid., p. 105.
58. Ibid., p. 107.
59. Spear, *History of Modern India*, op.cit., p. 103.
60. Hodson, *The Great Divide*, op.cit., p. 107.
61. Spear, *History of Modern India*, op.cit., p. 388.
62. Hodson, *The Great Divide*, op.cit., p. 120.
63. Ibid., p. 116.
64. Ibid., p. 125.
65. Ibid., p. 128.
66. Ibid., p. 129.
67. Ibid., p. 133.
68. Spear, *History of Modern India*, op.cit., p. 388.
69. Hodson, 'The Role of Lord Mountbatten', op.cit., pp. 117-26.
70. Idem, *The Great Divide*, op.cit., p. 228.
71. Ibid., p. 203.
72. Ibid., p. 232.
73. Ibid., p. 225.
74. Ibid., p. 245.
75. Ibid., p. 203.
76. Ibid., p. 247.
77. Ibid., p. 319.
78. Sumanta Niyogi, 'Colonial Historiography: Its Intellectual Origins and Perspective on Indian Nationalism', in *Journal of Historical Studies*, No.1 (Patna University, Patna, 1995), p. 3.
79. Hodson, *The Great Divide*, op.cit., p. 3.
80. 'What would move a Muslim peasant would differ from what would move a Hindu peasant', see Spear, 'A Third Force in India, 1920-40', op. cit., p. 497.
81. Idem, *History of Modern India*, op.cit., p. 355.
82. Ibid., p. 355.

Contributors

V.N. DATTA is an emeritus Professor of Modern History, University of Kurukshetra.

B.R. NANDA is a former Director, Nehru Memorial Museum & Library, New Delhi.

CHITTABRATA PALIT is a Professor of History, University of Jadavpur, Calcutta.

SUCHETA MHAJAN teaches history at the Delhi College of Arts and Commerce, University of Delhi.

S.K. CHAUBE is a retired Professor of Indian Politics, Department of Political Science, University of Delhi, and currently on a fellowship from the Lok Sabha Secretariat.

KWAJA A. KHALIQUE retired from the Indian Information Service, and is currently Chief Editor, Urdu Weekly, *Sadaqat*, New Delhi.

SALIL MISHRA teaches history at the Indira Gandhi Open University, New Delhi.

PARSHOTAM MEHRA is a retired Professor of History, Department of History and Central Asian Studies, University of Panjab, Chandigarh.

KANCHANMOY MAJUMDAR is a retired Professor of History, University of Nagpur.

JAYANTA SENGUPTA teaches history at the University of Jadavpur, Calcutta.

BIR GOOD GILL teaches history at the Guru Nanak Dev University, Amritsar.

K.S. SINGH is a former member of the Indian Administrative Service and former Director-General, Anthropological Survey of India.

DWIJENDRA TRIPATHI is a retired Professor of Business History, Indian Institute of Management, Ahmedabad.

SHRI PRAKASH is a retired Professor of Economics, North-East Hill University, Shillong, and currently Consultant, University Grants Commission, New Delhi.

The late PARTHA SARATHI GUPTA was a Professor of Modern European History, University of Delhi.

LAL BAHADUR VARMA is a retired Professor of History, University of Allahabad.

BISHWA MOHAN PANDEY teaches history, at the Government Post-Graduate College, Ranikhet, Almora, U.P.

Index